KARL
MARX

Francis Wheen is a writer, broadcaster and journalist. His previous book, a life of Tom Driberg, was shortlisted for the Whitbread Prize.

BOOK OF THE YEAR

According to:

John Banville
Lynn Barber
John Campbell
Nick Cohen
Terry Eagleton
Michael Foot
Sean French
Nick Hornby
Philip Kerr
Roger Lewis
Frank McLynn
Derwent May
Toby Mundy
Tom Paulin
Jeremy Paxman
Bem Pimlott
Kiernan Ryan
Richard Sennett
Barbara Trapido
A. N. Wilson
Jackie Wullschlager

Praise for *Karl Marx*:

'In his wonderfully entertaining biography, Wheen presents his subject as a man of both brilliance and frailty. Delving beneath the iconic status of the author of *Das Kapital*, Wheen captures Marx's humanity, critically yet sympathetically.' *Observer*

'A marvellous book which combines years of voracious reading with stylish writing and polemical wit. Wheen's object, triumphantly achieved, is to rescue Marx from those interminable haters and calumniators.' *Guardian*

'Wheen disproves the curious assumption of so many academics, that fluent writing is the inevitable counterpart of inadequate research . . . he approaches Marx rather as an enthusiastic naturalist might view a virile alligator; the beast is magnificent, but some of its habits are frankly disappointing . . . his combination of verve and forensic skill has infused much new life into the old revolutionary.' *TLS*

'This portrait is the first to show that the nineteenth century's most original political theorist also lived a life rich in unintentional comedy . . . With this vivid, thought-provoking biography, Francis Wheen rescues Marx from the smoke-filled rooms of forgotten political debate. Whatever anyone thinks about Marxism, this is a Marx anybody can believe in.' *Scotsman*

'Karl Marx has not been served well by his biographers . . . If the time is now more favourable to Marx biography, we had no right to expect one as vivid and enjoyable as this. A triumph.' *Financial Times*

'We learn that Marx was a serious drinker and an inveterate sponger . . . Until I read this litany of seediness and venality, I never had much time for the man. Now I think of him as someone I'd like to have known.' *Evening Standard*

'. . . And why is Karl Marx even more popular than Harry Potter?' *Independent*

'I once tried to indicate the hopelessness of a character in one of my novels by having him contemplate writing a biography of Karl Marx. The point of this has now been thoroughly spoiled by Francis Wheen's *Karl Marx*, which proved to be fascinating, funny, moving and – most startling of all – timely. His account of *Das Kapital* as a phantasmagoric Victorian novel is so compelling that I've started to read it.' Sean French, *Independent*

'I also very much enjoyed Francis Wheen's boils-and-all biography of Karl Marx and I shall never again stagger out of the Groucho and walk up Dean Street without glancing up at the flat where he used to live.' Philip Kerr, *Independent*

'Stripping away both the piety and the demonology, Wheen's book is fresh, funny, vivid and admirably short, revealing the contradictory man behind the forbidding bearded mask.' John Campbell, *Independent*

'Karl Marx making a comeback in the aftermath of the Soviet Union's collapse? It is hard to imagine but a touch of ironic genius is necessary for the achievement. Francis Wheen displays all these talents in his *Karl Marx*.' Michael Foot, *Observer*

'Most original biography: *Karl Marx* by Francis Wheen.' Frank McLynn, *Independent*

'Francis Wheen's biography *Karl Marx* has a passionate energy and commitment that made me cheer as I read it . . . Wheen's study is great fun, a bravura performance – well done yourself, I want to tell him.' Tom Paulin, *Guardian*

Also by Francis Wheen

Tom Driberg: His Life and Indiscretions

KARL
MARX

Francis Wheen

FOURTH ESTATE • *London*

This paperback edition first published in 2000
First published in Great Britain in 1999 by
Fourth Estate Limited
6 Salem Road
London W2 4BU
www.4thestate.co.uk

Copyright © Francis Wheen 1999

6

A catalogue record for this book is available from
the British Library.

ISBN 1-84115-114-9

Typeset by Avon Dataset Ltd,
Bidford on Avon B50 4JH
Printed and bound in Great Britain by
Clays Ltd St. Ives plc

For Julia

Contents

KARL
MARX

Introduction

There were only eleven mourners at Karl Marx's funeral on 17 March 1883. 'His name and work will endure through the ages,' Friedrich Engels predicted in a graveside oration at Highgate cemetery. It seemed an unlikely boast, but he was right.

The history of the twentieth century is Marx's legacy. Stalin, Mao, Che, Castro – the icons and monsters of the modern age have all presented themselves as his heirs. Whether he would recognise them as such is quite another matter. Even in his lifetime, the antics of self-styled disciples often drove him to despair. On hearing that a new French party claimed to be Marxist, he replied that in that case 'I, at least, am not a Marxist'. Nevertheless, within one hundred years of his death half the world's population was ruled by governments that professed Marxism to be their guiding faith. His ideas have transformed the study of economics, history, geography, sociology and literature. Not since Jesus Christ has an obscure pauper inspired such global devotion – or been so calamitously misinterpreted.

It is time to strip away the mythology and try to rediscover Karl Marx the man. There have been thousands of books about Marxism, but almost all have been written by academics and zealots for whom it is a near-blasphemy to treat him as a figure of flesh and blood – a Prussian émigré who became a middle-class English gentleman; an angry agitator who spent much of his adult life in the scholarly silence of the British Museum Reading Room; a gregarious and convivial host who fell out with almost all his friends; a devoted family man who impregnated his housemaid; and a deeply earnest philosopher who loved drink, cigars and jokes.

For the West, during the Cold War, he was the demonic begetter of all evil, the founder of an awesomely sinister cult, the man whose baleful influence must be suppressed. In the Soviet Union of the 1950s he assumed the status of a secular God, with Lenin as John the Baptist and, of course, Comrade Stalin himself as the redeeming Messiah. This alone has been quite enough to convict Marx as an accomplice in the massacres and purges: had he lived a few years longer, by now some enterprising journalist would probably have fingered him as a prime suspect in the Jack the Ripper murders too. But why? Marx himself certainly never asked to be included in the Holy Trinity, and would have been appalled by the crimes committed in his name. The bastard creeds espoused by Stalin, Mao or Kim Il Sung treated his work rather as modern Christians use the Old Testament: much of it simply ignored or discarded, while a few resonant slogans ('opium of the people', 'dictatorship of the proletariat') are wrenched out of context, turned upside down and then cited as apparently divine justification for the most brutal inhumanities. Kipling, as so often, had the right phrase:

> He that has a Gospel
> To loose upon Mankind,
> Though he serve it utterly –
> Body, soul and mind –
> Though he go to Calvary
> Daily for its gain –
> It is his Disciple
> Shall make his labour vain.

Only a fool could hold Marx responsible for the Gulag; but there is, alas, a ready supply of fools. 'In one way or another, the most important facts of our time lead back to one man – Karl Marx,'

Leopold Schwarzschild wrote in 1947, in the preface to his splenetic biography *The Red Prussian*. 'It will hardly be disputed that it is he who is manifested in the very existence of Soviet Russia, and particularly in the Soviet methods.' The resemblance between Marx's methods and those of Uncle Joe Stalin was apparently so indisputable that Schwarzschild did not bother to adduce any evidence for his preposterous assertion, contenting himself with the observation that 'the tree is known by its fruit' – which, like so many proverbs, is rather less axiomatic than it sounds. Should philosophers be blamed for any and every subsequent mutilation of their ideas? If Herr Schwarzschild found wasp-eaten windfalls in his orchard – or, perhaps, was served an overcooked apple pie for lunch – did he reach for an axe and administer summary justice to the guilty tree?

Just as halfwitted or power-hungry followers deified Marx, so his critics have often succumbed to the equal and opposite error of imagining him as an agent of Satan. 'There were times when Marx seemed to be possessed by demons,' writes a modern biographer, Robert Payne. 'He had the devil's view of the world, and the devil's malignity. Sometimes he seemed to know that he was accomplishing works of evil.' This school of thought – more of a borstal, really – reaches its absurd conclusion in *Was Karl Marx a Satanist?*, a bizarre book published in 1976 by a famous American hot-gospeller, the Reverend Richard Wurmbrand, author of such imperishable masterpieces as *Tortured for Christ* ('over two million copies sold') and *The Answer to Moscow's Bible*.

According to Wurmbrand, the young Karl Marx was initiated into a 'highly secret Satanist church' which he then served faithfully and wickedly for the rest of his life. No proof can be found, of course, but this merely strengthens the dog-collared detective's hunch: 'Since the Satanist sect is highly secret, we have only leads about the possibilities of his connections with it.' What are these 'leads'? Well, when he was a student Marx wrote a verse-play whose title, *Oulanem*, is more or less an anagram of Emanuel, the biblical name for Jesus – and thus 'reminds us of the inversions of the Satanist black mass'. Most incriminating; but there's more to come. 'Have you ever wondered,' Wurmbrand asks, 'about Marx's hairstyle? Men usually wore beards in his time, but not beards like this ... Marx's manner of bearing himself was characteristic of the disciples of Joanna Southcott, a Satanic priestess who considered herself in contact with the demon Shiloh.' In fact, the England inhabited by Marx had plenty of bushy-bearded gents, from the cricketer W. G. Grace to the politician Lord Salisbury. Were they, too, on speaking terms with the demon Shiloh?

After the end of the Cold War and the apparent triumph of God over Satan, countless wiseacres declared that we had reached what Francis Fukuyama smugly called the End of History. Communism was as dead as Marx himself, and the blood-curdling threat with which he concluded the *Communist Manifesto*, the most influential political pamphlet of all time, now seemed no more than a quaint historical relic: 'Let the ruling classes tremble at a communistic revolution. The proletarians have nothing to lose but their chains. They have a world to win. *Working men of all countries, unite!*' The only fetters binding the working class today are mock-Rolex watches, but these latter-day proletarians have much else which they'd hate to lose – microwave ovens, holiday timeshares and satellite dishes. They have bought their council houses and their shares in privatised utilities; they made a nice little windfall when their building society turned into a bank. In short, we are all bourgeois now. Even the British Labour Party has gone Thatcherite.

When I started researching this biography, many friends looked at me with pity and incredulity. Why, they wondered, would anyone wish to write about – still less read about – such a discredited, outmoded, irrelevant figure? I carried on regardless; and the more I studied Marx, the more astoundingly topical he seemed to be. Today's pundits and politicians who fancy themselves as modern thinkers like to mention the buzz-word 'globalisation' at every opportunity – without realising that Marx was already on the case in 1848. The globe-straddling dominance of McDonald's and MTV would not have surprised him in the least. The shift in financial power from the Atlantic to the Pacific – thanks to the Asian Tiger economies and the silicon boom towns of west-coast America – was predicted by Marx more than a century before Bill Gates was born.

There is, however, one development which neither Marx nor I had foreseen: that in the late 1990s, long after he had been written off even by fashionable liberals and post-modernist lefties, he would suddenly be hailed as a genius by the wicked old bourgeois capitalists themselves. The first sign of this bizarre reassessment appeared in October 1997, when a special issue of the *New Yorker* billed Karl Marx as 'the next big thinker', a man with much to teach us about political corruption, monopolisation, alienation, inequality and global markets. 'The longer I spend on Wall Street, the more convinced I am that Marx was right,' a wealthy investment banker told the magazine. 'I am absolutely convinced that Marx's approach is the best way to look at capitalism.' Since then, right-wing economists and journalists have been queuing up to pay similar homage. Ignore all that communist nonsense, they say: Marx was really 'a student of capitalism'.

Even this intended compliment serves only to diminish him. Karl Marx was a philosopher, a historian, an economist, a linguist, a literary critic and a revolutionist. Although he may not have had a 'job' as such, he was a prodigious worker: his collected writings, few of which were published in his lifetime, fill fifty volumes. What neither his enemies nor his disciples are willing to acknowledge is the most obvious yet startling of all his qualities: that this mythical ogre and saint was a human being. The McCarthyite witch-hunt of the 1950s, the wars in Vietnam and Korea, the Cuban Missile Crisis, the invasions of Czechoslovakia and Hungary, the massacre of students in Tiananmen Square – all these bloody blemishes on the history of the twentieth century were justified in the name of Marxism or anti-Marxism. No mean feat for a man who spent much of his adult life in poverty, plagued by carbuncles and liver pains, and was once pursued through the streets of London by the Metropolitan Police after a rather over-exuberant pub crawl.

I

The Outsider

A train grinds slowly through the Moselle valley – tall pines, terraced vineyards, prim villages, calm smoke in the winter sky. Gasping for breath in an overcrowded cattle truck, a young Spaniard captured while fighting with the French Resistance counts off the days and nights as he and his fellow prisoners are borne inexorably from Compiègne to the Nazi death camp at Buchenwald. When the train pulls up at a station he glances at the sign: TRIER. Suddenly a German boy on the platform hurls a rock at the grille behind which the doomed passengers cower.

Thus begins Jorge Semprun's great Holocaust novel, *The Long Voyage*, and nothing on that journey to extinction – not even the anticipation of horrors to come at Buchenwald – pierces the narrator's heart more agonisingly than the stone-throwing child. 'It's a goddamn dirty trick that this had to happen at Trier, of all places,' he laments.

'Why?' a puzzled Frenchman asks. 'You used to know it?'

'No, I mean I've never been here.'

'Then you know someone from here?'

'That's it, yes, that's it.' A childhood friend, he explains. But in fact he's thinking of an earlier son of Trier, a Jewish boy, born in the early hours of 5 May 1818.

'Blessed is he that hath no family,' Karl Marx sighed wearily in a letter to Friedrich Engels in June 1854. He was aged thirty-six at the time and had long since severed his own umbilical ties. His father was dead, as were three brothers and one of his five sisters; another sister died two years later, and even the survivors had little to do with him. Relations with his mother were icy and distant, not least because she had been inconsiderate enough to stay alive and thus keep the rebellious heir from his inheritance.

Marx was a bourgeois Jew from a predominantly Catholic city within a country whose official religion was evangelical Protestantism. He died an atheist and a stateless person, having devoted his adult life to predicting the overthrow of the bourgeoisie and the withering away of the nation-state. In his estrangement from religion, class and citizenship, he personified the alienation which he identified as the curse inflicted by capitalism upon humanity.

He may seem an odd representative of the oppressed masses, this respectable middle-class German, but his emblematic status would not have surprised Marx himself, who believed that individuals reflect the world they inhabit. His upbringing taught him all he needed to know about religion's seductive tyranny, arming him with the didactic eloquence and self-confidence to exhort humanity to throw off its shackles.

'He was a unique, an unrivalled storyteller,' his daughter Eleanor recorded, in one of the few surviving anecdotes from her father's childhood. 'I have heard my aunts say that as a little boy he was a terrible tyrant to his sisters, whom he would "drive" down the Markusberg at Trier full speed, as his horses, and, worse, would insist on their eating the "cakes" he made with dirty dough and dirtier hands. But they stood the "driving" and ate the "cakes" without a murmur, for the sake of the stories Karl would tell them as a reward for their virtue.' In later years – when the playful girls had become respectable married women – they were rather less indulgent towards their wayward sibling. Luise Marx, who emigrated to South Africa, once dined at his house while visiting London. 'She could not countenance her brother being the leader of the socialists,' a fellow guest reported, 'and insisted in my presence that they both belonged to the respected family of a lawyer who had the sympathy of everybody in Trier.'

Marx's determined efforts to cut loose from the influence of his family, religion, class and nationality were never wholly successful. As a venerable greybeard he remained forever the prodigal son, firing off begging letters to rich uncles or ingratiating himself with distant cousins who might soon be drawing up their wills. When he died, a daguerreotype photograph of his father was found in his breast pocket. It was placed in his coffin and interred in Highgate cemetery.

He was tethered – however unwillingly – by the force of his own logic. In a precocious schoolboy essay, 'Reflections of a Young Man on the Choice of Profession', the seventeen-year-old Karl Marx observed that 'we cannot always attain the position to which we believe we are called; our relations in society have to some extent already begun to be established before we are in a position to determine them'. His first biographer, Franz Mehring, may have exaggerated when he detected the germ of Marxism in this one sentence, but he had a point. Even in ripe maturity Marx insisted that human beings cannot be isolated or abstracted from their social and economic circumstances – or from the chilly shades of their forebears. 'The tradition of all the dead generations', he wrote in *The Eighteenth Brumaire of Louis Bonaparte*, 'weighs like a mountain on the mind of the living.'

One of Marx's paternal ancestors, Joshue Heschel Lwow, had become the rabbi of Trier as long ago as 1723, and the post had been something of a family sinecure ever since. His grandfather, Meier Halevi Marx, was succeeded as the town rabbi by Karl's uncle Samuel. Yet more dead generations were added to the load by Karl's mother, Henriette, a Dutch Jew in whose family 'the sons had been rabbis for centuries' – including her own father. As the oldest son of such a family, Karl might not have escaped his own rabbinical destiny but for those 'social and economic circumstances'.

Added to the weight of dead generations was the smothering spiritual tradition of Trier, oldest city in the Rhineland. As Goethe noted gloomily after a visit in 1793, 'Within its walls it is burdened, nay oppressed, with churches and chapels and cloisters and colleges and buildings dedicated to chivalrous and religious orders, to say nothing of the abbacies, Carthusian convents and institutions which invest, nay, blockade it.' During its annexation by France in the Napoleonic Wars, however, the inhabitants had been exposed to such unGermanic notions as freedom of the press, constitutional liberty and – more significantly for the Marx family – religious toleration. Though the Rhineland was reincorporated into imperial Prussia by the Congress of Vienna three years before Marx's birth, the alluring scent of French Enlightenment still lingered.

Karl's father, Hirschel, owned several Moselle vineyards and was a moderately prosperous member of the educated middle class. But he was also Jewish. Though never fully emancipated under French rule, Rhenish Jews had tasted just enough freedom to hunger for more. When Prussia wrested back the Rhineland from Napoleon, Hirschel petitioned the new government for an end to legal discrimination against himself and his 'fellow believers'. To no avail: the Jews of Trier were now subject to a Prussian edict of 1812 which effectively banned them from holding public office or practising in the professions. Unwilling to accept the social and financial penalties of second-class citizenship, Hirschel was reborn as Heinrich Marx, patriotic German and Lutheran Christian. His Judaism had long been an accident of ancestry rather than a deep or abiding faith. ('I received nothing from my family,' he said, 'except, I must confess, my mother's love.') The date of his baptism is unknown, but he had certainly converted by the time of Karl's birth: official records show that Hirschel began to work as an attorney in 1815, and in 1819 he celebrated the family's new respectability by moving from their five-room rented apartment into a ten-roomed property near the old Roman gateway to the city, Porta Nigra.

Catholicism might appear to have been the more obvious choice for what was, essentially, no more than a spiritual marriage of convenience: the Church to which he now belonged had barely 300 members in a city with a population of 11,400. But these adherents happened to include some of the most powerful men in Trier. As one historian has observed, 'To the Prussian state, the members of its established religion represented the solid, reliable and loyal core in a predominantly Roman Catholic, and somewhat dangerously gallicised, Rhineland.'

Not that Hirschel was immune to Gallic charm: during the years of Napoleonic dominance he had been steeped in free French ideas of politics, religion, life and art, becoming 'a real eighteenth-century "Frenchman" who knew his Voltaire and Rousseau by heart'. He was also an active member of Trier's Casino Club, where the more enlightened citizens gathered for political and literary debates. In January 1834, when Karl was fifteen, Heinrich organised a banquet at the club to pay tribute to the newly elected 'liberal' deputies to the Rhineland Assembly, winning raucous applause for his toast to the King of Prussia – 'to whose magnanimity we are indebted for the first institutions of popular representation. In the fullness of his omnipotence he has of his own free will directed that the Diets should assemble so that the truth might reach the steps of the throne.'

This extravagant flattery for a feeble and anti-Semitic king might sound sarcastic, and was probably taken thus by the more boisterous revellers. ('The fullness of his omnipotence', forsooth.) But Heinrich was perfectly sincere; no revolutionary he. Never-theless, the very mention of 'popular representation', however carefully muffled in sycophancy and moderation, was enough to alarm the authorities in Berlin: irony is often the dissident's only weapon in a land of censors and police spies, and the agents of the Prussian state – ever alert for mischief – were adept at detecting satire where none was intended. The local press was forbidden to print the speech. After a Casino Club gathering eight days later, at which members sang the Marseillaise and other revolutionary choruses, the government placed the building under police surveillance, reprimanded the provincial governor for permitting such treasonous assemblies and marked Heinrich Marx down as a dangerous troublemaker.

What did his wife make of all this? It is quite possible that he kept the news from her. Henriette Marx did not share her husband's intellectual appetites: she was an uneducated – indeed only semi-literate – woman whose interests began and ended with her family, over whom she fussed and fretted ceaselessly. She admitted to suffering from 'excessive mother love', and one of her few surviving letters to her son – written while he was at university – amply justifies the diagnosis: 'Allow me to note, dear Carl, that you must never regard cleanliness and order as something secondary, for health and cheerfulness depend on them. Insist strictly that your rooms are scrubbed frequently and fix a definite time for it – and you, my dear Carl, have a weekly scrub with sponge and soap. How do you get on about coffee, do you make it, or how is it? Please let me know everything about your household.' The picture of Mrs Marx as a congenital worrier was confirmed by Heinrich: 'You know your mother and how anxious she is . . .'

Once he had flown the nest, Karl had little more to do with his mother – except when he was trying, seldom with much success, to wheedle money out of the old girl. Many years later, after the death of Engels's lover Mary Burns, Marx sent his friend a brutal letter of condolence: 'I am being dunned for the school fees, the rent . . . Instead of Mary, ought it not to have been my mother, who is in any case a prey to physical ailments and has had her fair share of life?'

Karl Marx was born in the upstairs room of a house at 664 Brückergasse, a busy thoroughfare that winds down to the bridge over the Moselle river. His father had taken a lease on the building only one month earlier and moved out when Karl was fifteen months old. Yet this birthplace, of which he had no memories, was bought by the German Social Democratic Party in April 1928 and has ever since been a museum devoted to his life and times –

apart from a ghastly interlude between 1933 and 1945, when it was occupied by the Nazis and used as the HQ for one of their party newspapers. After the War, letters were sent out appealing for money to repair the damage done by Hitler's loutish squatters. One of the replies, dated 19 March 1947, came from the international secretary of the British Labour Party: 'Dear Comrade, I regret that the British Labour Party is not prepared as an organisation to support your international committee for the reconstruction of the Karl Marx house at Treves [the English name for Trier], since its resources are devoted to the upkeep of similar monuments of Karl Marx in England. Yours fraternally, Denis Healey.' A likely story: Londoners will search in vain for these monuments to which Healey allegedly 'devoted' his party's resources. Still, at least the house survives. A hundred yards away is the site of the old Trier synagogue at which so many of Marx's ancestors presided. The only token of its presence today is a sign attached to the lamppost at the street corner, which needs no translation: '*Hier stand die frühere Trierer Synagoge, die in der Pogromnacht im November 1938 durch die Nationalsozialisten zerstört wurde.*'

Little is known about Karl Marx's early boyhood, apart from his habit of forcing his sisters to eat mud pies. He appears to have been educated privately until 1830, when he entered the Trier High School – whose headmaster, Hugo Wyttenbach, was a friend of Heinrich Marx and a founder of the Casino Club. Although Karl later dismissed his schoolfellows as 'country bumpkins', the teachers were mostly liberal humanists who did their best to civilise the yokels. In 1832, after a rally at Hambach in support of free speech, police officers raided the school and found seditious literature – including speeches from the Hambach protest – circulating among the pupils. One boy was arrested, and Wyttenbach was placed under close surveillance. Two years later, the maths and Hebrew teachers were charged with the despicable crimes of 'atheism' and 'materialism' following the notorious Casino dinner of January 1834. To dilute Wyttenbach's influence, the authorities appointed a grim-faced reactionary named Loers as co-headmaster.

'I found the position of good Herr Wyttenbach extremely painful,' Heinrich told his son after attending Loers's installation ceremony. 'I could have wept at the offence to this man, whose only failing is to be much too kind-hearted. I did my best to show the high regard I have for him and, among other things, I told him how devoted you are to him. . .' But when Marx proved his devotion by refusing to speak to the conservative interloper, he earned a paternal scolding. 'Herr Loers has taken it ill that you did not pay him a farewell visit,' Heinrich wrote after Karl's matriculation in 1835. 'You and Clemens [another boy] were the only ones . . . I had to have recourse to a white lie and tell him we were there while he was away.' Here is the authentic voice of Heinrich Marx, angry but timid, unhappy but obedient, forever letting 'I dare not' wait upon 'I would', like the cat in the adage.

His son, by contrast, always preferred to imitate the action of a tiger. 'Social reforms,' Karl Marx wrote, when warning the working class not to expect any philanthropy from capitalism, 'are never carried out by the weakness of the strong; but always by the strength of the weak.' One could argue that he embodied this principle. Though his intellectual power seldom faltered, the body which sustained this tremendous creative fecundity was a very feeble vessel indeed. It was almost as if he decided to test on himself what he advocated for the proletariat, by defying his physical limitations and seeking out the strength of his own weakness.

Even in the full vigour of youth – before poverty, sleeplessness, bad diet, heavy drinking and constant smoking had taken their inevitable toll – he was a fragile specimen. 'Nine lecture courses seem to me rather a lot and I would not like you to do more than your body and mind can bear,' Heinrich Marx advised, soon after his seventeen-year-old son started at Bonn University in 1835. 'In providing really vigorous and healthy nourishment for your mind, do not forget that in this miserable world it is always accompanied by the body, which determines the well-being of the whole machine. A sickly scholar is the most unfortunate being on earth.

Therefore, do not study more than your health can bear.' Karl took no notice, then or ever: in later years he often toiled through the night, fuelled by cheap ale and foul cigars.

With his usual rash candour, the lad replied that he was indeed in poor health – thus provoking another earnest sermon from his Polonius of a father. 'Youthful sins in any enjoyment that is immoderate or even harmful in itself meet with frightful punishment. We have a sad example here in Herr Günster. True, in his case there is no question of vice, but smoking and drinking have worked havoc with his already weak chest and he will hardly live until the summer.' His mother, fretful as ever, added her own list of commandments: 'You must avoid everything that could make things worse, you must not get over-heated, not drink a lot of wine or coffee, and not eat anything pungent, a lot of pepper or other spices. You must not smoke any tobacco, not stay up too long in the evening, and rise early. Be careful also not to catch cold and, dear Carl, do not dance until you are quite well again.' Frau Marx, one can safely say, was no skylark.

Shortly after his eighteenth birthday Marx was excused military service because of his weak chest, though he may well have exaggerated his condition. (The suspicion of lead-swinging is strengthened by a letter from his father advising him on how to dodge the draft: 'Dear Karl, If you can, arrange to be given good certificates by competent and well-known physicians there, you can do it with a good conscience . . . But to be consistent with your conscience, do not smoke too much.') The supposed disability certainly didn't harm his enjoyment of student high jinks. An official 'Certificate of Release' issued after Marx's year at Bonn University, while praising his academic achievements ('excellent diligence and attention'), noted that 'he has incurred a punishment of one day's detention for disturbing the peace by rowdiness and drunkenness at night . . . Subsequently, he was accused of having carried prohibited weapons in Cologne. The investigation is still pending. He has not been suspected of participation in any forbidden association among the students.'

The university authorities didn't know the half of it. True, the Poets' Club – which he joined in his first term – was not a 'forbidden association', but neither was it quite so innocent as the name suggested: the discussion of poetry and rhetoric was a cover for more seditious talk. 'Your little circle appeals to me, as you may well believe, much more than alehouse gatherings,' Heinrich Marx wrote, happily imagining his boy improving the shining hour with earnest literary debate.

As it happened, Marx was no stranger to alehouses either. He was a co-president of the Trier Tavern Club, a society of about thirty university students from his home town whose main ambition was to get drunk as frequently and riotously as possible: it was after one of their revels that young Karl found himself detained for twenty-four hours, though the imprisonment did not prevent his chums from bringing him yet more booze and packs of playing cards to ease his sentence. During 1836 there was a series of fights in pubs between the Trier gang and a posse of young bloods from the Borussia Korps, who would force the student layabouts to kneel and swear allegiance to the Prussian aristocracy. Marx bought a pistol to defend himself against these humiliations, and when he visited Cologne in April the 'prohibited weapon' was discovered during a police search. It was only a begging letter from Heinrich Marx to a judge in Cologne which persuaded the authorities not to press charges. Two months later, after yet another fracas with the Borussia Korps, Marx accepted a challenge to a duel. The outcome of this contest between a short-sighted swot and a trained soldier was all too predictable, and he was lucky to get away with nothing worse than a small wound above his left eye. 'Is duelling then so closely interwoven with philosophy?' his father asked despairingly. 'Do not let this inclination, and if not inclination, this craze, take root. You could in the end deprive yourself and your parents of the finest hopes that life offers.'

After a year of 'wild rampaging in Bonn', Heinrich Marx was only too pleased to let his son transfer to the University of Berlin, where there would be fewer extra-curricular temptations. 'There is no question here of drinking, duelling and pleasant communal outings,' the philosopher Ludwig Feuerbach had observed while studying there ten years earlier. 'In no other university can you find such a passion for work ... Compared to this temple of work, the other universities are like public houses.' No wonder Heinrich was so eager to sign the necessary form consenting to the move. 'I not only grant my son Karl Marx permission, but it is my will that he should enter the University of Berlin next term for the purpose of continuing there his studies of Law...'

Any hopes that the wayward youth could now concentrate on his studies without distraction were quickly dashed: Karl Marx had fallen in love.

The one schoolfriend from Trier with whom Marx maintained any connection in adult life was Edgar von Westphalen, an amiable chump and dilettante with revolutionary inclinations. This enduring friendship had nothing to do with Edgar's qualities but everything to do with his sister, the lovely Johanna Bertha Julie Jenny von Westphalen, known to all as Jenny, who became the first and only Mrs Karl Marx.

She was quite a catch. Revisiting his home town many years later, Karl wrote fondly to Jenny, 'Every day and on every side I am asked about the *quondam* "most beautiful girl in Trier" and the "queen of the ball". It's damned pleasant for a man, when his wife lives on like this as an "enchanted princess" in the imagination of a whole town.' It may seem surprising that a twenty-two-year-old princess of the Prussian ruling class – the daughter of Baron Ludwig von Westphalen – should have fallen for a bourgeois Jewish scallywag four years her junior, rather than some dashing grandee with a braided uniform and a private income; but Jenny was an intelligent, free-thinking girl who found Marx's intellectual swagger irresistible. After ditching her official fiancé, a respectable young second lieutenant, she became engaged to Karl in the summer vacation of 1836. He was so proud that he couldn't stop himself from boasting to his parents, but the news was kept from Jenny's family for almost a year.

The reasons for this long concealment are obvious enough at first glance. Baron Ludwig von Westphalen, a senior official of the Royal Prussian Provincial Government, was a man of doubly aristocratic lineage: his father had been Chief of the General Staff during the Seven Years' War and his Scottish mother, Anne Wishart, was descended from the Earls of Argyll. Such a thoroughbred magnifico would scarcely wish his daughter to saddle herself with the untitled descendant of a long line of rabbis.

On closer inspection, however, the secrecy is more puzzling; for von Westphalen was neither a snob nor a reactionary. After a conventional upper-class marriage which had produced four conventional upper-class children – one of whom, Ferdinand, later became a fiendishly oppressive Minister of the Interior in the Prussian government – the Baron was now married to Caroline Heubel, a plain, decent daughter of the German middle class, who was the mother of Jenny and Edgar. (His first wife, Lisette Veltheim, had died in 1807.) No longer obliged to put on airs and graces or fuss about his social status, Baron Ludwig had relaxed into his more natural character – cultured, liberal and benign. As a Protestant in a Catholic city, he may have felt himself to be something of an outsider; certainly, he sympathised with life's outcasts. In official reports to Berlin he drew attention to the 'great and growing poverty' of the lower classes in Trier, though without proposing any cause or cure. He was an almost perfect specimen of the well-meaning liberal conservative, distressed by the privations of the poor but enjoying his own amplitude of life.

Rather like Heinrich Marx, in fact. The two men met soon after von Westphalen was posted to Trier in 1816 and discovered that they had much in common, including a love of literature and Enlightenment philosophy. Though they were unquestioning monarchists and patriots, both argued – *sotto voce* and with the utmost politeness – for some mild reforms that might temper the excesses of Prussian absolutism. Like Heinrich Marx, Ludwig von Westphalen joined the Casino Club and was therefore treated with wary suspicion by his superiors in Berlin.

The two wives had nothing in common at all. Caroline von Westphalen was a lively and generous hostess, forever organising poetry readings or musical soirées; Henriette Marx was narrow-minded, inarticulate and socially awkward. To the Marx children, the von Westphalens' house on Neustrasse was a haven of light and life. Sophie Marx and Jenny von Westphalen were intimate friends for most of their childhood: when the five-year-old Jenny first set eyes on her future husband, he was still a babe-in-arms. Like her brother, who was one year older than Karl, Jenny soon fell under the spell of this dark-eyed, domineering infant ('he was a terrible tyrant') and never escaped.

The Baron, too, began to notice their precocious playmate. Unlike his own son, Edgar, the Marx boy had a hunger for knowledge and a quick intelligence with which to digest it. On long walks together, the old man would recite long passages from Homer and Shakespeare to his young companion. Marx came to know much of Shakespeare by heart – and used it to good effect, salting and peppering his adult writings with apt quotations and analogies from the plays. 'His respect for Shakespeare was boundless: he made a detailed study of his works and knew even the least important of his characters,' Marx's son-in-law Paul Lafargue recalled. 'His whole family had a real cult for the great English dramatist; his three daughters knew many of his works by heart. When after 1848 he wanted to perfect his knowledge of English, which he could already read, he sought out and classified all Shakespeare's original expressions.'

In later life Marx relived those happy hours with von Westphalen by declaiming scenes from Shakespeare – as well as Dante and Goethe – while leading his family up to Hampstead Heath for Sunday picnics. 'The children are constantly reading Shakespeare,' he reported to Engels, with immense paternal pride, in 1856. At the age of twelve, Marx's daughter Jenny compared his former secretary Wilhelm Pieper with Benedick from *Much*

Ado About Nothing – whereupon her eleven-year-old sister, Laura, pointed out that Benedick was a wit but Pieper was merely a clown, 'and a cheap clown too'. During the long years of exile in London, Marx's only forays into English culture were occasional outings to watch the leading Shakespearean actors Salvini and Irving. It is no coincidence that one of the Marx children, Eleanor, went on the stage and another, little Jenny, yearned to do likewise. As Professor S. S. Prawer has commented, anyone in Marx's household was obliged to live 'in a perpetual flurry of allusions to English literature'. There was a quotation for every occasion – to flatten a political enemy, to enliven a dry economic text, to heighten a family joke, or to authenticate an intense emotion. In a love-letter to his wife, written thirteen years after their wedding, Marx revealed once again the Baron von Westphalen's enduring influence:

> There you are before me, large as life, and I lift you up in my arms and I kiss you all over from top to toe, and I fall on my knees before you and cry: 'Madame, I love you.' And love you I do, with a love greater than was ever felt by the Moor of Venice ... Who of my many calumniators and venomous-tongued enemies has ever reproached me with being called upon to play the romantic lead in a second-rate theatre? And yet it is true. Had the scoundrels possessed the wit, they would have depicted 'the productive and social relations' on one side and, on the other, myself at your feet. Beneath it they would have written: 'Look to this picture and to that.'

That last phrase, as Jenny would not have needed telling, was plucked from *Hamlet*.

Why, then, were Karl and Jenny so reluctant to tell her parents of the betrothal? Perhaps Karl thought that the difference in their ages would count against him: marriages to older women were still rare enough to seem a crime against the laws of nature. Or perhaps they feared that, for all his generosity of spirit, the old man would try to dissuade his adored daughter from throwing in her lot with a brilliant but volatile nonconformist. Life with Karl Marx would never be dull, but it held little promise of stability or prosperity.

Apart from Jenny von Westphalen, the most important passion of Marx's youth was a dead philosopher, G. W. F. Hegel. It followed much the same course as many love affairs: shy wariness, followed by the intoxicating thrill of a first embrace, followed by rejection of the beloved as the *amour fou* wanes. But he remained grateful for this initiation into the secrets of adulthood. Long after repudiating Hegelianism and declaring his intellectual independence, Marx spoke affectionately of the man who led him out of innocence. He had earned the right to chide Hegel with the robust honesty of an intimate friend; strangers were permitted no such licence.

'The mystificatory side of Hegelian dialectic I criticised nearly thirty years ago, at a time when it was still the fashion,' he wrote in 1873. 'But just as I was working at the first volume of *Capital*, it was the good pleasure of the peevish, arrogant, mediocre epigones, who now talk big in cultured Germany, to treat Hegel in the same way as the brave Moses Mendelssohn in Lessing's time treated Spinoza, i.e. as a "dead dog". I therefore openly avowed myself the pupil of that mighty thinker, and even here and there, in the chapter on the theory of value, coquetted with the modes of expression peculiar to him. The mystification which dialectic suffers in Hegel's hands by no means prevents him from being the first to present its general form of working in a conscious and comprehensive manner.' It was very rare indeed for Marx to pay such a compliment to someone with whom he had disagreed: usually, those who fell foul of him could expect to be condemned as curs and jackasses for ever afterwards. Heinrich Heine was an exception, since Marx believed that one had to forgive great poets their shortcomings; and it seems he had a similar rule for great though flawed philosophers. For the second-raters, however – the poetasters, the posturing ninnies, the self-important numskulls – no epithet was too harsh. When he saw Hegel attacked by lesser minds, Marx knew at once whose side he was on.

For one thing, he was still in the old boy's debt, as he admitted all those years later. Hegel used a radical methodology to reach conservative conclusions. What Marx did was to keep the dialectical framework but discard the mystical mumbo-jumbo – rather like a man who buys a deconsecrated chapel and converts it into a habitable, secular dwelling.

What is dialectic? As any schoolchild with a set of magnets – or, for that matter, any dating agency – will confirm, opposites can attract. If it were not so, the human race would be extinct. Female mates with male, and from their sweaty embrace a new creature emerges who will, eventually, repeat the process. Not always, of course, but often enough to ensure the survival and progress of the species.

The dialectic performs much the same function for the human mind. An idea, stripped naked, has a passionate grapple with its antithesis, from which a synthesis is created; this in turn becomes the new thesis, to be duly seduced by a new demon lover. Two wrongs may make a right – but, soon after its birth, that right becomes another wrong which must be subjected to the same intimate scrutiny as its forebears, and thus we go forward. Marx's own engagement with Hegel was itself something of a dialectical process, from which emerged the nameless infant that was to become historical materialism.

I simplify, of course; but one is obliged to simplify Hegel since much of his work would otherwise remain impenetrably obscure. As an eighteen-year-old, soon after arriving at Berlin University, Marx himself had mocked this opaqueness and ambiguity in a series of epigrams titled 'On Hegel':

Words I teach all mixed up into a devilish muddle,
    Thus, anyone may think just what he chooses to think;

Never, at least, is he hemmed in by strict limitations.
    Bubbling out of the flood, plummeting down from the cliff,
So are his Beloved's words and thoughts that the Poet devises;
    He understands what he thinks, freely invents what he feels.
Thus, each may for himself suck wisdom's nourishing nectar;
    Now you know all, since I've said plenty of nothing to you!

Marx included the poem in a notebook of verse 'dedicated to my dear father on the occasion of his birthday as a feeble token of everlasting love'. The old man must have been delighted to learn that his son hadn't succumbed to the epidemic of Hegel-worship which was infecting almost every institution in the land. In one of his letters to Berlin, Heinrich warned Karl against the contagious influence of Hegelians – 'the new immoralists who twist their words until they themselves do not hear them; who christen a flood of words a product of genius because it is devoid of ideas'.

Someone as limitlessly curious and disputatious as Karl Marx was unlikely to resist for long. Hegel had held the chair of philosophy at Berlin from 1818 until his death in 1831, and by the time Marx enrolled at the university, five years later, his intellectual heirs were still fighting over the legacy. In his youth Hegel had been an idealistic supporter of the French Revolution, but like so many radicals – then as now – he became comfortable and complaisant in middle age, believing that a truly mature man should recognise 'the objective necessity and reasonableness of the world as he finds it'. The world in question – the Prussian state – was a complete and final manifestation of what he called the Divine Spirit or Idea (the *Geist*). This being so, there was nothing left for philosophers to discuss. Any further questioning of the status quo was the merest vanity.

Naturally, this line of argument made him very popular indeed with the Prussian authorities, who brandished it as proof that their system of government was not only inevitable but unimprovable. 'All that is real is rational,' Hegel had written; and since the state was undoubtedly real, in the sense that it *existed*, it must therefore be rational and above reproach. Those who championed the subversiveness of his earlier work – the so-called Young Hegelians – preferred to cite the second half of that famous dictum: 'All that is rational is real.' An absolute monarchy, buttressed by censors and secret police, was palpably irrational and therefore unreal, a mirage or spectre that would disappear as soon as anyone dared to touch it.

As a student in the Berlin law faculty, Marx had a front-row seat at the arena. His lecturer in jurisprudence was Friedrich Karl von Savigny, a thin, severe reactionary who, though not a Hegelian, nevertheless agreed that the development of a country's law and government was an organic process reflecting the character and tradition of its people. To challenge Prussian absolutism was to defy nature: one might as well demand a reform in the structure of oak trees, or the abolition of rain. The alternative view was represented by the chubby and cheerful professor of criminal law, Eduard Gans, a radical Hegelian who believed that institutions should be subjected to rational criticism rather than mystical veneration.

For his first year at Berlin, Marx struggled to ignore the temptations of philosophy: he was, after all, meant to be studying law. Besides, hadn't he already rejected the devilish Hegel and all his works? He distracted himself by writing lyrical verse, but produced only 'diffuse and inchoate expressions of feeling, nothing natural, everything built out of moonshine, complete opposition between what is and what ought to be, rhetorical reflections instead of poetic thoughts . . .' (Out of the quarrel with others, as W. B. Yeats said, we make rhetoric; from the quarrel with ourselves, we make poetry.) He then set about composing a philosophy of law – 'a work of about 300 pages' – only to discover the same old gulf between what is and what ought to be: 'What I was pleased to call the metaphysics of law, i.e. basic principles, reflections, definitions of concepts, [was] divorced from all actual law and every actual form of law.' Worse still, having failed to bridge the gap between theory and practice he found himself unable to reconcile the *form* of law with its content. His mistake – for which he blamed von Savigny – 'lay in my belief that matter and form can and must develop separately from each other, and so I obtained not a real form but something like a desk with drawers into which I then poured sand'.

His labours weren't entirely wasted. 'In the course of this work,' he revealed, 'I adopted the habit of making extracts from all the books I read' – a habit he never lost. His reading list from this period shows the breadth of these intellectual explorations: who else, while composing a philosophy of law, would think it worthwhile to make a detailed study of Johann Joachim Winckelmann's *History of Art*? He translated Tacitus's *Germania* and Ovid's *Tristia*, and 'began to learn English and Italian by myself, i.e. out of grammars'. In the next semester, while devouring dozens of textbooks on civil procedure and canon law, he translated Aristotle's *Rhetoric*, read Francis Bacon and 'spent a good deal of time on Reimarus, to whose book on the artistic instincts of animals I applied my mind with delight'.

All good exercise for the brain, no doubt; but even the artistic animals couldn't rescue his *magnum opus*. Abandoning the 300-page manuscript in despair, young Karl turned again to 'the dances of the Muses and the music of the Satyrs'. He dashed off a short 'humoristic novel', *Scorpion and Felix*, a nonsensical torrent of whimsy and persiflage that was all too obviously written under the spell of Sterne's *Tristram Shandy*. It does, however, have one passage that deserves quotation:

Every giant . . . presupposes a dwarf, every genius a hidebound philistine, and every storm at sea – mud, and as soon as the first disappear, the latter begin, sit down at the table, sprawling out their long legs arrogantly.

The first are too great for this world, and so they are thrown out. But the latter strike root in it and remain, as one may see from the facts, for champagne leaves a lingering repulsive aftertaste, Caesar the hero leaves behind him the play-acting Octavianus, Emperor Napoleon the bourgeois king Louis Philippe . . .

No previous writer on Marx appears to have noticed the resemblance between this jokey conceit and the famous opening paragraph of *The Eighteenth Brumaire of Louis Bonaparte*, written fifteen years later:

> Hegel remarks somewhere that all facts and personages of great importance in world history occur, as it were, twice. He forgot to add: the first time as a great tragedy, the second as a miserable farce. Caussidière for Danton, Louis Blanc for Robespierre, the Montagne of 1848–1851 for the Montagne of 1793–1795, and the London constable [Louis Bonaparte] with the first dozen indebted lieutenants that came along for the little corporal [Napoleon] with his band of marshals! The eighteenth Brumaire of the idiot for the eighteenth Brumaire of the genius!

Apart from that suggestive echo, there is little in *Scorpion and Felix* that need detain us; and even less in *Oulanem*, an overwrought verse drama that groans under the weight of Goethe's influence. After these experiments, Marx finally accepted the death of his literary ambitions. 'Suddenly, as if by a magic touch – oh, the touch was at first a shattering blow – I caught sight of the distant realm of true poetry like a distant fairy palace, and all my creations crumbled into nothing.' The discovery had cost him many a sleepless night and much anguish. 'A curtain had fallen, my holy of holies was rent asunder, and new gods had to be installed.' Suffering some kind of physical breakdown, he was ordered by his doctor to retreat to the countryside for a long rest. He took a house in the tiny village of Stralau, on the banks of the River Spree just outside Berlin.

At this point, he seems to have become slightly unhinged. Still striving to ignore the siren voice of Hegel ('the grotesque craggy melody of which did not appeal to me'), he wrote a twenty-four-page dialogue on religion, nature and history – only to find that 'my last proposition was the beginning of the Hegelian system'. He had been delivered into the hands of his enemy. 'For some days my vexation made me quite incapable of thinking; I ran about madly in the garden by the dirty water of the Spree, which "washes souls and dilutes the tea". [A quotation from Heinrich Heine.] I even joined my landlord in a hunting excursion, rushed off to Berlin and wanted to embrace every street-corner loafer.' Interestingly, Hegel himself had undergone a similar crack-up at the time when he was jettisoning his ideals and embracing 'maturity'. It is no coincidence that both Hegel and Marx wrote at length about the problem of alienation – the estrangement of humans from themselves and their society. For in the nineteenth century 'alienation' had a secondary meaning as a synonym for derangement or insanity: hence, mental pathologists (or 'mad-doctors') were known as alienists.

While he was convalescing – restoring his strength with long walks, regular meals and early nights – Marx read Hegel from beginning to end. Through a friend at the university he was introduced to the Doctors' Club, a group of Young Hegelians who met regularly at the Hippel café in Berlin for evenings of noisy, boozy controversy. Members included the theology lecturer Bruno Bauer and the radical philosopher Arnold Ruge, both of whom were to become intellectual collaborators with Marx – and, a few years later, his sworn enemies.

On the night of 10 November 1837, Marx wrote a very long letter to his father describing his conversion, and the intellectual peregrinations that had led him to it. 'There are moments in one's life,' he began, 'which are like frontier posts marking the completion of a period but at the same time clearly indicating a new direction. At such a moment of transition we feel compelled to view the past and the present with the eagle eye of thought in order to become conscious of our real position. Indeed, world history itself likes to look back in this way and take stock . . .'

No false modesty there: at the age of nineteen he was already trying on the clothes of a Man of Destiny and finding that they fitted him handsomely. Now that he had begun the next stage of life, he wanted to erect a memorial to what he had lived through – 'and where could a more sacred dwelling place be found for it than in the heart of a parent, the most merciful judge, the most intimate sympathiser, the sun of love whose warming fire is felt at the innermost centre of our endeavours!'

Ornate flattery got him nowhere. Heinrich was neither sympathetic nor merciful as he read, with rising horror, the full story of his son's intellectual adventures. To have a Hegelian in the family was shaming enough; worse still was the realisation that the boy had been squandering his time and talents on philosophy when he should have been concentrating solely on obtaining a good law degree and a lucrative job. Had he no consideration for his long-suffering parents? No duty to God, who had blessed him with such magnificent natural gifts? And what of his responsibility for his wife-to-be – 'a girl who has made a great sacrifice in view of her oustanding merits and her social position in abandoning her brilliant situation and prospects for an uncertain and duller future and chaining herself to the fate of a younger man'? Even if Karl cared nothing for his fretful mother and ailing father, he must surely feel obliged to secure a happy and prosperous future for the gorgeous Jenny; and this could hardly be achieved by sitting in a smoke-filled room poring over books about arty animals:

God's grief!!! Disorderliness, musty excursions into all departments of knowledge, musty brooding under a gloomy oil-lamp, running wild in a scholar's dressing-gown and with unkempt hair instead of running wild over a glass of beer; unsociable withdrawal with neglect of all decorum ... And is it here, in this workshop of senseless and inexpedient erudition, that the fruits are to ripen which will refresh you and your beloved, and the harvest to be garnered which will serve to fulfil your sacred obligations!?

This stinging reprimand – which is also a brilliant description of Marx's lifelong working methods – was delivered in December 1837, when Heinrich was already dangerously ill with tuberculosis. It sounds like the last desperate howl of a dying man who has placed all his hopes in the next generation – only to see those hopes crumpled like so much waste paper. Fortifying himself with a fistful of pills prescribed by his doctor, he hurled grievances galore at the wastrel son. Karl scarcely ever replied to his parents' letters; he never enquired after their health; he had spent almost 700 thalers of their money in one year, 'whereas the richest spend less than 500'; he had weakened his mind and body chasing abstractions and 'giving birth to monsters'; he never returned home during university holidays, and ignored the existence of his brothers and sisters. Even Jenny von Westphalen, who had previously been praised to the skies, was now revealed as yet another irritant: 'Hardly were your wild goings-on in Bonn over, hardly were your old sins wiped out – and they were truly manifold – when, to our dismay, the pangs of love set in . . . While still so young, you became estranged from your family. . .' True enough; but this litany of complaint was scarcely calculated to reunite them. Karl's parents begged him to visit Trier for a few days during the Easter vacation of 1838; he refused.

The truth was that Marx had left his family behind. The distance between them can be gauged by a letter from Heinrich in March 1837 suggesting that Karl make his name by writing a heroic ode: 'It should redound to the honour of Prussia and afford the opportunity of allotting a role to the genius of the monarchy . . . If executed in a patriotic and German spirit with depth of feeling, such an ode would itself be sufficient to lay the foundation for a reputation.' Did the old man really think that his son would wish to glorify either Germany or its monarchy? Perhaps not. 'I can only propose, advise,' he conceded ruefully. 'You have outgrown me; in this matter you are in general superior to me, so I must leave it to you to decide as you will.'

Heinrich Marx died, aged fifty-seven, on 10 May 1838. Karl

did not attend the funeral. The journey from Berlin would be too long, he explained, and he had more important things to do.

2

The Little Wild Boar

During his three years at Berlin University, Marx was seldom in
the lecture hall and often in debt. The death of his father meant
an end to the regular stipends but also relieved the paternal
pressure to apply himself to legal studies. 'It would be stupid,'
Bruno Bauer advised, 'if you were to devote yourself to a practical
career. Theory is now the strongest practice, and we are absolutely
incapable of predicting to how large an extent it will become
practical.' The task of the Young Hegelians was to infiltrate the
academy and establish their theories as the new received wisdom.
Marx began work on a doctoral thesis which would qualify him
for a lectureship, taking as his subject 'The Difference Between
the Democritean and Epicurean Philosophy'.

He could not have chosen a less propitious moment, since it
coincided with a new and thoroughgoing purge of Hegel's left-
wing disciples. Eduard Gans, the last Hegelian in the faculty of
law, died unexpectedly in 1839 and was replaced by the severely
reactionary Julius Stahl. Bauer himself was evicted from the
theology department soon afterwards and forced to seek refuge at
the University of Bonn. As recently as 1836 Bauer had argued,
with some vehemence, that religion should remain above and
beyond philosophical criticism; now he was proclaiming his
atheism from the rooftops. He urged Marx to get on with the
dissertation and join him in Bonn as soon as possible. Another
young radical predicted that 'if Marx, Bruno Bauer and Feuerbach
come together to found a theological–philosophical review, God

would do well to surround Himself with all His angels and indulge in self-pity, for these three will certainly drive Him out of His heaven'. Luckily for God, He had Prussian friends in high places. After the accession of Friedrich Wilhelm IV to the throne in 1840 the persecution of dissidents was redoubled, strict censorship imposed on all publications and academic freedom extinguished.

Stranded in inhospitable Berlin, Marx no longer bothered to attend the university. By day he sat in his lodgings, reading and writing and smoking; in the evenings he colloquised and caroused with the kindred souls at the Doctors' Club, who were keeping their spirits up by meeting almost daily. Though his explorations of Epicurus and Democritus might seem harmless enough, he knew that there was no question of submitting his thesis to the Berlin professors – especially since it would be scrutinised by F. W. von Schelling, a veteran anti-Hegelian philosopher who was brought into the university in 1841 at the personal command of the new king to root out unhealthy influences. Despite its apparently dry subject, Marx's comparative study of Democritus and Epicurus was actually a daring and original piece of work in which he set out to show that theology must yield to the superior wisdom of philosophy, and that scepticism will triumph over dogma. His argument was laid down like a gauntlet on the first page:

> As long as a single drop of blood pulses in her world-conquering and totally free heart, philosophy will continually shout at her opponents the cry of Epicurus: 'Impiety does not consist in destroying the gods of the crowd but rather in ascribing to the gods the ideas of the crowd.' Philosophy makes no secret of it. The proclamation of Prometheus – 'In one word, I hate all gods' – is her own profession, her own slogan against all gods in heaven and earth who do not recognise man's self-consciousness as the highest divinity. There shall be none other beside it.

In the spirit of belligerent mischief that was to be such a feature of his later polemics, Marx added a brief appendix mocking his own tutor's loss of liberal faith. Quoting from an essay Schelling had written more than forty years earlier – 'The time has come to proclaim to the better part of humanity the freedom of minds, and not to tolerate any longer that they deplore the loss of their fetters' – he asked, 'When the time had already come in 1795, how about the year 1841?'

Schelling did not have a chance to reply. Marx submitted his thesis instead to the University of Jena, which had a reputation for awarding degrees without delay or debate. He was obliged to attach his leaving certificate from Bonn (which mentioned the escapades with drink and firearms) and a reference from the Deputy Royal Government Plenipotentiaries at Berlin University, who found 'nothing specially disadvantageous to note from the point of view of discipline' except that 'on several occasions he has been the object of proceedings for debt'. The Dean of Philosophy at Jena, Dr Carl Friedrich Bachmann, decided that these trifling misdemeanours could be disregarded, since the essay on Democritus and Epicurus 'testifies to intelligence and perspicacity as much as to erudition, for which reason I regard the candidate as pre-eminently worthy'. On 15 April 1841, just nine days after sending his dissertation to Jena, Karl Marx collected a Ph.D.

Herr Doktor Marx was now ready to launch himself in the world. But for the next year he shuttled aimlessly between Bonn, Trier and Cologne, apparently uncertain of what to do next. His thesis had been dedicated 'to his dear fatherly friend, Ludwig von Westphalen . . . as a token of filial love', and during several visits to Trier he pointedly ignored his own surviving parent, devoting himself to the ailing Baron (who was to die in March 1842) and the patient Jenny, whose adoration of her 'little wild boar' was as intense as ever in spite of his lengthy absences. 'My little heart is so full, so overflowing with love and yearning and ardent longing for you, my infinitely loved one,' she wrote. 'It is certain, isn't it, that I can marry you?' Of course, of course, he agreed, but not just yet. The marriage would have to be postponed until he had found gainful employment, since his wretched mother had stopped his allowance and withheld his share of Heinrich Marx's estate.

In July 1841 Marx went to stay with Bruno Bauer in Bonn, where the two reprobates spent an uproarious summer shocking the local bourgeoisie – getting drunk, laughing in church, galloping through the city streets on donkeys and (rather more subversively) penning an anonymous spoof, *The Last Trump of Judgement Against Hegel the Atheist and the Anti-Christ*. At first glance this was a pious broadside, supposedly written by a devout and conservative Christian who wished to prove that Hegel was a revolutionary atheist; but its true intent soon became apparent, as did the identity of the authors. One Hegelian newspaper commented knowingly that every '*bauer*' (the German word for 'peasant') would understand the real meaning. Bruno Bauer was expelled from the university, and with him went Marx's last chance of academic preferment.

'In a few days I have to go to Cologne,' Marx told the radical Hegelian philosopher Arnold Ruge in March 1842, 'for I find the proximity of the Bonn professors intolerable. Who would want to have to talk always with intellectual skunks, with people who study only for the purpose of finding new dead ends in every corner of the world!' A month later, he was having second thoughts: 'I have abandoned my plan to settle in Cologne, since life there is too noisy for me, and an abundance of good friends does not lead to better philosophy . . . Thus Bonn remains my residence for the time being; after all, it would be a pity if no one remained here for the holy men to get angry with.'

But the lure of Cologne was hard to resist, since the 'noise' of which he complained sounded remarkably like an echo of the Doctors' Club meetings in the Hippel café – the main difference being the quality of the alcohol. 'How glad I am that you are happy,' Jenny wrote to Karl in August 1841, 'and that you drank champagne in Cologne, and that there are Hegel clubs there, and that you have been dreaming . . .' Champagne seemed a more appropriate lubricant than the ale favoured in Berlin: Cologne was the wealthiest and largest city in the Rhineland, which was itself the most politically and industrially advanced province in the whole of Prussia, and the local bankers and businessmen had lately begun to agitate for a form of government more suited to a modern economy than the wheezing, ancient apparatus of absolute monarchy and bureaucratic oppression under which they laboured. As Marx himself pointed out often enough in later years, the nature of society is dictated by its forms of production; now that industrial capitalism had established itself, the talk in the bars of Cologne was that democracy, a free press and a unified Germany would have to follow. It was no surprise, then, that the city acted as a magnet for heretical thinkers and Bohemian malcontents who offered their wealth of knowledge in exchange for the tycoons' knowledge of wealth. The child of this union was the *Rheinische Zeitung*, a liberal newspaper founded in the autumn of 1841 by a group of wealthy manufacturers and financiers (including the President of the Cologne Chamber of Commerce) to challenge the dreary, conservative *Kölnische Zeitung*.

With hindsight, it was sublimely inevitable that Marx would write for the paper and quickly install himself as its presiding genius. But although Marxism has often been caricatured as a doctrine of 'historical inevitability', he knew very well that individual destinies are not preordained – though he did tend to underestimate the importance of accident and coincidence in shaping a life. What if Bruno Bauer had not been driven out of academe? What if Dr Marx had found a university sinecure instead of being forced – *faute de mieux* – to express his restless intelligence through journalism?

Chance may have helped to decide his fate; but it was a chance he had himself been seeking. This was another of those frontier posts marking the unexplored territory beyond. Hegel had served his purpose, and since leaving Berlin Marx's thoughts had been moving from idealism to materialism, from the abstract to the actual. 'Since every true philosophy is the intellectual quintessence of its time,' he wrote in 1842, 'the time must come when philosophy not only internally by its content, but also externally through its form, comes into contact and interaction with the real world of its day.' He had come to despise the nebulous and blurry arguments of those German liberals 'who think freedom is honoured by being placed in the starry firmament of the imagination instead of on the solid ground of reality'. It was thanks to these ethereal dreamers that freedom in Germany had remained no more than a sentimental fantasy. His new direction would, of course, require another exhaustive and exhausting course of self-education, but that was no discouragement to such an insatiable auto-didact.

He composed his first journalistic essay in February 1842, while visiting the dying Baron von Westphalen in Trier, and sent it to Arnold Ruge in Dresden for inclusion in his new Young Hegelian journal, the *Deutsche Jahrbücher*. The article was a brilliant polemic against the latest censorship instructions issued by King Friedrich Wilhelm IV – and, with glorious if unintended irony, the censor promptly banned it. The *Deutsche Jahrbücher* itself was closed down a few months later, by order of the federal parliament.

Grumbling about the 'sudden revival of Saxon censorship', Marx hoped for better luck in Cologne, where several of his friends were already installed at the *Rheinische Zeitung*. The editor, Adolf Rutenberg, was a bibulous comrade from the Doctors' Club (and brother-in-law to Bruno Bauer), but since he was usually sozzled the burden of producing the paper fell mostly on Moses Hess, a rich young socialist. Moses Hess later became a fierce enemy, as did almost *all* of Marx's friends, but at this time his attitude to the combative youngster was reverential. He wrote to his friend Berthold Auerbach:

He is a phenomenon who made a tremendous impression on me in spite of the strong similarity of our fields. In short you can prepare yourself to meet the greatest – perhaps the only genuine – philosopher of the current generation. When he makes a public appearance, whether in writing or in the lecture hall, he will attract the attention of all Germany ... Dr Marx (that is my idol's name) is still a very young man – about twenty-four at the most. He will give medieval religion and philosophy their *coup de grâce*; he combines the deepest philosophical seriousness with the most biting wit. Imagine Rousseau, Voltaire, Holbach, Lessing, Heine and Hegel fused into one person – I say fused not juxtaposed – and you have Dr Marx.

Marx had the same effect on almost everyone he encountered at this time. Though the men in the Berlin Doctors' Club and the Cologne Circle were eight or ten years older than him, most treated him as their senior. When Friedrich Engels arrived in Berlin to do his military service, a few months after Marx's departure, he found that the young Rhinelander was already a legend. A poem written by Engels in 1842 includes a vivid description of his future collaborator – whom he hadn't yet met – based entirely on the breathless reminiscences of fellow intellectuals:

Who runs up next with wild impetuosity?
A swarthy chap of Trier, a marked monstrosity.
He neither hops nor skips, but moves in leaps and bounds,
Raving aloud. As if to seize and then pull down
To Earth the spacious tent of Heaven up on high,
He opens wide his arms and reaches for the sky.
He shakes his wicked fist, raves with a frantic air,
As if ten thousand devils had him by the hair.

He was indeed swarthy (hence his lifelong nickname, 'Moor') and the effect was accentuated by thick black hair which seemed to sprout from almost every pore on his cheeks, arms, ears and nose.

It is easy to overlook the obvious, which may be why so few writers on Marx have noticed what is staring them in the face: that he was, like Esau, an hairy man. In the recollections of those who knew him, however, the awe-inspiring effect of that magnificent mane is mentioned again and again. Here is Gustav Mevissen, a Cologne businessman who invested in the *Rheinische Zeitung* in 1842: 'Karl Marx from Trier was a powerful man of twenty-four whose thick black hair sprang from his cheeks, arms, nose and ears. He was domineering, impetuous, passionate, full of boundless self-confidence . . .' And the poet George Herwegh, who came to know Marx in Paris: 'Luxuriant black hair over-shadowed his forehead. He was superbly suited to play the role of the last of the scholastics.' Pavel Annenkov, who encountered Marx in 1846: 'He was most remarkable in his appearance. He had a shock of deep black hair and hairy hands . . . he looked like a man with the right and power to command respect.' Friedrich Lessner: 'His brow was high and finely shaped, his hair thick and pitch-black . . . Marx was a born leader of the people.' Carl Schurz: 'The somewhat thick-set man, with broad forehead, very black hair and beard and dark sparkling eyes, at once attracted general attention. He enjoyed the reputation of having acquired great learning . . .' Wilhelm Liebknecht, writing in 1896, still trembled to recall the moment half a century earlier when he had first 'endured the gaze of that lion-like head with the jet-black mane'.

This apparently careless luxuriance was contrived quite deliberately. Both Marx and Engels understood the power of the hirsute, as they proved in a sneering aside half-way through their pamphlet on the poet and critic Gottfried Kinkel, written in 1852:

London provided the much venerated man with a new, complex arena in which to receive even greater acclaim. He did not hesitate: he would have to be the new lion of the season. With this in mind he refrained for the time being from all political activity and withdrew into the seclusion of his home in order to grow a beard, without which no prophet can succeed.

Perhaps for the same reason, Marx grew a set of whiskers at university and cultivated them with pride throughout his adulthood until he was as woolly as a flock of sheep. (A Prussian spy in London, reporting to his Berlin masters in 1852, thought it significant that 'he does not shave at all'.)

Friedrich Engels, too, seems to have formulated a political theory of facial hair at an early age. 'Last Sunday we had a moustache evening,' the nineteen-year-old Engels wrote to his sister in October 1840. 'I had sent out a circular to all moustache-capable young men that it was finally time to horrify all philistines, and that that could not be done better than by wearing moustaches. Everyone with the courage to defy philistinism and wear a moustache should therefore sign. I had soon collected a dozen moustaches, and then the 25th of October, when our moustaches would be a month old, was fixed as the day for a common moustache jubilee.' This pogonophiles' party, held in the cellar of Bremen town hall, concluded with a defiant toast:

> Philistines shirk the burden of bristle
> By shaving their faces as clean as a whistle.
> We are not philistines, so we
> Can let our mustachios flourish free.

Though the growth later spread over his cheeks and chin, Engels's wispy beard was no match for the magnificent Marxist plumage. The image of Karl Marx familiar from countless posters, revolutionary banners and heroic busts – and the famous headstone in Highgate cemetery – would lose much of its iconic resonance without that frizzy aureole.

Marx was no great orator – he had a slight lisp, and the gruff Rhenish accent often led to misunderstandings – but the mere presence of this bristling boar was enough to inspire and intimidate. The historian Karl Friedrich Köppen, a *habitué* of the Doctors' Club, found himself paralysed whenever he was in Marx's company. 'Once again I now have thoughts of my own,' he wrote soon after his fearsome friend had left Berlin in 1841, 'ideas that I have (so to speak) produced myself, whereas all my earlier ones came from some distance away, namely from the Schützenstrasse [where Marx lived]. Now I can really work once more, and I am pleased to be walking around amongst complete idiots without feeling that I am one myself . . .' After reading an article by Bruno Bauer on the politics of Christianity, Köppen told Marx that 'I subjected this idea to police-examination and asked to see its passport, whereupon I observed that it too emanates from the Schützenstrasse. So you see, you are an absolute storehouse of ideas, a complete factory or (to use the Berlin slang) you have the brain of a swot.'

When Marx started working for the *Rheinische Zeitung*, colleagues noticed that his restless intellectual impetuosity also manifested itself in an endearing absent-mindedness. The journalist Karl Heinzen loved to watch Marx sitting in a tavern, gazing myopically at a newspaper over his morning coffee, 'and then suddenly going to another table and reaching for papers that were just not available; or when he ran to the censor to protest about the cutting out of an article and then, instead of the article in question, stuffed into his pocket some other newspaper or even a handkerchief and hared off'.

Equally attractive, to those with strong stomachs, was Marx's taste for revelry and rough-housing. Heinzen describes one evening when he had to lead Marx home after several bottles of wine:

As soon as I was in the house, he shut the doors, hid the key and jeered comically at me that I was his prisoner. He asked me to follow him up into his study. On arrival I sat myself down on the sofa to see what on earth this marvellous crank would get up to. He immediately forgot that I was there, sat down astride a chair with his head leaning forward against the back, and began to declaim in a strong singing tone which was half mournful and half mocking, 'Poor lieutenant, poor lieutenant! Poor lieutenant, poor lieutenant!' This lament concerned a Prussian lieutenant whom he 'corrupted' by teaching him the Hegelian philosophy . . .

After he had lamented the lieutenant for a while, he started up and suddenly discovered that I was in the room. He came over to me, gave me to understand that he had me in his power, and, with a malice that recalled an imp rather than the intended devil, he began to attack me with threats and cuffs. I begged him to spare me that sort of thing, because it went against the grain to pay him back in the same coin. When he did not stop I gave him a serious warning that I would deal with him in a way which he would certainly feel and when that too did no good I saw myself compelled to dispatch him into the corner of the room. When he got up I said that I found his personality boring and asked him to open the front door. Now it was his turn to be triumphant. 'Go home then, strong man,' he mocked, and added a most comical smirk. It was as though he was chanting the words from Faust, 'There is one imprisoned inside . . .' At least, the sentiment was similar, although his unsuccessful imitation of Mephistopheles made the situation comic in the extreme. In the end I warned him that if he would not open the door for me, then I would get it open myself and he would have to pay for the damage. Since he only answered with mocking sneers, I went down, tore the front door off its lock and called out to him from the street that he should shut the house up to prevent the entry of thieves. Dumb with amazement that I had escaped from his spell, he leaned out of the window and goggled at me with his small eyes like a wet goblin.

The sequel is all too predictable: a few years later, Marx denounced Heinzen as a loutish philistine ('flat, bombastic, bragging, thrasonical') and was in turn condemned by his sometime prisoner as 'an untrustworthy egoist'. Engels then entered the lists, calling Heinzen 'the most stupid person of the century' and threatening to box his ears; Heinzen replied that he could not be intimidated by 'a frivolous dilettante'. And so, interminably, on. Even as late as 1860, after emigrating to the United States, Heinzen still nursed his grudge – describing Marx in one article as a cross between a cat and an ape, a sophist, a mere dialectician, a liar and an intriguer, noted for his yellow dirty complexion, black dishevelled hair, small eyes possessed by 'a spirit of wicked fire', snubby nose, unusually thick lower lip, a head that suggested anything but nobility or idealism and a body always dressed in dirty linen.

Marx was often accused of being an intellectual bully, especially by those who felt the full force of his invective. (One of his tirades against Karl Heinzen, published in 1847, runs to nearly thirty pages.) He undoubtedly delighted in his talent for inflicting verbal violence. His style, as a friend noted admiringly, is what the *stylus* originally was in the hands of the Romans – a sharp-pointed steel pencil for writing and for stabbing. 'The style is the dagger used for a well-aimed thrust at the heart.' Heinzen thought it not so much a dagger as a full battery of artillery – logic, dialectics, learning – used to annihilate anyone who would not see eye to eye with him. Marx, he said, wanted 'to break windowpanes with cannon'. Nevertheless, the charge of bullying cannot be upheld. Marx was no coward, tormenting only those who wouldn't retaliate: his choice of victims reveals a courageous recklessness which explains why he spent most of his adult life in exile and political isolation.

For proof, one need look no further than his first article for the *Rheinische Zeitung*, published in May 1842, in which he delivered a withering exegesis of the Rhine Provincial Assembly's debates on freedom of the press. Naturally he criticised the oppressive intolerance of Prussian absolutism and its lickspittles; this was brave enough, if unsurprising. But, with an exasperated cry of 'God save me from my friends!', he was even more scathing about the feeble-mindedness of the liberal opposition. Whereas the enemies of press freedom were driven by a pathological emotion which lent feeling and conviction to their absurd arguments, 'the *defenders* of the press in this Assembly have on the whole *no real relation* to what they are defending. They have never come to know freedom of the press as a *vital need*. For them, it is a matter of the head, in which the heart plays no part.' Quoting Goethe – who had said that a painter can succeed only with a type of feminine beauty which he has loved in at least one living being – Marx suggested that freedom of the press also has its beauty, which one must have loved in order to defend it. But the so-called liberals in the Assembly seemed to lead complete and contented lives even while the press was in fetters.

Having made enemies of both the government and the opposition, he was soon turning against his own confrères as well. Georg Jung, a successful Cologne lawyer involved in the *Rheinische Zeitung*, thought him 'a devil of a revolutionary', and the radical young Turks on the staff had high hopes when Marx was appointed to the editor's chair in October 1842. They were to be disappointed. He set out his editorial policy in the form of a reply to the *Augsburger Allgemeine Zeitung*, which had accused its rival of flirting with communism:

> The *Rheinische Zeitung*, which does not even admit that communist ideas in their present form possess even *theoretical reality*, and therefore can still less desire their *practical realisation*, or even consider it possible, will subject these ideas to thoroughgoing criticism ... Such writings as those of Leroux, Considérant, and above all the sharp-witted work by Proudhon, cannot be criticised on the basis of superficial flashes of thought, but only after long and profound study.

No doubt he had half an eye on the censor – and on the paper's shareholders, bourgeois capitalists to a man. But he meant it all the same. Marx disliked the posturing of colleagues such as the tipsy Rutenberg (who was still working in the office, though his job consisted mainly of inserting punctuation marks) and Moses Hess. He was even more irritated by the antics of the Young Hegelian pranksters in Berlin, now calling themselves 'The Free', who lived up to the name by freely criticising everything – the state, the Church, the family – and advocating ostentatious libertinism as a political duty. He regarded them as tiresome, frivolous self-publicists. 'Rowdiness and blackguardism must be loudly and resolutely repudiated in a period which demands serious, manly and sober-minded persons for the achievement of its lofty aims,' he told his readers.

There was, of course, an element of hypocrisy here: as his Cologne drinking companions testify, he was not always either serious or sober, and the solemn disapproval of attention-grabbing stunts came a little oddly from a man who, only a few months earlier, had been clattering through the streets of Bonn astride a donkey. But the assumption of editorial responsibility had concentrated his mind wonderfully: juvenile japes were no longer acceptable. The most persistent nuisance was Eduard Meyen, leader of the licentious Berlin clique, who submitted 'heaps of scribblings, pregnant with revolutionising the world and empty of ideas'. During the weak, undiscriminating stewardship of Rutenberg, Meyen and his gang had come to regard the *Rheinische Zeitung* as their private playground. But the new editor made it clear that he would no longer permit them to drench the newspaper in a watery torrent of verbiage. 'I regard it as inappropriate, indeed even immoral, to smuggle communist and socialist doctrines, hence a new world outlook, into incidental theatrical criticisms etc.,' he wrote. 'I demand a quite different and more thorough discussion of communism, if it should be discussed at all.'

Marx's own ability to discuss communism was hampered by the fact that he knew nothing about it. His years of academic study had taught him all the philosophy, theology and law that he was ever likely to need, but in politics and economics he was still a novice. 'As editor of the *Rheinische Zeitung*,' he admitted many years later, 'I experienced for the first time the embarrassment of having to take part in discussions on so-called material interests.'

His first venture into this unexplored territory was a long critique of the new law dealing with thefts of wood from private forests. By ancient custom, peasants had been allowed to gather fallen branches for fuel, but now anyone who picked up the merest twig could expect a prison sentence. More outrageously still, the offender would have to pay the forest-owner the value of the wood, such value to be assessed by the forester himself. This legalised larceny forced Marx to think, for the first time, about the questions of class, private property and the state. It also allowed him to exercise his talent for demolishing a thoughtless argument with its own logic. Reporting a comment by one of the knightly halfwits in the provincial assembly – 'It is precisely because the pilfering of wood is not regarded as theft that it occurs so often – he let rip with a characteristic *reductio ad absurdum*: 'By analogy with this, the legislator would have to draw the conclusion: It is because a box on the ear is not regarded as a murder that it has become so frequent. It should be decreed therefore that a box on the ear is murder.'

This may not have been communism but it was quite naughty enough to worry Prussian officialdom – especially since the paper's circulation and reputation were growing rapidly. 'Do not imagine that we on the Rhine live in a political Eldorado,' Marx wrote to Arnold Ruge, whose *Deutsche Jahrbücher* had taken a fearsome battering from the authorities in Dresden. 'The most unswerving persistence is required to push through a newspaper like the *Rheinische Zeitung*.' For most of 1842, the resident censor at the paper was Laurenz Dolleschall, a doltish police officer who had once banned an advertisement for Dante's *Divine Comedy* on the grounds that 'the divine is not a fit subject for comedy'. After receiving the proofs each evening he blue-pencilled any articles he didn't understand (most of them), whereupon the editor would spend hours persuading him that it was all quite harmless – while the printers waited, long into the night. Marx liked to quote Dolleschall's anguished wail whenever his superiors chided him for letting through some piece of devilry: 'Now my living's at stake!' One can almost sympathise with the hapless jobsworth, since any censor unlucky enough to have to haggle with Karl Marx every working day might well conclude that a policeman's

lot is not a happy one. A story told by the left-wing journalist
Wilhelm Blos shows what Dolleschall had to endure:

> One evening the censor had been invited, with his wife and
> nubile daughter, to a grand ball given by the President of the
> Province. Before leaving he had to finish work on the censor-
> ship. But precisely on this evening the proofs did not arrive at
> the accustomed time. The censor waited and waited, because
> he could not neglect his official duties, and yet he had to put in
> an appearance at the President's ball – quite apart from the
> openings this would give to his nubile daughter. It was near ten
> o'clock, the censor was extremely agitated and sent his wife
> and daughter on in front to the President's house and dis-
> patched his servant to the press to get the proofs. The servant
> returned with the information that the press was closed. The
> bewildered censor went in his carriage to Marx's lodgings,
> which was quite a distance. It was almost eleven o'clock.
>
> After much bell-ringing, Marx stuck his head out of a third-
> storey window.
>
> 'The proofs!' bellowed up the censor.
>
> 'Aren't any!' Marx yelled down.
>
> 'But —'
>
> 'We're not publishing tomorrow!'
>
> Thereupon Marx slammed the window shut. The anger of
> the censor, thus fooled, made his words stick in his throat. He
> was more courteous from then on.

His employers, however, were not. The provincial governor who
hosted the ball, Oberpräsident von Schaper, complained in
November that the tone of the paper was 'becoming more and
more impudent' and demanded the dismissal of Rutenberg (whom
he wrongly assumed to be the culprit) from the editorial board.
Since Rutenberg was a pie-eyed liability anyway, this was no great
sacrifice. Marx composed a grovelling letter assuring His Excel-
lency that the *Rheinische Zeitung* wished only to echo 'the

benedictions which at the present time the whole of Germany conveys to His Majesty the King in his ascendant career'. As Franz Mehring commented many years later, the letter displayed 'a diplomatic caution of which the life of its author offers no other example'.

It failed to mollify Herr Oberpräsident. In mid-December he recommended to the censorship ministers in Berlin that they should prosecute the newspaper – and the anonymous author of the article on wood-gathering – for 'impudent and disrespectful criticism of the existing government institutions'. On 21 January 1843 a mounted messenger arrived from Berlin bearing a ministerial edict revoking the *Rheinische Zeitung's* licence to publish, with effect from the end of March. Loyal readers throughout the Rhineland – from Cologne, Düsseldorf, Aachen and Marx's home town of Trier – sent petitions to the king begging for a reprieve, but to no effect. A second censor was installed to prevent any monkey business in the final weeks. 'Our newspaper has to be presented to the police to be sniffed at,' Marx grumbled to a friend, 'and if the police nose smells anything unChristian or unPrussian, the newspaper is not allowed to appear.'

Since no explanation was given for the ban, Marx could only speculate. Had the authorities panicked when they noticed the paper's swelling popularity? Had he been too outspoken in his defence of the other victims of censorship, such as Ruge's *Deutsche Jahrbücher*? The likeliest reason, he guessed, was a long article published only a week before the edict, in which he had accused the authorities of ignoring the wretched economic plight of Moselle wine-farmers who were unable to compete with the cheap, tariff-free wines being imported into Prussia from other German states.

Little did he realise – though he might have been gratified to hear it – that there were more potent forces working behind the scenes. The Prussian king had been asked to suppress the paper by no less a figure than Tsar Nicholas I of Russia, his closest and most necessary ally, who had taken exception to an anti-Russian diatribe in the 4 January issue of the *Rheinische Zeitung*. At a ball in the Winter Palace four days later, the Prussian ambassador to the court of St Petersburg was harangued by the Tsar about the 'infamy' of the liberal German press. The ambassador sent an urgent dispatch to Berlin reporting that the Russians could not understand 'how a censor employed by Your Majesty's government could have passed an article of such a nature'. And that was that.

'Today the wind has changed,' one of the *Rheinische Zeitung*'s censors wrote on the day after Karl Marx had vacated the editor's chair. 'I am well content.' Marx himself was pretty happy too. 'I had begun to be stifled in that atmosphere,' he confided to Ruge. 'It is a bad thing to have to perform menial duties even for the sake of freedom; to fight with pinpricks, instead of with clubs. I have become tired of hypocrisy, stupidity, gross arbitrariness, and of our bowing and scraping, dodging, and hair-splitting over words. Consequently, the government has given me back my freedom.'

He had no future in Germany, but since most of the people and institutions for which he cared were now dead – his father, the Baron von Westphalen, the *Deutsche Jahrbücher*, the *Rheinische Zeitung* – there was nothing to keep him anyway. What mattered was that, at the age of twenty-four, he was already wielding a pen that could terrify the crowned heads of Europe. When Arnold Ruge decided to quit the country and set up a journal-in-exile, the *Deutsche-Französische Jahrbücher*, Marx gladly accepted an invitation to join him. There was only one caveat: 'I am engaged to be married and I cannot, must not and will not leave Germany without my fiancée.'

Seven years after pledging himself to Jenny, even the thick-skinned Karl Marx was beginning to feel prods and stabs of guilt. 'For my sake,' he admitted in March 1843, 'my fiancée has fought the most violent battles, which almost undermined her health, partly against her pietistic aristocratic relatives, for whom "the Lord in heaven" and "the lord in Berlin" are equally objects of a religious cult, and partly against my own family, in which some priests and other enemies of mine have ensconced themselves. For years, therefore, my fiancée and I have been engaged in more unnecessary and exhausting conflicts than many who are three times our age.' But the trials and torments of this long betrothal could not all be blamed on others. While Karl was making whoopee in Berlin or fomenting trouble in Cologne, Jenny stayed at home in Trier wondering if he would still love her tomorrow. Sometimes these anxieties surfaced in her letters – which were then misinterpreted by Marx as evidence of her own inconstancy. 'I was shattered by your doubt of my love and faithfulness,' she complained in 1839. 'Oh, Karl, how little you know me, how little you appreciate my position, and how little you feel where my grief lies . . . If only you could be a girl for a little while and, moreover, such a peculiar one as I am.'

It was, as she tried to explain, different for girls. Condemned to passivity by Eve's original sin, they could only wait, hope, suffer and endure. 'A girl, of course, cannot give a man anything but love and herself and her person, just as she is, quite undivided and for ever. In ordinary circumstances, too, the girl must find her complete satisfaction in the man's love, she must forget everything in love.' But how could she forget everything while premonitions of grief buzzed in her head like angry bees? 'Ah, dear, dear sweetheart, now you get yourself involved in politics too,' she wrote in August 1841, while Marx was gallivanting in Bonn with Bruno Bauer. 'That is indeed the most risky thing of all. Dear little Karl, just remember always that here at home you have a sweetheart who is hoping and suffering and is wholly dependent on your fate.'

Actually, his political agitation was the least of her worries: it was dangerous, to be sure, but also thrillingly heroic. She expected nothing less from her 'wild black boar', her 'wicked knave'. What stopped Jenny surrendering to happiness was fear of the agony 'if your ardent love were to cease'. There were good reasons for these misgivings. While studying in Berlin, he fell under the spell of the famous romantic poet Bettina von Arnim – who was old enough to be his mother – and on one occasion, with clodhopping insensitivity, even took her back to Trier to meet his young bride-to-be. Jenny's friend Betty Lucas witnessed the miserable encounter:

> I entered Jenny's room one evening, quickly and without knocking, and saw in the semi-darkness a small figure crouching on a sofa, with her feet up and her knees in her hands, resembling more a bundle than a human figure, and even today, ten years later, I understand my disappointment when this creature, gliding from the sofa, was introduced to me as Bettina von Arnim . . . The only words her celebrated mouth uttered were complaints about the heat. Then Marx entered the room and she asked him in no uncertain tone to accompany her to the Rheingrafenstein, which he did, although it was already nine o'clock and it would take an hour to get to the rock. With a sad glance at his fiancée he followed the famous woman.

How could a half-educated girl compete with such sirens? Marx's intellectual strength intimidated Jenny. When chatting to aristocratic mediocrities in gilded ballrooms she was witty, lively and supremely self-assured. When she was in the presence of her beloved, one look from those dark and fathomless eyes was enough to strike her dumb: 'I cannot say a word for nervousness, the blood stops flowing in my veins and my soul trembles.'

One need hardly add that Jenny was a child of the Romantic Age. Like many restless spirits of that generation she read and reread Shelley's *Prometheus Unbound*, whose hero was shackled to a rock for defying the gods and enlightening mankind. ('Prometheus,' Marx declared in his doctoral thesis, 'is the most eminent saint and martyr in the philosophical calendar.' An allegorical cartoon published after the suppression of the *Rheinische Zeitung* showed Marx himself in Promethean guise, chained to a printing press while a Prussian eagle pecked at his liver.) Unable to keep pace with Karl's striding impetuosity, she began to dream that he too would have to be hobbled:

> So, sweetheart, since your last letter I have tortured myself with the fear that for my sake you could become embroiled in a quarrel and then in a duel. Day and night I saw you wounded, bleeding and ill, and, Karl, to tell you the whole truth, I was not altogether unhappy in this thought: for I vividly imagined that you had lost your right hand, and, Karl, I was in a state of rapture, of bliss, because of that. You see, sweetheart, I thought that in that case I could really become quite indispensable to you, you would then always keep me with you and love me. I also thought that then I could write down all your dear, heavenly ideas and be really useful to you.

Though she conceded that this fantasy might sound 'queer', in fact it is a common enough romantic motif – the dark, dangerous hero who must be maimed or emasculated before he can win a woman's heart. Only a few years later Charlotte Brontë used the same idea in the denouement of *Jane Eyre*.

Jenny's wish was granted, more or less. During their four decades of marriage Marx was often 'bleeding and ill'; and, since his handwriting was indecipherable to the untrained eye, he depended on her to transcribe his dear, heavenly ideas. Rapture, however, proved rather more elusive in real life than in her giddy dreams.

Half Prometheus, half Mr Rochester: if this is how his adoring fiancée saw him, the attitude of her more conventional relations can well be imagined. To marry a Jew was shocking enough, but to marry a jobless, penniless Jew who had already achieved national notoriety was quite intolerable. Her reactionary half-brother Ferdinand, the head of the family since their father's death, did his utmost to prevent the union, warning that Marx was a ne'er-do-well who would bring disgrace on the entire tribe of von Westphalens. To escape the incessant gossip and brow-beating, Jenny and her mother – who supported her loyally if anxiously throughout – fled from Trier to the fashionable spa resort of Kreuznach, fifty miles away. It was there, at 10 a.m. on 19 June 1843, that the twenty-five-year-old Herr Marx, Doctor of Philosophy, married Fräulein Johanna Bertha Julia Jenny von Westphalen, aged twenty-nine, 'of no particular occupation'. The only guests were Jenny's goofy brother Edgar, her mother and a few local friends. None of Karl's relations attended. The bride wore a green silk dress and a garland of pink roses. The wedding present from Jenny's mother was a collection of jewellery and silver plate embellished with the Argyll family crest, a legacy from the von Westphalens' Scottish ancestors. The Baroness also gave them a large box of cash to help them through the first few months of married life but unfortunately the newlyweds took this treasure chest with them on a honeymoon trip up the Rhine, encouraging any indigent friends they happened to meet on the way to help themselves. The money was all gone within a week.

A few days before the wedding ceremony, at Jenny's insistence, Karl had signed an unusual contract promising that the couple would have 'legal common ownership of property' – save that 'each spouse shall for his or her own part pay the debts he or she has made or contracted, inherited or otherwise incurred before marriage'. One must assume that this was an attempt to placate Jenny's mother, who was well aware of Marx's hopelessness with money. But the contract was never enforced, even though he was seldom out of debt thereafter. During the next few years, the Argyll family silver spent more time in the hands of pawnbrokers than in the kitchen cupboard.

In that post-nuptial summer of 1843, the new Mr and Mrs Karl Marx were able to live on next to nothing as guests at the Baroness's house in Kreuznach while waiting to learn from Ruge when – and where – his new journal would be born. It was an idyllic little interlude. In the evenings, Karl and Jenny would stroll down to the river, listening to the nightingales singing from the woods on the far bank. By day, the editor-elect of the *Deutsche-Französische Jahrbücher* retreated to a workroom, reading and writing with furious intensity.

Marx always liked to work out his ideas on paper, scribbling down thoughts as they occurred to him, and a surviving page from his Kreuznach notebooks shows the process in action:

Note. Under Louis XVIII, the constitution by grace of the king (Charter imposed by the king); under Louis Philippe, the king by grace of the constitution (imposed kingship). In general we can note that the conversion of the subject into the predicate, and of the predicate into the subject, the exchange of that which determines for that which is determined, is always the most immediate revolution. Not only on the revolutionary side. The king makes the law (old monarchy), the law makes the king (new monarchy).

Once Marx had started on one of these riffs, playing with his beloved contradictions, there was no stopping him. Mightn't the simple grammatical inversion that turned old monarchs into new also explain where German philosophy had gone wrong? Hegel, for instance, had assumed that 'the Idea of the State' was the subject, with society as its predicate, whereas history showed the reverse to be the case. There was nothing wrong with Hegel that couldn't be cured by standing him on his head: religion does not make man, man makes religion; the constitution does not create the people, but the people create the constitution. Top down and bottom up, it all made perfect sense.

The credit for this discovery belongs to the German philosopher Ludwig Feuerbach, whose *Introductory Theses to the Reform of Philosophy* had been published in March 1843. 'Being is subject, thought predicate,' he argued. 'Thought arises from being, not being from thought.' Marx stretched the logic much further by extending it from abstract philosophy to the real world – above all, the world of politics, the state and society. Feuerbach, a former

pupil of Hegel, had already travelled quite a distance from his
mentor's idealism towards materialism (his most memorable
aphorism, still to be found in dictionaries of quotations, was
'Man is what he eats'); but it was a studiously cerebral materialism, unrelated to the social and economic conditions of his time
or place. Marx's foray into journalism had convinced him that
radical philosophers shouldn't spend their lives atop a lofty pillar
like some ancient Greek anchorite; they must come down and
engage with the here and now.

Feuerbach was one of the first writers from whom Marx
solicited a contribution to the *Deutsche-Französische Jahrbücher* as
soon as he knew that its publication was assured. On 3 October
1843, just before setting off to join Ruge in Paris, he wrote to
suggest a demolition job on the Prussian court philosopher F. W.
von Schelling, his old antagonist from Berlin University. 'The
entire German police is at his disposal, as I myself experienced
when I was editor of the *Rheinische Zeitung*. That is, a censorship
order can prevent anything against the holy Schelling from getting
through . . . But just imagine Schelling exposed in Paris, before
the French literary world! . . . I confidently expect a contribution
from you in the form you may find most convenient.' As further
enticement, he added a cheeky postscript: 'Although she does not
know you, my wife sends greetings. You would not believe how
many followers you have among the fair sex.'

Feuerbach was not seduced. He replied that, in his opinion, it
would be rash to move from theory to practice until the theory
itself had been honed to perfection. Marx, by contrast, believed
the two were – or ought to be – inseparable. Praxis makes perfect,
and the most necessary practice for philosophers at this time was
'merciless criticism of all that exists'. The critique of Hegel had
been inspired by Feuerbach; now Feuerbach himself, having served
his purpose, must expect to be criticised in turn – most notably in
the *Theses on Feuerbach*, written in the spring of 1845, which
conclude with the most succinct summary of the difference
between anchorites and activists: 'The philosophers have only

interpreted the world, in various ways; the point is to *change* it.'

Unlike most of the thinkers whom Marx chewed up and spat out, Feuerbach earned his lasting gratitude. 'I am glad to have an opportunity of assuring you of the great respect and – if I may use the word – love which I feel for you,' he wrote to Feuerbach in 1844. 'You have provided – I don't know whether intentionally – a philosophical basis for socialism ... The unity of man with man, which is based on the real differences between men, the concept of the human species brought down from the heaven of abstraction to the real earth, what is this but the concept of *society*!'

In his last weeks at Kreuznach, Marx wrote two important essays which were to appear in the *Deutsche-Französische Jahrbücher*. The first, 'On the Jewish Question', is usually mentioned only *en passant*, if at all, in Marxist hagiographies. But it has provided powerful ammunition for his enemies.

Was Marx a self-hating Jew? Although he never denied his Jewish origins, he never drew attention to them either – unlike his daughter Eleanor, who proudly informed a group of workers from the East End of London that she was 'a Jewess'. In his later correspondence with Engels, he sprayed anti-Semitic insults at his enemies with savage glee: the German socialist Ferdinand Lassalle, a frequent victim, was described variously as the Yid, Wily Ephraim, Izzy and the Jewish Nigger. 'It is now quite plain to me – as the shape of his head and the way his hair grows also testify – that he is descended from the negroes who accompanied Moses' flight from Egypt, unless his mother or paternal grandmother interbred with a nigger,' Marx wrote in 1862, discussing the ever-fascinating subject of Lassalle's ancestry. 'Now, this blend of Jewishness and Germanness, on the one hand, and basic negroid stock, on the other, must inevitably give rise to a peculiar product. The fellow's importunity is also niggerlike.'

Some passages from 'On the Jewish Question' have an equally rancid flavour if taken out of context – which they usually are.

What is the secular basis of Judaism? Practical need, self-interest.

What is the secular cult of the Jew? Haggling.

What is his secular God? Money...

We therefore recognise in Judaism the presence of a universal and contemporary anti-social element whose historical evolution – eagerly nurtured by the Jews in its harmful aspects – has arrived at its present peak, a peak at which it will inevitably disintegrate.

The emancipation of the Jews is, in the last analysis, the emancipation of mankind from Judaism.

Those critics who see this as a foretaste of *Mein Kampf* overlook one essential point: in spite of the clumsy phraseology and crude stereotyping, the essay was actually written as a defence of the Jews. It was a retort to Bruno Bauer, who had argued that Jews should not be granted full civic rights and freedoms unless they were baptised as Christians. Although (or perhaps because) Bauer was an ostentatious atheist, he thought Christianity a more advanced phase of civilisation than Judaism, and therefore one step closer to the joyful deliverance which would follow the inevitable destruction of all religion – just as a gravedigger might regard a doddery dowager as a more promising potential customer than the local Queen of the May.

This perverse justification for official bigotry, which allied Bauer with the most reactionary boobies in Prussia, was demolished with characteristic brutality. True, Marx seemed to accept the caricature of Jews as inveterate moneylenders – but then so did almost everyone else. (The German word '*Judentum*' was commonly used at the time as a synonym for 'commerce'.) More significantly, he didn't blame or accuse them: if they were forbidden to participate in political institutions, was it any wonder that they exercised the one power permitted to them, that of making money? Cash and religion both estranged humanity from itself, and so 'the emancipation of the Jews is, in the last analysis, the emancipation of mankind from Judaism'.

From Judaism, *nota bene*, not from the Jews. Ultimately, mankind must be freed from the tyranny of all religions, Christianity included, but in the meantime it was absurd and cruel to deny Jews the same status as any other citizen. Marx's commitment to equal rights is confirmed by a letter he sent from Cologne in March 1843 to Arnold Ruge: 'I have just been visited by the chief of the Jewish community here, who has asked me for a petition for the Jews to the Provincial Assembly, and I am willing to do it. However much I dislike the Jewish faith, Bauer's view seems to me too abstract. The thing is to make as many breaches as possible in the Christian state and to smuggle in as much as we can of what is rational.' It is also borne out by the other major work on which he started during the post-honeymoon summer of 1843, 'Towards a Critique of Hegel's *Philosophy of Right*: An Introduction', which was completed in Paris a few months later and published in the spring of 1844.

Though its title may be familiar only to the initiated, the essay itself is as famous as the article on Judaism is obscure. Many of those who have never read a word of Marx still quote the epigram about religion being the opium of the people. It is one of his most potent metaphors – inspired, one guesses, by the 'Opium War' between the British and Chinese, fought from 1839 to 1842. But do those who parrot the words actually understand them? Thanks to his self-appointed interpreters in the Soviet Union, who hijacked the phrase to justify their persecution of old believers, it is usually taken to mean that religion is a drug dispensed by wicked rulers to keep the masses in a state of dopey, bubble-brained quiescence.

Marx's point was rather more subtle and sympathetic. Though he insisted that 'the criticism of religion is the prerequisite of all criticism', he understood the spiritual impulse. The poor and wretched who expect no joy in this world may well choose to console themselves with the promise of a better life in the next; and if the state cannot hear their cries and supplications, why not appeal to an even mightier authority who promised that no prayer would go unanswered? Religion was a justification for oppression – but also a refuge from it. 'Religious suffering is at one and the same time the expression of real suffering and a protest against real suffering. Religion is the sigh of the oppressed creature, the heart of a heartless world and the soul of soulless conditions. It is the opium of the people.'

Most eloquent. Elsewhere in the essay, however, his verbal facility occasionally degenerates into mere word-juggling for its own sake – or, to be blunt, showing off. Here he is on Martin Luther and the German Reformation:

> He destroyed faith in authority, but only by restoring the authority of faith. He transformed the priests into laymen, but only by transforming the laymen into priests. He freed mankind from external religiosity, but only by making religiosity the inner man. He freed the body from the chains, but only by putting the heart in chains.

Or on the difference between France and Germany:

> In France it is enough to be something for one to want to be everything. In Germany no one may be anything unless he renounces everything. In France partial emancipation is the basis of universal emancipation. In Germany universal emancipation is the *conditio sine qua non* of any partial emancipation.

After a few paragraphs of this pyrotechnic flamboyance, one suspects that the display itself has become an end rather than a means.

To wish away Marx's stylistic excess is, however, to miss the point. His vices were also his virtues, manifestations of a mind addicted to paradox and inversion, antithesis and chiasmus. Sometimes this dialectical zeal produced empty rhetoric, but more often it led to startling and original insights. He took nothing for granted, turned everything upside down – including society itself. How could the mighty be put down from their seat, and the humble exalted? In the critique of Hegel he set out his answer for the first time: what was required was 'a class with radical chains, a class of civil society which is not a class of civil society, a class which is the dissolution of all classes ... This dissolution of society as a particular class is the *proletariat*.' That last word resounds like a clap of thunder over a parched landscape. Never mind that neither Germany nor France yet had a proletariat worth the name: a storm was coming.

Marx's theory of class struggle was to be refined and embellished over the next few years – most memorably in the *Communist Manifesto* – but its outline was already clear enough: 'Every class, as soon as it takes up the struggle against the class above it, is involved in a struggle with the class beneath it. Thus princes struggle against kings, bureaucrats against aristocrats, and the bourgeoisie against all of these, while the proletariat is already beginning to struggle against the bourgeoisie.' The role of emancipator therefore passes from one class to the next until universal liberation is finally achieved. In France, the bourgeoisie had already toppled the nobility and the clergy, and another upheaval seemed imminent. Even in stolid old Prussia, medieval government could not prolong its reign indefinitely. With a parting jibe at Teutonic efficiency – 'Germany, which is renowned for its thoroughness, cannot make a revolution unless it is a thorough one' – he set off for Paris. It was, he sensed, the only place to be at this moment in history. 'When all the inner conditions are met, the day of the German resurrection will be heralded by the crowing of the Gallic cock.'

3

The Grass-eating King

'And so – to Paris, to the old university of philosophy and the new capital of the new world!' Marx wrote to Ruge in September 1843. 'Whether the enterprise comes into being or not, in any case I shall be in Paris by the end of this month, since the atmosphere here makes one a serf, and in Germany I see no scope at all for free activity.' The revolutions of 1789 and 1830 had made the French capital a natural rallying point. It was a city of plotters and poets and pamphleteers, sects and salons and secret societies – 'the nerve-centre of European history, sending out electric shocks at intervals which galvanised the whole world'. All the best-known political thinkers of the age were Frenchmen: the mystical Christian socialist Pierre Leroux, the utopian communists Victor Considérant and Etienne Cabet, the liberal orator and poet Alphonse de Lamartine (or, to give him his full glorious appellation, Alphonse Marie Louis de Prat de Lamartine). Above all there was Pierre Joseph Proudhon, libertarian anarchist, who had won instant fame in 1840 with his book *What Is Property?* – a question he answered on page one with the simple formulation 'property is theft'. All these political picadors would eventually be tossed and gored by Karl Marx – most notably Proudhon, whose *magnum opus* on 'the philosophy of poverty' provoked Marx's lacerating riposte, *The Poverty of Philosophy*. For the moment, however, the newcomer would be content to listen and learn.

There was music in the cafés at night, revolution in the air. With the 'bourgeois monarchy' of Louis Philippe tottering, another high-voltage excitement seemed inevitable and imminent. 'The bourgeois King's loss of prestige among the people is demonstrated by the many attempts to assassinate that dynastic and autocratic prince,' Ruge reported. 'One day when he dashed by me in the Champs-Elysées, well hidden in his coach, with hussars in front and behind and on both sides, I observed to my astonishment that the outriders had their guns cocked ready to fire in earnest and not just in the usual burlesque style. Thus did he ride by with his bad conscience!' Ruge, Marx and the poet Georg Herwegh – the presiding triumvirate of the *Deutsche-Französische Jahrbücher* – arrived in Paris in the autumn of 1843. Ruge travelled from Dresden in a 'large omnibus' accompanied by his wife, a swarm of children and a large leg of veal. Inspired by the utopian Charles Fourier, he proposed that the three couples should form a 'phalanstery' or commune, in which the women would take it in turns to shop, cook and sew. 'Frau Herwegh summed up the situation at first glance,' her son Marcel recorded many years later. 'How could Frau Ruge, the nice, small Saxon woman, get on with the very intelligent and even more ambitious Frau Marx, whose knowledge was far superior to hers? How could Frau Herwegh, who had only been married so short a time and was the youngest of them, find herself attracted by this communal life?' Georg and Emma Herwegh had a taste for luxury – and, since her father was a rich banker, the means to indulge it. They declined Ruge's invitation. But Karl and Jenny (who was now four months pregnant) decided to give it a try. They moved into Ruge's apartment at 23 Rue Vanneau, next door to the offices of the *Jahrbücher*.

The experiment in patriarchal communism lasted for about a fortnight before the Marxes decamped and found lodgings of their own further down the street. Ruge was a prim, puritanical homebody who couldn't tolerate his co-editor's disorganised and impulsive habits: Marx, he complained, 'finishes nothing, breaks off everything and plunges ever afresh into an endless sea of books . . . He has worked himself sick and not gone to bed for three, even four, nights on end . . .' Shocked by these 'crazy methods of working', Ruge was downright scandalised by Marx's leisures and pleasures. 'His wife gave him for his birthday a riding switch costing 100 francs,' he wrote a few months later, 'and the poor devil cannot ride nor has he a horse. Everything he sees he wants to "have" – a carriage, smart clothes, a flower garden, new furniture from the Exhibition, in fact the moon.' It's an implausible shopping list: Marx was uninterested in luxuries or fripperies. If he did desire such things it was undoubtedly on behalf of Jenny, who delighted in them. These early months in Paris were the first and only time in her married life when she could afford to indulge the appetite, since Karl's salary was augmented by a donation of 1,000 thalers sent from Cologne by former shareholders in the *Rheinische Zeitung*. Besides, he wanted her to enjoy a last spree before being cribbed and confined by the demands of maternity. On May Day 1844 she gave birth to a baby girl, Jenny – more often known by the diminutive 'Jennychen' – whose dark eyes and black crest of hair gave her the appearance of a miniature Karl.

The novice parents, though doting, were hopelessly incompetent, and by early June it was agreed that the two Jennys should spend several months with the Baroness von Westphalen in Trier learning the rudiments of motherhood. 'The poor little doll was quite miserable and ill after the journey,' Jenny wrote to Karl on 21 June, 'and turned out to be suffering not only from constipation but downright overfeeding. We had to call in the fat pig [Robert Schleicher, the family doctor], and his decision was that it was essential to have a wet-nurse since with artificial feeding she would not easily recover . . . It was not easy to save her life, but she is now almost out of danger.' Better still, the wet-nurse agreed to come back to Paris with them. But in spite of Jenny's happiness ('my whole being expresses satisfaction and *affluence*'), she couldn't entirely dispel her old forebodings. 'Dearest heart, I am greatly worried about our future . . . If you can, do set my mind at rest about this. There is too much talk on all sides about a *steady* income.' A steady income was one necessity of life that always eluded Karl Marx.

His job in Paris, which seemed to promise financial security, turned out to be even more temporary than his last editorship. Only one issue of the *Deutsche-Französische Jahrbücher* appeared before the breach with Ruge became irreparable – and it scarcely lived up to the cross-border promise of its title. Though France was well supplied with writers, not one of them was willing to contribute. To fill the gap, Marx included his essays on the Jewish question and on Hegel, together with an edited version of his correspondence with Ruge over the previous year or two. The only non-German voice was that of an exiled Russian anarcho-communist, Michael Bakunin. 'Marx was then much more advanced than I was,' he recalled. 'He, although younger than I, was already an atheist, an instructed materialist, and a conscious socialist . . . I eagerly sought his conversation, which was always instructive and witty, when it was not inspired by petty hate, which alas! was only too often the case. There was, however, never any frank intimacy between us – our temperaments did not permit. He called me a sentimental idealist, and he was right; I called him vain, perfidious and sly, and I was right too.'

For all its obvious deficiencies, the first and last issue of the *Jahrbücher* did have one contributor of international stature – the romantic poet Heinrich Heine, whom Marx had revered since childhood and befriended soon after arriving in Paris. Heine was a painfully thin-skinned creature who often burst into tears at the slightest criticism; Marx was a pitiless critic of magnificent insensitivity. For once, however, he restrained his icon-smashing inclinations, in deference to a genuine hero of literature. Heine became a regular visitor to the Marxes' apartment in the Rue Vanneau, reading aloud from works in progress and asking the young editor to suggest emendations. On one occasion he arrived to find Karl and Jenny frantic with worry over little Jennychen, who had an attack of the cramps and was – or so they believed – at death's door. Heine took charge at once, announcing that 'the child must have a bath'. And so, according to Marx family legend, the girl's life was saved.

Heine was not a communist, at least in the Marxian sense. He cited the tale of a Babylonian king who thought himself God but fell miserably from the height of his conceit to crawl like an animal on the ground and eat grass: 'This story is found in the great and splendid Book of Daniel. I recommend it for the edification of my good friend Ruge, and also to my much more stubborn friend Marx, and also to Messrs Feuerbach, Daumer, Bruno Bauer, Hengstenberg, and the rest of the crowd of godless self-appointed gods.' He contemplated the victory of the proletariat with dread, fearing that art and beauty would have no place in this new world. 'The more or less clandestine leaders of the German communists are great logicians, the most powerful among them having come from the Hegelian school,' he wrote in 1854, referring to Marx. 'These doctors of revolution and their relentlessly determined pupils are the only men in Germany with some life in them and the future belongs to them, I fear.' Shortly before his death in 1856 he wrote a last will and testament begging forgiveness from God if he had ever written anything 'immoral', but Marx was prepared to overlook this lapse into piety – which in anyone else would have provoked his most savage scorn. As Eleanor Marx wrote, 'He loved the poet as much as his works and looked as generously as possible on his political weaknesses. Poets, he explained, were queer fish and they must be allowed to go their own ways. They should not be assessed by the measure of ordinary or even extraordinary men.'

The *Jahrbücher* may have been a financial disaster but it enjoyed great *succès d'estime*, not least because of Heinrich Heine's satirical odes on King Ludwig of Bavaria. Hundreds of copies sent to Germany were confiscated by the police, who had been warned by the Prussian government that its contents were an incitement to high treason. An order went out that Marx, Ruge and Heine should be arrested at once if they attempted to return to their fatherland. In Austria, Metternich promised 'severe penalties' against any bookseller caught stocking this 'loathsome and disgusting' document.

Arnold Ruge, taking fright, left Marx in the lurch by suspending publication and refusing to pay him the promised salary. Some historians have claimed that the quarrel needn't have become terminal 'had not other personal differences, especially on fundamental matters of principle, been developing between them for some time'. But in fact the most 'fundamental matter of principle' was a ridiculous squabble over the sex life of their colleague Georg Herwegh, who had already betrayed his new bride by starting an affair with the Comtesse Marie d'Agoult, a former mistress of the composer Liszt and mother of the girl who became Cosima Wagner. 'I was incensed by Herwegh's way of living and his laziness,' Ruge wrote to his mother. 'Several times I referred to him warmly as a scoundrel, and declared that when a man gets married he ought to know what he is doing. Marx said nothing and took his departure in a perfectly friendly manner. Next morning he wrote to me that Herwegh was a genius with a great future. My calling him a scoundrel filled him with indignation, and my ideas on marriage were philistine and inhuman. Since then we have not seen each other again.'

Although Marx often railed against promiscuity and libertinism with the puritanical ferocity of a Savonarola – if only to disprove the charge that communism was synonymous with communal sex – he observed the amorous escapades of his friends with amusement and, perhaps, a touch of envy. Jenny certainly feared as much. 'Although the spirit is willing, the flesh is weak,' she wrote from Trier in August 1844, two months after leaving her husband alone in Paris. 'The real menace of unfaithfulness, the seductions and attractions of a capital city – all those are powers and forces whose effect on me is more powerful than anything else.' She needn't have worried. Among the seductions and attractions of Paris, the rustle of a countess's skirt could not begin to compete with the clamour of politics. In the summer of 1844 Marx took up an offer to write for *Vorwärts!*, a biweekly communist journal

sponsored by the composer Meyerbeer and now edited by Karl
Ludwig Bernays, who had collaborated on the *Deutsche-Französische
Jahrbücher*.

As the only uncensored radical paper in the German language
appearing anywhere in Europe, *Vorwärts!*, provided a refuge for all
the old gang of émigré poets and polemicists, including Heine,
Herwegh, Bakunin and Arnold Ruge. Once a week they would
gather at the first-floor office on the corner of the Rue des Moulins
and the Rue Neuve des Petits for an editorial conference presided
over by Bernays and his publisher, Heinrich Börnstein, who
recalled:

Some would sit on the bed or on the trunks, others would stand
and walk about. They would all smoke terrifically and argue
with great passion and excitement. It was impossible to open
the windows, because a crowd would immediately have gathered in the street to find out the cause of the violent uproar,
and very soon the room was concealed in such a thick cloud of
tobacco smoke that it was impossible for a newcomer to
recognise anyone present. In the end, we ourselves could not
even recognise each other.

Which was probably just as well, if both Marx and Ruge were in
attendance: otherwise the 'violent uproar' might have degenerated
into fisticuffs.

The two enemies continued their feud in the public prints
instead. In July 1844, signing himself merely 'A Prussian', Ruge
wrote a long article for *Vorwärts!* about the Prussian King's brutal
suppression of the Silesian weavers, who had smashed the
machines which were threatening their livelihoods. He regarded
the weavers' revolt as an inconsequential nothing, since Germany
lacked the 'political consciousness' necessary to transform an
isolated act of disobedience into a full-dress revolution.

Marx's reply, published ten days later, argued that the fertiliser
of revolutions was not 'political consciousness' but class con-

sciousness, which the Silesians had in abundance. Ruge (or 'the alleged Prussian', as Marx called him) thought that a social revolution without a political soul was impossible; Marx dismissed this 'nonsensical concoction', maintaining that all revolutions are both social and political in so far as they dissolve the old society and overthrow the old power. Even if the revolution occurred in just one factory district, as with the Silesian weavers, it still threatened the whole state because 'it represents man's protest against a dehumanised life'. This was too optimistic by half. The only lasting influence of the revolt was that it inspired one of Heine's most celebrated verses, 'The Song of the Silesian Weavers', which was published in the same issue of *Vorwärts!*.

'The German proletariat is the theoretician of the European proletariat, just as the English proletariat is its economist, and the French proletariat its politician,' Marx wrote in his riposte to Ruge, prefiguring a later assessment by Engels that Marxism itself was a hybrid of these three bloodlines. The twenty-six-year-old Marx was already well versed in German philosophy and French socialism; now he set about educating himself in the dismal science. During the summer of 1844 he read his way systematically through the main corpus of British political economy – Adam Smith, David Ricardo, James Mill – and scribbled a running commentary as he went along. These notes, which run to about 50,000 words, were not discovered until the 1930s, when the Soviet scholar David Ryazanov published them under the title *Economic and Philosophical Manuscripts*. They are now more commonly known as the Paris manuscripts.

Marx's work has often been dismissed as 'crude dogma', usually by people who give no evidence of having read him. It would be a useful exercise to force these extempore critics – who include the present British prime minister, Tony Blair – to study the Paris manuscripts, which reveal the workings of a ceaselessly inquisitive, subtle and undogmatic mind.

The first manuscript begins with a simple declaration: 'Wages are determined by the fierce struggle between capitalist and worker. The capitalist inevitably wins. The capitalist can live longer without the worker than the worker can without him.' From this premiss all else follows. The worker has become just another commodity in search of a buyer; and it isn't a seller's market. Whatever happens, the worker loses out. If the wealth of society is decreasing, the worker suffers most. But what of a society which is prospering? 'This condition is the only one favourable to the worker. Here competition takes place among the capitalists. The demand for workers outstrips supply. But . . .'

But indeed. Capital is nothing more than the accumulated fruits of labour, and so a country's capitals and revenues grow only 'when more and more of the worker's products are being taken from him, when his own labour increasingly confronts him as alien property and the means of his existence and of his activity are increasingly concentrated in the hands of the capitalist' – rather as an intelligent chicken (if such an unlikely creature existed) would be most conscious of its impotence when at its most fertile, laying dozens of eggs only to see them snatched away while still warm.

Furthermore, in a prosperous society there will be a growing concentration of capital and more intense competition. 'The big capitalists ruin the small ones and a section of the former capitalists sinks into the class of the workers which, because of this increase in numbers, suffers a further depression of wages and becomes ever more dependent on the handful of big capitalists. Because the number of capitalists has fallen, competition for workers hardly exists any longer, and because the number of workers has increased, the competition among them has become all the more considerable, unnatural and violent.'

So, Marx concludes, even in the most propitious economic conditions, the only consequence for the worker is 'overwork and early death, reduction to a machine, enslavement to capital'. The division of labour makes him more dependent still, introducing competition from machines as well as men. 'Since the worker has been reduced to a machine, the machine can confront him as a competitor.' Finally, the accumulation of capital enables industry to turn out an ever greater quantity of products. This leads to overproduction and ends up either by putting a large number of workers out of a job or by reducing their wages to a pittance. 'Such,' Marx concluded with bleak irony, 'are the consequences of a condition of society which is most favourable to the worker, i.e. a condition of *growing* wealth. But in the long run the time will come when this state of growth reaches a peak. What is the situation of the worker then?' Pretty miserable, you won't be surprised to learn.

The odds were hopelessly stacked in capital's favour. A big industrialist can sit on the products of his factory until they fetch a decent price, whereas the worker's only product – the sweat of his brow – loses its value completely if it is not sold at every instant. A day's missed toil is as worthless in the market as yesterday morning's newspaper, and can never be recovered. 'Labour is life, and if life is not exchanged every day for food it suffers and soon perishes.' Unlike other commodities, labour can be neither accumulated nor saved – not by the labourer, at any rate. The employer is more fortunate, since capital is 'stored-up labour' with an indefinite shelf-life.

The only defence against capitalism was competition, which raises wages and cheapens prices. But for this very reason the big capitalists would always try to thwart or sabotage competitiveness. Just as the old feudal landlords operated a monopoly of land – for which the demand was almost limitless, but the supply finite – so the new breed of industrialists sought a monopoly of production. It was therefore foolish to conclude, as Adam Smith had, that the interest of the landlord or the capitalist is identical with that of society. 'Under the rule of private property, the interest which any individual has in society is in inverse proportion to the interest which society has in him, just as the interest of the moneylender in the spendthrift is not at all identical with the interest of the spendthrift.'

Marx had a strong if critical respect for Smith and Ricardo. As with Hegel, he used their own words and logic to expose the shortcomings of their theories. And the most obvious shortcoming was this: 'Political economy proceeds from the fact of private property. It does not explain it.' Classical economists treated private property as a primordial human condition, rather as theology explained the existence of evil by reference to man's first disobedience and the fruit of that forbidden tree whose mortal taste brought death into the world.

But there was nothing fixed or immutable about it. Already, thanks to the Industrial Revolution, power had transferred from feudal landlords to corporate grandees: the aristocracy of money had supplanted the aristocracy of land. 'We refuse to join in the sentimental tears which romanticism sheds on this account,' Marx commented sternly. Feudal landowners had been inefficient boobies who made no attempt to extract the maximum profit from their property, basking in the 'romantic glory' of their noble indifference. It was thoroughly desirable that this benign myth should be exploded, and that 'the root of landed property – sordid self-interest – should manifest itself in its most cynical form'. By reducing the great estates to mere commodities, with no arcadian mystique, capitalism was at least transparent in its intentions. The medieval motto *nulle terre sans seigneur* (no land without its master) gave way to a more vulgar but honest admission: *l'argent n'a pas de maître* (money knows no master).

Under this tyranny, almost everyone and everything is 'objectified'. The worker devotes his life to producing objects which he does not own or control. His labour thus becomes a separate, external being which 'exists outside him, independently of him and alien to him, and begins to confront him as an autonomous power; the life which he has bestowed on the object confronts him as hostile and alien'. No Marxian scholar or critic has drawn attention to the obvious parallel with Mary Shelley's *Frankenstein*, the tale of a monster which turns against its creator. (In view of Marx's fascination with the Promethean legend, one might also note the novel's subtitle: *A Modern Prometheus*.) While suffering from an eruption of boils in December 1863, Marx described one particularly nasty specimen as 'a second Franken-stein on my back'. 'It struck me as a good theme for a short story,' he wrote to Engels. 'From the front, the man who regales *his inner man* with port, claret, stout and a truly massive mass of meat. From the front, the guzzler. But behind, on his back, the *outer man*, a damned carbuncle. If the devil makes a pact with one to sustain one with consistently good fare in circumstances like these, may the devil take the devil, I say.' Marx mentioned this pustulent incubus to his daughter Eleanor, who was eight years old at the time. 'But it is your own flesh!' she pointed out.

The concept of self-alienation was drummed into Marx's children from infancy, mainly through the fairy stories which he invented to amuse them. 'Of the many wonderful tales [he] told me, the most wonderful, the most delightful one, was "Hans Röckle",' Eleanor wrote in a memoir:

It went on for months and months; it was a whole series of stories . . . Hans Röckle himself was a Hoffmann-like magician, who kept a toyshop, and who was always 'hard up'. His shop was full of the most wonderful things – of wooden men and women, giants and dwarfs, kings and queens, workmen and masters, animals and birds, as numerous as Noah got into the ark, tables and chairs, carriages, boxes of all sorts and sizes. And though he was a magician, Hans could never meet his obligations either to the devil or the butcher, and was therefore – much against the grain – constantly obliged to sell his toys to the devil. These then went through wonderful adventures – always ending in a return to Hans Röckle's shop.

Easy enough in a fairy tale. But how could a worker recover the fruits of labour without recourse to magic? For Hegel, alienation had been simply a fact of life, the shadow that falls between the conception and the creation, between the desire and the spasm.

Once an idea had become an object – whether a machine or a book – it was 'externalised' and thus divorced from its producer. Estrangement was the inevitable conclusion of all labour.

For Marx, alienated labour was not an eternal and inescapable problem of human consciousness but the result of a particular form of economic and social organisation. A mother, for instance, isn't automatically estranged from her baby the moment it emerges from the womb, even though parturition is undoubtedly an example of Hegel's 'externalisation'. But she would feel very alienated indeed if, every time she gave birth, the squealing infant was immediately seized from her by some latter-day Herod. This, more or less, was the daily lot of the workers, forever producing what they could not keep. No wonder they felt less than human. 'The result is,' Marx observed, in a characteristic paradox, 'that man (the worker) feels that he is acting freely only in his most animal functions – eating, drinking and procreating, or at most in his dwelling and adornment – while in his human functions he is nothing more than an animal.'

What was the alternative? By the time he wrote the Paris manuscripts, in 1844, Marx already had a formidable talent for spotting the structural faults of society – the rising damp, the rotted timbers, the joists that couldn't sustain the weight placed on them – and explaining why the wrecking ball was urgently required. But his skills as a surveyor and demolisher were not yet matched by any great architectural vision of his own. 'The supersession of private property is . . . the complete *emancipation* of all human senses and attributes,' he wrote. 'Only through the objectively unfolded wealth of human nature can the wealth of subjective *human* sensitivity – a musical ear, an eye for the beauty of form, in short, *senses* capable of human gratification – be either cultivated or created.' Communism alone could resolve the conflict between man and nature, and between man and man. 'It is the solution to the riddle of history,' he announced, with a grandiloquent flourish, 'and knows itself to be the solution.'

Maybe so; but what exactly *was* it? Unable to elaborate on his rather vague humanism, Marx preferred to say what it was not. No solution to the riddle of history could be found in the petty-bourgeois platitudes of Proudhon ('his homilies about home, conjugal love and suchlike banalities'), or in the pipe-dreams of egalitarians such as Fourier and Babeuf, who – driven by 'envy and desire to level down' – would not abolish private property but merely redistribute it. Their imaginary Happy Valley was 'a community of *labour* and *equality of wages*, which are paid out by the communal capital, the *community* as universal capitalist'. Material possession would still be the purpose of existence, the only difference being that all men – including the former capitalists – would be reduced to the category of 'worker'. And what of the women? Since marriage was itself a form of exclusive private property, presumably the crude communists intended that 'women are to go from marriage into general prostitution' – thus becoming the property of all. Marx recoiled in horror from this 'bestial' prospect.

One can see why the attempt at communal living with Herr and Frau Ruge was so unsuccessful. For all his mockery of bourgeois morals and manners, Marx was at heart a supremely bourgeois patriarch. When drinking or corresponding with male friends, he loved nothing better than a dirty joke or a titillating sexual scandal. In mixed company, however, he displayed a protective chivalry that any Victorian paterfamilias would have admired. 'As father and husband, Marx, in spite of his wild and restless character, is the gentlest and mildest of men,' a police spy observed with surprise in the 1850s. The German socialist Wilhelm Liebknecht – his companion on many a pub-crawl – found Marx's prudishness touching and rather comical. 'Although in political and economic discussion he was not wont to mince his words, often making use of quite coarse phrases, in the presence of children and of women his language was so gentle and refined that even an English governess could have had no cause for complaint. If in such circumstances the conversation should turn upon some delicate subject, Marx would fidget and blush like a sixteen-year-old maiden.'

In August 1844, while Jenny was still on her extended maternity leave in Trier and Karl toiled alone over his economic notebooks at their apartment in the Rue Vanneau, the twenty-three-year-old Friedrich Engels passed through Paris en route from England to Germany. Although the two men had met once before – when Engels visited the office of the *Rheinische Zeitung* on 16 November 1842 – it had been a cool and unmemorable encounter: Engels was wary of the impetuous young editor who 'raves as if ten thousand devils had him by the hair', as Edgar Bauer had forewarned him; Marx was equally suspicious, guessing that since Engels lived in Berlin he was probably an accomplice to the Free Hegelian follies of the brothers Bruno and Edgar Bauer. Engels redeemed himself soon afterwards by moving from Berlin to Manchester, and was allowed to write several articles for the *Rheinische Zeitung*, but what really stirred Marx's interest was a brace of essays submitted to the *Deutsche-Französische Jahrbücher* – a review of Thomas Carlyle's *Past and Present*, and a lengthy *Critique of Political Economy* which Marx described as a work of genius. One can see why: though he had already decided that abstract idealism was so much hot air, and that the engine of history was driven by economic and social forces, Marx's practical knowledge of capitalism was nil. He had been so engaged by his dialectical tussle with German philosophers that the condition of England – the first industrialised country, the birthplace of the proletariat – had escaped his notice. Engels, from his vantage point in the cotton mills of Lancashire, was well placed to enlighten him.

By the time they renewed their acquaintance in August 1844, Marx's attitude had thus changed from mistrust to respectful curiosity, and after a few aperitifs at the Café de la Régence – an old haunt of Voltaire and Diderot – Engels was invited back to the Rue Vanneau to continue the conversation. It lasted for ten intense days, fuelled by copious quantities of midnight oil and red wine, at the end of which they pledged undying friendship.

Strangely, neither of them ever wrote about this epic dialogue.

Engels's account, in a preface written more than forty years later, runs to one sentence: 'When I visited Marx in Paris in the summer of 1844, our complete agreement in all theoretical fields became evident and our joint work dates from that time.' *C'est tout*: one would hardly guess from his brisk summary that Engels's stopover in Paris might justly be described as ten days that shook the world.

Friedrich Engels's ancestors had lived in Wuppertal for more than two centuries, earning their living in agriculture and then – rather more lucratively – in the textile trade. His father, also Friedrich Engels, had diversified and expanded the enterprise by founding cotton mills in Manchester (1837) and Barmen and Engelskirchen (1841), in partnership with two brothers named Ermen.

Friedrich junior was born on 28 November 1820. The household was pious, industrious, its strict orthodoxy relieved only slightly by the cheerful disposition of his mother, Elise, whose sense of humour was 'so pronounced that even in old age she would sometimes laugh till the tears ran down her cheeks'. The father, a far more severe character, watched his eldest son anxiously for any deviation from the paths of righteousness. 'Friedrich brought home middling reports for last week,' he wrote to Elise on 27 August 1835. 'As you know, his manners have improved; but in spite of severe punishment in the past, he does not seem to be learning implicit obedience even from the fear of chastisement. Today I was once more vexed by finding in his desk a dirty book from a lending library, a romance of the thirteenth century. May God guard the boy's heart, for I am often troubled over this son of ours who is otherwise so full of promise.' God was apparently not paying attention: young Engels soon moved on to far more dangerous 'dirty books'.

He did conform to parental expectations in one respect by entering the family firm – though with no great enthusiasm. In his final school report, at Michaelmas 1837, the headmaster noted that young Friedrich 'believed himself inclined' to go into business 'as his external career'. Internally, he was already germinating other plans. But he needed an income, and a job at Ermen & Engels would be a useful sinecure that guaranteed financial security and plenty of free time.

He began his apprenticeship in Bremen, where his father found him a place as an unpaid clerk in an export business run by Heinrich Leupold. 'He's a terribly nice fellow, oh so good, you can't imagine,' Engels said of the boss. In a letter to his old schoolfriends Friedrich and Wilhelm Graeber, dated 1 September 1838, he apologises for not writing at greater length 'because the Principal is sitting here'. But, as the next paragraph indicates, Leupold wasn't a hard taskmaster:

> Excuse me for writing so badly, I have three bottles of beer under my belt, hurrah, and I cannot write much more because this must go to the post at once. It is already striking half-past three and letters must be posted by four o'clock. Good gracious, thunder and lightning, you can see that I've got some beer inside me . . . What a lamentable state! The old man, i.e. the Principal, is just going out and I am all mixed up, I don't know what I'm writing. There are all sorts of noises going on in my head.

Indeed there were. When not attending to his minimal duties in the office, or writing squiffy letters after lunch, or lying in a hammock studying the ceiling through a haze of cigar smoke, or lolloping on horseback around the suburbs of Bremen, Engels was already listening to those cranial noises. He composed choral music – much of it plagiarised from old hymns – and tried his hand at poetry. One of his poems, 'The Bedouin', was accepted for publication by the *Bremisches Conversationsblatt* in September 1838. Noteworthy as his first published work, it also marked his first encounter with the censoriousness of bourgeois editors.

As written by Engels, the poem began by lamenting that the Bedouin – 'sons of the desert, proud and free' – had been robbed of that pride and freedom, and were now mere performing

exhibits for the amusement of tourists. It ended with a stirring
battle-cry:

> Go home again, exotic guests!
> Your desert robes do not belong
> With our Parisian coats and vests,
> Nor with our literature your song!

The idea, he explained later, was 'to contrast the Bedouin, even
in their present condition, and the audience, who are quite alien
to these people'. But in the published text this was replaced with
a new final stanza, added by the editor himself without the
author's permission:

> They jump at money's beck and call,
> And not at Nature's primal urge.
> Their eyes are blank, they're silent, all
> Except for one who sings a dirge.

Thus an angry exhortation was reduced to nothing more than a
melancholy, rueful shrug of the shoulders. Engels was understandably displeased: in his primitive fashion he had already
noticed that society is shaped by economic imperatives, but the
editor would not allow him to name or condemn the culprits. 'It
has become clear to me,' he concluded after this unhappy début,
'that my rhyming achieves nothing.'

His literary tastes were becoming more political and prosaic.
He bought a topical pamphlet, *Jacob Grimm über seiner Entlassung*,
which described the dismissal by Göttingen University of seven
liberal professors who had dared to protest at the oppressive
regime of Ernst August, the new King of Hanover. 'It is
extraordinarily good and written with a rare power.' He read no
fewer than seven pamphlets on the 'Cologne affair' – the refusal,
in 1837, of the Archbishop of Cologne to obey the King of
Prussia. 'I have read things here and come across expressions – I

am getting good practice, especially in literature – which one would never be allowed to print in our parts, quite liberal ideas, etc . . . really wonderful.' In one of his letters to the Graebers, emboldened by beer, he referred to Ernst August as 'the old Hanoverian he-goat'.

The most obviously 'progressive' voices of the time came from the Young Germany group of writers, disciples of Heine who advocated free speech, the emancipation of women, an end to religious tyranny, and abolition of hereditary aristocracy. 'Who can have anything against that?' Engels asked, half-mockingly. He was impatient with their easy, vague liberalism, but in the absence of anything more rigorous or analytical he had nowhere else to turn. 'What shall I, poor devil, do now? Go on swotting on my own? Don't feel like it. Turn loyal? The devil if I will!' So, *faute de mieux*, he became a Young German himself. 'I cannot sleep at night, all because of the ideas of the century. When I am at the post office and look at the Prussian coat of arms, I am seized with the spirit of freedom. Every time I look at a newspaper I hunt for advances of freedom. They get into my poems and mock at the obscurantists in monk's cowls and in ermine.'

Back home in Barmen his parents knew nothing of their son's democratic fever: he did his best to keep them in ignorance, then and for many years afterwards. Even in middle age, when he and Marx were joyfully awaiting the imminent crisis of capitalism, Engels was always on his best behaviour during Friedrich senior's visits to Manchester, playing the part of a dutiful heir who could be trusted with the family fortune – just as, out riding with the Cheshire Hunt, he was able to pass himself off as a conservative local businessman. His communism, his atheism, his sexual promiscuity: these all belonged to his separate life.

To those in the know, Engels's true opinions of his parents and their milieu were obvious as early as March 1839, when he wrote a coruscating attack on the smug, complacent burghers of Barmen and Elberfeld for the *Telegraph für Deutschland*, a Young Germany newspaper. The eighteen-year-old author hid behind the pseudonym 'Friedrich Oswald' – a necessary precaution, since the articles were nothing less than journalistic parricide. In the 'gloomy streets' of Elberfeld, he reported, all the alehouses were full to overflowing on Saturday and Sunday nights:

> and when they close at about eleven o'clock, the drunks pour out of them and generally sleep off their intoxication in the gutter ... The reasons for this state of affairs are perfectly clear. First and foremost, factory work is largely responsible. Work in low rooms where people breathe in more coal fumes and dust than oxygen – and in the majority of cases beginning already at the age of six – is bound to deprive them of all strength and joy in life. The weavers, who have individual looms in their homes, sit bent over them from morning till night, and desiccate their spinal marrow in front of a hot stove. Those who do not fall prey to mysticism are ruined by drunkenness.

As the reference to mysticism implies, Engels had already identified religion as a handmaiden of exploitation and hypocrisy: 'For it is a fact that the pietists among the factory owners treat their workers worst of all; they use every possible means to reduce the workers' wages on the pretext of depriving them of the opportunity to get drunk, yet at the election of preachers they are always the first to bribe their people.' He even named some of these snivelling pharisees, though he forbore to mention his own father.

The 'Letters from Elberfeld' caused outrage. 'Ha, ha, ha!' he wrote to Friedrich Graeber, one of the few to be let in on the secret. 'Do you know who wrote the article in the *Telegraph*? The author is the writer of these lines, but I advise you not to say anything about it. I could get into a hell of a lot of trouble.'

In the spring of 1841 Engels left Bremen for military service in Berlin, enlisting in the Household Artillery. The choice of Berlin, capital city of Young Hegelianism, was no accident: though his army uniform gave him a camouflage of respectability and reassured his parents, he spent every spare moment immersing himself in radical theology and journalism. He pulled off a similar trick in the autumn of 1842 when dispatched to the Manchester branch of Ermen & Engels: while apparently training himself in the family business, as a dutiful heir should, he took the opportunity to investigate the human consequences of capitalism. Manchester was the birthplace of the Anti-Corn Law League, the centre of the 1842 General Strike, a city teeming with Chartists, Owenites and industrial agitators of every kind. Here, if anywhere, he would discover the nature of the beast. By day he was a quietly diligent young manager at the Cotton Exchange; after hours he changed sides, exploring the *terra incognita* of proletarian Lancashire to gather facts and impressions for his early masterpiece, *The Condition of the Working Class in England* (1845). Often accompanied by his new lover, a redheaded Irish factory girl called Mary Burns, he ventured into slum districts which few other men of his class had ever seen. Here, for example, is his picture of 'Little Ireland', the area of Manchester south-west of the Oxford Road:

Masses of refuse, offal and sickening filth lie among standing pools in all directions; the atmosphere is poisoned by the effluvia from these, and laden and darkened by the smoke of a dozen tall factory chimneys. A horde of ragged women and children swarm about here, as filthy as the swine that thrive upon the garbage heaps and in the puddles. In short, the whole rookery furnishes such a hateful and repulsive spectacle as can hardly be equalled in the worst court on the Irk. The race that lives in these ruinous cottages, behind broken windows, mended with oilskin, sprung doors, and rotten door-posts, or in dark, wet cellars, in measureless filth and stench, in this atmosphere penned in as if with a purpose, this race must really have reached the lowest stage of humanity. This is the impression and the line of thought which the exterior of this district forces upon the beholder. But what must one think when he hears that in each of these pens, containing at most two rooms, a garret and perhaps a cellar, on the average twenty human beings live?

What gave the book its power and depth was Engels's skilful interweaving (he was a textile man, after all) of firsthand observation with information from parliamentary commissions, health officials and copies of Hansard. The British state may have done little or nothing to improve the lot of the workers, but it had collected a mass of data about the horrors of industrial life which was available to anyone who cared to retrieve it from a dusty library shelf. Newspaper reports, particularly from criminal trials, provided yet more details. 'On Monday, 15 January, 1844,' Engels noted:

> two boys were brought before the police magistrate because, being in a starving condition, they had stolen and immediately devoured a half-cooked calf's foot from a shop. The magistrate felt called upon to investigate the case further, and received the following details from the policeman. The mother of the two boys was the widow of an ex-soldier, afterwards policeman, and had had a very hard time since the death of her husband . . . When the policeman came to her, he found her with six of her children literally huddled together in a little back room, with no furniture but two old rush-bottomed chairs with the seats gone, a small table with two legs broken, a broken cup and a small dish. On the hearth was scarcely a spark of fire, and in one corner lay as many old rags as would fill a woman's apron, which served the whole family as a bed.

Engels was astonished to discover that the organs of the British bourgeoisie provided so much incriminating evidence against themselves. After quoting several gruesome cases of disease and starvation, published in the middle-class *Manchester Guardian*, he exulted: 'I delight in the testimony of my opponents.' One need only study the citations from government Blue Books and *The Economist* in the first volume of *Capital* to see how much Karl Marx learned from this technique.

Marx and Engels complemented each other perfectly. While Engels couldn't begin to match Marx's erudition, having missed out on university, he had invaluable firsthand knowledge of the machinery of capitalism. But the 'complete agreement in all theoretical fields' didn't extend to their respective habits and styles. One might almost say that the two characters were Thesis and Antithesis incarnate. Marx wrote in a cramped scrawl, with countless deletions and emendations as blotchy testimony to the effort it cost him; Engels's script was neat, businesslike, elegant. Marx was squat and swarthy, a Jew tormented by self-loathing; Engels was tall and fair, with more than a hint of Aryan swagger. Marx lived in chaos and penury; Engels was a briskly efficient worker who held down a full-time job at the family firm while maintaining a formidable output of books, letters and journalism – and often ghost-writing articles for Marx as well. Yet he always found the time to enjoy the comforts of high bourgeois life: horses in his stables, plenty of wine in his cellar and mistresses in the bedroom. During the long years when Marx was almost drowning in squalor, fending off creditors and struggling to keep his family alive, the childless Engels pursued the carefree pleasures of a prosperous bachelor.

In spite of the obvious disparity of advantage, Engels knew that he would never be the dominant partner. He deferred to Marx from the outset, accepting that it was his historic duty to support and subsidise the indigent sage without complaint or jealousy – even, come to that, without much gratitude. 'I simply cannot understand,' he wrote in 1881, nearly forty years after that first meeting, 'how anyone can be envious of genius; it's something so very special that we who have not got it know it to be unattainable right from the start; but to be envious of anything like that one must have to be frightfully small-minded.' Marx's

friendship, and the triumphant culmination of his work, would
be reward enough.

They had no secrets from each other, no taboos: if Marx found
a huge boil on his penis he didn't hesitate to supply a full
description. Their voluminous correspondence is a gamey stew
of history and gossip, political economy and schoolboy smut,
high ideals and low intimacies. In a letter to Engels on 23 March
1853, to take a more or less random example, Marx discusses the
rapid increase in British exports to the Turkish dominions,
Disraeli's position in the Conservative Party, the passage of the
Canadian Clergy Reserves Bill through the House of Commons,
the harassment of refugees by the British police, the activities of
German communists in New York, an attempt by Marx's publisher
to swindle him, the condition of Hungary – and the alleged
flatulence of the Empress Eugénie: 'That angel suffers, it seems,
from a most indelicate complaint. She is passionately addicted to
farting and is incapable, even in company, of suppressing it. At one
time she resorted to horse-riding as a remedy. But this having now
been forbidden her by Bonaparte, she "vents" herself. It's only a
noise, a little murmur, a nothing, but then you know that the
French are sensitive to the slightest puff of wind.'

As stateless cosmopolitans they even evolved their own private
language, a weird Anglo-Franco-Latino-German mumbo-jumbo.
All other quotations in this book have been translated to spare
readers the anguish of puzzling over the Marxian code, but one
brief sentence will give an idea of its expressive if incomprehensible syntax: 'Diese excessive technicality of ancient law zeigt
Jurisprudenz as feather of the same bird, als d. religiösen
Formalitäten z. B. Auguris etc. od. d.. Hokus Pokus des medicine
man der savages.' Engels learned to understand this gibberish
with ease; more impressively still, he was able to read Marx's
handwriting, as was Jenny. Apart from those two close collaborators, however, few have managed the task without tearing their
hair out. After Marx's death, Engels had to give a lengthy course
of instruction in paleography to the German Social Democrats

who wished to organise the great man's unpublished papers.

Engels served Marx as a kind of substitute mother – sending him pocket money, fussing over his health and continually reminding him not to neglect his studies. In the earliest surviving letter, written in October 1844, he was already chivvying Marx to finish his political and economic manuscripts: 'See to it that the material you've collected is soon launched into the world. It's high time, heaven knows!' And again on 20 January 1845: 'Do try and finish your political economy book, even if there's much in it that you yourself are dissatisfied with, it doesn't really matter; minds are ripe and we must strike while the iron's hot . . . So try and finish *before* April, do as I do, set yourself a date by which you will *definitely have finished*, and make sure it gets into print quickly.'

Fat chance. Marx was led astray by Engels himself, who made the mistake of proposing that they collaborate on a pamphlet demolishing Bruno Bauer and his troupe of clowns, under the working title *Critique of Critical Criticism*. He emphasised that it should be no more than forty pages long, since 'I find all this theoretical twaddle daily more tedious and am irritated by every word that has to be expended on the subject of "man", by every line that has to be read or written against theology and abstraction . . .'

Engels dashed off his portion of twenty pages while still at the flat in the Rue Vanneau, and then returned home to the Rhineland. He was 'not a little surprised', several months later, to hear that the pamphlet was now a swollen monstrosity of more than 300 pages and had been renamed *The Holy Family*. 'If you have retained my name on the title page it will look rather odd,' he pointed out. 'I contributed practically nothing to it.' But this was not the only reason for wanting his name removed. 'The *Critical Criticism* has still not arrived!' he told Marx in February 1845. 'Its new title, *The Holy Family*, will probably get me into hot water with my pious and already highly incensed parent, though you, of course, could not have known that.' The angry parent was, of course, his bigoted and despotic father, who had begun to fear for the boy's Christian soul. 'If I get a letter, it's sniffed all over before it reaches me,' he grumbled. 'I can't eat, drink, sleep, let out a fart, without being confronted by the same accursed lamb-of-God expression.' One day, when Engels staggered home at two in the morning, the suspicious patriarch asked if he had been arrested. Not at all, Engels replied reassuringly: he had simply been discussing communism with Moses Hess. 'With Hess!' his father spluttered. 'Great heavens! What company you keep!'

He didn't know the half of it. 'Now all my old man has to do is to discover the existence of the *Critical Criticism* and he will be quite capable of flinging me out of the house. And on top of it all there's the constant irritation of seeing that nothing can be done with these people, that they positively *want* to flay and torture themselves with their infernal fantasies, and that one can't even teach them the most platitudinous principles of justice.'

The Holy Family, or Critique of Critical Criticism: Against Bruno Bauer and Consorts was published in Frankfurt in the spring of 1845. Rereading the book more than twenty years later, Marx was 'pleasantly surprised to find that we have no need to feel ashamed of the piece, although the Feuerbach cult now makes a most comical impression on one'. Few other readers have shared his satisfaction. By the time Marx started writing this scornful epic, the brothers Bruno, Edgar and Egbert Bauer – the holy family of the title – had already slipped from militant atheism and communism into mere buffoonery, rather like the Dadaists or Futurists of the 1930s. All they deserved or needed was a quick slap, not a full-scale bombardment. Who shoots a housefly with a blunderbuss?

Marx's scattergun hit other targets who were no more worthy of his attentions. There were several chapters of invective against Eugène Sue, an author of popular sentimental novels, whose only offence was to have been praised in Bruno Bauer's *Allgemeine Literatur-Zeitung*. Though Sue may well have been every bit as dire as Marx suggested, the punishment was absurdly disproportionate to the crime: try to imagine, by way of a modern equivalent, a *magnum opus* by Professor George Steiner attacking *The Bridges of Madison County*. Even Engels had to admit that Marx was wasting his sourness on the desert air. 'The thing's too long,' he wrote. 'The supreme contempt we two evince towards the *Literatur-Zeitung* is in glaring contrast to the twenty-two sheets [352 pages] we devote to it. In addition most of the criticism of speculation and of abstract being in general will be incomprehensible to the public at large, nor will it be of general interest. Otherwise the book is splendidly written . . .'

Or, as the tactful curate said on being served a rotten egg by his bishop, 'No, my lord, parts of it are excellent!'

4

The Mouse in the Attic

Had Marx confined himself to twitting obscure Hegelians and second-rate novelists, he might have been left in peace. But he couldn't resist the chance to tease a bigger and more dangerous beast. In the summer of 1844, after surviving an assassination attempt, King Friedrich Wilhelm IV of Prussia issued this brief message of thanks to his loyal subjects before departing on holiday: 'I cannot leave the soil of the Fatherland, although only for a short time, without expressing publicly the deeply felt gratitude in My and the Queen's name by which Our heart has been moved.' Marx thought this hilarious – and said so, *con brio*, in an article for *Vorwärts!*. The King's syntax, he wrote, seemed to imply that the royal bosoms were moved by the royal name:

> If amazement at this peculiar movement makes one think again, one sees that the relative conjunction '*by which* our heart has been moved' refers not to the name but to the more remotely situated *gratitude* . . . The difficulty is due to the combination of three ideas: (1) that the King is leaving his homeland, (2) that he is leaving it only for a short time, (3) that he feels a need to thank the people. The too compressed utterance of these ideas makes it appear that the King is expressing his *gratitude* only because he is leaving his homeland . . .

If Marx thought that he could get away with this lèse-majesté, he had forgotten that monarchs have their own masonic solidarity.

On 7 January 1845, at an audience with King Louis Philippe in Paris, the Prussian envoy Alexander von Humboldt handed over two items – a valuable porcelain vase, and a letter from Friedrich Wilhelm IV protesting at the outrageous insults and libels published by *Vorwärts!*. Louis Philippe agreed that there were indeed far too many German philosophers in Paris: the magazine was closed down two weeks later, and the interior minister François Guizot ordered Marx's expulsion from France.

Where now? The only king in mainland Europe still willing to accept refugees was Leopold I of Belgium, though even he demanded a written promise of good behaviour. ('To obtain permission to reside in Belgium I agree to pledge myself, on my word of honour, not to publish in Belgium any work on current politics. [signed] Dr Karl Marx.') While Jenny stayed on for a few days to sell their furniture and linen, Marx left Paris in the company of Heinrich Bürgers, a young journalist from *Vorwärts!* who was quitting the country in disgust at 'the punishment inflicted on the man who was my friend and faithful guide in my studies'. As their two-man coach rattled through Picardy, Bürgers tried vainly to lift his mentor's spirits with choruses from German drinking songs.

A good night's sleep was rather more restorative. The next morning Marx was already impatient for action, telling Bürgers to hurry up with his breakfast because 'we must go and see Freiligrath today'. Ferdinand Freiligrath, a quondam court poet to Friedrich Wilhelm IV, had fled to Belgium some weeks earlier to escape arrest after publishing a treasonous *Confession of Faith*. Once a regular butt of the old *Rheinische Zeitung*, he was now granted instant absolution as a convert to the anti-Prussian cause. Other new arrivals from the radical diaspora included Moses Hess, Karl Heinzen, the Swiss radical Sebastian Seiler, the former artillery officer Joseph Weydemeyer (who was to become a lifelong friend), a gaggle of Polish socialists – and, most importantly, Friedrich Engels, who needed little persuasion to escape from the stifling propriety of Barmen and follow Marx into exile. Jenny's brother Edgar von Westphalen, the lovable if incontinent puppy of the family, came too.

By the time Marx's wife and daughter joined him, he was already back in the old routine – reading, writing, boozing, scheming. 'We were madly gay,' Weydemeyer recalled. There were long mornings in cafés and even longer nights of card-playing and tipsy conversation. For once, even the family finances were in credit: two days before leaving Paris Marx was paid a 1,500-franc advance by a publisher in Darmstadt for his embryonic work on political economy, and a whip-round by Engels added another 1,000 francs to the kitty, mostly from supporters in Germany. Engels also handed over the fee for his own book, *The Condition of the Working Class in England*, so that 'at least the curs shan't have the satisfaction of seeing their infamy cause you pecuniary embarrassment'. But, he added presciently, 'I fear that in the end you'll be molested in Belgium too, so that you'll be left with no alternative but England.'

Jenny, pregnant once more, tried to conceal her disappointment at forsaking the shops and *salons* of Paris for boring old Brussels, but her mother was worried enough by this latest domestic upheaval to send her maidservant from Trier, Helene Demuth, on permanent loan. The twenty-five-year-old Demuth, who spent the rest of her life holding the Marx household together through countless crises and vicissitudes, was a small, graceful woman of peasant stock – round faced, blue eyed and always immaculately neat and well groomed even when surrounded by squalor. Her domestic efficiency was formidable and unflagging. As late as 1922, an Englishwoman who had visited the Marxes as a girl still recalled Helene's excellent cooking: 'Her jam tarts are a sweet and abiding memory to this day.' Not that she was a meek little drudge: she guarded her new employers with tigerish ferocity, and any guests who outstayed their welcome could expect a severe mauling.

For the first couple of months Marx and his family lodged in hotels or the spare rooms of friends. But as soon as they found a

more permanent billet – a small terraced house at 5 Rue
D'Alliance, at the eastern end of the city – Jenny set off with her
daughter and maid for a summer vacation in the Baroness von
Westphalen's residence in Germany, leaving Karl to make the
place habitable. 'The little house should do,' Jenny wrote from
Trier. A room would have to be set aside for childbirth, but 'having
concluded my important business on the upper floor, I shall
remove downstairs again. Then you could sleep in what is now
your study and pitch your tent in the immense drawing-room –
that would present no difficulty. The children's noise downstairs
would then be completely shut off, you would not be disturbed
upstairs, I could join you when things were quiet ... What a
colony of paupers there is going to be in Brussels!' On 26
September, only a fortnight after travelling back from Trier, Jenny
added to the colonial population by giving birth to another
daughter, Laura.

Marx had promised the Belgian authorities not to publish
anything on current politics, but thought he was quite within his
rights to *participate* in politics and to pursue his studies in economic
history. Hence the summons to Engels, by now an indispensable
lieutenant. In the summer of 1845 the two men paid a six-week
visit to England, partly to take advantage of the well-stocked
libraries in Manchester and London but also to meet the leaders
of the Chartists, the first working-class movement in the world.
On their return, Engels rented a house next door to the Marxes
and set about organising the socialist flotsam of Brussels into a
comparable political force.

First, however, there was the small matter of Marx's book. The
research trip to Britain and the long hours he spent in Brussels's
municipal library must have raised the hopes of his publisher,
Karl Leske, who was expecting the *Critique of Economics and Politics*
by the end of the summer. But Marx had already set the
manuscript aside after writing no more than a table of contents.
'It seemed to me very important,' he explained to Leske, 'to
precede my *positive* development with a polemical piece against

German philosophy and German socialism up till the present. This is necessary in order to prepare the public for the viewpoint adopted in my Economy, which is diametrically opposed to German scholarship past and present . . . If need be, I could produce numerous letters I have received from Germany and France as proof that this work is most eagerly awaited by the public.'

Not so: his 'polemical piece', *The German Ideology*, didn't find a publisher until 1932. The only public demand for it came from Marx himself, who was now being caricatured by the Young Hegelians as an unthinking disciple of Ludwig Feuerbach. This infuriated him: Feuerbach's demystification of Hegel had indeed been a glorious moment of revelation, like Keats's first glimpse of Chapman's Homer, but Marx had long since concluded that the critique merely substituted one myth for another. Feuerbach, the man who had turned Hegel upside down, was now due for the same treatment – or, as Marx put it, a 'settlement of accounts'.

His exercise in philosophical bookkeeping began in the spring of 1845 when he scribbled down the brief notes now known as the *Theses on Feuerbach*. 'The chief defect of all previous materialism (that of Feuerbach included) is that things, reality, sensuousness, are conceived only in the form of the *object*, or of *contemplation*, but not as *sensuous human activity*, *practice*.' Feuerbach had exposed the secular basis of religion, but then allowed the secular realm itself to float off into clouds of abstraction. 'The question whether objective truth can be attributed to human thinking,' Marx argued, 'is not a question of theory but is a *practical* question . . . All social life is essentially *practical* . . . The philosophers have only *interpreted* the world in various ways; the point is to *change* it.' Theory without practice was a form of scholastic masturbation – pleasurable enough, but ultimately infertile and of no consequence. Nevertheless, Marx and Engels proceeded to spend the winter of 1845–6 theorising like billy-o as they composed their *German Ideology*.

The book begins with one of Marx's attention-grabbing generalisations: 'Hitherto men have always formed wrong ideas about themselves, about what they are and what they ought to be.' This is followed by another favourite trick, the provocative parable:

> Once upon a time a valiant fellow had the idea that men were drowned in water only because they were possessed with the *idea of gravity*. If they were to get this notion out of their heads, say by avowing it to be a superstitious, a religious concept, they would be sublimely proof against any danger from water. His whole life long he fought against the illusion of gravity, of whose harmful consequences all statistics brought him new and manifold evidence. This valiant fellow was the type of the new revolutionary philosophers in Germany.

These thinkers were sheep labouring under the delusion that they were wolves, whose vapid bleating 'merely imitates in a philosophic form the conceptions of the German middle class'.

One sheep was Ludwig Feuerbach himself, whose conception of the world was 'confined on the one hand to mere contemplation of it, and on the other to mere feeling'. He thus failed to notice that even the simplest natural objects are in fact products of historical circumstance. For instance: 'The cherry-tree, like almost all fruit-trees, was, as is well known, only a few centuries ago transplanted by *commerce* into our zone, and therefore only by this action of a definite society in a definite age has it become a "sensuous certainty".' To Feuerbach, the cherry-tree was simply *there*, one of nature's altruistic gifts.

Oddly enough, although the book had been intended as a settling of accounts with Feuerbach, he merited no more than a couple of short chapters. Bruno Bauer – 'Saint Bruno' – was dispatched with similar speed. But 300 unreadable pages were devoted to the follies of Max Stirner, an anarchic Young Hegelian author who proposed that heroic egoism and self-indulgence would liberate individuals from their imaginary oppression. Though Stirner's existentialist credo deserved its come-uppance, a quick stiletto jab would have done the job far more effectively than Marx's verbose sarcasm – which, ironically, looked very much like an example of the self-indulgent egoism that Stirner advocated.

For all its *longueurs*, however, *The German Ideology* is a most revealing account of what the twenty-seven-year-old Marx had learned from his philosophical and political adventures. Having rejected God, Hegel and Feuerbach in quick succession, he and Engels were now ready to unveil their own scheme of practical theory or theoretical practice – otherwise known as historical materialism. 'The premises from which we begin,' they announced, 'are not arbitrary ones, not dogmas, but real premises from which abstraction can only be made in the imagination. They are the real individuals, their activity and the material conditions of their life . . . These premises can thus be verified in a purely empirical way.' Whereas Feuerbach had argued that you are what you eat, Marx and Engels insisted that you are what you produce – and how you produce it. 'The division of labour inside a nation leads at first to the separation of industrial and commercial from agricultural labour, and hence to the separation of town and country and to the conflict of their interests. Its further development leads to the separation of commercial from industrial labour . . .' And so on. These various refinements in the division of labour reflected the development of property – from primitive tribal property to ancient communal and state property, thence to feudal or estate property and onwards to bourgeois property. 'The social structure and the state are continually evolving out of the life-process of definite individuals . . . It is not consciousness that determines life, but life that determines consciousness.' Slavery could not be abolished without the steam engine or the mule jenny, just as serfdom could not be abolished without improvements in agriculture, and in general 'people cannot be liberated as long as they are unable to obtain food and drink, housing and clothing in adequate quality and quantity'.

What would this liberation feel like? Though the new materialism of Marx and Engels was presented as the negation of idealism,
their own vision of paradise turned out to be a pastoral idyll –
bizarrely ironic in view of Marx's contempt for country life, which
he usually described as 'rural idiocy'. Under the present division
of labour, they noted, each man was trapped in an exclusive
sphere of activity:

> He is a hunter, a fisherman, a shepherd, or a critical critic, and
> must remain so if he does not want to lose his means of
> livelihood; whereas in communist society, where nobody has
> one exclusive sphere of activity but each can become accom-
> plished in any branch he wishes, society regulates the general
> production and thus makes it possible for me to do one thing
> today and another tomorrow, to hunt in the morning, fish in
> the afternoon, rear cattle in the evening, criticise, just as I have
> a mind, without ever becoming hunter, fisherman, shepherd or
> critic.

A rather exhausting Nirvana, some might think. Engels certainly
enjoyed hunting and criticising, but did his heart really thrill at
the promise of postprandial cattle-rearing?

The Marxist paradise was evoked rather more enticingly in the
interminable diatribe against Stirner, who had suggested that the
division of labour applied only to those tasks which any reasonably
trained person could perform – baking or ploughing, for instance.
No one, he maintained, could have done Raphael's works for
him. This was an unfortunate example: Raphael had teams of
assistants and pupils to complete his frescoes, as Marx and Engels
were quick to point out. Besides, the communists didn't believe
that everyone should or could produce the work of a Raphael,
but only that a potential Raphael must be allowed to develop
without hindrance.

Sancho [i.e. Stirner] imagines that Raphael produced his pictures independently of the division of labour that existed in Rome at the time. If he were to compare Raphael with Leonardo da Vinci and Titian, he would see how greatly Raphael's works of art depended on the flourishing of Rome at that time, which occurred under Florentine influence, while the works of Leonardo depended on the state of things in Florence, and the works of Titian, at a later period, depended on the totally different development of Venice. Raphael as much as any other artist was determined by the technical advances in art made before him, by the organisation of society and the division of labour . . . In a communist society there are no painters but only people who engage in painting among other activities.

Activities such as hunting, fishing and sheep-shearing, presumably. The question of who would clean the lavatories or hew the coal was neither asked nor answered. When a German smart aleck tried to catch him out by wondering aloud who would polish the shoes under communism, Marx replied crossly, 'You should.' A friend once suggested that she couldn't imagine Marx living contentedly in an egalitarian society. 'Neither can I,' he agreed. 'These times will come, but we must be away by then.'

Since its belated publication this century, extravagant claims have been made for *The German Ideology* as a 'comprehensive exposition' of the Marxist conception of history. Marx himself was more realistic about its limitations. 'We abandoned the manuscript to the gnawing criticism of the mice,' he wrote, 'all the more willingly as we had achieved our main purpose – self-clarification.' The tattered pages of the surviving manuscript do indeed appear to have been nibbled at the margin by small rodents, possibly of an unreconstructed Hegelian tendency.

Having sorted out the theory to their satisfaction, Marx and

Engels moved swiftly on to the practice – 'to win over the European, and in the first place the German, proletariat to our conviction'. And where was the German proletariat to be found? In Paris, London and Brussels, of course.

The earliest organisation of exiled German communists, the League of Outlaws, had been founded in Paris in 1834. Its members were mostly middle-class intellectuals – 'the most sleepy-headed elements', as Engels called them – who soon dozed off altogether. The clandestine League of the Just, which split away from it in 1836, was an altogether livelier outfit run by self-educated artisans who spent many a happy evening plotting putsches and conspiracies. Their politics, however, still amounted to little more than a vague egalitarianism derived from the eighteenth-century utopian Gracchus Babeuf. After participating in the botched Parisian uprising of May 1839 several of the League's leaders fled to London, where they set up a respectable-sounding German Workers' Educational Association as a front for their secret society. The most important of these figures were Karl Schapper, a burly typesetter and sometime forestry worker who had won his revolutionary spurs during the storming of a Frankfurt police station in 1833; Heinrich Bauer, a witty little cobbler from Franconia; and Joseph Moll, a watchmaker from Cologne of medium height but huge physical courage. 'How often,' Engels wrote, 'did Schapper and he victoriously defend the entrance to a hall against hundreds of onrushing opponents!' (Heroic to the last, Moll was shot dead on a German battlefield during the Baden uprising of 1849.)

Engels came to know the triumvirate while he was visiting London in 1843. They were the first working-class revolutionaries he had ever met, and to an impressionable bourgeois youngster their status as 'real men' easily outweighed the narrowness and naïvety of their ideology. Besides, they were undoubtedly efficient, having rebuilt the League of the Just as a thriving concern in London and created a network of supporters in Switzerland, Germany and France. Where workers' associations were banned by law, their 'lodges' masqueraded as choral societies or gymnastic clubs.

Although these conspirators still looked to Paris as the mother-city of revolutions, they no longer treated French philosophy with quite the old awe or deference. For the League now had a theoretician of its own, the journeyman tailor Wilhelm Weitling, whose book *Mankind As It Is and As It Ought To Be* had been published by the League in 1838.

Weitling, the illegitimate son of a German washerwoman, had the pious, anguished demeanour of a martyred prophet. He would have been quite at home among the travelling chiliastic preachers of the Middle Ages, or the communist millenarian sects that flourished at the time of the English Civil War, but he had little in common with the thinkers or agitators of nineteenth-century revolution. His creed was a home-made cocktail of the Book of Revelation and the Sermon on the Mount, in which the cloying sweetness of Sunday-school homily was spiced up with a dash of fire and brimstone. When not warning of imminent Armageddon he babbled happily of a return to Eden, an Arcadia in which hatred and envy would be unknown. It was as if one of the four horsemen of the Apocalypse had suddenly dismounted to stroke a passing cat.

Still, there was no denying the power of his evangelism. 'The respect he enjoyed in our circles was boundless,' wrote Friedrich Lessner, another communist tailor from Germany. 'He was the idol of his followers.' And, because of his wanderings through Europe, these disciples formed an impressive multinational brigade. Escaping to Switzerland after the failed French rebellion of 1839, he established branches of the League of the Just in Geneva and Zurich which eventually brought him to the attention of Swiss officialdom. During a raid on his lodgings the police found more incriminating evidence of his wickedness – an autobiographical manuscript, *The Gospel of a Poor Sinner*, in which he likened himself to Jesus Christ as an impoverished outcast who had been crucified for daring to speak out against injustice. This impudence earned him six months in jail for blasphemy, followed by deportation to Germany – where he was soon arrested again, this time for deserting from the army to avoid national service. By the time he reached London, in 1844, the thirty-six-year-old tailor was a legendary figure who drew large crowds of expatriate German socialists and English Chartists with his revivalist rhetoric. In one of his favourite *coups de théâtre*, he would hitch up an elegant trouser leg (as a tailor himself, Weitling always wore well-cut suits) to reveal the livid scars left by the chains and shackles of his jailers.

It's hard to imagine anyone less likely to appeal to Marx than this vain utopian dreamer, whose political programme was summarised in a toe-curling preface to his book *Guarantees of Harmony and Freedom*: 'We wish to be free as the birds in the sky; we wish to dart through life like them, carefree in joyful flight and sweet harmony.' The best way of achieving lift-off, Weitling suggested, was to recruit a 40,000-strong army of convicted thieves and robbers – who, driven on by their burning grudge against private property, would bring down the mighty from their seats and usher in a new age of peace and joy. 'Criminals are a product of the present order of society,' he wrote, 'and under communism they would cease to be criminals.' In Weitling's earthly paradise everyone would be provided with identical clothes (designed by himself, no doubt), and those who wished to wear anything else would have to earn it by working overtime. Eating would take place in communal canteens, though policy on cutlery had still to be decided. ('These tailors are really astounding chaps,' Engels commented after meeting some of Weitling's followers. 'Recently they were discussing quite seriously the question of knives and forks.') When people reached the age of fifty they would be removed from the labour force and dispatched to a retirement colony – a sort of communist Eastbourne, though perhaps without the bowls club.

One can almost hear Marx snorting with derision at this

twaddle. But he hesitated to condemn it publicly. Although he had proclaimed in 1844, with patriotic hyperbole, that 'the German proletariat is the theoretician of the European proletariat', the truth was that until the mid-1840s he had met very few German workers. ('What the proletariat does we know not and indeed could hardly know,' Engels reminded him in March 1845.) At first, therefore, his reaction to the emergence of a truly working-class thinker from his homeland was like that of Dr Johnson to the dog walking on its hind legs: it is not done well but you are surprised to find it done at all – and, consequently, you reward the performing mutt with extravagant praise. 'Where among the bourgeoisie – including its philosophers and learned writers – is to be found a book about the emancipation of the bourgeoisie – *political* emancipation – similar to Weitling's work *Guarantees of Harmony and Freedom*?' Marx wondered. 'It is enough to compare the petty faint-hearted mediocrity of German political literature with this *vehement* and brilliant literary début of the German workers, it is enough to compare these gigantic *infant shoes* of the proletariat with the dwarfish, worn-out political shoes of the German bourgeoisie, and one is bound to prophesy that the German Cinderella will one day have the figure of an athlete . . .'

The itinerant Cinderella never did go to the ball, either in glass slippers or running shoes. Though Messrs Schapper, Bauer and Moll gave Weitling a generous reception when he arrived in London in 1845, they quickly concluded that his ideas were too cranky by half. He was grievously disappointed by their unwillingness to invest in his many ingenious schemes – the creation of a new universal language, the invention of a machine for making ladies' straw hats – and even more upset when they refused to elect him as president of their association. At the beginning of 1846 he went off to try his luck in Brussels.

'If I tell you what kind of life we have been leading here, you would certainly be surprised at the communists,' Joseph Weydemeyer wrote to his fiancée in February. 'To crown the

folly, Marx, Weitling, Marx's brother-in-law and I sat up the
whole night playing. Weitling got tired first. Marx and I slept a
few hours on the sofa and idled away the whole of the next day
in the company of his wife and his brother-in-law in the most
priceless manner. We went to a tavern early in the morning,
then we went by train to Villeworde, which is a little place
nearby, where we had lunch and then returned in the most
cheerful mood by the last train.' It will be noticed that Weitling,
after retiring early, played no part in the morning-after amuse-
ments: his halo of sanctity made him uncongenial company,
especially for bourgeois intellectuals. As Engels wrote, 'He was
now the great man, the prophet, driven from country to country,
who carried a prescription for the realisation of heaven on earth
ready-made in his pocket, and who imagined that everybody
was out to steal it from him.'

When Heinrich Heine met Weitling, he was outraged by 'the
fellow's utter lack of respect while he conversed with me. He did
not remove his cap and, while I was standing before him, he
remained sitting with his right knee raised by the aid of his right
hand to his very chin and steadily rubbing the raised leg with his
left hand just above the ankle'. Cue the old trick with the trouser
leg and the prison scars; but even this left Heine unmoved. 'I
confess that I recoiled when the tailor Weitling told me about
these chains. I, who had once in Münster kissed with burning lips
the relics of the tailor John of Leyden – the chains he had worn,
the pincers with which he had been tortured and which are
preserved in the Münster City Hall – I who had made an exalted
cult of the dead tailor, now felt an insurmountable aversion for
this living tailor, Wilhelm Weitling, though both were apostles
and martyrs in the same cause.'

Marx and Engels had a similar revulsion, especially when
Weitling took to addressing them as 'my dear young fellows', but
they did their best to conceal it, if only out of respect for his
proletarian status and his long years of persecution. Early in 1846
they invited him to become a founder member of the new

Communist Correspondence Committee in Brussels, whose purpose was to maintain 'a continuous interchange of letters' with the League of the Just and other fraternal associations in western Europe. Since the committee was the original Adam from which all the many subsequent Communist Parties were descended, it may be worth listing the eighteen founding signatories: Karl Marx, Friedrich Engels, Jenny Marx, Edgar von Westphalen, Ferdinand Freiligrath, Joseph Weydemeyer, Moses Hess, Hermann Kriege, Wilhelm Weitling, Ernst Dronke, Louis Heilberg, Georg Weerth, Sebastian Seiler, Philippe Gigot, Wilhelm Wolff, Ferdinand Wolff, Karl Wallau, Stephan Born. Like most of its twentieth-century successors this communist cell asserted its authority by purging anyone suspected of deviation from official correctness; inevitably, Weitling was picked out as the first sacrificial victim.

The occasion for his ritual humiliation was a meeting on the evening of 30 March 1846 attended by half a dozen members plus an outside observer, Pavel Annenkov, a young Russian 'aesthetical tourist' who had lately turned up in Brussels with a letter of introduction from one of Marx's old Paris friends. Though not a socialist, Annenkov was fascinated by the character of his host:

> Marx was the type of man who is made up of energy, will and unshakeable conviction. He was most remarkable in his appearance. He had a shock of deep black hair and hairy hands and his coat was buttoned wrong; but he looked like a man with the right and power to demand respect, no matter how he appeared before you and no matter what he did . . . He always spoke in imperative words that would brook no contradiction and were made all the sharper by the almost painful impression of the tone which ran through everything he said. This tone expressed the firm conviction of his mission to dominate men's minds and prescribe them their laws. Before me stood the embodiment of a democratic dictator.

The dapper Weitling, by contrást, looked more like a commercial traveller than a hero of the working class.

After introductions had been effected, everyone gathered around the small green table in Marx's living-room to discuss the tactics of revolution. Engels, tall and erect and dignified, spoke of the need to agree on a single common doctrine for the benefit of those workers who lacked the time and opportunity to study theory. Before he could finish, however, Marx was already spoiling for a fight. 'Tell us, Weitling,' he interrupted, glaring across the table, 'you who have made such a noise in Germany with your preaching: on what grounds do you justify your activity and what do you intend to base it on in future?'

Weitling, expecting nothing more than an evening of liberal commonplaces, was taken aback by this abrupt challenge. He launched into a long, rambling monologue, often pausing to repeat or correct himself as he explained that his aim was not to create new economic theories but to adopt those that were 'most appropriate'. Marx moved in for the kill. To rouse the workers without offering any scientific ideas or constructive doctrine, he said, was 'equivalent to vain dishonest play at preaching which assumes an inspired prophet on the one side and on the other only the gaping asses'.

Weitling's pale cheeks coloured. In trembling voice, he protested that a man who had rallied hundreds of people under the same banner in the name of justice and solidarity could not be treated like this. He consoled himself by remembering the countless letters of thanks that he had received, and by the thought that his 'modest spade-work was perhaps of greater weight for the common cause than criticism and armchair analysis of doctrines far from the world of the suffering and afflicted people'. This attempt to play the proletarian card was more than Marx could bear. Leaping from his seat, and thumping the table so hard that the lamp on it shook and rang, he yelled, 'Ignorance never yet helped anybody!' The meeting was adjourned in uproar. 'As Marx paced up and down the room, extraordinarily irritated and angry,' Annenkov reported, 'I hurriedly took leave of him and his interlocutors and went home, amazed at all I had seen and heard.' No one who knew Marx well would have been so amazed: throughout his life he found it both necessary and enjoyable to denounce the false gods and posturing messiahs of the communist movement.

Surprisingly, Weitling continued to visit Marx's house for some weeks afterwards, and was present in May for another show trial. The defendant, condemned in absentia this time, was the young Westphalian student Hermann Kriege, who had lately emigrated to edit a German-language newspaper in New York. At a meeting on 11 May, the following motion was passed with only Weitling voting against:

1. The line taken by the editor of the *Volks-Tribun*, Hermann Kriege, is not communist.
2. Kriege's childish pomposity in support of this line is compromising in the highest degree to the Communist Party, both in Europe and America, inasmuch as he is held to be the representative of German communism in New York.
3. The fantastic emotionalism which Kriege is preaching in New York under the name of 'communism' must have an extremely damaging effect on the workers' morale if it is adopted by them.

In support of their indictment Marx and Engels produced a 'Circular Against Kriege', deriding the soppy sentimentalism of his newspaper, the *Volks-Tribun*, which described women as 'the flaming eyes of humanity', 'true priestesses of love' and 'beloved sisters' whose sacred duty was to lead men into 'the kingdom of bliss'. What is a woman, Kriege had asked in an editorial, 'without the man whom she can love, to whom she can surrender her trembling soul?' Marx and Engels said that this amorous slobbering 'presents communism as the love-imbued opposite of selfishness and reduces a revolutionary movement of world-historical importance to the few words: love – hate, communism – selfishness ... We leave Kriege to reflect for himself on the enervating effect this love-sickness cannot fail to have on both sexes and the mass hysteria and anaemia it must produce in the "virgins".'

The original eighteen members thus dwindled to sixteen – and soon to fifteen, as Moses Hess resigned before he too could be expelled. With Marx's growing reputation as a 'democratic dictator', new recruits for his letter-writing circle were hard to find. In May, while seeing off Weitling and Kriege, he invited Pierre-Joseph Proudhon to join the club. 'So far as France is concerned, we all of us believe that we could find no better correspondent than yourself. As you know, the English and Germans have hitherto estimated you more highly than have your own compatriots ... Let us have an early reply, and rest assured of the sincere friendship of yours most sincerely, Karl Marx.' The professions of respect and friendship, and the assurance that the committee was engaged in a civilised 'exchange of ideas', were undermined by Marx's scrawled postscript: 'PS I must now denounce to you Mr Grün of Paris. The man is nothing more than a literary swindler, a species of charlatan, who seeks to traffic in modern ideas. He tries to conceal his ignorance with pompous and arrogant phrases but all he does is make himself ridiculous with his *gibberish* ... In his book on "French socialists", he has the audacity to describe himself as tutor to Proudhon ... Beware of this parasite.'

Alas! Proudhon was actually rather fond of Karl Grün, a well-known publicist for 'True Socialism', and thought the warning ill-judged and distasteful. 'Grün is in exile, with no wealth, with a wife and two children to support, living by his pen. What would you wish him to exploit in order to earn a livelihood, if not modern ideas? ... I see nothing here except misfortune and extreme necessity, and I pardon the man.' Marx's vindictiveness worried Proudhon far more than Grün's harmless vanity. 'Let us, if you wish, collaborate in trying to discover the laws of society,' he proposed.

> But for God's sake, after we have demolished all the dogmatisms *a priori*, let us not of all things attempt in our turn to instill another kind of dogma into the people . . . With all my heart I applaud your idea of bringing all opinions out into the open. Let us have decent and sincere polemics. Let us give the world an example of learned and farsighted tolerance. But simply because we are at the head of the movement, let us not make ourselves the leaders of a new intolerance . . . Let us never regard a question as exhausted, and even when we have used up our last argument, let us begin again, if necessary, with eloquence and irony. Under these conditions I will gladly enter into your association. Otherwise – no!

Marx could not allow such a snub to go unpunished – as Proudhon had anticipated towards the end of his letter: 'This, my dear philosopher, is where I am at the moment; unless, of course, I am mistaken and the occasion arises to receive a caning from you, to which I subject myself with good grace . . .' The occasion for this larruping arose only a few months later when Proudhon produced a two-volume work on *The Philosophy of Poverty*. Marx retaliated with a 100-page philippic titled *The Poverty of Philosophy*, published in both Paris and Brussels in June 1847, which ridiculed the Gallic guru for his fathomless ignorance. In the foreword he wrote:

> Monsieur Proudhon has the misfortune of being peculiarly misunderstood in Europe. In France, he has the right to be a bad economist, because he is reputed to be a good German philosopher. In Germany, he has the right to be a bad philosopher, because he is reputed to be one of the ablest of French economists. Being both a German and an economist at the same time, we desire to protest against this double error. The reader will understand that in this thankless task we have often

had to abandon our criticism of M. Proudhon in order to criticise German philosophy, and at the same time to give some observations on political economy.

Though the ad hominem swipes at Proudhon are entertaining enough, it is these 'observations' on economics and philosophy that give the book its lasting value. With *The German Ideology* consigned to a mouse-infested attic, *The Poverty of Philosophy* is the first published work in which Marx set out his materialist idea of history. Economic categories such as 'the division of labour' were, he argued, only the theoretical and transitory expression of actual conditions of production. But Proudhon – 'holding things upside down like a true philosopher' – thought these actual conditions were only the incarnation of timeless economic laws, from which he concluded that the division of labour was an eternal and inevitable fact of life. Marx overturned this topsy-turvy logic in a justly famous paragraph:

M. Proudhon the economist understands very well that men make cloth, linen or silk materials in definite relations of production. But what he has not understood is that these definite social relations are just as much produced by men as linen, flax, etc. Social relations are closely bound up with productive forces. In acquiring new productive forces men change their mode of production; and in changing their mode of production, in changing the way of earning their living, they change all their social relations. The hand-mill gives you society with the feudal lord; the steam-mill, society with the industrial capitalist.

To Marx's unforgiving eye, Proudhon's socialist manifesto looked suspiciously like a reluctant acceptance of the status quo. Workers shouldn't organise to demand higher wages, Proudhon warned, since they would then have to pay their own bill in the form of higher prices. Nor was there anything to be gained from revolutionary violence. In fact, it was hard to tell what he did advocate, beyond a vague reliance on 'providence'.

When, Marx demanded, did meek acquiescence ever achieve anything? On the final page of *The Poverty of Philosophy*, his simmering indignation boiled over:

> The antagonism between the proletariat and the bourgeoisie is a struggle of class against class, a struggle which carried to its highest expression is a total revolution. Indeed, is it at all surprising that a society founded on the *opposition* of classes should culminate in its brutal *contradiction*, the shock of body against body, as its final denouement?
>
> Do not say that social movement excludes political movement. There is never a political movement which is not at the same time social.
>
> It is only in an order of things in which there are no more classes and class antagonisms that *social evolutions* will cease to be *political revolutions*. Till then, on the eve of every general reshuffling of society, the last word of social science will always be: 'Combat or death, bloody struggle or extinction. Thus the question is inexorably put.' (George Sand.)

Proudhon made no public riposte to *The Poverty of Philosophy*, but his own copy has furious marginal scribbles on almost every page – 'Absurd', 'A lie', 'Prattle', 'Plagiarism', 'Brazen slander' and 'Actually, Marx is jealous'. An entry in one of his notebooks describes Marx as 'the tapeworm of socialism'.

The Communist Correspondence Committee would have to find someone else to represent it in France. Engels moved to Paris in August 1846 to reconnoitre. 'Our affair will prosper greatly here,' he reported after talking to August Hermann Ewerbeck, a local leader of the League of the Just. 'What remains here of the Weitlingians, a small clique of tailors, is now in process of being thrown out ... The cabinet-makers and tanners, on the other hand, are said to be capital fellows.' Ewerbeck had identified four or five of them who might be reliable enough to join the correspondence network. (The assumption that all revolutionaries must be artisans was hard to dislodge: that same month the Parisian *Journal des Economistes* described Marx as 'a shoemaker' with a penchant for 'abstract formulas'.)

A few weeks later, having attended several meetings of the League, Engels seemed less cheerful. Ewerbeck, though amiable and well-intentioned, was a ghastly old bore who specialised in hair-splitting disquisitions on 'true value' and lectures on old German etymology. Worse still, he and his members treated the effusions of Proudhon and Grün as holy writ. 'It is disgraceful that one should still have to pit oneself against such barbaric nonsense. But one must be patient, and I shall not let the fellows go until I have driven Grün from the field and have swept the cobwebs from their brains.'

He staged his *coup* in mid-October by initiating a debate at the League on the pros and cons of communism, thus forcing the Parisian artisans to decide whether they were avowedly communist or merely 'in favour of the good of mankind', as preferred by Grün and his followers. Engels warned that if the vote went against him he 'didn't give a fig for them' and would attend no more meetings. 'By dint of a little patience and some terrorism,' he told Marx, 'I have emerged victorious with the great majority behind me.' Grün's chief disciple, an old carpenter called Eisermann, was so intimidated by Engels's verbal battering-ram that he never showed his face again.

These noisy exchanges soon came to the attention of the French police chief, Gabriel Delessert. When Engels heard that expulsion orders might be issued against himself and Ewerbeck, he decided to keep away from the League until the hue and cry had subsided. 'I am indebted to Mr Delessert for some delicious encounters with *grisettes* and for a great deal of pleasure,' he confessed roguishly, 'since I wanted to take advantage of the days and nights which might well be my last in Paris.' After satisfying his carnal appetite he spent a week in Sarcelles at the house of Karl

Ludwig Bernays, Marx's old editor at *Vorwärts!*, but found the atmosphere intolerably fetid: 'The stench is like five thousand unaired featherbeds, multiplied by the release therein of innumerable farts – the result of Austrian vegetable cookery.' He also wrote a satirical pamphlet 'pullulating with smutty jokes' about Lola Montez, the Spanish dancer whose influence over King Ludwig of Bavaria was a cause of scandalised amusement to both Marx and Engels. No publisher would take it, and the manuscript has long since disappeared.

As one can infer from all these *divertissements*, Engels was short of intellectual stimulation. 'If at all possible, do come here some time in April,' he begged Marx in early March:

> By 7 April I shall be moving – I don't yet know where to – and about that time I shall also have a little money. So for a time we could enjoy ourselves famously, squandering our all in taverns . . . If I had an income of 5,000 fr. I would do nothing but work and amuse myself with women until I went to pieces. If there were no Frenchwomen, life wouldn't be worth living. But so long as there are *grisettes*, well and good! That doesn't prevent one from sometimes wishing to discuss a decent topic or enjoy life with a measure of refinement, neither of which is possible with anyone in the whole band of my acquaintances. You must come here.

Perhaps all that carousing had addled the Engels brain. Three months before he wrote this letter Jenny Marx had given birth to her first son, Edgar, a brother for two-year-old Jennychen and one-year-old Laura. As the sole provider for an effete wife, three small children and a housemaid, Marx could ill afford to go off on a bachelors' bender in gay Paree. Unemployed and virtually unemployable, he couldn't even raise the fare for a rather more important excursion, to London, where the League of the Just summoned a conference in June to discuss a merger with the Brussels correspondence circle.

It was not so much a merger as a takeover. Marx had refused to join forces with the Londoners – Schapper, Bauer, Moll – until they reconstituted themselves as a Communist League, jettisoning the simpering pieties with which the League of the Just had been associated. They were now willing to meet his demands. Proudhon, Grün and Weitling were to be ritually denounced for 'hostility to the communists', and the old League slogan that Marx so despised – 'All Men Are Brothers' – was replaced by the imperative 'Working Men of All Countries, Unite!'

Two months after the Communist League's inaugural meeting in London, the correspondence committee in Brussels converted itself into a branch (or 'community') of the League, with Marx as president. Under the new rules, each community must have at least three and at most twelve members, each of whom had to 'give his word of honour to work loyally and to observe secrecy'. It was, after all, an illegal organisation. Following the Londoners' example, however, Marx also founded a more open and less political Workers' Association which staged quasi-parliamentary debates as well as 'singing, recitation, theatricals and the like'. More than 100 workers joined in the first couple of weeks. 'However minor it may be,' Marx wrote to George Herwegh, 'public activity is infinitely refreshing.'

His interests were represented at the June congress in London by another German communist from Brussels, Wilhelm Wolff, as well as the delegate from the League's Paris branch, a certain F. Engels, who had arrived with a draft statement of principles for the new Communist League. Though not formally adopted, this was sent to communities elsewhere in Europe 'for serious and mature consideration'. As a circular from HQ explained, 'We have tried on the one hand to refrain from all system-making and all barrack-room communism, and on the other to avoid the fatuous and vapid sentimentality of the tearful, emotional communists [i.e. utopians such as Weitling] . . . We hope that the Central Authority will receive from you very many proposals for additions and amendments, and we will call on you again to discuss the project with particular zest.' No one received the invitation with more zest than Marx, who within a year had transformed Engels's embryonic credo into one of the most influential books ever published.

5

The Frightful Hobgoblin

The *Manifesto of the Communist Party* may be the most widely read political pamphlet in human history, but it is also the most misleadingly titled: no such party existed. Nor, come to that, was it conceived as a manifesto. What the members of the Communist League wanted in 1847 was a 'profession of faith', and an early draft written by Engels in June 1847 shows that they were still wedded to the initiation rituals favoured by the French underground sects:

QUESTION 1: Are you a Communist?

ANSWER: Yes.

QUESTION 2: What is the aim of the Communists?

ANSWER: To organise society in such a way that every member of it can develop and use all his capabilities and powers in complete freedom and without thereby infringing the basic conditions of this society.

QUESTION 3: How do you wish to achieve this aim?

ANSWER: By the elimination of private property and its replacement by community of property.

And so on for another seven pages, culminating in Question 22 ('Do Communists reject the existing religions?'), to which the correct answer is that communism 'makes all existing religions superfluous and supersedes them'. From a modern vantage point, this laborious Q&A exercise is irresistibly reminiscent of the

Monty Python sketch in which Marx appears on a TV quiz show hosted by Eric Idle:

> IDLE: The development of the industrial proletariat is conditioned by what other development?
> MARX: The development of the industrial bourgeoisie.
> IDLE: Yes it is indeed. Well done, Karl! You're on your way to a lounge suite! Now Karl, number two. The struggle of class against class is a what struggle?
> MARX: A political struggle.
> IDLE: Good! One final question, and that beautiful non-materialistic lounge suite will be yours. Ready, Karl? You're a brave man. Your final question: who won the English FA Cup in 1949?
> MARX: Er, er, the workers' control of the means of production? The-the struggle of the urban proletariat?
> IDLE: No, it was Wolverhampton Wanderers, who beat Leicester 3–1.
> MARX: Oh, shit!

Engels's catechism might have been appropriate for a secret society such as the old League of Outlaws or the League of the Just – but this was the furtive, conspiratorial tradition from which Marx wanted to rescue the new Communist League. Why, he demanded, should revolutionaries hide their views and intentions?

Engels took the point, admitting that 'since a certain amount of history has to be narrated in it, the form hitherto adopted is quite unsuitable'. Returning to Paris in October after an extended stay in Brussels, he discovered that Moses Hess had prepared another draft 'Confession' which reeked of utopianism and hardly mentioned the proletariat. Engels ridiculed this document, line by line, at a meeting of the local Communist League – 'and was not yet half-way through when the lads declared themselves *satisfaits*', as he reported triumphantly to Marx in Brussels. 'Completely unopposed, I got them to entrust me with the task of drafting a new one which will be discussed next Friday by the district and will be sent to London *behind the backs of the communities*. Naturally not a soul must know about this, otherwise we shall all be unseated and there'll be a deuce of a row.'

Within days Engels had finished his new version, less like a credo and more like an exam paper, with a long historical account of the origins and development of the proletariat, as well as 'all kinds of secondary matter'. Nevertheless, it was still written in the call-and-response style of its predecessor. ('What is communism? *Answer*: Communism is the doctrine of the conditions for the emancipation of the proletariat. What is the proletariat? *Answer*: The proletariat is that class of society which procures its means of livelihood entirely and solely from the sale of its labour . . .') 'Give a little thought to the Confession of Faith,' he wrote to Marx on 23 November 1847. 'I think we would do best to abandon the catechetical form and call the thing Communist *Manifesto*.' Five days later the two men met at Ostend, en route for London and the second congress of the Communist League.

The venue for the congress was the HQ of the German Workers' Educational Association, above the Red Lion pub in Great Windmill Street, Soho; and the intensity of the debate can be gauged by the fact that it continued for ten days – no doubt with occasional forays downstairs for urgently needed refreshment. Few contemporary records survive, but Marx's dominant presence was described years later in a memoir by Friedrich Lessner, a journeyman tailor from Hamburg who had been living in London since April 1847:

Marx was a born leader of the people. His speech was brief, convincing and compelling in its logic. He never said a superfluous word; every sentence was a thought and every thought was a necessary link in the chain of his demonstration. Marx had nothing of the dreamer about him. The more I realised the difference between the communism of Weitling's time and that of the *Communist Manifesto*, the more clearly I saw that Marx represented the manhood of socialist thought.

By the end of the ten-day marathon, Marx and Engels had carried all before them. The June congress, which Marx had not attended, had declared merely that the League 'aims at the emancipation of humanity by spreading the theory of the community of property and its speediest possible practical introduction'. The rules adopted at the second congress were far more combative and robust: 'The aim of the League is the overthrow of the bourgeoisie, the rule of the proletariat, the abolition of the old bourgeois society which rests on the antagonism of classes, and the foundation of a new society without classes and without private property.' The delegates agreed these basic principles unanimously, and Marx and Engels were commissioned to draw up a manifesto summarising the new doctrine as soon as possible.

Marx seemed in no great hurry to comply. After returning to Brussels in mid-December, he delivered a course of lectures to the German Workers' Association on political economy, arguing that capital was not an inanimate object but a 'social relation'. He wrote several articles for the *Deutsche-Brüsseler-Zeitung*, defending the communists and anticipating with relish the coming revolution in France. He gave a long speech on free trade. At a New Year's Eve party given by the Workers' Association he proposed a toast to Belgium – 'forcefully expressing appreciation of the benefits of a liberal constitution, of a country where there is freedom of discussion, freedom of association, and where a humanitarian seed can flourish to the good of all Europe'. (Little did he guess that within a couple of months he would be denouncing the 'unprecedented brutality' and 'reactionary fury' of this erstwhile liberal paradise, when the Belgian government kicked him out of the country at twenty-four hours' notice.) From 17 to 23 January he visited Ghent to establish a local branch of the Democratic Association.

Most authors will recognise the symptoms: ceaseless procrastination, a quest for distractions, a willingness to do anything except the job in hand. Most publishers, likewise, will sympathise with the growing impatience of the London leaders of the Communist League, who dispatched an ultimatum to Brussels on 24 January 1848:

> The Central Committee charges its regional committee in Brussels to communicate with Citizen Marx, and to tell him that if the Manifesto of the Communist Party, the writing of which he undertook to do at the recent congress, does not reach London by 1 February of the current year, further measures will have to be taken against him. In the event of Citizen Marx not fulfilling his task, the Central Committee requests the immediate return of the documents placed at Citizen Marx's disposal.

Marx was usually at his best when up against a deadline, and this final warning seems to have done the trick. Though every modern edition of the *Manifesto* carries the names of Marx and Engels – and Engels's ideas undoubtedly had an influence – the text that finally reached London at the beginning of February was written by Karl Marx alone, in his study at 42 Rue d'Orléans, scribbling furiously through the night amid a thick fug of cigar smoke.

Kierkegaard says somewhere that life must be lived forwards but can only be understood backwards. This applies also to eras and epochs: the reality of a particular age may not become apparent until it is drawing to a close. Or, as Hegel wrote in his *Philosophy of Right*, 'the owl of Minerva spreads his wings only with the falling of the dusk'. When Marx wrote the *Communist Manifesto*, in January 1848, he imagined he could see the wise owl once more preparing for flight: the brief but brilliant era of bourgeois capitalism had served its transitional purpose and would soon be buried under its own contradictions. By driving hitherto isolated workers into mills and factories, modern industry had created the very conditions in which the proletariat could associate and combine into a dominant force. 'What the bourgeoisie, therefore, produces, above all, is its own grave-diggers,' he noted with satisfaction at the end of the manifesto's first section. 'Its fall and the victory of the proletariat are equally inevitable.'

Perhaps because he thought he was rehearsing a funeral oration, he could afford to be generous to his vanquished foe. Those who have never read Marx, but know of him merely as some kind of bloodthirsty bogeyman whose name is invoked to terrify the middle classes, are often surprised to discover how much praise he lavished on the bourgeoisie. He was not a man to underestimate the enemy's achievement:

> The bourgeoisie, historically, has played a most revolutionary part. The bourgeoisie, wherever it has got the upper hand, has put an end to all feudal, patriarchal, idyllic relations. It has pitilessly torn asunder the motley feudal ties that bound man to his 'natural superiors', and has left remaining no other nexus between man and man than naked self-interest, than callous 'cash payment'. It has drowned the most heavenly ecstasies of religious fervour, of chivalrous enthusiasm, of philistine sentimentalism, in the icy water of egotistical calculation. It has resolved personal worth into exchange value, and in place of the numberless indefeasible chartered freedoms has set up that single, unconscionable freedom – Free Trade. In one word, for exploitation, veiled by religious and political illusions, it has substituted naked, shameless, direct, brutal exploitation . . .

> The bourgeoisie has disclosed how it came to pass that the brutal display of vigour in the Middle Ages, which Reactionists so much admire, found its fitting complement in the most slothful indolence. It has been the first to show what man's activity can bring about. It has accomplished wonders far surpassing Egyptian pyramids, Roman aqueducts and Gothic cathedrals; it has conducted expeditions that put in the shade all former Exoduses of nations and crusades.

One modern critic has described the manifesto as 'a lyrical

celebration of bourgeois works'. And so it is, after a fashion: Marx was celebrating capitalism as a temporary phenomenon, as the harbinger of a true revolution. But what he took to be its death throes were in fact nothing more than birth pangs. The signs he misinterpreted – the howls, the thrashing limbs, the blood-spattered sheets – are even more conspicuous today than in his own time, though he is seldom given any credit for noticing them. 'The bourgeoisie has through its exploitation of the world market given a cosmopolitan character to production and consumption in every country,' he pointed out. 'In place of the old wants, satisfied by the productions of the country, we find new wants, requiring for their satisfaction the products of distant lands and climes.' Anyone surveying the fruit and veg counter in a supermarket – piled high with mangoes, avocados, sugar-snap peas and out-of-season strawberries – will see what he meant.

While importing exotica, the bourgeoisie foists its own products, tastes and habits on everyone else: 'In one word, it creates a world after its own image.' To recognise the truth of this, one need only visit Beijing – the capital of an avowedly communist state – where the city centre now looks eerily like Main Street, USA, with McDonald's, Kentucky Fried Chicken, Haagen-Dazs and Pizza Hut, plus several branches of Chase Manhattan and Citibank in which to deposit the profits.

'As in material, so also in intellectual production,' the *Manifesto* continued. 'The intellectual creations of individual nations become common property ... The bourgeoisie, by the rapid improvement of all instruments of production, by the immensely facilitated means of communication, draws all, even the most barbarian nations, into civilisation.' One can argue about whether Arnold Schwarzenegger, John Grisham and non-stop MTV really constitute 'civilisation', but the essential truth of his perception can't be denied. He also understood that the pace of technological change would become ever more frantic, creating a sort of permanent revolution where any computer software bought more than a couple of years ago is all but obsolete. 'The bourgeoisie

cannot exist without revolutionising the instruments of production, and thereby the relations of production, and with them
the whole relations of society . . . Constant revolutionising of
production, uninterrupted disturbance of all social conditions,
everlasting uncertainty and agitation distinguish the bourgeois
epoch from all earlier ones. All fixed, fast-frozen relations, with
their train of ancient and venerable prejudices and opinions, are
swept away, all new-formed ones become antiquated before they
can ossify. All that is solid melts into air . . .'

To mark the *Manifesto*'s 150th anniversary, in 1998, countless
academics and politicians were trotted out to gloat over the old
boy's imbecility. A British intellectual, Lord Skidelsky, sneered
that Marx had 'got it wrong' by predicting imminent revolution –
and that his work was, therefore, no longer worth a second glance.
As it happens, revolution *did* break out within days of the
Manifesto's publication, first in Paris and then, with the speed of
brushfire, across much of continental Europe. But it was doused
just as quickly, and bourgeois triumphalism began its long reign.
In that sense, Marx's optimism was misplaced, even though his
vision of the global market was uncannily prescient.

How could he be so wrong and yet so right? When he is in
prophetic mood, Marx sometimes thinks like a chess player
devising a fatal pincer movement on the black king six moves
hence – not noticing, all the while, that his opponent can mate
him far sooner. If the other player makes a mistake, Marx's
calculations will be vindicated. And even if Marx loses, he can
argue that he would have been proved right if only the battle had
continued for a few minutes longer.

We know these chess players well – brilliant strategy, fragile
tactics – and Marx was indeed one of them. Though unbeatable
at draughts or checkers, he lacked the artful patience required for
the infinite complexities of the chessboard. His style was noisy,
argumentative, hot-tempered. In the early 1850s, soon after his
arrival in London, he ended many an evening in wild fury as yet
another German exile cornered his king. 'One day,' Wilhelm

Liebknecht recalled, 'Marx announced triumphantly that he had discovered a new move by which he would drive us all under cover. The challenge was accepted. And really – he defeated us all one after the other. Gradually, however, we learned victory from defeat, and I succeeded in checkmating Marx. It had become very late, and he grimly demanded revenge for next morning, in his house.'

At 11 a.m. the following day Liebknecht duly presented himself at Marx's rooms in Dean Street, to find that the great man had sat up all night refining and perfecting his 'new move'. Once again, it seemed to work at first, and Marx celebrated his victory by calling for drinks and sandwiches. But then the struggle commenced in earnest: throughout the afternoon and evening the two men faced each other grimly across the black-and-white battlefield until, at midnight, Liebknecht succeeded in checkmating his opponent twice in succession. Marx was ready to continue until dawn, but his strong-willed housekeeper Helene Demuth had had enough: 'Now,' she ordered the bleary-eyed contestants, 'you stop!'

Early the next day Liebknecht was roused from his bed by a knock on the door. It was Helene, bearing a message: 'Mrs Marx begs that you play no more chess with Moor in the evening – when he loses the game, he is most disagreeable.'*

Liebknecht never played chess with Marx again; but his description of the Marxian technique – 'he tried to make up what he lacked in science by zeal, impetuousness of attack and surprise' – might be applied to the *Communist Manifesto*. Kings, queens, bishops and knights would all be forced into submission sooner or later, beaten down by the sheer determination of their challengers. Like the 'new move' of which he was so proud, the manifesto was a weapon of revenge against his smugly superior adversaries, forged and fashioned during sleepless nights of brooding rage. His equally smug detractors today are therefore missing the point.

* See Postscript 3 for the only surviving record of an actual chess game played by Marx.

Any text from the 1840s will include passages that now seem slightly quaint or outdated; the same could be said of many party election manifestos or newspaper editorials published only a year or two ago. It was never intended as a timeless sacred text, though generations of disciples have sometimes treated it as such. The very first paragraph – with its references to Metternich, Guizot and the Tsar – emphasises that this is a perishable commodity, written at a specific moment for a particular purpose, without a thought for posterity.

The truly remarkable thing about the manifesto, then, is that it has any contemporary resonance at all. In a London bookshop recently I counted no fewer than nine English editions on sale. Even Karl Marx, who never suffered from false modesty, could scarcely have expected that his little tract would still be a best-seller at the end of the millennium.

The unforgettable first sentence of the *Communist Manifesto* has the force of a thunderbolt. 'A frightful hobgoblin stalks through Europe . . .' That, at least, was how it appeared in the first English edition, published by the *Red Republican* newspaper in 1850 and translated by Helen Macfarlane, a feminist Chartist who knew Marx and Engels and was greatly admired by both of them. Somehow, alas, the frightful hobgoblin never caught on. The version that everyone now knows is the translation by Samuel Moore, first published in 1888 and reprinted countless times since: 'A spectre is haunting Europe – the spectre of Communism. All the powers of old Europe have entered into a holy alliance to exorcise this spectre: Pope and Tsar, Metternich and Guizot, French Radicals and German police spies.'

This opening salvo was out of date almost as soon as Marx fired it. The original German edition of the manifesto was published on or about 24 February 1848, having been set up in type by the Workers' Educational Association in London (using a new Gothic font they had bought) and then rushed to a printer near Liverpool Street by the eager young Friedrich Lessner. 'We were intoxicated with enthusiasm,' Lessner recalled. By the time he collected the finished copies – bound in appropriately jaunty yellow paper – word was already arriving from France that the revolution had begun, with fighting and barricades in the streets of Paris. François Guizot, the man who had signed Marx's expulsion order in 1845, was dismissed as prime minister on 23 February; King Louis-Philippe abdicated the next day, with his throne literally ablaze. Another of Marx's *bêtes noires*, the Austrian chancellor Metternich, was toppled within three weeks. On 18 March the turmoil spread to Berlin.

The Gallic cock had crowed, and all Europe was suddenly awake. 'Our age, the age of democracy, is breaking,' Engels wrote in an ecstatic dispatch for the *Deutsche-Brüsseler-Zeitung*. 'The flames of the Tuileries and the Palais Royal are the dawn of the proletariat. Everywhere the rule of the bourgeoisie will now come crashing down, or be dashed to pieces. Germany, we hope, will follow. Now or never will it raise itself from its degradation . . .' Germany – or rather the King of Prussia – had other ideas. His spies in Belgium had been watching the *Deutsche-Brüsseler-Zeitung* with mounting horror:

> This noxious paper [a police agent reported] must indisputably exert the most corrupting influence upon the uneducated public at whom it is directed. The alluring theory of the dividing-up of wealth is held out to factory workers and day labourers as an innate right, and a profound hatred of the rulers and the rest of the community is inculcated into them. There would be a gloomy outlook for the fatherland and for civilisation if such activities succeeded in undermining religion and respect for the laws and in any great measure infected the lower class of the people.

As early as April 1847 the Prussian ambassador was demanding the suppression of this incendiary rag, which 'attacked His Majesty's government with revolting scurrility and savagery'.

Nothing happened. But with the proclamation of a French Republic, the Belgian police panicked. In the late afternoon of 3 March 1848, Marx received a royal decree signed by King Leopold I of Belgium, ordering him to quit the country within twenty-four hours and never return.

By happy coincidence, he was already planning his departure. Paris was where the action was, and he had just been sent a comradely invitation from Ferdinand Flocon, the editor of *La Réforme* and now a member of the provisional government in France. 'What an ass Flocon is!' Engels had written only four months earlier, dismissing him as a dunderhead 'who sees everything through the eyes of a third-rate Parisian clerk in a fourth-rate bank'. If Flocon was aware of the contempt which Marx and Engels felt for him, his message did not betray it:

Good and loyal Marx,

The soil of the French Republic is a field of refuge and asylum for all friends of liberty.

Tyranny exiled you, now free France opens its doors to you and to all those who are fighting for the holy cause, the fraternal cause of all peoples.

Marx needed no further encouragement to pack his bags – and for the rest of the evening he did just that. At 1 a.m., however, ten police officers burst into the house and dragged him off to a prison cell at the town hall, where he was locked up with a 'raving madman' who spent much of the night trying to punch him on the nose. The official reason given for the detention was that his 'passport was not in order', even though he presented his captors with no fewer than three passports that were all correctly stamped and dated, together with the expulsion order signed by the King. But the police's suspicions of Marx may not have been quite as capricious as they seem. In mid-February his mother had belatedly sent him the huge sum of 6,000 gold francs as his share of old Heinrich Marx's legacy, and most of this windfall was immediately put to subversive use. According to one of Marx's most recent biographers, David McLellan, 'the police suspected (there was no evidence) that he was using it to finance the revolutionary movement'. There is in fact ample evidence – not least from Jenny Marx herself. 'The German workers [in Brussels] decided to arm themselves,' she admitted. 'Daggers, revolvers, etc., were procured. Karl willingly provided money, for he had just come into an inheritance. In all this the government saw conspiracy and criminal plans: Marx receives money and buys weapons, he must therefore be got rid of.'

The tone of injured innocence is hardly justified by her confession: if the authorities could connect her husband with the arsenal of 'daggers, revolvers, etc.', he would be in the soup right up to his bushy eyebrows. Deeply alarmed, she scampered off to break the news of his arrest to a left-wing lawyer, leaving the three small children in the care of Helene. When she returned home in the early hours the door was guarded by a policeman who told her, with perfect politeness, that if she wanted to talk to Monsieur Marx he would be happy to escort her. But as soon as they reached the police station Jenny was arrested for 'vaga-bondage' – on the grounds, apparently, that she didn't have her papers with her – and thrown into a dark cell with 'prostitutes of the lowest order'.

When Jenny appeared in court the next day, an examining magistrate expressed sarcastic surprise that the police hadn't arrested her babies while they were about it. She and Karl were released without charge at three o'clock in the afternoon – which left them just two hours to put their affairs in order, collect the children and catch the train to Paris. Jenny hastily sold a few possessions but had to leave her family silver and best linen in the care of a friendly bookseller. The Marxes were then forced to travel with a police escort all the way to the border, presumably to give them a final taste of Belgian hospitality.

Already weary from their night in the cells, Karl and Jenny had an exhausting transmigration. There were no spare seats and scarcely any standing room, since most of the available space had been commandeered by Belgian troops heading south to guard the frontier against revolutionary contagion. On the French leg of the journey, passengers had to alight and continue by omnibus once they reached Valenciennes, where Luddite coachmen had taken advantage of the mayhem to uproot tracks and destroy the engines that were stealing their livelihood.

Reaching Paris on 5 March, Marx found the streets smothered by a rough porridge of broken glass and paving stones. As if to make up for what he had missed, he plunged into the struggle without delay. The very next day he informed the London Communist League that the executive headquarters had been transferred to Paris; on 9 March the League unanimously approved his proposal that all members should wear a 'blood-red ribbon' on their coats. Since the League was still a semi-clandestine outfit, he also founded a German Workers' Club, whose committee was announced in the newspaper *La Réforme* as 'H. Bauer, shoemaker; Hermann, cabinet-maker; J. Moll, watch-maker; Wallau, printer; Charles Marx; Charles Schapper.' Karl Schapper was in fact a compositor by trade, but it's hard to imagine what sort of artisanal status Marx could have claimed; 'troublemaker', perhaps.

That was certainly how he was regarded by some fellow exiles – particularly his old colleague Georg Herwegh and the former Prussian army officer Adalbert von Bornstedt, who had conceived a mad romantic scheme to form a 'German legion' which would march triumphantly into their homeland and liberate it. After that, they would invade Russia. 'Oh, just for one day, dare it!' was Herwegh's recruiting slogan. The French provisional government, only too glad to see the back of these quixotic foreigners, offered free billets and a daily wage of fifty centimes for every volunteer.

Marx accused Herwegh and Bornstedt of 'behaving like scoundrels', dismissing their plan as an arrogant adventure that was bound to end ignominiously. He was right: Herwegh's raggle-taggle army, probably numbering no more than a thousand, set off for Germany on April Fools' Day and was comprehensively routed as soon as it crossed the border.

What was required for a German revolution, Marx argued, was not a regiment of poets and professors brandishing second-hand bayonets, but ceaseless agitation and propaganda. As soon as Engels joined him in Paris, on 21 March, they produced a handbill headed 'Demands of the Communist Party in Germany', which was swiftly reprinted by democratic newspapers in Berlin, Trier and Düsseldorf. One modern critic has claimed that this seventeen-point programme was 'calculated to intimidate the bourgeoisie'. Far from it: since Germany had no proletariat worth the name, Marx realised that the first stage of his campaign must be a bourgeois revolution. By his standards, the 'demands' were therefore surprisingly modest. They included only four of the ten points from the *Communist Manifesto* – progressive income tax, free schooling, state ownership of all means of transport and the creation of a national bank. To emphasise his intentions, Marx added that the state bank would substitute paper money for metal coins, thus cheapening the universal means of exchange and liberating gold and silver for use in foreign trade. 'This measure,' he wrote, 'is necessary in order to bind the interests of the conservative bourgeoisie to the cause of the revolution.'

There were further notable concessions. The *Communist Manifesto* had advocated 'abolition of all right of inheritance' (though this hadn't inhibited Marx from accepting a paternal legacy of 6,000 francs); the 'Demands' suggested merely that inheritance should be 'curtailed'. Where the *Manifesto* had proposed the nationalisation of all land, in the 'Demands' he limited this to 'princely and other feudal estates'. He even tried to woo the peasants and small tenant farmers – whom he privately despised – by offering them state mortgages, free legal advice and an end to all feudal tithes and obligations. To show how moderate these 'Demands of the Communist Party' were, one need only point out that many of them – including universal adult suffrage, the payment of salaries to parliamentary representatives and the transformation of Germany into a 'single indivisible republic' – have since been accepted by governments whose capitalist credentials are beyond question.

Pandering to the peasants and petty bourgeois was all very well, but Marx's most urgent task now was to raise the consciousness of the Teutonic masses. In late March and early April the Communist League's supporters in Paris departed for Germany, mostly to their home towns, to start the process of education and organisation. Karl Schapper went to Nassau, Wilhelm Wolff to Breslau. 'The League has dissolved; it is everywhere and nowhere,' wrote Stephan Born, a revolutionary typesetter who installed himself in Berlin. (Born, whose real name was the delicious Simon Buttermilch, later abandoned communism and became a schoolmaster in Switzerland.)

Marx's preferred weapon, as so often, was journalism. 'A new daily newspaper will be published in Cologne,' he announced. 'It will be called the *Neue Rheinische Zeitung* and will be edited by Herr Karl Marx.' There were good reasons for the choice of location. Cologne, the capital of the Rhineland, was a city he knew well from his spell as editor of the previous *Rheinische Zeitung*. He was still friendly with some of the old shareholders and expected them to back his new venture. Perhaps more importantly, the Code Napoleon – a bequest from the years of French occupation – was still in force there, allowing some measure of press freedom.

The Marxes left Paris in the first week of April 1848 accompanied by Engels and Ernst Dronke, a twenty-six-year-old German radical who already had a novel, a prison sentence and a daring jailbreak to his credit. After a brief stopover in Mainz, they went their separate ways: Engels to Wuppertal, in the hope of persuading his father and friends to invest in the new paper; Dronke to an uncle in Koblenz; Jenny and the children to Trier, where they intended to stay with her mother for a few weeks until Karl had obtained a residence permit.

As soon as he arrived in Cologne, Marx duly asked the police authorities to restore his Prussian citizenship, which had been relinquished in 1845. He claimed that he wished to settle there with his family to write 'a book about economics', discreetly omitting his plan for a popular daily newspaper. The authorities turned him down anyway, thus leaving open the possibility of expulsion if he became too much of a nuisance.

Engels, too, was being thwarted at every turn. 'There's damned little prospect for the shares here,' he wrote from Barmen on 25 April. 'The fact is, *au fond*, that even these radical bourgeois here see us as their future main enemies and have no intention of putting into our hands weapons which we would shortly turn against themselves.' As well they might, since that was precisely Marx's intention. 'Nothing whatever is to be got out of my old man,' Engels continued. 'Sooner than present us with 1,000 thalers, he would pepper us with a thousand balls of grapeshot.' In the end, Marx had to raid what remained of his own inheritance to ensure that the paper began publication on 1 June 1848. The starting date should have been 1 July, but 'the renewed insolence of the reactionaries' persuaded him that there was no time to be lost. ('Our readers will therefore have to bear with us,' he wrote in the inaugural issue, 'if during the first days we cannot offer the abundant variety of news and reports that our wide-spread connections should enable us to do. In a few days we shall be able to satisfy all requirements.')

The editorial board was controlled by former members of the Communist League, including the revolutionary poet Georg Weerth, Ernst Dronke, and the journalists Ferdinand Wolff and Wilhelm Wolff. (To avoid confusion, these unrelated Wolffs were nicknamed 'Red Wolf' and 'Lupus'.) But as Engels admitted, the newspaper was essentially 'a simple dictatorship by Marx'. According to Stephan Born, who visited the office some months later, even the tyrant's most loyal subjects sometimes found it hard to cope with his chaotic autocracy. 'The most bitter complaints about Marx came from Engels. "He is no journalist," he said, "and will never become one. He pores for a whole day over a leading article that would take someone else a couple of hours as though it concerned the handling of a deep philosophical problem. He changes and polishes and changes the change and owing to his unremitting thoroughness can never be ready on time." It was a real release for Engels to be able once in a while to sound off about what annoyed him.' Though Marx was undoubtedly a deadline-hugger, Born may be exaggerating. The *Neue Rheinische Zeitung* was published daily, often with a hefty supplement to accommodate all the news and features that wouldn't fit into the main section; on special occasions it had an afternoon edition as well. If the editor had been quite as dilatory as Born alleged, the paper would never have gone to press at all.

What distinguished the *Neue Rheinische Zeitung* from the rest of the 'democratic' press in Germany was its preference for information over long-winded theory. By carefully shepherding the facts to suit his purposes, Marx believed he could achieve far more than any number of scholarly liberals brooding on the meaning of republicanism. He also paid close attention to the activities of Chartists in Britain and latter-day Jacobins in France, hoping that these would alert his readers to the necessary antagonism between the bourgeoisie and proletariat – an antagonism he dared not spell out any more explicitly. (The first thing he did on arriving in Cologne was to take out subscriptions to three English newspapers, *The Times*, the *Telegraph* and the *Economist*.)

The twelve months that Marx spent in Germany during 1848 and 1849 are often referred to as 'the mad year', and he certainly seems to have been in a frothing rage for much of the period – not least with himself, as he tried to marry two wholly irreconcilable impulses. The dilemma was obvious to anyone who studied the *Communist Manifesto*, where he had argued that communists should encourage the proletariat to support the bourgeoisie 'whenever it acts in a revolutionary way' while simultaneously instilling into the workers 'the clearest possible recognition of the hostile antagonism between bourgeoisie and proletariat'. The middle classes – can't live with 'em, can't live without 'em.

The bourgeois liberals, including several of his shareholders, were putting their faith in two democratic institutions that had been established after the riots of March, the German National Assembly in Frankfurt and the Prussian Assembly in Berlin. An editor who wanted to reassure anxious middle-class readers of his intentions might have been well advised to give these infant parliaments the benefit of the doubt, at least for a month or two. But impatience got the better of him: in the very first issue there was a mordant and merciless account of the Frankfurt assembly, written by Engels.

'For a fortnight Germany has had a Constituent National Assembly elected by the German people as a whole,' he reported. 'The first act of the National Assembly should have been to proclaim loudly and publicly this sovereignty of the German people. Its second act should have been the drafting of a German constitution based on the sovereignty of the people.' Instead, the 'elected philistines' – most of whom were lawyers and schoolmasters – had wasted their time with 'new amendments and new digressions ... long-winded speeches and endless confusion'. Whenever it looked as if a decision might be taken, the representatives would defer the question and adjourn for dinner. Several businessmen who had put money into the newspaper withdrew their support immediately. 'It cost us half our shareholders,' Engels confessed. Having thus antagonised the moderates, Marx then picked a fight with the most popular socialist in town, Andreas Gottschalk, who was not only president of the newly formed Cologne Workers' Association but also the leading figure in the local branch of the Communist League.

The violent animosity between the two men is hard to explain or justify – though jealousy may have had something to do with it. As he had already shown elsewhere, Marx disliked organisations or institutions which he couldn't dominate; and Gottschalk, a doctor who was much loved for his medical work among the poor, had rather more disciples than the irascible editor. The *Neue Rheinische Zeitung* was selling 5,000 copies, a huge circulation by the standards of the day; but Gottschalk's Cologne Workers' Association had a membership of 8,000 within weeks of its inception.

Marx condemned Gottschalk as a left-wing sectarian who had jeopardised the 'united front' of bourgeoisie and proletariat by founding an exclusively working-class pressure group – and, worse still, by demanding a boycott of elections for the parliaments in Berlin and Frankfurt. Given Marx's own readiness to lampoon the National Assembly as a nest of pettifogging time-wasters, some might think this criticism reeked of humbug. Even more perversely, he complained that Gottschalk was willing to accept a limited constitutional monarchy instead of outright republicanism. Yet Marx himself declared, in an editorial on 7 June, 'We do not make the utopian demand that at the outset a *united indivisible German republic* should be proclaimed.'

Poor old Gottschalk thus found himself damned for timidity and over-zealousness at the same time; no wonder he resigned from the Communist League weeks after Marx's noisy arrival in Cologne. Even when Gottschalk and his friend Friedrich Anneke were arrested and charged with incitement to violence, at the beginning of July, the *Neue Rheinische Zeitung* seemed curiously dispassionate. 'We are reserving our judgement since we are still lacking definite information about their arrest and the manner in which it was carried out,' Marx commented in a brief editorial on 4 July. 'The workers will be sensible enough not to let themselves be provoked into creating a disturbance.' The next day's paper had a fuller report, which concentrated on the treatment of Anneke by his arresting officers: it accused the public prosecutor, Herr Hecker, of arriving at the house half an hour after the police to give them time to beat up the suspect and terrorise his pregnant wife. 'Herr Hecker replied that he had given no orders to commit brutalities,' Marx noted sarcastically. 'As if Herr Hecker could order brutalities!' Of the hapless Gottschalk, however, there was scarcely a mention.

Gottschalk stayed in jail for the next five months awaiting trial.

A cynic might suspect that Marx wasn't entirely unhappy at his rival's absence from the scene, since it gave him a chance to impose his own political authority and unite the quarrelling factions. But Marx was never a natural conciliator. Carl Schurz, a student from Bonn, watched his performance at a gathering of Cologne democrats held in August 1848:

> He could not have been much more than thirty years old at that time, but he was already the recognised head of the advanced socialistic school . . . I have never seen a man whose bearing was so provoking and intolerable. To no opinion which differed from his own did he accord the honour of even condescending consideration. Everyone who contradicted him he treated with abject contempt; every argument that he did not like he answered either with biting scorn at the unfathomable ignorance that had prompted it, or with opprobrious aspersions upon the motives of him who had advanced it. I remember most distinctly the cutting disdain with which he pronounced the word 'bourgeois'; and as a 'bourgeois' – that is, as a detestable example of the deepest mental and moral degeneracy – he denounced everyone who dared to oppose his opinion . . . It was very evident that not only had he not won any adherents, but had repelled many who otherwise might have become his followers.

It should be pointed out that this was written more than fifty years later, long after Schurz had emigrated to America and become a thoroughly respectable statesman, serving as a US senator and Secretary for the Interior. Nevertheless, it rings horribly true. Since Marx was seldom capable of remaining on civil terms with even his closest comrades, it was absurd to imagine that he could bring harmony to an already fractious coalition of liberals and leftists, peasants and proletarians. In his speeches and editorials he insisted that Germany must have a democratic government 'of the most heterogeneous elements' rather than a dictatorship of brilliant communists such as himself; but the vehemence with which he delivered these views – flinging insults and derision at anyone who dared disagree – suggested that this was a man who wouldn't recognise pluralism if it was presented to him on a silver salver with watercress garnish.

The Prussian authorities weren't fooled for a moment by his posturings as a benign reformist. Inspector Hünermund of the Cologne police had warned his superiors of 'the politically unreliable Dr Marx' as early as April, and when the *Neue Rheinische Zeitung* printed its caustic account of Anneke's arrest they seized their chance. On 7 July Marx was hauled up before the examining magistrate for 'insulting or libelling the Chief Public Prosecutor', while policemen ransacked his office for any scrap of paper which might identify the anonymous author of the offending article. Two weeks later he was taken in for further interrogation, and in August his colleagues Dronke and Engels were called as witnesses. On 6 September the *Zeitung* reported a worrying new development: 'Yesterday one of our editors, Friedrich Engels, was again summoned to appear before the examining magistrate in the investigation against Marx and consorts, but this time not as a witness but as co-accused.'

The harassment of 'Marx and consorts' did not cow or silence them; if anything, they became more reckless. 'A characteristic feature of the Rhineland,' Engels told a meeting of Cologne democrats in mid-August, 'is hatred of Prussian officialdom and dyed-in-the-wool Prussianism; it is to be hoped that this attitude will endure.' As he must have known, Prussian officialdom did not care to have its tail tweaked. The army, in particular, seemed to be entirely out of control, merrily sabotaging the so-called 'Government of Action' that had been formed only a couple of months earlier. In August the Prussian assembly in Berlin demanded the sacking of any military officers who were unwilling to accept the new constitutional system. The Minister of War took no notice, and on 8 September the government was toppled by a vote of no confidence from the assembly, proposed by representatives of the Left and Centre.

Marx himself happened to be in Berlin at the time, returning from a fund-raising trip to Vienna. 'Indescribable rejoicing broke out when news of the government's defeat became known to the assembled crowd,' he reported back to Engels, who was running the newspaper in his absence. 'Thousands of people joined this procession and to the accompaniment of endless hurrahs the masses rolled across the Opera House Square. Never before has such an expression of joy been seen here.'

It was a pyrrhic victory. Caught up in the euphoria of the crowd, Marx had blithely assumed that there would now be a government of the Centre Left. A moment's reflection might have shown him that the King of Prussia would never tolerate such an affront. Sure enough, by the time Marx returned to Cologne the counter-revolution had begun. Defying the wishes of the people's representatives in Berlin, the King began composing a new cabinet of reactionary bureaucrats and army officers. 'The Crown and the Assembly confront each other,' Marx wrote on 14 September. 'It is possible that arms will decide the issue. The side that has the greater courage and consistency will win.'

A heroic delusion, of course: bravery would count for little against the full might of state intimidation. Soon after dawn on 25 September the Cologne police arrested several leaders of the newly formed Committee of Public Safety, including Karl Schapper and Hermann Becker; they came for Engels, too, but he had made himself scarce. At lunchtime Marx addressed a mass meeting in the old marketplace, warning workers not to react to these 'police provocations' by taking to the barricades. The time was not yet ripe for street fighting.

But time, like quinces and avocado pears, has a trick of going rotten before it is ripe. A state of martial law was declared in Cologne on 25 September, and the military commander immediately suspended publication of the *Neue Rheinische Zeitung*. Marx issued a leaflet to subscribers explaining that 'the pen has to submit to the sabre', but promised that the paper would appear again before long 'in an enlarged format'.

With several of the journalists already jailed and shareholders refusing to subsidise a newspaper in limbo, this seemed rather optimistic – especially since Marx's most valuable colleague, Engels, had scarpered as soon as he heard that the police were after him, pausing briefly in Barmen to break the news to his horrified parents before fleeing to the sanctuary of Belgium. The rival *Kölnische Zeitung*, patriotic and law-abiding as ever, published the warrant for his arrest:

> Name: *Friedrich Engels*; occupation: merchant; place of birth and residence: Barmen; religion: Evangelical; age: 27 years; height: 5 feet 8 inches; hair and eyebrows: dark blond; forehead: ordinary; eyes: grey; nose and mouth: well-proportioned; teeth: good; beard: brown; chin and face: oval; complexion: healthy; figure: slender.

A splendid advertisement for the revolutionary lifestyle. The owner of this healthy complexion and well-proportioned nose arrived in Brussels on 5 October, accompanied by Ernst Dronke, but the two fugitives had only just sat down to dinner in their hotel when a police posse dragged them off to the Petits-Carmes prison, taking full advantage of the law against 'vagabonds' which had proved so effective with Jenny Marx. Two hours later Engels and Dronke were driven to the railway station in a sealed carriage and escorted on to the next train for Paris.

As soon as the *Neue Rheinische Zeitung* resumed publication after the lifting of martial law, on 12 October, Marx wrote a furious editorial about the 'brutal treatment' of his friends. 'It is clear from this that the Belgian government is increasingly learning to recognise its position,' he commented:

> The Belgians gradually become policemen for all their neighbours, and are overjoyed when they are complimented on their

quiet and submissive behaviour. Nevertheless, there is something ridiculous about the good Belgian policeman. Even the earnest *Times* only jestingly acknowleged the Belgian desire to please. Recently it advised the Belgian nation, after it had got rid of all the [workers'] clubs, to turn itself into one big club with the motto: '*Ne risquez rien!*' It goes without saying that the official Belgian press, in its cretinism, also reprinted this piece of flattery and welcomed it jubilantly.

The struggle to save Germany's infant democracy was reaching its climax, with a revolutionary uprising in Vienna and street battles in Berlin. No sooner had Marx been elected president of the Cologne Workers' Association, on 22 October, than the editor of the Association's newspaper was sentenced to a month's imprisonment for defaming Herr Hecker. Encouraged by this small victory over his tormentors, the vengeful public prosecutor brought several new lawsuits against Marx, claiming that his speeches were tantamount to 'high treason'. Absurdly, he also started libel proceedings over an item published by the *Neue Rheinische Zeitung* under the byline 'Hecker', even though the article was plainly a valedictory message to the German people from the republican Friedrich Hecker, who was leaving to start a new life in America. Nevertheless, Cologne's tinpot Torquemada alleged that readers would assume it reflected his own views. As Marx asked incredulously, did the plaintiff really think that 'this newspaper, with its inventive maliciousness, has signed its own proclamation "Hecker" in order to make the German people believe that Hecker, the public prosecutor, is emigrating to New York, that Hecker, the public prosecutor, proclaims the German republic, that Hecker, the public prosecutor, officially sanctions pious revolutionary wishes?' Probably not: but it was yet another opportunity to hound and harass the enemies of the Prussian state.

Instead of hastening back to his fatherland for the denouement of these various dramas – half-tragedy, half-farce – Engels forgot about them altogether. After a few days' rest in Paris, he set off alone on a strange, meandering ramble through the French countryside in the vague direction of Switzerland – though with many a pleasant detour along the way. As he admitted, 'one does not readily part from France'. Comrades in Cologne might be fighting for their lives and liberties, but he was in no particular hurry to join them. Could it be that he had lost his nerve?

Engels's unpublished journal of this month-long odyssey, which scarcely mentions the crisis engulfing Germany, is written with all the saucer-eyed wonder of a novice tourist. 'What country in Europe can compare with France in wealth, in the variety of its gifts of nature and products, in its universality?' he gushes. 'And what wine! What a diversity, from Bordeaux to Burgundy, from Burgundy to the heavy St Georges, Lünel and Frontignan of the south, and from that to sparkling champagne!' He seems to have been more or less squiffy all the time – especially in Auxerre, which he reached in time to celebrate the new Burgundian vintage. 'The 1848 harvest was so infinitely rich that not enough barrels could be found to take all the wine. And what is more, of such quality – better than '46, perhaps even better than '34!'

It wasn't only the wine that intoxicated: 'At every step I found the gayest company, the sweetest grapes and the prettiest girls.' After expert and exhaustive research, he concluded that the 'cleanly washed, smoothly combed, slimly built' women of Burgundy were preferable to their 'earthy' and 'tousled' counterparts between the Seine and the Loire. 'It will therefore be readily believed that I spent more time lying in the grass with the vintners and their girls, eating grapes, drinking wine, chatting and laughing, than marching up the hill.'

One can see why the journey took so long – and why he was flat broke when he finally arrived in Switzerland. Appealing to both his father and Marx for donations, and hearing nothing from either, he wrote again to Cologne wondering nervously if the editor had disowned him for going AWOL. 'Dear Engels,' Marx replied. 'I am truly amazed that you should still not have received any money from me. *I* (not the dispatch department) sent you 61 thalers ages ago . . . To suppose that I could leave you in the lurch for even a moment is sheer fantasy. You will always remain my friend and confidant as I hope to remain yours, K. Marx.' He added a cheerfully combative PS: 'Your old man's a swine and we shall write him a damned rude letter.' But it soon dawned on him that this might not be an effective fund-raising technique. 'I have devised an infallible plan for extracting money from your old man, as we now have none,' he wrote on 29 November, after further consideration. 'Write me a begging letter (as crude as possible) in which you retail your past vicissitudes, but in such a way that I can pass it on to your mother. The old man's beginning to get the wind up.' Billy Bunter, it may be recalled, used a similar appeal to maternal sympathy when trying to extract postal orders from his father, and it was no more successful for him than for Marx and Engels.

By Christmas, Engels was bored of 'sinful living' and 'lazing about in foreign parts'. In a letter from Berne he offered a preposterous new excuse for his truancy: 'If there are sufficient grounds for believing that I shall not be detained for questioning, I shall come at once. After that they may, so far as I'm concerned, place me before 10,000 juries, but when you're arrested for questioning you're not allowed to smoke, and I won't let myself in for that.'

After being reassured that he needn't sacrifice his cigars for the cause, Engels returned to Germany in January – only to find that the revolution was all but over. A new government had been formed under the reactionary Count Brandenburg, bastard son of Frederick William II, and the King had dissolved the Prussian assembly. 'The bourgeoisie did not raise a finger; they simply allowed the people to fight for them,' Marx grumbled in the *Neue Rheinische Zeitung*, admitting that his vision of a grand alliance between the workers and the middle classes had been no more than a pipedream. The Prussian débâcle proved that a bourgeois revolution was impossible in Germany; nothing short of a republican insurrection would now suffice. But the German working class was unable to gird up its loins for action without encouragement from abroad – specifically, from France. After brooding on the lessons of the previous year, he published a revised revolutionary menu on 1 January 1849:

> The overthrow of the bourgeoisie in France, the triumph of the French working class, the emancipation of the working class in general, is therefore the rallying cry of European liberation.
>
> But *England*, the country that turns whole nations into its proletarians, that takes the whole world within its immense embrace . . . *England* seems to be the rock against which the revolutionary waves break, the country where the new society is stifled in the womb.

Every social upheaval in France was bound to be thwarted by the industrial and commercial power of the English middle class, 'and only a world war can overthrow the Old England, as only this can provide the Chartists, the party of the organised English workers, with the conditions for a successful rising against their gigantic oppressors'. This seasonal game of consequences – which, more than a century later, would come to be known as the domino theory – led to an inescapable and apocalyptic conclusion. 'The table of contents for 1849 reads: *Revolutionary uprising of the French working class, world war.*'

And for afters? During 1848 the working class had been thoroughly worsted whenever and wherever it raised its head above the barricades – in France, Prussia, Austria and not least England itself, where a mass demonstration in Kennington, South London, marked the end of the Chartist threat. But with his talent for paradox and perversity, Marx could discern potential triumph in every disaster, silver linings behind every cloud, a new dawn lurking in even the most Stygian night. So what if the counter-revolutions had succeeded? This would spur the workers into a proper cavalry charge next time. He put his faith in the old tactic of *réculer pour mieux sauter*.

As it turned out, 1849 was merely a gloomy postscript to 1848. One month after publishing the New Year message, Marx and Engels stood trial on the by now familiar charge of insulting the public prosecutor. In an hour-long speech from the dock, Marx showed what a brilliant mind the legal profession had lost when he declined to follow his father's career, deconstructing Articles 222 and 367 of the Napoleonic penal code until there was nothing left but a handful of dust. He lectured the jury on the important if pedantic distinction between insulting remarks and calumny; he argued that the prosecutor must prove not only the insult but the *intention* to insult, since Article 367 allowed a journalist to publish 'facts' even if they caused offence. In his exegesis of Article 222 (which forbade insults against public officials) he pointed out that the penal code, unlike Prussian law, did not include the crime of *lèse-majesté*; and since the King of Prussia wasn't an official he could not avail himself of Article 222 either. 'Why am I permitted to insult the King, whereas I am not permitted to insult the chief public prosecutor?'

Marx presented much of this defence calmly and forensically, without his customary rhetorical tricks or embellishments, but in his peroration he at last appealed to the jurors' political conscience:

> I prefer to follow the great events of the world, to analyse the course of history, than to occupy myself with local bosses, with the police and prosecuting magistrates. However great these gentlemen may imagine themselves in their own fancy, they are *nothing*, absolutely *nothing*, in the gigantic battles of the present time. I consider we are making a real sacrifice when we decide to break a lance with these opponents. But, firstly, it is the duty of the press to come forward on behalf of the oppressed in its immediate neighbourhood . . . The first duty of the press now is *to undermine all the foundations of the existing political state of affairs*.

He sat down to loud applause from the crowded courtroom: Marx and Engels had won their acquittal. But there was little time for celebration. The very next day, 8 February, Marx was back in the dock with two of his colleagues from the Rhenish District Committee of Democrats, this time accused of 'incitement to revolt'.

The prosecution arose from the turmoil of November 1848 when members of the Prussian National Assembly – then being forced out of their debating chamber at gunpoint by government troops – had ruled that taxes should be withheld in protest. In a proclamation dated 18 November 1848, Marx's committee declared that the forcible collection of taxes 'must be resisted everywhere and in every way', and that a people's militia should be formed 'to repulse the enemy'. Since this was undoubtedly an incitement to revolt, as Marx admitted in court, the only question was 'whether the accused were authorised by the decision of the National Assembly on the refusal to pay taxes to call in this way for resistance to the state power [and] to organise an armed force against that of the state'. After a very brief discussion the jury decided unanimously that he had behaved with perfect con-stitutional propriety. In the words of the *Deutsche Londoner Zeitung*, a liberal weekly for German refugees in England: 'In political trials the government nowadays has no luck at all with the juries.' But the government had other shots in its locker. The un-fortunately named Colonel Friedrich Engels, deputy commandant of the Cologne garrison, informed the Rhineland *Oberpräsident* that Marx was 'becoming increasingly more audacious now that he has been acquitted by the jury, and it seems to me high time that this man was deported, as one certainly does not have to put up with an alien who is no more than tolerated in our midst, befouling everything with his poisonous tongue, especially as our home-grown vermin are doing that quite adequately'.

While Colonel Engels waited for an answer, two of his NCOs from the 8th Infantry Company took it upon themselves to engage in a spot of freelance bullying by turning up at Marx's house on the afternoon of 2 March and demanding to know who had written a recent article in the *Neue Rheinische Zeitung* about military corruption, which had apparently caused grave offence to 'the whole of the 8th Company'. The editor pointed out that the article in question was in fact an advertisement, for which he had no responsibility. His uniformed visitors, literally rattling their sabres, warned that 'evil would result' if he refused to name the author. By way of reply, Marx drew their attention to the butt of a pistol protruding from his dressing-gown pocket. The two men quickly took their leave.

'Relaxation of discipline must have gone very far,' Marx wrote to Colonel Engels, 'and all sense of law and order must have ceased if, like a robber band, a Company can send delegates to an individual citizen and attempt with threats to extort this or that confession from him . . . I must beg you, Sir, to institute an inquiry into this incident and to give me an explanation for this singular presumption. I would be sorry to be obliged to have recourse to publicity.' Marx's pen was a more effective threat than the sabres of the NCOs. The wretched commandant assured him that the men had been reprimanded, and thanked the *Neue Rheinische Zeitung* for its discretion in not reporting the incident. Magnanimous in victory, Marx told the Colonel that the newspaper's silence demonstrated 'how great is its consideration for the prevailing mood of unrest'.

A likely story. Though Marx was indeed being castigated by leftists such as Dr Gottschalk (now released from jail) for lack of militancy, what he did publish was quite provocative enough – including savage mockery of the 'bureaucratic–feudal–military despotism' presided over by the King and his aristocratic new Interior Minister, Baron von Manteuffel. 'The governments are openly preparing for *coups d'état* which are intended to complete the counter-revolution,' he predicted on 12 March. 'Consequently, the people would be fully justified in preparing for an insurrection.' He did add that the people shouldn't be decoyed into this 'clumsily laid trap' – but only because he thought there would soon be a far better opportunity. On 8 May, after an eruption of riots and guerrilla warfare in Dresden and the Palatinate, the *Neue Rheinische Zeitung* brought the glad tidings that 'the revolution is drawing nearer and nearer'.

'Wonder was expressed,' Engels wrote many years later, 'that we carried on our activities so unconcernedly within a Prussian fortress of the first rank, in the face of a garrison of 8,000 troops and confronting the guardhouse; but, on account of the eight rifles with bayonets and 250 live cartridges in the editorial room, and the red Jacobin caps of the compositors, our house was reckoned by the officers likewise as a fortress which was not to be taken by a mere *coup de main*.' In fact, the fortress surrendered without a shot being fired. On 16 May the Prussian authorities prosecuted half of the editorial staff and recommended the other half – the non-Prussians, including Marx – for deportation. Nothing more could be done. In the final issue, printed defiantly in bright red ink, the editors announced that 'their last word everywhere and always will be: *emancipation of the working class*!' Marx and his journalists then left the building, clutching their weapons and baggage, with a band playing and the red flag flying proudly from the rooftop.

After liquidating everything – including the newspaper's printing machinery, which he owned personally, and the furniture from his house – Marx managed to settle all outstanding debts. But he was left penniless. Jenny's family silver was despatched to a pawnshop, this time in Frankfurt, while she and the children set off once again to stay with her mother in Trier. Marx and Engels headed for Frankfurt in the hope of persuading left-wing deputies in the National Assembly to support the insurgent troops from south-western Germany, who were still fighting the good fight on behalf of the 'provisional government' in Baden and the Palatinate. No one would listen, so the next day they travelled to Baden and urged the revolutionary forces to march on Frankfurt uninvited. Again their appeals were ignored, though they had a friendly encounter with their old colleague Willich, who was now in charge of a partisan corps. Engels, a lifelong student of military strategy, couldn't resist the chance to put on a uniform and join a real war. Enlisting as a volunteer, he soon became Willich's chief adjutant, jointly directing operations and campaigns, and during the next few weeks he fought in four skirmishes – all of which were lost. His most important discovery, he told Jenny Marx, was 'that the much-vaunted bravery under fire is quite the most ordinary quality one can possess. The whistle of bullets is really quite a trivial matter.' He saw little evidence of cowardice, but plenty of 'brave stupidity'.

Marx, who had neither the inclination nor the physique for soldiering, realised that there was nothing more he could do in Germany. At the beginning of June he departed for Paris, travelling on a false passport, and introduced himself to the French as the official envoy of the Palatinate revolutionary government. By the time he arrived, however, Paris was in the grip of a royalist reaction and a cholera epidemic. 'For all that,' he wrote cheerfully to Engels on 7 June, 'never has a colossal eruption of the revolutionary volcano been more imminent than it is in Paris today . . . I consort with the whole of the revolutionary party and in a few days' time I shall have *all* the revolutionary journals at my disposal.'

Within a few days there were no revolutionary journals to be had. When the Montagnard faction in the French National Assembly called for a mass demonstration on 13 June, government troops simply dragooned the protesters from the streets and arrested the ringleaders. Thus ended the revolutions begun in 1848: the Gallic cock, having crowed and strutted, had its neck wrung.

Jenny, pregnant with their fourth child, joined her husband in Paris at the beginning of July. 'If my wife were not in an *état par trop intéressant*, I would gladly leave Paris as soon as it was financially possible to do so,' he wrote to Engels. But the decision was no longer up to him. The triumphant reactionaries were busily seeking out and evicting foreign revolutionists from the newly placid capital, and on the sunny morning of 19 March a police sergeant turned up on the Marxes' doorstep at 45 Rue de Lille to deliver an official order banishing him to the *département* of Morbihan, in Brittany. The only surprise is that he wasn't expelled sooner: it seems that the police had been unable to find him for several weeks, perhaps because he had taken the precaution of renting his lodging under the pseudonym 'Monsieur Ramboz'.

He managed to delay the inevitable by appealing to the Ministry of the Interior. On 16 August the Parisian commissioner informed him that the order had been confirmed, though Jenny was given permission to stay for another month. Marx described Morbihan as 'the Pontine marshes of Brittany', a malaria-infested swamp which would undoubtedly kill him and his family, all of whom were in wretched health. 'I need hardly say,' he told Engels, 'that I shall not consent to this veiled attempt on my life. So I am leaving France.' Neither Germany nor Belgium would let him in, and the Swiss refused his application for a passport – not that he particularly wanted to live in their 'mousetrap' of a country anyway. And so he turned to the last refuge of the rootless revolutionary. When the SS *City of Boulogne* sailed into Dover on 27 August 1849 its captain notified the Home Office of 'all Aliens who are now on board my said ship', as required by law: they included a Greek actor, a French gentleman, a Polish professor and one Charles Marx, who gave his profession as 'Dr'.

'You must leave for London at once,' Marx wrote to Engels, who was recuperating from his military exertions by wining and womanising in Lausanne. 'I count on this *absolutely*. You *cannot* stay in Switzerland. In London we shall get down to business.'

6

The Megalosaurus

Karl Marx's final refuge was the largest and wealthiest metropolis in the world. London had been the first city to reach a population of 1,000,000, a great wen that continued to swell without ever quite bursting. When the journalist Henry Mayhew went up in a hot-air balloon in the hope of comprehending its entirety, he could not tell 'where the monster city began or ended, for the buildings stretched not only to the horizon on either side, but far away into the distance . . . where the town seemed to blend into the sky'. Census figures show that 300,000 newcomers settled in the capital between 1841 and 1851 – including hundreds of refugees who, like Marx, were lured by its reputation as a sanctuary for political outcasts.

But this 'super-city de luxe' was also the dark, dank monster that looms up from the opening paragraphs of *Bleak House*, written three years after Marx's arrival:

Implacable November weather. As much mud in the streets, as if the waters had but newly retired from the face of the earth, and it would not be wonderful to meet a Megalosaurus, forty feet long or so, waddling like an elephantine lizard up Holborn Hill. Smoke lowering down from chimney-pots, making a soft black drizzle, with flakes of soot in it as big as full-grown snowflakes – gone into mourning, one might imagine, for the death of the sun.

Beyond the plush salons of Mayfair and Piccadilly lay a sprawling, uncharted shanty town of slums and sweatshops, brothels and blacking factories. 'It is like the heart of the universe and the flood of human effort rolls out of it and into it with a violence that almost appals one's very sense,' Thomas Carlyle wrote to his brother. 'O that our father saw Holborn in a fog! with the black vapour brooding over it, absolutely like fluid ink; and coaches and wains and sheep and oxen and wild people rushing on with bellowings and shrieks and thundering din, as if the earth in general were gone distracted.' Disease was commonplace – unsurprisingly, since sewers ran into the Thames, which provided much of the water supply. Only a month before Marx came to London, when the city was enduring one of its periodic cholera epidemics, *The Times* published the following cry for help on its letters page:

> Sur, May we beg and beseech you proteckshion and power. We are, Sur, as it may be, living in a Wilderniss, so far as the rest of London knows anything of us, or as rich and great people care about. We live in muck and filthe. We aint got no privez, no dust bins, no drains, no water splies, and no drain or suer in the whole place. The Suer Corporation, in Greek Street, Soho Square, all great, rich and powerfool men, take no notice whatsomedever of our complaints. The Stenche of a Gully-hole is disgustin. We al of us suffer, and numbers are ill, and if the Colera comes Lord help us.

In some districts, one child in every three died before its first birthday.

The marvels and monstrosities of Victorian London which so astonished many foreign visitors were invisible to Marx. For all his talents as a reporter and social analyst, he was often curiously oblivious to his own immediate surroundings: unlike Dickens, who plunged into the grime to bring back vivid firsthand observations, he preferred to rely on newspapers or Royal

Commissions for information. Nor did he show the slightest interest in the tastes and habits of his new compatriots – their dress, their games, their popular songs. True, in July 1850 he became 'all flushed and excited' after noticing a working model of an electric railway engine in the window of a Regent Street shop, but even then it was the economic implications rather than the thrill of novelty that excited him. 'The problem is solved – the consequences are indefinable,' he told his fellow gawpers, explaining that just as King Steam had transformed the world in the last century so now the electric spark would set off a new revolution. 'In the wake of the economic revolution the political must necessarily follow, for the latter is only the expression of the former.' It seems unlikely that anyone else in the Regent Street crowd had paused to consider the political consequences of this Trojan iron horse; to Marx, however, it was all that mattered. Had he encountered Dickens's megalosaurus in the mud of Holborn Hill he would scarcely have given it a second glance.

Work was the only reliable distraction from the wretchedness of his plight. Without pausing to acclimatise himself, he set about establishing a new HQ for the Communist League at the London offices of the German Workers' Education Society, one of the many political groups of the revolutionary diaspora. By mid-September he had also been elected to a Committee to Aid German Refugees. 'I am now in a really difficult situation,' he wrote to Ferdinand Freiligrath on 5 September 1849, little more than a week after arriving in England. 'My wife is in an advanced state of pregnancy, she is obliged to leave Paris on the 15th and I don't know how I am to raise the money for her journey and for settling her in here. On the other hand there are excellent prospects of my being able to start a monthly review here . . .'

Few refugees required aid more urgently than the Marxes. Jenny reached London on 17 September, sick and exhausted, with 'my three poor persecuted small children'. Jennychen had been born in France, Laura and Edgar in Belgium, and this record of peripatetic parturition was maintained by their second son, who entered the world on 5 November 1849 to the sound of exploding fireworks as Londoners held their annual celebration of the failure of Guido (Guy) Fawkes to blow up the Houses of Parliament in 1605. In homage to the great conspirator, the boy was christened Heinrich Guido and instantly nicknamed 'Fawkesy' (later Germanicised into 'Foxchen').

Marx had a most endearing passion for sobriquets and pseudonyms. Sometimes, of course, these were a political necessity: hence the comical alias 'Monsieur Ramboz', adopted while he was lying low in Paris. Even in liberal London, where there was little need for subterfuge, he sometimes signed his letters 'A. Williams' to evade any police finks in the postal sorting office. But most of the monikers he bestowed so liberally on friends and family were purely whimsical. Engels, the armchair soldier, was addressed by his imaginary rank, 'General'. The housekeeper Helene Demuth was 'Lenchen' or, occasionally, 'Nym'. Jennychen enjoyed the title if not the trappings of 'Qui Qui, Emperor of China', while Laura became 'Kakadou' and 'the Hottentot'. Marx, known to intimates as 'Moor', encouraged his children to call him 'Old Nick' and 'Charley'. Confusingly, the surest sign of his contempt for someone was the regular use of their Christian name: the poet Kinkel, anti-hero of Marx's pamphlet *Great Men of the Exile*, was always referred to as 'Gottfried'.

'You know that my wife has made the world richer by one citizen?' Marx wrote to Joseph Weydemeyer in Frankfurt, soon after Fawkesy's début. The chirpy tone concealed a fearful apprehension: how on earth was he to provide for four young children and an ailing wife? Like Mr Micawber, he persuaded himself that something was bound to turn up. In October he had moved into a house in Anderson Street, Chelsea (then as now one of the more fashionable and expensive districts) at a rent of £6 a month, far more than he could afford.

A penniless, deracinated exile in a strange land might seem to need all the friends he can muster; but not Marx. The only ally he required was Engels – who, faithful as ever, moved to London on

12 November, loins girded for battle with the backsliders and traitors. At a meeting of the German Workers' Education Society six days later, Marx changed the name of the refugees' aid committee to distinguish it from a rival group founded by such namy-pamby 'liberals' as Gustav von Struve, Karl Heinzen and the Marxes' newly acquired family doctor, Louis Bauer. With severe formality, he informed Dr Bauer that 'in view of the inimical relations now obtaining between the two societies to which we belong – in view of your direct attacks upon the refugee committee here, at any rate upon my friends and colleagues in the same – we must break off social relations . . . Yesterday evening I thought it unseemly, in the presence of my wife, to express my views on this collision. While expressing my utmost obligation to you for your medical assistance, I would beg you to send me your account.' As soon as the bill was presented, however, Marx accused the doctor of trying to fleece him and refused to pay.

By Christmas, Engels was able to report to another German comrade that 'all in all, things are going quite well here. Struve and Heinzen are intriguing with all and sundry against the Workers' Society and ourselves, but without success. They, together with some wailers of moderate persuasion who have been thrown out of our society, form a select club at which Heinzen airs his grievances about the noxious doctrines of the communists.' When *The Times* described Heinzen as a 'shining light of the German Social Democratic Party', Engels sent a stern rebuttal to the *Northern Star*, a Chartist paper: 'Herr Heinzen, so far from serving as a shining light to the party in question, has, on the contrary, ever since 1842, strenuously, though unsuccessfully, opposed everything like Socialism and Communism'. It was just like the old times in Paris or Brussels – a whirligig of intriguing, score-settling and striving for mastery. At the Society's clubroom in Great Windmill Street, Soho, Marx soon took charge of vetting newcomers and laying down the law.

Wilhelm Liebknecht, who fled to London in 1850, left a vivid account of the intimidating methods by which Marx established his dominance. At a Society picnic shortly after his arrival he was taken aside by 'Père Marx', who began a minute inspection of the shape of his skull. Unable to find any obvious abnormalities, Marx invited him to the 'private parlour' at Great Windmill Street the following day for a more thorough scrutiny:

> I did not know what a private parlour was, and I had a presentiment that now the 'main' examination was impending, but I followed confidingly. Marx, who had made the same sympathetic impression on me as the day previous, had the quality of inspiring confidence. He took my arm and led me into the private parlour; that is to say, the private room of the host – or was it a hostess? – where Engels, who had already provided himself with a pewter-pot full of dark-brown stout, at once received me with merry jokes . . . The massive mahogany table, the shining pewter-pots, the foaming stout, the prospect of a genuine English beefsteak with accessories, the long clay pipes inviting to a smoke – it was really comfortable and vividly recalled a certain picture in the English illustrations of 'Boz'. But an examination it was for all that.

The examiners had done their homework. Citing an article written by Liebknecht for a German newspaper in 1848, Marx accused him of philistinism and 'South German sentimental haziness'. After a long plea in mitigation, the candidate was pardoned. But his ordeal had not finished: the Communists' resident phrenologist, Karl Pfaender, was then summoned to carry out a further investigation of Liebknecht's cranial contours. 'Well, my skull was officially inspected by Karl Pfaender and nothing was found that would have prevented my admission into the Holiest of Holies of the Communist League. But the examinations did not cease . . .' Marx, who was only five or six years older than the 'young fellows' such as Wilhelm Liebknecht, quizzed them as if he were a professor testing a rather dim class of undergraduates, wielding his colossal knowledge and fabulous memory as instruments of torture. 'How he rejoiced when he had tempted a "little student" to go on the ice and demonstrated in the person of the unfortunate the inadequateness of our universities and of academic culture.'

Marx was undoubtedly a tremendous show-off and a sadistic intellectual thug. But he was also an inspiring teacher, who educated the young refugees in Spanish, Greek, Latin, philosophy and political economy. 'And how patient he was in teaching, he who otherwise was so stormily impatient!' From November 1849 he delivered a long course of lectures under the title 'What is Bourgeois Property?', which drew capacity crowds to the upstairs room at Great Windmill Street. 'He stated a proposition – the shorter the better – and then demonstrated it in a lengthier explanation, endeavouring with the utmost care to avoid all expressions incomprehensible to the workers,' Liebknecht recalled. 'Then he requested his audience to put questions to him. If this was not done he commenced to examine the workers, and he did this with such pedagogic skill that no flaw, no misunderstanding escaped him . . . He also made use of a blackboard, on which he wrote the formulas – among them those familiar to all of us from the beginning of *Capital*.'

The denizens of Great Windmill Street maintained a busy timetable. On Sundays, there were lectures on history, geography and astronomy, followed by 'questions of the present position of the workers and their attitude to the bourgeoisie'. Discussions about communism occupied most of Monday and Tuesday, but later in the week the curriculum included singing practice, language teaching, drawing lessons and even dancing classes. Saturday evening was devoted to 'music, recitations and reading interesting newspaper articles'. In spare moments, Marx would stroll up to Rathbone Place, just off Oxford Street, where a group of French émigrés had opened a salon in which fencing with sabres, swords and foils could be practised. According to Liebknecht, Marx's cut-and-thrust technique was crude but effective. 'What he lacked in science, he tried to make up in aggressiveness. And unless you were cool, he could really startle you.'

As with the sword, so with the mightier pen: when not brandishing an épée he was preparing to unsheathe yet another newspaper with which he could stab and gore the philistines. At the beginning of 1850, the following announcement appeared in the German press: 'The *Neue Rheinische Zeitung. Politisch-ökonomische Revue* edited by Karl Marx will appear in January 1850 . . . The review will be published in monthly issues of at least five printers' sheets at a subscription price of 24 silver groschen per quarter.' The business manager was to be Conrad Schramm, another footloose German revolutionary who had come to London a few months earlier.

Marx's ambitions for the review were heroically grand. 'I have little doubt that by the time three, or maybe two, monthly issues have appeared, a world conflagration will intervene,' he predicted. In the meantime, however, there was the small but tiresome problem of finance. Convinced that 'money is to be had only in America', Marx decided to send Conrad Schramm on a transatlantic fund-raising tour – until it belatedly dawned on him that such a lengthy journey would incur even more expense.

The new journal, which limped through five issues before expiring, was jinxed from the start. The first issue was postponed when Marx fell ill for a fortnight; the typesetters' inability to decipher his scrawl caused further delay; he argued continually with the publisher and distributor, suspecting them of being in league with the censors. The miracle is that it ever appeared at all.

There were many good things in the *Revue* – notably a long series in which Marx employed all his dialectical ingenuity to challenge the received wisdom that the French revolution of 1848 had failed. 'What succumbed in these defeats was not the revolution. It was the pre-revolutionary traditional appendages, results of social relationships which had not yet come to the point of sharp class antagonisms . . .' Success would have been a disaster in disguise: it was only by a series of rebuffs that the revolutionary party could free itself of illusory notions and opportunistic leaders. 'In a word: the revolution made progress, forged ahead, not by its immediate tragi-comic achievements, but on the contrary by the creation of a powerful, united counter-revolution.' Having proved this contrarian thesis to his own satisfaction ('The revolution is dead! – *Long live the revolution!*'), he moved on to discuss Louis Napoleon's spectacular victory in the presidential elections of December 1848. Why had the French voted, in such overwhelming numbers, for this preposterous deadbeat – 'clumsily cunning, knavishly naïve, doltishly sublime, a calculated superstition, a pathetic burlesque, a cleverly stupid anachronism, a world-historic piece of buffoonery and an undecipherable hieroglyphic'? Simple: the very blankness of this junior Bonaparte allowed all classes and types to reinvent him in their own image. To the peasantry, he was the enemy of the rich; to the proletariat, he represented the overthrow of bourgeois republicanism; to the *haute* bourgeoisie, he offered the hope of royalist restoration; to the army, he promised war. Thus it happened that the most simple-minded man in France acquired the most complex significance: 'Just because he was nothing, he could signify everything.'

For all its boldness and brilliance, the *Revue* did not go out of its way to woo subscribers. As E. H. Carr has pointed out, 'the whole was tactfully seasoned with pungent attacks on the other German refugees in London, who were almost the only potential readers of the journal'. The circulation was tiny, and revenue negligible. In May 1850, Jenny Marx wrote beseechingly to Weydemeyer in Frankfurt: 'I beg you to send us as soon as possible any money that has come in or comes in from the *Revue*. We are in dire need of it.' Marx himself was stoical about the failure of a project in which he had invested so much hope and energy. As Jenny noted admiringly, he never lost his good humour or robust confidence in the future even during the 'most frightful moments' – of which there were all too many in 1850. 'Pray do not be offended by my wife's agitated letters,' he reassured Weydemeyer. 'She is nursing her child, and our situation here is so extraordinarily wretched that an outburst of impatience is excusable.'

This brisk summary barely hinted at the true horror of their struggle for survival. In a long and heart-rending letter written in May 1850, Jenny Marx described a scene that might have come from a Dickens novel:

Let me describe for you, as it really was, just one day in our lives, and you will realise that few refugees are likely to have gone through a similar experience. Since wet-nurses here are exorbitantly expensive, I was determined to feed my child myself, however frightful the pain in my breast and back. But the poor little angel absorbed with my milk so many anxieties and unspoken sorrows that he was always ailing and in severe pain by day and by night. Since coming into the world, he has never slept a whole night through – at most, two or three hours. Latterly, too, there have been violent convulsions, so that the child has been hovering constantly between death and a miserable life. In his pain he sucked so hard that I got a sore on my breast – an open sore; often blood would spurt into his little, trembling mouth. I was sitting thus one day when suddenly in came our landlady, to whom we had paid over 250 Reichstahlers in the course of the winter, and with whom we had contractually agreed that we should subsequently pay, not her, but her landlord by whom she had formerly been placed under distraint; she now denied the existence of this contract, demanded the £5 we still owed her and, since this was not ready to hand . . . two bailiffs entered the house and placed under distraint what little I possessed – beds, linen, clothes, everything, even my poor infant's cradle, and the best of the toys belonging to the girls, who burst into tears. They threatened to take everything away within two hours – leaving me lying on the bare boards with my shivering children and my sore breast. Our friend Schramm left hurriedly for town in search of help. He climbed into a cab, the horses took fright, he jumped out of the vehicle and was brought bleeding back to the house where I was lamenting in company with my poor, trembling children.

The following day we had to leave the house, it was cold, wet and overcast, my husband went to look for lodgings; on his mentioning four children, no one wanted to take us in. At last a friend came to our aid, we paid, and I hurriedly sold all my beds so as to settle with the apothecaries, bakers, butchers and milkman who, their fears aroused by the scandal of the bailiffs, had suddenly besieged me with their bills. The beds I had sold were brought out on to the pavement and loaded on to a barrow – and then what happens? It was long after sunset, English law prohibits this, the landlord bears down on us with constables in attendance, declares we might have included some of his stuff with our own, that we are doing a flit and going abroad. In less than five minutes a crowd of two or three hundred people stands gaping outside our door, all the riff-raff of Chelsea. In go the beds again; they cannot be handed over to the purchaser until tomorrow morning after sunrise; having thus been enabled, by the sale of everything we possessed, to pay every farthing, I removed with my little darlings into the two little rooms we now occupy in the German Hotel, 1 Leicester Street, Leicester Square, where we were given a humane reception in return for £5.10 a week.

A few days later the Marxes found temporary shelter in the house of a Jewish lace dealer at 64 Dean Street, Soho, where they spent a miserable summer teetering on the edge of destitution. Jenny was pregnant again, and constantly ill. By August things were so bad that she had to go to Holland and throw herself on the mercy of Karl's maternal uncle Lion Philips, a wealthy Dutch businessman (whose eponymous company flourishes to this day, selling all manner of electronic products from television sets to pop-up toasters). She needn't have bothered: Philips, who was 'very ill-disposed by the unfavourable effect the revolution had had on his business', offered only an avuncular embrace and a small present for little Fawkesy. When she warned that they would have to emigrate to America if he couldn't rescue them, Philips replied that he thought this an excellent idea. 'I am afraid, dear Karl, I am coming home to you quite empty-handed, disappointed, torn apart and tortured by a fear of death,' Jenny wrote. 'Oh, if you knew how much I am longing to see you and the little ones. I cannot write anything about the children, my eyes begin to tremble . . .'

Many revolutionaries exiled in London were artisans – typesetters, cobblers, watchmakers. Others earned a few pounds by teaching English or German. But Marx was congenitally unsuited to any regular employment. He did consider emigration but discovered that tickets for the voyage would be 'hellishly expensive'; if he had known that assisted passages were available, he might have taken the next boat. As usual, Engels saved the day, sacrificing his own journalistic ambitions in London to take a job at the Manchester office of his father's textile firm, Ermen & Engels. He remained there for almost twenty years. 'My husband and all the rest of us have missed you sorely and have often longed to see you,' Jenny wrote soon after his departure, in December 1850. 'However, I am very glad that you have left and are well on the way to becoming a great cotton lord.'

He had no desire to become anything of the kind, regarding 'vile commerce' as a penance that had to be endured. Though Engels soon assumed the outward appearance of a Lancashire businessman – joining the more exclusive clubs, filling his cellar with champagne, riding to hounds with the Cheshire Hunt – he never forgot that the main purpose was to support his brilliant but impecunious friend. He acted as a kind of secret agent behind enemy lines, sending Marx confidential details of the cotton trade, expert observations on the state of international markets and – most essentially – a regular consignment of small-denomination banknotes, pilfered from the petty cash box or guilefully prised out of the company's bank account. (As a precaution against mail theft he snipped them in two, posting each half in a separate envelope.) It is a measure of how slackly the office was run that neither his father nor his business partner in Manchester, Peter Ermen, ever noticed anything amiss.

Nevertheless, Engels was careful not to arouse their suspicions, even if this sometimes meant leaving the Marx family penniless. 'I am writing today just to tell you that I am unfortunately still not in a position to send you the £2 I promised you,' he wrote in November. 'Ermen has gone away for a few days and, since no proxy has been authorised with the bank, we are unable to make any remittances and have to content ourselves with the few small payments that happen to come in. The total amount in the cash box is only about £4 and you will therefore realise that I must wait a while.' When his father visited the Manchester office a few months later, Engels negotiated himself an 'expense and entertainment allowance' of £200 a year. 'With such a salary, all should be well, and if there are no ructions before the next balance sheet and if business prospers here, he'll have quite a different bill to foot – even this year I'll exceed the £200 by far,' he reported. 'Since business has been very good and he is now more than twice as wealthy as he was in 1837, it goes without saying that I shan't be needlessly scrupulous.' Engels senior soon had second thoughts, deciding that Friedrich was spending far too much money and must make do with £150. Though the prodigal son chafed at this 'ludicrous imposition', it didn't cramp his generosity unduly. By 1853 he was able to boast that 'last year, thank God, I gobbled up half of my old man's profits from the business here'. He could even afford to maintain two residences: at one, a smart townhouse, he entertained the local nobs and nabobs, while in the other he established a *ménage à trois* with his lover Mary Burns and her sister Lizzie.

On 15 June 1850, shortly before Engels began his long northern exile, the London *Spectator* printed a letter from Messrs 'Charles Marx' and 'Fredc. Engels' of 64 Dean Street, Soho. 'Really, Sir, we should never have thought that there existed in this country so many police spies as we have had the good fortune of making the acquaintance of in the short space of a week,' they wrote. 'Not only that the doors of the houses where we live are closely watched by individuals of a more than doubtful look, who take down their notes very coolly every time one enters the house or leaves it; we cannot make a single step without being followed by them wherever we go. We cannot get into an omnibus or enter a coffeehouse without being favoured with the company of at least one of these unknown friends.'

And quite right too, *Spectator* readers might have thought, especially since the authors proudly identified themselves as revolutionaries who had fled from the land of their birth. But Marx and Engels forestalled this objection with a cunning appeal to English vanity and Hunnophobia, revealing that in their previous sanctuaries – France, Belgium, Switzerland – they had been unable to escape the baleful power of the Prussian King. 'If, through his influences, we are to be made to leave this last refuge left to us in Europe, why then Prussia will think herself the ruling power of the world ... We believe, Sir, that under these circumstances, we cannot do better than bring the whole case before the public. We believe that Englishmen are interested in anything by which the old-established reputation of England, as the safest asylum for refugees of all parties and all countries, may be more or less affected.'

In spite of the amused tone, Marx desperately needed re-assurance that good old England would not let him down. Since a recent assassination attempt on King Frederick William IV, the Prussian Minister of the Interior had intensified his campaign against 'political conspirators' by dispatching police spies and *agents provocateurs* to the capitals of Europe – particularly to London, and most particularly to Dean Street, Soho. And no wonder: for the Minister of the Interior was none other than Jenny's reactionary half-brother Ferdinand von Westphalen. Having failed to prevent Marx from marrying into his family seven years earlier, he was hell-bent on revenge.

In the *Spectator* letter, Marx alleged that a fortnight before the shooting of King Frederick William 'persons whom we have every reason to consider as agents either of the Prussian government or the Ultra-Royalists presented themselves to us, and almost directly engaged us to enter into conspiracies for organising regicide in Berlin and elsewhere. We need not add that these persons found no chance of making dupes of us.' Their aim, as he explained, was to persuade the British authorities to 'remove from this country the pretended chiefs of the pretended conspiracy'. One of these unidentified agents was Wilhelm Stieber, later the chief of Bismarck's secret service, who came to London during the spring of 1850 masquerading as a journalist called Schmidt. Stieber had been instructed to keep a close eye on Karl Marx, and after infiltrating the communist HQ at 20 Great Windmill Street he sent back an urgent cable confirming all von Westphalen's suspicions about his nefarious brother-in-law. 'The murder of Princes is formally taught and discussed,' he reported:

At a meeting held the day before yesterday at which I assisted and over which Wolff and Marx presided, I heard one of the orators call out 'The Moon Calf [Queen Victoria] will likewise not escape its destiny. The English steel wares are the best, the axes cut particularly sharply here, and the guillotine awaits every Crowned Head.' Thus the murder of the Queen of England is proclaimed by Germans a few hundred yards only from Buckingham Palace . . . Before the close of the meeting Marx told his audience that they might be perfectly tranquil, their men were everywhere at their posts. The eventful moment was approaching and infallible measures are taken so that not one of the European crowned executioners can escape.

An earlier biographer of Karl Marx has claimed that 'this report is oddly convincing'. In fact, it is manifestly absurd – as the British government of the time recognised. Although the Prussian Minister of the Interior forwarded the dispatch to London, Lord

Palmerston consigned it to the Foreign Office files where it remains to this day. As far as one can tell, he did not even bother to alert Scotland Yard. When the Austrian ambassador in London complained to the Home Secretary, Sir George Grey, that Marx and his fellow members of the Communist League were discussing regicide, he was rewarded with a brief, supercilious lecture on the nature of liberal democracy: 'Under our laws, mere discussion of regicide, so long as it does not concern the Queen of England and so long as there is no definite plan, does not constitute sufficient grounds for the arrest of the conspirators.' A plot to assassinate Queen Victoria was precisely the sort of pointless stunt that Marx abhorred. He despised those revolutionaries who preferred flamboyant gestures to the dull but necessary process of preparing for the economic crisis which would precipitate the victory of the proletariat. Indeed, it was his very doggedness on this point that destroyed the Communist League in London, as the more impatient committee members chafed at his insistence that they must bide their time.

The leader of the malcontents was August Willich, Engels's old military commander from the '49 campaign in Baden, who had been making a thorough nuisance of himself since joining the German diaspora in England. 'He would come to visit me,' Jenny Marx wrote many years later, 'because he wanted to pursue the worm that lives in every marriage and lure it out.' Almost everything about Willich was calculated to irritate Marx – his posturing and preening, his colourful clothes, his noisy attention seeking. By the summer of 1850 he was openly denouncing Jenny's husband as a 'reactionary'. Marx, never one to miss an opportunity for vituperation, retaliated by dismissing him as an 'uneducated, four-times cuckolded jackass'. At a riotous meeting of the League's central committee on 1 September, Willich challenged Marx to a duel.

As Willich was a crack shot who could hit the ace of hearts at twenty paces, Marx had enough sense to refuse; but his eager lieutenant Conrad Schramm, who had never fired a pistol in his life, picked up the gauntlet at once and departed with Willich to Antwerp – duels being illegal in Britain – for a final reckoning. Karl and Jenny feared the worst, especially when they heard that that Willich was taking Emmanuel Barthélemy as his second. Barthélemy, a fierce-eyed muscular ruffian, had been convicted of murdering a policeman at the age of seventeen and still wore on his shoulder the indelible brand of a galley convict. Having fled to London only a few weeks earlier, after escaping from a French prison, he had already been heard to say that '*traîtres*' such as Marx and his cronies should be killed. Given his prowess with pistol and sabre, as demonstrated at the salon in Rathbone Place, this was no idle threat.

What hope did the bold but feeble Schramm have against the formidable expertise of Willich and Barthélemy? On the appointed day, Marx and Jenny sat miserably in their rooms with Wilhelm Liebknecht, counting the minutes until their young comrade died. The next evening Barthélemy himself came to the door and announced in a sepulchral voice that '*Schramm a une balle dans la tête!*' Bowing stiffly, he then left without another word.

'Of course, we gave up Schramm for lost,' Liebknecht wrote. 'The next day, while we were just talking about him sadly, the door is opened and in comes with a bandaged head but gaily laughing the sadly mourned one and relates that he had received a glancing shot which had stunned him – when he recovered consciousness, he was alone on the sea coast with his second and his physician.' Assuming that the wound was fatal, Willich and Barthélemy had caught the next steamer back from Ostend.

Thus ended Marx's dream of running the Communist League from England. At its final meeting, on 15 September 1850, he proposed that the Central Committee should be transferred to Cologne since the bickering London agitators were incapable of providing leadership of any kind. A fair point – except that the Communists of Cologne had quite enough problems of their own. The Prussian government had redoubled its persecution of subversives since the attempted assassination of King Frederick

William IV, and by the summer of 1851 all eleven members of the Cologne Central Committee were in jail awaiting trial on conspiracy charges. Poor old Marx, who had looked forward to a well-earned respite from the Communist League, found himself reluctantly dragged back into its affairs as he began to lobby and protest on behalf of the German 'conspirators'. It was not mere altruism: to his fury, he had been fingered by the prosecutor as the evil genius behind the bloodthirsty schemes and *coups* of which the defendants were accused. He worked day and night, setting up defence committees, raising funds, scribbling indignant letters to the newspapers. 'A complete office has now been set up in our house,' Jenny told a friend. 'Two or three people are writing, others running errands, others scraping pennies together so that the writers may continue to exist and prove the old world of officialdom guilty of the most outrageous scandal. And in between whiles my three merry children sing and whistle, often to be harshly told off by their papa. What a bustle!'

Seven of the eleven defendants were imprisoned. The Communist League was dead, and many years were to pass before Marx joined any other organisation. Understandably weary of Committees and Societies and Leagues, which demanded so much and achieved so little, he retreated into the British Museum reading room, ten minutes' walk from Dean Street, and applied himself to the ambitious task of producing a comprehensive, systematic explanation of political economy – the monumental project which was to become *Capital*.

At the end of 1850 – after six wretched months at 64 Dean Street – Karl and Jenny Marx found a more permanent home a hundred yards up the road, in two rooms on the top floor of number 28. Today the building is an expensive restaurant presided over by the modish chef Marco-Pierre White; a small blue plaque on the front, affixed by the defunct Greater London Council, records that 'Karl Marx 1818–1883 lived here 1851–56'. This is the only official monument to his thirty-four years in England, a country which has never known whether to feel pride or shame at its connection with the father of proletarian revolution. Appropriately enough, the dates on the sign are inaccurate.

The *annus horribilis* was nearly over, but it had a few more cruelties to inflict. Two weeks before the Marxes moved into 28 Dean Street their little gunpowder plotter, Heinrich Guido 'Fawksey', died suddenly after a fit of convulsions. 'A few minutes before, he was laughing and joking,' Marx told Engels. 'You can imagine what it is like here. Your absence at this particular moment makes us feel very lonely.' Jenny was quite distraught, 'in a dangerous state of excitation and exhaustion', while Karl expressed his grief in characteristic style by denouncing the perfidy of his comrades. The main target this time was Conrad Schramm, that erstwhile Hotspur who had risked his life only a few weeks earlier to defend Marx's honour.

'For two whole days, 19 and 20 November, he never showed his face in our house,' Marx raged, 'then came for a moment and immediately disappeared again after one or two fatuous remarks. He had volunteered to accompany us on the day of the funeral; he arrived a minute or two before the appointed hour, said not a word about the funeral, but told my wife that he had to hurry away so as not to be late for a meal with his brother.' Schramm thus joined an ever-lengthening list of traitors. Rudolf Schramm, Conrad's brother, was already on it, having had the effrontery to organise a meeting of Germans in London without inviting associates of Marx and Engels.

Another of these outcasts was Eduard von Müller-Tellering, a former correspondent for the *Neue Rheinische Zeitung* who was known as 'a first-class brawler' but met his match when he tried to pick a fight with Marx. As so often with these internecine vendettas, the original *casus belli* was laughably petty. Tellering asked Engels, at very short notice, for a ticket to a ball organised by the German Workers' Educational Society; Engels, explaining that the application was too late, couldn't resist pointing out that Tellering had never attended any meetings of the Society, nor even collected his membership card – 'and only the day before yesterday an individual in a similar situation was expelled from the society'. Taking the hint, the Society's 'court of honour', presided over by Willich, rescinded Tellering's membership. He replied with a volley of libellous attacks on the Marx–Engels clique – or, as it was often called by now, the Marx Party.

At this point the party leader himself entered the fray. 'For the letter you wrote yesterday to the Workers' Society, I would send you a challenge, were you still capable of giving satisfaction,' Marx thundered. 'I await you on a different field to strip you of the hypocritical mask of revolutionary fanaticism behind which you have so far skilfully contrived to hide your petty interests, your envy, your unassuaged vanity and your angry discontent over the world's lack of appreciation for your great genius – a lack of appreciation that began with your failure to pass your examination.' It was Marx who had encouraged Tellering's journalistic ambitions and had recommended him to the Society; it was now Marx who consigned the unworthy servant to the outer darkness. After one final, flailing counter-strike – a pamphlet of hysterical anti-Semitic insults – Tellering emigrated to the United States and was never heard of again.

Marx revelled in conflict and was always alert to any slight, real or imagined. Tellering and Rudolf Schramm were 'those wretches'; the leaders of the Democratic Association – a rival group to the German Workers' Educational Society – were 'charlatans and swindlers'; another group of newly arrived refugees was 'a fresh swarm of democratic scallywags'. If these wretches and scallywags were so negligible, one might well ask, why couldn't he ignore them? When libelled in print by an obscure politician in Switzerland named Karl Vogt, did he really have to compose a 200-page polemic – *Herr Vogt* – by way of reply? Marx was not alone in disliking the vain and boastful revolutionary poet Gottfried Kinkel, but no one else thought it necessary to subject Kinkel's absurdities to a hundred closely printed pages of scabrous mockery, published under the sarcastic title *The Great Men of the*

Exile. Whenever well-wishers suggested that a lion should not waste his time fighting with dung-beetles, Marx would reply that the merciless exposure of utopian charlatans was nothing less than his revolutionary duty: 'Our task must be unsparing criticism, directed even more against our self-styled friends than against our declared enemies.'

Besides, he enjoyed the sport. One need only read some of the incidental pen portraits in *The Great Men of the Exile* to see what pleasure he took in skewering them. Rudolf Schramm: 'A rowdy, loudmouthed and extremely confused little mannikin whose life-motto came from *Rameau's Nephew*: "I would rather be an impudent windbag than nothing at all." ' Gustav Struve: 'At the very first glimpse of his leathery appearance, his protuberant eyes with their sly, stupid expression, the matt gleam on his bald pate and his half Slav, half Kalmuck features one cannot doubt that one is in the presence of an unusual man . . .' Arnold Ruge: 'It cannot be said that this noble man commends himself by his notably handsome exterior; Paris acquaintances were wont to sum up his Pomeranian-Slav features with the word "ferret-face" . . . Ruge stands in the German revolution like the notices seen at the corner of certain streets: It is permitted to pass water here.'

Far from dissipating his vigour, these wild jeremiads actually seemed to renew it. The volcanic rage that erupted over obscure deviationists or dullards was the same fiery passion that illuminated his exposures of capitalism and its contradictions. To work at his best, Marx needed to keep himself in a state of seething fury – whether at the endless domestic disasters that beset him, at his wretched ill health or at the halfwits who dared to challenge his superior wisdom. While writing *Capital*, he vowed that the bourgeois would have good reason to remember the carbuncles which caused him such pain and kept his temper foul. The Vogts and the Kinkels served the same purpose – not so much butterflies upon a wheel as festering boils on the bum.

His living conditions might have been expressly designed to keep him from lapsing into contentment. The furniture and fittings in the two-room apartment were all broken, tattered or torn, with a half-inch of dust over everything. In the middle of the front living-room, overlooking Dean Street, was a big table covered with an oilcloth on which lay Marx's manuscripts, books and newspapers, as well as the children's toys, rags and scraps from his wife's sewing basket, several cups with broken rims, knives, forks, lamps, an inkpot, tumblers, Dutch clay pipes and a thick veneer of tobacco ash. Even finding somewhere to sit was fraught with peril. 'Here is a chair with only three legs, on another chair the children have been playing at cooking – this chair happens to have four legs,' a guest reported. 'This is the one which is offered to the visitor, but the children's cooking has not been wiped away; and if you sit down, you risk a pair of trousers.'

One of the few Prussian police spies who gained admission to this smoke-filled cavern was shocked by Marx's chaotic habits:

He leads the existence of a real bohemian intellectual. Washing, grooming and changing his linen are things he does rarely, and he likes to get drunk. Though he is often idle for days on end, he will work day and night with tireless endurance when he has a great deal of work to do. He has no fixed times for going to sleep and waking up. He often stays up all night, and then lies down fully clothed on the sofa at midday and sleeps till evening, untroubled by the comings and goings of the whole world.

Marx's reluctance to go to bed seems eminently reasonable, since his whole *ménage* – including the housekeeper, Helene 'Lenchen' Demuth – had to sleep in one small room at the back of the building. How Karl and Jenny ever found the time or privacy for procreation remains a mystery; one assumes that they seized their chances while Lenchen was out taking the children for a walk. With Jenny ill and Karl preoccupied, the task of preserving any semblance of domestic order fell entirely on their servant. 'Oh, if you knew how much I am longing for you and the little ones,' Jenny wrote to Karl during her fruitless expedition to Holland in

1850. 'I know that you and Lenchen will take care of them. Without Lenchen I would not have peace of mind here.'

Lenchen was indeed attending to Jenny's usual duties – including those of the conjugal bed. Nine months later, on 23 June 1851, she gave birth to a baby boy. On the birth certificate for young Henry Frederick Demuth, later known as Freddy, the space for the father's name and occupation were left blank. The child was given to foster parents soon afterwards, probably a working-class couple called Lewis in east London. (The evidence here is only circumstantial: Lenchen's son changed his name to Frederick Lewis Demuth and spent his entire adult life in the borough of Hackney. He became a skilled lathe-operator in several East End factories, a stalwart of the Amalgamated Engineering Union and a founder member of Hackney Labour Party. Remembered by colleagues as a quiet man who never talked about his family, he died on 28 January 1929.)

Since Freddy was born in the small back room at 28 Dean Street – and Lenchen's swelling stomach would have been all too obvious in the preceding weeks – this apparently miraculous conception could not be hidden from Jenny. Though deeply upset and angry, she agreed that the news would provide lethal ammunition to Marx's enemies should it ever get out. So began one of the first and most successful cover-ups ever organised for the greater good of the communist cause. There were plenty of rumours that Marx had fathered an illegitimate child, but the first public reference to Freddy's true paternity did not appear until 1962, when the German historian Werner Blumenberg published a document found in the vast Marxist archive at the International Institute of Social History, Amsterdam. It is a letter written on 2 September 1898 by Louise Freyberger, a friend of Helene Demuth and housekeeper to Engels, describing her employer's deathbed confession:

I know from General [Engels] himself that Freddy Demuth is Marx's son. Tussy [Marx's youngest daughter, Eleanor] went on at me so, that I asked the old man straight out. General was very astonished that Tussy clung to her opinion so obstinately. And he told me that if necessary I was to give the lie to the gossip that he disowned his son. You will remember that I told you about it long before General's death.

Moreover this fact that Frederick Demuth was the son of Karl Marx and Helene Demuth was again confirmed by General a few days before his death in a statement to Mr Moore [Samuel Moore, translator of the *Communist Manifesto* and *Capital*], who then went to Tussy at Orpington and told her. Tussy maintained that General was lying and that he himself had always admitted he was the father. Moore came back from Orpington and questioned General again closely. But the old man stuck to his statement that Freddy was Marx's son, and said to Moore, 'Tussy wants to make an idol of her father.'

On Sunday, that is to say the day before he died, General wrote it down himself for Tussy on the slate, and Tussy came out so shattered that she forgot all about her hatred of me and wept bitterly on my shoulder.

General gave us . . . permission to make use of the information only if he should be accused of treating Freddy shabbily. He said he would not want his name slandered, especially as it could no longer do anyone any good. By taking Marx's part he had saved him from a serious domestic conflict. Apart from ourselves and Mr Moore and Mr Marx's children (I think Laura knew about the story even though perhaps she had not heard it exactly), the only others that knew that Marx had a son were Lessner and Pfänder. After the Freddy letters had been published, Lessner said to me, 'Of course Freddy is Tussy's brother, we knew all about it, but we could never find out where the child was brought up.'

Freddy looks comically like Marx and, with that really Jewish face and thick black hair, it was really only blind prejudice that could see in him any likeness to General. I have seen the letter that Marx wrote to General in Manchester at that time (of course General was not yet living in London then); but I believe General destroyed this letter, like so many others they exchanged.

That is all I know about the matter. Freddy has never found out, either from his mother or from General, who his father really is . . .

I am just reading over again the few lines you wrote me about the question. Marx was continually aware of the possibility of divorce, since his wife was frantically jealous. He did not love the child, and the scandal would have been too great if he had dared to do anything for him.

Since it was made public in 1962 most Marxist scholars have accepted this document as conclusive proof of Karl's infidelity. But there are one or two sceptics. Eleanor Marx's biographer Yvonne Kapp has described the Freyberger letter as a 'high fantasy' which 'forfeits credence on many points'; nevertheless, she concedes, 'there can be no reasonable doubt that he [Freddy] was Marx's son'. Professor Terrell Carver, the author of a life of Engels, goes much further. He refuses to believe that either Marx or Engels could have sired Freddy Demuth, and dismisses the letter as a forgery – 'possibly by Nazi agents aiming to discredit socialism'. He points out that the version in the Amsterdam archive is a typewritten copy whose provenance is unknown, and the original (if there was one) has never been traced.

Certainly, some of the allegations in the document defy all logic or common sense. Take the 'letter' which Marx is supposed to have sent Engels at the time of the birth, and which Louise Freyberger claims to have seen. Since Freyberger was born in 1860 and did not go to work for Engels until 1890, this means that he must have kept it among his papers for many decades. Why, having taken the trouble to preserve it, did he then destroy the only evidence which would 'give the lie to the gossip that he disowned his son'?

There is also a rather obvious psychological implausibility. When Jenny Marx discovered that her servant and her husband had been canoodling behind her back – and while she herself was pregnant – she would probably have evicted the treacherous Lenchen from the household forthwith, or at least regarded her with cold mistrust. Yet the two women remained affectionate partners for the rest of their lives. 'Research into the life of Frederick Demuth and of his relations has yielded nothing concerning the identity of his father, and even Engels's alleged claim that he had somehow accepted paternity has no other supporting facts,' Professor Carver concludes. 'The surviving correspondence and memoirs certainly provide no positive support for Louise Freyberger's story.'

This is not quite true. Although the papers of Marx and Engels were carefully weeded by their executors, who did not wish to embarrass or injure the grand old men of communism, a few telling fragments have survived. The first is a letter from Eleanor Marx to her sister Laura, dated 17 May 1882, which shows that Marx's daughters had accepted the story of Engels's paternity: 'Freddy has behaved admirably in all respects and Engels's irritation against him is as unfair as it is comprehensible. We should none of us like to meet our pasts, I guess, in flesh and blood. I know I always meet Freddy with a sense of guilt and wrong done. The life of that man! To hear him tell of it all is a misery and shame to me.' Ten years later, on 26 July 1892, Eleanor returned to the subject: 'It may be that I am very "sentimental" – but I can't help feeling that Freddy has had great injustice all through his life. Is it not wonderful when you come to look things squarely in the face, how rarely we seem to practise all the fine things we preach – to others?' In the light of that earlier letter, her jibe is clearly aimed at Engels.

Both Karl Marx and his wife left small but telling clues to the truth. Jenny's autobiographical essay, 'A Short Sketch of an Eventful Life', written in 1865, includes a curious parenthetical revelation: 'In the early summer of 1851 an event occurred which

I do not wish to relate here in detail, although it contributed to increase our worries, both personal and others.' The event in question can only have been the arrival of Freddy. If Helene Demuth had been impregnated by some other lover, why would it have caused Jenny such lasting and personal grief?

Odder still is a letter sent by Marx to Engels on 31 March 1851, when Helene was six months pregnant. After an epic grumble about his debts, his creditors and his tight-fisted mother, Marx adds, 'You will admit that this is a pretty kettle of fish and that I am up to my neck in petty-bourgeois muck . . . But finally, to give the matter a tragi-comic turn, there is in addition a *mystère* which I will now reveal to you *en très peu de mots*. However, I've just been interrupted and must go and help nurse my wife. The rest, then, in which you also figure, in my next.' By the time of the next letter, two days later, he had changed his mind. 'I'm not writing to you about the *mystère* since, *coûte que coûte* [whatever it costs], I shall be coming in any case to see you at the end of April. I must get away from here for a week.'

What was the *mystère* if not Lenchen's gestation? The coy lapses into French euphemism prove it beyond doubt, since this was his usual language of gynaecological embarrassment. (During Jenny's pregnancies he often told Engels that she was in '*un état trop intéressant*'.) His reluctance to give any more details in writing is amply explained later in the same letter: 'My wife, alas, has been delivered of a girl, and not a *garçon*. And, what is worse, she's very poorly.' Was it Frau Marx or her new daughter, Franziska, who was 'poorly'? Probably both. We know from Jenny's memoir that she was depressed during the early summer of 1851, and Marx's letter of 31 March confirms this: 'My wife was brought to bed on 28 March. Though the confinement was an easy one, she is now very ill in bed, the causes being domestic rather than physical.' By the beginning of August, with two nursing mothers sharing the cramped quarters at Dean Street, other émigrés were beginning to gossip about old father Marx. 'My circumstances are very dismal,' he confessed to his friend Weydemeyer. 'My wife will go

under if things continue like this much longer. The constant
worries, the slightest everyday struggle wears her out; and on top
of that there are the infamies of my opponents who have never
yet so much as attempted to attack me as to the substance, who
seek to avenge their impotence by casting suspicions on my civil
character and by disseminating the most unspeakable infamies
about me. Willich, Schapper, Ruge and countless other democratic
rabble make this their business.' Rudolf Schramm, brother of the
duellist Conrad, had been whispering to acquaintances that
'whatever the outcome of the revolution, Marx is *perdu*'.

'I, of course, would make a joke of the whole dirty business,'
Marx wrote. 'Not for one moment do I allow it to interfere with
my work but, as you will understand, my wife, who is poorly and
caught up from morning till night in the most disagreeable of
domestic quandaries, and whose nervous system is impaired, is
not revived by the exhalations from the pestiferous democratic
cloaca daily administered to her by stupid tell-tales. The tactlessness of some individuals in this respect can be colossal.' What
was all that about, if not the mysterious conception of little
Freddy Demuth? It is noteworthy that Marx doesn't actually deny
the 'unspeakable' rumours while deploring the tactlessness of
those who broadcast them.

Things could hardly get worse; but they did. At Easter 1852,
shortly after her first birthday, Franziska had a severe attack of
bronchitis. On 14 April, Marx scribbled a brief letter to Engels:
'Dear Frederic, Only a couple of lines to let you know that our
little child died this morning at a quarter past one.' This
unemotional announcement does not begin to describe the agony
and despair that now enveloped the Marx household. For that,
we must turn to Jenny's 'Short Sketch of an Eventful Life'. 'She
suffered terribly. When she died we left her lifeless little body in
the back room, went into the front room and made our beds on
the floor. Our three living children lay down by us and we all
wept for the little angel whose livid, lifeless body was in the next
room.' At first the Marxes couldn't even afford to hire an

undertaker, but a French neighbour in Dean Street took pity on them and lent them two pounds. 'That money was used to pay for the coffin in which my child now rests in peace. She had no cradle when she came into the world and for a long time was refused a last resting place.'

Marx had been in London for little more than two years and had already been bereaved twice over. Engels identified the probable reason: 'If only,' he lamented in his letter of condolence, 'there were some means by which you and your family could move into a more salubrious district and more spacious lodgings!' Whether or not penury killed Franziska, it certainly interfered with her burial. For the previous few weeks Marx had been hoping to stabilise his finances with donations from American sympathisers, but on the very morning of the funeral he had a message from Weydemeyer, now living in New York, warning that there was little chance of salvation from that quarter. 'You will realise that Weydemeyer's letter made a very unpleasant impression here, particularly on my wife,' Marx told Engels. 'For two years now she has seen all my enterprises regularly come to grief.'

7

The Hungry Wolves

One morning in April 1853 a baker turned up at 28 Dean Street to warn that he would deliver no more bread until his outstanding bills were paid. He was greeted by Edgar Marx, a chubby-cheeked six-year-old who was already as street-smart as any Artful Dodger. Edgar's smallness had earned him the nickname 'Musch' ('fly') in infancy, but this had later been amended to 'Colonel Musch' in tribute to his tactical nous.

'Is Mr Marx at home?' the man enquired.

'No, he ain't upstairs,' the cockney urchin replied – and then, grabbing three loaves, shot off like an arrow.

Musch's father was immensely proud of the lad, but he could hardly expect all creditors to be rebuffed so easily. Throughout the years in Soho the Marxes lived in a state of siege: grubby police spies from Prussia lurked all too conspicuously outside, keeping note of the comings and goings, while irate butchers and bakers and bailiffs hammered on the door.

His letters to Engels are a ceaseless litany of wretchedness and woe. 'A week ago I reached the pleasant point where I am unable to go out for want of the coats I have in pawn, and can no longer eat meat for want of credit. Piffling it all may be, but I'm afraid that one day it might blow up into a scandal.' (27 February 1852.) 'My wife is ill. Little Jenny is ill. Lenchen has some sort of nervous fever. I could not and cannot call the doctor because I have no money to buy medicine. For the past eight to ten days I have been feeding the family solely on bread and potatoes, but whether I shall be able to get hold of any today is doubtful . . . How am I to get out of this infernal mess?' (8 September 1852.) 'Our misfortunes here have reached a climax.' (21 January 1853.) 'For the past ten days there hasn't been a sou in the house.' (8 October 1853.) 'At present I have to pay out twenty-five per cent [of household income] to the pawnshop alone, and in general am never able to get things in order because of arrears . . . The total absence of money is the more horrible – quite apart from the fact that family wants do not cease for an instant – as Soho is a choice district for cholera, the mob is croaking right and left (e.g. an average of three per house in Broad Street) and "victuals" are the best defence against the beastly thing.' (13 September 1854.) 'While I was upstairs busy writing my last letter to you, my wife down below was besieged by hungry wolves all of whom used the pretext of the "heavy times" to dun her for money which she had not got.' (8 December 1857.) 'I've just received a *third and final warning* from the rotten rate collector to the effect that, if I haven't paid by Monday, they'll put a broker in the house on Monday afternoon. If possible, therefore, send me a few pounds . . .' (18 December 1857.)

These 'few pounds' added up to a fairly lavish subsidy. Even in 1851, one of Marx's most poverty-stricken years, he received at least £150 from Engels and other supporters – a sum on which a lower-middle-class family could live in some comfort. That autumn he was appointed European correspondent of the *New York Daily Tribune*, the world's best-selling newspaper, for which he regularly submitted two articles a week at £2 apiece. Though his earnings from the *Tribune* dwindled slightly after 1854, by then he was also collecting £50 a year for his contributions to the *Neue Oder-Zeitung* in Breslau. In short, from 1852 onwards he had an income of at least £200. The annual rent for Dean Street was only £22. Why, then, was he always so catastrophically broke?

If Marx had been the careless bohemian depicted in so many police reports, he might have managed pretty well. In fact he

belonged to the class of distressed gentlefolk, desperate to keep
up appearances and unwilling to forgo bourgeois habits. For most
of the 1850s he could scarcely afford to feed his own children and
yet he insisted on employing a secretary, the young German
philologist Wilhelm Pieper, even though Jenny Marx was eager to
do the job.

Pieper, described by Jenny as a 'slovenly flibbertigibbet',
managed the rare feat of being both frivolous and dogmatic at the
same time. He was also tactless, loutish, extravagantly boastful
and insatiably libidinous. Some female visitors to the Marx
household were reduced to tears by his boorish political harangues
– and others by his brazen salaciousness. He regarded himself as
'Byron and Leibniz rolled into one'. More to the point, he was a
useless secretary. His main duty was to transcribe and translate
Marx's newspaper articles, but the translations were so erratic
that Engels usually had to redo them from scratch. Anyway, from
the spring of 1853 Marx felt confident enough to write in English
himself. 'I can't conceive what you still need him for,' Engels
muttered. Later that summer Pieper spent a fortnight in hospital,
where a little board at the end of the bed broadcast his shame for
all to see: 'Wilhelm Pieper, *syphilis secundarius*.' Though he promised
to be more discriminating in future, the pell-mell seductions
continued and before long he was back in hospital with a second
dose.

One day a letter arrived for him at Dean Street, addressed in a
female hand, requesting a rendezvous. Since the signature meant
nothing to Pieper he passed it to Jenny Marx – who recognised
that it was their former wet-nurse, 'a fat old Irish slattern'. Karl
and Jenny teased him about this latest admirer; but, as Marx
noticed, 'he kept his rendezvous with the old cow'. A few weeks
later he was declaring his boundless love for a greengrocer's
daughter from south London, described by Marx as a tallow
candle in green spectacles – 'her entire person green like verdigris
rather than veg., and greens to boot without any meat or flesh
whatever'. The main purpose of the courtship, it transpired, was

that Pieper hoped to touch her father for a loan of twenty quid, but like all his schemes it ended in disaster: the greengrocer refused to lend him a penny and the infatuated daughter then rushed over to Dean Street proposing that they elope together at once.

Pieper sometimes disappeared for weeks on end, either chasing an alluring petticoat or trying a new career – as journalist, proofreader, City clerk, lamp salesman, schoolmaster – but his dreams of love and money never came to anything; and so he would return to Dean Street in a bedraggled state pleading for shelter and sustenance. 'I am, *hélas*, once again saddled with Pieper,' Marx moaned in July 1854, 'who looks like a half-starved sucking pig seethed in milk, after having lived for a fortnight with a whore he describes as *un bijou*. He has frittered away some £20 in a fortnight and now both his purses are equally depleted. In this weather it is a bore to have the fellow hanging around from morning to night and night to morning. And it disrupts one's work.' Because of the cramped conditions in the flat Pieper had to share a bed with Marx. Worse still, Pieper insisted on playing him some of Richard Wagner's new work – 'music of the future' – which Marx thought horrible.

In 1857, Pieper announced that he had been offered a post as the German master at a private school in Bognor, apparently hoping that Marx would press him to stay on more favourable terms. At long last, however, his bluff was called – and Jenny slipped effortlessly into his place. 'It transpired that his "indispensability" was merely a figment of his own imagination,' Marx wrote, neglecting to add that he too had fallen for the myth. 'My wife fulfils the function of secretary without all the bother created by the noble youth . . . I do not need him in any way.' Since she had already proved this on several occasions while Marx was ill and Pieper off whoring, why did it take him so long to notice? He had been irritated by the unreliable factotum for years, privately referring to him as a feather-brained clown and a silly ass. 'The combination of dilettantism and sententiousness, vapidity and pedantry makes him ever harder to stomach. And, as so often in the case of such laddies, there lurks, beneath an apparently sunny temperament, much irritability, moodiness and crapulous despondency.'

The employment of Pieper was a needless extravagance from the outset, but had been allowed to continue because Marx thought it unseemly for a chap in his position *not* to have a confidential secretary – as well as regular seaside holidays, piano lessons for the children, and all the other costly appurtenances of respectability. However empty his pockets, he simply refused to accept a 'sub-proletarian' way of life, as he put it. What to other refugees might seem luxuries therefore became 'absolute necessities' while more imperative exigencies, such as paying the grocer, were treated as an optional extra.

These inverted priorities are apparent in a begging letter sent to Engels in June 1854, when Jenny was recovering from illness and Dr Freund, her GP, was clamouring for settlement of overdue medical bills. 'I find myself in a fix,' Marx wrote, explaining that his quarterly accounts were hopelessly in the red, 'since I had £12 to pay out for the household, and the total received was considerably reduced because of unwritten articles, besides which the chemist's bills alone swallowed up a large part of the budget.' The heart-tugging effect of this appeal was sabotaged in the very next sentence when he mentioned that Jenny, the children and housekeeper were about to take a fortnight's holiday at a villa in Edmonton – after which 'she might then be so far restored by the country air as to manage the journey to Trier'. If Marx was too skint to pay his own doctor, Engels might have wondered, how could he afford a fare to Germany? The question certainly occurred to his long-suffering creditors when they learned that Jenny had equipped herself with a new wardrobe of clothes for the trip. Marx affected not to understand their indignation, maintaining that the daughter of a German baron 'could naturally not arrive in Trier looking shabby'.

He was ridiculously proud of having married a bit of posh. Hence the visiting cards he had printed for her ('Mme Jenny

Marx, *née* Baronesse de Westphalen'), which he sometimes
flourished in the hope of impressing tradesmen and Tories.
'The sea is doing my wife a lot of good,' he noted after one of
Jenny's holidays. 'In Ramsgate she has made the acquaintance
of refined and, *horribile dictu*, clever Englishwomen. After years
during which she has enjoyed only inferior company, if any at
all, intercourse with people of her own kind seems to agree with
her.' Jenny had few such opportunities, and Marx was haunted
by guilt at the squalid fate he had inflicted on the former princess
of Trier society. There was a most humiliating reminder of how
far they had sunk when he was arrested while trying to pawn
Jenny's Argyll family silver – the police suspecting, reasonably
enough, that a scruffy German refugee couldn't have acquired
these ducal heirlooms legitimately. Marx spent a night in the
cells before Jenny managed to convince them of her aristocratic
bona fides.

Unable to keep his wife in the fashion appropriate to 'people
of her own kind', Marx could at least strive to do better by his
children. The girls must marry well, of course, and to attract the
right kind of suitor they would need ballgowns, dancing classes
and all the other social advantages money could buy, even if the
money in question had to be cadged from someone else. Engels,
long accustomed to being that someone else, never questioned his
friend's assumption that it was worth living beyond one's means
to avoid losing caste, and that an expensive show of finery would
actually pay dividends in the long run. 'I for my part wouldn't
care a damn about living in Whitechapel,' Marx claimed, but 'it
could hardly be suitable for growing girls.' In their teenage years
the Marx daughters attended a 'ladies' seminary' which charged
£8 a quarter, besides which they were enrolled for private tuition
in French, Italian, drawing and music. 'It is true my house is
beyond my means,' he admitted to Engels in 1865, after moving
to a mansion in north London. 'But it is the only way for the
children to establish themselves socially with a view to securing
their future . . . I believe you yourself will be of the opinion that,

even from a purely commercial point of view, to run a purely proletarian household would not be appropriate in the circumstances, although that would be quite all right if my wife and I were by ourselves or if the girls were boys.'

Even Engels couldn't cover the entire cost of grooming a bevy of eligible débutantes. After much brow-furrowing, he decided that Marx's hope of salvation lay in a loan from the People's Provident Assurance Society: 'Though I've racked my brains I can think of no other method of raising money in England. It seems to me that the moment has come for you to have a go at your mater . . .' A more obvious method – to get a job – had apparently not entered his businesslike brain, though on other occasions he was quick to recommend it as a cure-all for fellow refugees. 'I wish some of our lads in London would really settle down to a more or less steady job,' he told Marx once, with no ironic intent, 'for they're becoming inveterate loafers.'

During his thirty-four years in London there were only two occasions when Marx sought gainful employment. In a letter of 1852 to Joseph Weydemeyer, by then living in the United States, we learn of a 'newly invented lacquer varnish' to which Marx had been alerted by his new chum Colonel Bangya, a mysterious Hungarian émigré who later turned out to be an undercover agent for half the crowned heads of Europe. Weydemeyer was to take a stall at the International Industrial Exhibition in New York, where customers would be so dazzled by the invention that 'it might set you up in funds at one stroke' – and, of course, yield a handsome profit for its joint backers in London. 'Write to me at once, giving full details of the expenses you thereby incur,' Marx advised. Nothing more was heard of this magical varnish, which seems to have met the same fate as Weitling's ingenious contraption for making ladies' straw hats. Ten years later, when his debts were even ghastlier than usual, Marx applied in desperation for a job as a railway clerk but was rejected because of his unreadable handwriting.

Without his benefactor, Marx wrote, 'I would long ago have been obliged to start a "trade" '. The retching disgust represented by those inverted commas is almost audible. As it was, thanks to Engels's generosity, he could spend most of his days in the reading room of the British Museum, resuming his long-neglected study of economics. After the dissolution of the Communist League in 1852 he had no political chores to distract him, and he dealt with the demands of the New York *Tribune* by subcontracting much of the work to Engels. 'You've got to help me, now that I'm so busy with political economy,' he pleaded on 14 August 1851. 'Write a series of articles on Germany, from 1848 onwards. Witty and uninhibited.' So the first major series under Marx's byline in the *Tribune* – 'Revolution and Counter-revolution in Germany', which appeared in nineteen instalments between October 1851 and October 1852 – was in fact written wholly by Engels. An article on the progress of the Russo-Turkish war, published as an anonymous editorial in December 1853, showed such expert knowledge of military strategy that New York gossip attributed it to a famous American soldier of the time, General Winfield Scott. The editor, Charles Dana, cited these rumours in a letter to Jenny Marx as proof of her husband's brilliance – little guessing that the author was, once again, 'General' Engels, sometime foot-soldier in the Palatinate campaign.

'Engels really has too much work,' Marx admitted, 'but being a veritable walking encyclopedia, he's capable, drunk or sober, of working at any hour of the day or night, is a fast writer and devilish quick on the uptake.' Though happy enough to take on this extra burden, Engels was so exhausted by his long hours at the cotton factory that he couldn't be expected to write *everything*. Nor did Marx want him to: the *Tribune*'s huge and influential readership – its weekly edition alone sold more than 200,000 copies – was an irresistible lure for a man more accustomed to addressing audiences of a few dozen in the upstairs room of a London pub. Sometimes he sent a rough outline to Manchester which Engels then fleshed out; on other occasions – when, say, the newspaper wanted something on warfare, or 'the Eastern question' – the secret ghost-writer would have to do it all himself, since Marx 'hadn't a clue' about such things.

Even so, Marx can probably take the credit for at least half of the 500-odd articles that he submitted to the *Tribune*. In his wearier moments he sometimes neglected the old journalistic injunction to grab the reader's attention from the outset ('The Parliamentary debates of the week offer but little of interest' is the unimprovable opening sentence of a dispatch from March 1853) but most of these commentaries, particularly on British politics, have his inky fingerprints all over them. Here, for example, is an account of the 1852 election: 'Days of general election are in Britain traditionally the bacchanalia of drunken debauchery, conventional stock-jobbing terms for the discounting of political consciences, the richest harvest time of the publicans . . . They are saturnalia in the ancient Roman sense of the word. The master then turned servant, the servant turned master. If the servant be turned master for one day, on that day brutality will reign supreme.' His remarks on the violent insurrection by Sepoys, native soldiers in the Anglo-Indian army, are better still: 'There is something in human history like retribution; and it is a rule of historical retribution that its instrument be forged not by the offended, but by the offender. The first blow dealt to the French monarchy proceeded from the nobility, not from the peasants. The Indian revolt does not commence with the Ryots, tortured, dishonoured and stripped by the British, but with the Sepoys, clad, fed, petted, fatted and pampered by them.'

It is surprising – or, rather, depressingly unsurprising – that none of his journalistic jabs has found its way into a dictionary of quotations. Has anyone ever impaled Palmerston more lethally? 'What he aims at is not the substance, but the mere appearance of success. If he can do nothing, he will devise anything. Where he dares not interfere, he intermeddles. Not able to vie with a strong enemy, he improvises a weak one . . . In his eyes, the movement of history is nothing but a pastime, expressly invented

for the private satisfaction of the noble Viscount Palmerston of
Palmerston.' Or how about this, on the wretched and squirming
Lord John Russell? 'No other man has verified to such a degree
the truth of the biblical axiom that no man is able to add an inch
to his natural height. Placed by birth, connections and social
accidents on a colossal pedestal, he always remained the same
homunculus – a malignant and distorted dwarf on the top of a
pyramid.'

Had he but world enough and time, Marx could have kept this
up indefinitely and made his name as the sharpest polemical
journalist of the century. But at his back he could always hear the
nagging voice of conscience, whispering, '*C'est magnifique, mais ce
n'est pas la guerre.*' As early as April 1851 Marx claimed to be 'so far
advanced that I will have finished the whole economic stuff in
five weeks' time. And having done that, I shall complete the
political economy at home and apply myself to another branch
of learning at the Museum.' For the next couple of months he sat
in the reading room from nine in the morning until seven in the
evening most days. 'Marx lives a very retired life,' Wilhelm Pieper
reported, 'his only friends being John Stuart Mill and Loyd [the
economist Samuel Jones Loyd], and whenever one goes to see
him one is welcomed with economic categories in lieu of
greetings.'

But there was still no end to the Herculean task he had set
himself. 'The material I am working on is so damnably involved
that, no matter how I exert myself, I shall not finish for another
six to eight weeks,' he told Weydemeyer in June. 'There are,
moreover, constant interruptions of a practical kind, inevitable
in the wretched circumstances in which we are vegetating here.
But for all that, for all that, the thing is rapidly approaching
completion. There comes a time when one has forcibly to break
off.'

This shows a comical lack of self-knowledge. Marx would
happily 'break off' from old friendships or political associations
with impetuous nonchalance, but he had no such facility for letting

go of his work – especially not *this* work, this vast compendium of statistics and history and philosophy which would at last expose all the shameful secrets of capitalism. The more he wrote and studied, the further the book seemed from completion: as with Casaubon's interminable 'Key to All Mythologies' in *Middlemarch*, there were always new leads to be pursued, obscure research to be quarried. (As it happens, Marx loved the novels of George Eliot. 'Well, our friend Dakyns is a sort of Felix Holt, less the affectation of that man, and plus the knowledge,' he wrote to his daughter Jenny after visiting the geologist J. R. Dakyns in 1869. 'I could of course not forbear making a little fun of him and warning him to fight shy of any meeting with Mrs Eliot who would at once make literary property out of him.')

'The main thing,' Engels advised in November 1851, 'is that you should once again make a public début with a big book . . . It's absolutely essential to break the spell created by your prolonged absence from the German book market.' But for the next four years the project was set aside, a victim of those 'constant interruptions' – many of which, one might add, were entirely of his own making. Immediately after the French *coup* of December 1851 he began writing *The Eighteenth Brumaire of Louis Bonaparte* at the request of the new American weekly *Die Revolution*, founded by his friend Joseph Weydemeyer: big books might be beyond him, but he had lost none of his pamphleteering *brio*.

Alas, some of his more questionable skills hadn't deserted him either. In the spring of 1852 Marx wasted several months composing *The Great Men of the Exile*, his verbose satire on the 'more noteworthy jackasses' and 'democratic scallywags' of the socialist diaspora. The chief villain in this rogues' gallery was Gottfried Kinkel, an occasional poet and sometime political prisoner who was now being lionised by grand London hostesses such as the Baroness von Brüningk, *châtelaine* of an agreeable salon in St John's Wood. Marx spent the whole of June in Manchester with Engels, salting the text with ever more elaborate insults against Kinkel and the other scallywags. 'The process of curing these stockfish,' he wrote, 'makes us laugh till we cry.' Luckily for his reputation, the *folie à deux* remained a private joke. When Marx entrusted the manuscript to Colonel Bangya for delivery to a German publisher, the treacherous rogue promptly sold it to the Prussian police. It languished unseen for nearly a century, and anyone reading the book today may well judge that this was no great loss.

But he wasn't finished with the stockfish. In July rumours reached him that Kinkel, during a fund-raising tour of America, had told an audience in Cincinnati, 'Marx and Engels are no revolutionaries, they're a couple of blackguards who have been thrown out of public houses by the workers in London.' Marx challenged him to deny the story: 'I await your answer by return of post. Silence will be regarded as an admission.' Kinkel replied that since he had been attacked by Marx in the *Neue Rheinische Zeitung* in 1950, while still imprisoned in Germany, 'I have wanted to have nothing more to do with you'.

> If you believe that you can . . . provide proof that I untruthfully said or published anything detrimental to your own or Mr Engels's honour, I must point out to you, as I would to anyone with whom I have neither personal nor political contacts, the usual way which, under the law, is open to everyone who feels himself insulted or libelled. Except in this way, I shall have no further dealings with you.

Marx was peeved that his challenge hadn't been taken up. ('How coolly everything is rejected that might smack of a duel and the like.') A libel case was out of the question, as a British court could hardly pass judgment on insults delivered in Cincinnati. Assuming that Kinkel would ignore any further correspondence with a Soho postmark, Marx contrived an elaborate ruse. He persuaded the Chartist leader Ernest Jones to address an envelope to Kinkel (guessing that his own spidery scrawl would be instantly recognised) and then asked Wilhelm Wolff to post it from Windsor.

The *billet-doux* inside, on coloured paper adorned with a posy of forget-me-nots and roses, was full of the predictable sweet nothings that Marx bestowed on his enemies. Revealing that he now had sworn statements from witnesses in Cincinnati, he thundered, 'Your letter – and this is precisely why it was *provoked* – provides a new and striking proof that the said Kinkel is a cleric whose baseness is equalled only by his cowardice.'

Marx took great pride in his schoolboy jape. 'The cream of the jest,' he gloated, 'will only become plain to Kinkel later on, with the appearance of the first instalment of *The Great Men of the Exile*. Namely, that shortly *before* this fearsome attack on Gottfried, I diverted myself by doing him direct and personal injury, while at the same time justifying myself in the eyes of the émigré louts. To that end I needed something in "black and white" from Johann etc. Now for greater matters . . .'

These 'greater matters' turned out to be yet more internecine squabbles, prompted by the opening of the long-postponed trial of Cologne Communists in October 1852. Since the most incriminating exhibits at the trial were minute-books and reports advocating armed insurrection, supposedly purloined from the Communist League in London, Marx spent the summer and autumn collecting affidavits to confirm that the documents were forgeries. When the trial was over he felt obliged to write an article defending himself against the slanders on 'the Marx group' that had been aired in the Cologne courtroom – and, by the by, putting the knife into the Willich–Schapper faction from the Communist League. Inevitably enough, this article soon grew into a book, *Revelations Concerning the Communist Trial in Cologne*, which, with equal inevitability, was denounced by August Willich. Marx then dashed off another pamphlet, *The Knight of the Noble Conscience*, savaging his erstwhile comrade's 'overweening conceit' and 'foul insinuations'. And so on, and so on . . .

With unusual discretion, he omitted one damaging fact about the ignoble knight. During 1852 Willich was given free lodging at the Baroness von Brüningk's house in north London, and according to a story relayed by Marx to Engels, she 'used to enjoy flirting with this old he-goat, as with the other ex-lieutenants. One day the blood rushes to the head of our ascetic, he makes a brutally brutish assault upon *madame*, and is ejected from the house with *éclat*. No more love! No more free board!' With his London reputation in tatters Willich emigrated to America shortly afterwards, where he fought with great courage in the Civil War. Even Marx was forced to concede, many years later, that the old he-goat had at least partly redeemed himself.

Why, one must ask again, did Marx fritter away his talents on these extravagant vendettas? One explanation is that his domestic chaos was unconducive to grander or more taxing work. ('All one can do,' he sighed, 'is produce miniature dunghills.') Perhaps, too, the ancient scar from that undergraduate duel had never quite healed. When the London German newspaper *How Do You Do?* hinted that he was secretly in cahoots with his brother-in-law Ferdinand von Westphalen, the fiercely oppressive Prussian Minister of the Interior, Marx strode down to the office and challenged the editor to a duel. The terrified hack published an apology at once. In October 1852 he used the same threat against Baron von Brüningk, who had accused him of spreading a rumour that the coquettish Baroness was a Russian spy. Marx proposed a meeting at which he would demonstrate his innocence – 'and should my explanation not suffice, I shall be prepared to give you the satisfaction customary among gentlemen'. The dispute was eventually settled without bloodshed by a formal exchange of letters. But one month later he was at it again, this time sending a splenetic message to the left-wing historian Karl Eduard Vehse who was apparently broadcasting 'insolent' and 'impertinent' gossip in Dresden about Marx's pamphlet on *The Great Men of the Exile*. 'Should this letter cause you offence,' he concluded after several ripe paragraphs of invective, 'you need only come to London; you know where I live and may be assured that you will always find me prepared to give you the satisfaction customary in such cases.'

The only people likely to receive satisfaction from this communist cannibalism were the Prussian authorities: Marx's vendettas against men such as Willich were far more effective than the bungled attempts at sabotage and entrapment by their own Keystone Cops. Though aware that he was giving aid and comfort to the enemy, Marx argued that the conspirators he attacked were the truly dangerous enemies because their siren song of instant revolution might lure socialists into some sort of premature and disastrous stunt. Fake messiahs, if left unexposed, were far more attractive to the masses than genuine monarchs. The *ad hominem* pamphlets, and the threats of pistols at dawn, were therefore essential political interventions rather than mere manifestations of pique and wounded pride – or so he convinced himself. 'I am,' he said, 'engaged in a fight to the death with the sham liberals.' The most deadly weapon against these poltroons would be a finished copy of his *magnum opus*, demonstrating once and for all why revolutionaries could never succeed without first doing their economic homework. 'The democratic simpletons to whom inspiration comes "from above" need not, of course, exert themselves thus,' he sneered. 'Why should these people, born under a lucky star, bother their heads with economic and historical material? It's really all *so simple*, as the doughty Willich used to tell me. All so simple to these addled brains!'

Marx's enemies, then and since, have attributed his dislike of Willich and the other 'great men of the exile' to pure jealousy. After the failure of the 1848 revolutions many of the heroes of that glorious defeat had come to London garlanded with campaign medals and romantic glamour – men such as Mazzini from Italy, Louis Blanc from France, Kossuth from Hungary, Kinkel from Germany. Society hostesses vied for their attention; lavish banquets were held in their honour; portraits were commissioned. Gottfried Kinkel, who had fled to England after a daring escape from Spandau jail, was eulogised by Dickens in *Household Words*. He then gave a series of lectures on drama and literature for which tickets were sold at an amazing one guinea a head. As

Marx commented, 'No running around, no advertisement, no charlatanism, no importunity was beneath him; in return, however, he did not go unrewarded. Gottfried sunned himself complacently in the mirror of his own fame and in the gigantic mirror of the Crystal Palace of the world.' Though trapped in poverty, obscurity and near starvation, Marx never envied these swaggering world-liberators their *réclame*. He often quoted Dante's maxim, *Segui il tuo corso, e lascia dir le genti* – go your own way and let tongues wag. What he admired in the British co-operative pioneer Robert Owen was that whenever any of his ideas became popular he would immediately say something outrageous to make himself unpopular all over again.

'He loathed fine speakers and woe betide anyone who engaged in phrasemongering,' Liebknecht observed. 'He kept impressing upon us "young fellows" the necessity for logical thought and clarity in expression and forced us to study . . . While the other emigrants were daily planning a world revolution and day after day, night after night, intoxicating themselves with the opium-like motto "Tomorrow it will begin!", we, the "brimstone band", the "bandits", the "dregs of mankind", spent our time in the British Museum and tried to educate ourselves and prepare arms and ammunition for the future fight.' His favourite story about the perils of posturing concerned Louis Blanc, a very small but exceedingly vain man, who turned up at Dean Street early one morning and was asked by Lenchen to wait in the front parlour while Marx dressed. Peeping through the connecting door, which had been left slightly ajar, Karl and Jenny had to bite their lips to stop laughing: the great historian and politician, former member of the French provisional government, was strutting in front of a shabby mirror in the corner, contemplating himself with delight and frisking like a March hare. After a minute or two of this entertainment Marx coughed to announce his presence. The foppish tribune wrenched himself away from the narcissistic pleasures of the looking-glass and 'hastily adopted as natural an attitude as he was capable of'.

The applause of the multitude was worthless until the workers were 'spiritually soaked' in socialist ideas – through education not elocution, political organisation rather than preening. And where better to begin the task? England was not only the cradle of capitalism but also the birthplace of Chartism. While his fellow exiles contented themselves with secret societies and salons, the natives had already recruited a huge army of proletarian resistance. 'The English working men are the first-born sons of modern industry,' Marx declared. 'They will then, certainly, not be the last in aiding the social revolution produced by that industry.'

Chartism took its name and inspiration from the People's Charter of May 1838, which had six fundamental demands: universal male suffrage; secret ballots; annual parliaments; salaries for MPs; abolition of the property qualification for MPs; an end to rotten boroughs. Though beset by constant arguments between the advocates of violent insurrection and those who put their trust in 'moral force', the Chartists remained a potent threat to the established order for much of the next decade. One of their newspapers, the *Northern Star*, sold more than 30,000 copies a week, and since most of these were bought in pubs or factories the actual readership was far higher. Pitched battles were fought with the police, most notably in Birmingham and Monmouthshire, after which several of the leaders were jailed or transported. A Chartist petition presented to Parliament in 1842 – unsurprisingly rejected – had 3,317,702 signatures and was more than six miles long. That summer a two-week general strike in support of the Charter paralysed the Midlands, the North of England and parts of Wales.

In April 1848, as Europe's *anciens régimes* tottered and fell, the Chartists announced that they would assemble on Kennington Common, just south of the Thames, and march on Parliament. The news provoked such panic among the governing classes that the Duke of Wellington himself, victor of Waterloo, was brought out of retirement to prevent the demonstrators from crossing the river. It was Chartism's last hurrah. Three years later, big crowds did gather in the centre of town – but for the International Exhibition in Hyde Park. With its industrial wealth, middle-class resilience and ubiquitous police, England had apparently weathered the revolutionary storms rather better than its Continental neighbours. Even so, a kind of submerged radicalism lingered on. Henry Mayhew's book *London Labour and the London Poor*, published in 1851, recorded that 'the artisans are almost to a man red-hot proletarians, entertaining violent opinions'.

Karl Marx had little time for the Chartists' leader, Feargus O'Connor, a brilliant but increasingly demented Irish demagogue. He was more impressed by O'Connor's two lieutenants, George Julian Harney and Ernest Jones, whom he had met briefly during his first visit to England in the summer of 1845. Engels wrote a series of articles about Germany for Harney's *Northern Star* that year and invited him to join the communists' correspondence network soon afterwards. Harney and Jones both attended the second congress of the Communist League in November 1847, at which Marx and Engels were asked to compose their manifesto.

Alarmed by the galloping optimism of these German revolutionists, Harney tugged desperately on the reins. 'Your prediction that we will get the Charter in the course of the present year, and the abolition of private property within three years, will certainly not be realised,' he warned Engels in 1846. 'The *body* of the English people, without becoming a slavish people, are becoming an eminently pacific people . . . Organised conflicts such as we may look for in France, Germany, Italy and Spain cannot take place in this country. To organise, to conspire a revolution in this country would be a vain and foolish project.' Engels ignored the cautionary signals. Immediately after the Kennington Common rally of April 1848 he told his communist brother-in-law, Emil Blank, that the English bourgeoisie would be 'in for a surprise when once the Chartists make a start. The business of the procession was a mere bagatelle. In a couple of months, my friend G. Julian Harney . . . will be in Palmerston's shoes. I'll bet you twopence and in fact any sum.' After a couple of months – and indeed a couple of years – Palmerston was still Foreign Secretary.

What went wrong? On 1 January 1849, Marx reviewed the failed revolutions of 1848 and looked ahead to the coming year in the *Neue Rheinische Zeitung*. '*England*, the country that turns whole nations into proletarians, that takes the whole world within its immense embrace, that has already defrayed the cost of a European Restoration, the country in which class contradictions have reached their most acute and shameless form – *England* seems to be the rock against which the revolutionary waves break, the country where the new society is stifled even in the womb.' The world market was dominated by England, and England was dominated by the bourgeoisie. 'Only when the Chartists head the English government will the social revolution pass from the sphere of utopia to that of reality.'

In short, the future of world revolution depended on Harney and his colleagues – a heavy responsibility for Marx to lay upon them, though also a handsome tribute to their prowess. Alas for his prediction, they were already disintegrating into factions and splinter groups. Encouraged by Marx and Engels, George Julian Harney broke with O'Connor in 1849 and founded a succession of evanescent if lively journals – the *Democratic Review*, the *Red Republican* (whose greatest achievement, during its brief six months of existence, was to publish the first English translation of the *Communist Manifesto*) and the *Friend of the People*.

To the disgust of Marx and Engels, Harney practised what he preached about the 'brotherhood of man' – a phrase Marx detested, since there were many men whose brother he would never wish to be under any circumstances. The emollient Harney spread his political favours widely, applauding Marx's 'rascally foes' among the Continental democrats – Mazzini, Ledru-Rollin, Louis Blanc, Ruge, Schapper – and somehow contriving to keep in with all sides when the Communist League fell apart. Marx

thought him not so much wicked as merely impressionable –
'impressionable, that is, to famous names, in whose shadow he
feels touched and honoured'. In his private correspondence with
Engels, Marx nicknamed the indiscriminate cheerleader 'Citizen
Hiphiphiphurrah' – or sometimes 'Our Dear', a mocking
reference to his cloyingly fond and attentive wife, Mary Harney.
'I am *fatigué* of this public incense so tirelessly used by Harney to
fill the nostrils of *les petits grands hommes*,' he complained in February
1851.

Still, Harney's ideological promiscuity had one merit: it left
Marx once again without any loyal allies. 'I am greatly pleased by
the public, authentic isolation in which we two, you and I, now
find ourselves,' he wrote to Engels. 'It is wholly in accord with our
attitude and our principles. The system of mutual concessions,
half-measures tolerated for decency's sake, and the obligation to
bear one's share of public ridicule in the party along with these
jackasses, all this is now over ... I hardly see anyone here [in
London] save Pieper and live in complete retirement.'

Engels agreed wholeheartedly:

I find this inanity and want of tact on Harney's part more
irritating than anything else. But *au fond* it is of little moment.
At long last we have again the opportunity – the first time in
ages – to show that we need neither popularity, nor the support
of any party in any country, and that our position is completely
independent of such ludicrous trifles. From now on we are only
answerable for ourselves and, come the time when these gentry
need us, we shall be in a position to dictate our own terms.
Until then we shall at least have some peace and quiet ... How
can people like us, who shun official appointments like the
plague, fit into a 'party'? And what have we, who spit on
popularity, who don't know what to make of ourselves if we
show signs of growing popular, to do with a 'party', i.e. a herd
of jackasses who swear by us because they think we're of the
same kidney as they? Truly, it is no loss if we are no longer held

to be the 'right and adequate expression' of the ignorant curs with whom we have been thrown together over the past few years.

Like another Marx, they disdained any club that would want them as members: 'merciless criticism of everyone' was now their policy. 'What price all the tittle-tattle the entire émigré crowd can muster against you,' Engels asked, 'when you answer it with your political economy?'

This lofty contempt for tittle-tattle was gloriously disingenuous: Marx and Engels had an undiminished thirst for émigré gossip, and for the rest of their lives they never missed a chance to amuse or infuriate each other by trading scuttlebutt. The spluttering indignation reached new heights in February 1851 when Harney helped to organise a London banquet at which the guest of honour was Louis Blanc. Two of Marx's few remaining allies among the London expatriates, Conrad Schramm and Wilhelm Pieper, were sent along to observe the proceedings – only to find themselves dragged out of the hall, denounced as spies and then kicked and punched by a 200-strong crowd, including many members of Harney's ill-named 'Fraternal Democrats'. Schramm appealed for help to one of the stewards, Landolphe, but to no avail. Then, as Marx informed Engels, 'who should arrive but Our Dear; instead of intervening energetically, however, he stammered something about knowing these people and would have launched into long explanations. A fine remedy, of course, at such a moment.' Engels suggested that Pieper and Schramm avenge themselves by giving Landolphe a box on the ears. Marx, predictably enough, felt that nothing less than a duel would provide the necessary satisfaction – and 'if anybody is to be done an injury, it must be the little Hiphiphiphurrah Scotsman, George Julian Harney, and no other, and then it is Harney who will have to practise shooting.'

Citizen Hiphiphiphurrah's only use to Marx and Engels thereafter was as the butt for jokes. However, they stayed on friendly terms with Ernest Jones, who had not attended the infamous banquet. Having spent his childhood in Germany, Jones was deemed to be 'unEnglish' – the highest compliment they could pay any British citizen. (In 1846, still in the first flush of infatuation, Engels had described Harney as 'more of a Frenchman than an Englishman'.) Marx contributed to Jones's periodical, the *People's Paper*, and in his articles elsewhere continued to praise the Chartists' insistence on widening the franchise. 'After the experiments which undermined universal suffrage in France in 1848, the Continentals are prone to underrate the importance and meaning of the English Charter,' he wrote in the *Neue Oder-Zeitung*. 'They overlook the fact that two-thirds of the population of France are peasants and over one-third towns-people, whereas in England more than two-thirds live in towns and less than one-third in the countryside. Hence the results of universal suffrage in England must likewise be in inverse pro-portion to the results in France, just as town and country are in the two states.' In France, the suffrage was a political demand, supported to a greater or lesser extent by almost every 'educated' person. In Britain, it was a social question, marking the divide between aristocracy and bourgeoisie on the one side and 'the people' on the other. English agitation for suffrage had gone through 'historical development' before it became a slogan of the masses; in France, the slogan came first, without any preceding gestation. Here we see once more the curious ambivalence of Marx's attitude to his adoptive country. Unlike its peasant-infested neighbours, England had a large and sophisticated metropolitan proletariat: it was therefore more 'advanced' and ready for revolution. Yet England also possessed an immensely self-confident bourgeosie, the rock against which revolutionary waves broke in vain. Sometimes he persuaded himself that a political cataclysm in Britain was not only inevitable but imminent; at other times he was reduced to angry despair by the doltish conservatism of the inhabitants. But what could one expect? Marx, more than any other thinker of his generation, was a connoisseur of paradox and contradictions – since it was these very contradictions which guaranteed capitalism's demise.

'There is one great fact, characteristic of this our nineteenth century, a fact which no party dares deny,' he said in April 1856, at a London dinner celebrating the fourth anniversary of the *People's Paper*. 'On the one hand, there have started into life industrial and scientific forces which no epoch of the former human history had ever suspected. On the other hand, there exist symptoms of decay, far surpassing the horrors recorded of the latter times of the Roman empire. In our days everything seems pregnant with its contrary.' Machinery, blessed with the power of shortening and fructifying people's labour, had instead starved and overworked them. The new sources of wealth, by some inverse alchemy, had become sources of want. And Britain – the wealthiest and most modern industrial society in the world – was also the most ripe for destruction. 'History is the judge – its executioner, the proletarian.'

Even an after-dinner audience of English Jacobins, fortified with 'the choicest viands and condiments of the season', might have raised a quizzical eyebrow at this apocalyptic rhetoric. Could England – the financial and industrial centre of the world, the hub of the greatest empire ever seen, the throbbing heart of capitalism – really be so flimsy and frangible? To Marx, the paradox was more apparent than real. It was an 'old and historically established maxim' that obsolete social forces summon all their strength before their final death agony, and were therefore weakest when they seemed most intimidating. 'Such is today the English oligarchy.'

One wonders if any of his listeners recalled the rather more cautious tone of his essay on the civil war in France, written for the *Neue Rheinische Zeitung* in 1850. 'The original process always takes place in England: it is the demiurge of the bourgeois cosmos,' he had argued then. But while England luxuriated in bourgeois prosperity 'there can be no talk of a real revolution ... A new revolution is possible only in consequence of a new crisis.'

He had been waiting ever since, with some impatience, for the crisis to arrive – reading the runes, seeking out portents. 'Provided nothing untoward happens within the next six weeks, this year's cotton crop will amount to 3,000,000 bales,' Engels informed him in July 1851. 'If the CRASH in the market coincides with such a gigantic crop, things will be cheery indeed. Peter Ermen is already fouling his breeches at the very thought of it, and the little tree frog's a pretty good barometer.' A collapse in the fortunes of the textile industry would also have put an end to Marx's regular subsidies from the petty-cash box at Ermen & Engels, but this was apparently a price worth paying for the general ruination of all the little tree frogs. He licked his lips at 'the very pleasing prospect of a trade crisis'. By September, however, there was no sign of one. Instead, the discovery of gold in the South Australian state of Victoria might actually open up new markets and precipitate an expansion of world trade and credits, like the California gold rush of 1848. 'One must hope the Australian gold business won't interfere with the trade crisis,' Engels fretted. He consoled himself with the thought that even if capitalism was rescued by Antipodean success, at least they would have been right about something: 'In six months' time the circumnavigation of the world by steam will be fully under way and our predictions concerning the supremacy of the Pacific Ocean will be fulfilled even more quickly than we could have anticipated.' Australia – that 'united states of deported murderers, burglars, rapists and pickpockets' – would then startle the world by showing what wonders could be performed by a nation of undisguised rascals. 'They will beat California hollow.' Anyway, the demand for Lancashire cotton was still slumping most agreeably, and soon 'we shall have such overproduction as will warm the cockles of your heart'.

A month later there was another cockle-warming bulletin from Marx's Trojan horse in the capitalist citadel. 'The iron trade is totally paralysed, and two of the main banks which supply it with money – those in Newport – have gone broke . . . There is the prospect, if not actually the certainty, of next spring's convulsions on the Continent coinciding with quite a nice little crisis. Even Australia seems incapable of doing very much; since California, the discovery of gold has become an old story and the world has grown blasé about it . . .' Two days after Christmas 1851, Marx sent a cheerful end-of-year message to the poet Ferdinand Freiligrath: 'From what Engels tells me, the city merchants now also share our view that the crisis, held in check by all kinds of factors (including, e.g., political misgivings, the high price of cotton last year) etc., must blow up at the latest next autumn. And since the latest events I am more than ever convinced that there will be no serious revolution without a trade crisis.' The downfall of Russell's Whig administration in February 1852, and the installation of a Tory cabinet headed by Lord Derby, seemed likely to speed the happy day. 'In England our movement can progress only under the Tories,' Marx explained. 'The Whigs conciliate all over the place and lull everyone to sleep. On top of that there is the commercial crisis which is looming ever closer and whose early symptoms are erupting on every hand. *Les choses marchent.*' Free trade and a falling cotton price might keep the English economy afloat until the autumn, but then the fun would begin.

Engels was not so sure. Although the crisis certainly ought to come by the end of 1852 'according to all the rules', the strength of Indian markets and the cheapness of raw materials suggested otherwise. 'One is almost tempted to forecast that the present period of prosperity will be of exceptionally long duration. At any rate it may well be that the thing will last until the spring.' It did; and perhaps Marx wasn't entirely disappointed. 'The revolution may come sooner than we would like,' he wrote in August, noting a spate of bankruptcies and below-average harvests. 'Nothing could be worse than the revolutionaries having to provide bread.' Here he was hoist by his own explosive logic: if the revolution depended on economic catastrophe, as he insisted, it would of course inherit a breadless world. Nevertheless, for the next couple of years he still felt cheerfully certain that there were bad times just around the corner. 'The state of the winter crops being what it is, I feel convinced that the crisis will become due.' (January 1853.) 'Present conditions . . . in my view must soon lead to an earthquake.' (March 1853). '*Les choses marchent merveilleusement.* All hell will be let loose in France when the financial bubble bursts.' (September 1853.)

In the absence of a terminal economic crisis, Marx began to wonder if some other spark could light the conflagration. The Crimean War, perhaps? 'We must not forget that there is a sixth power in Europe,' he wrote in the *New York Daily Tribune* on 2 February 1854, 'which at given moments asserts its supremacy over the whole of the five so-called "Great" Powers and makes them tremble, every one of them. That power is the Revolution . . . A signal only is wanted, and this sixth and greatest European power will come forward, in shining armour, and sword in hand, like Minerva from the head of the Olympian. This signal the impending European war will give . . .'

No such luck. Apparently forgetting his insistence that revolution was possible only as the consequence of an economic débâcle, he scanned the horizon for some other dark cloud. On 24 June 1855 the Chartists held a rally in Hyde Park to protest against the new Sunday Trading Bill, which would ban the opening of pubs and the printing of newspapers on the sabbath. Ladies and gentlemen riding along Rotten Row had to run the gauntlet of demonstrators; some were forced to dismount and flee. 'We were spectators from beginning to end,' Marx wrote in the *Neue Oder-Zeitung*, 'and do not think we are exaggerating in saying that *the English revolution began yesterday in Hyde Park.*'

A similar gathering one week later drew an even bigger crowd – and another vivid dispatch from Marx to the *Neue Oder-Zeitung*. 'At once the constabulary rushed from ambush, whipped their truncheons out of their pockets, began to beat up people's heads until the blood ran profusely, yanked individuals here and there out of the vast multitude (a total of 104 were thus arrested) and dragged them to the improvised blockhouses.' But the character

of the scene was quite different from the improvised class war of
the previous weekend:

> Last Sunday the masses were confronted by the ruling class as
> individuals. This time it appeared as the state power, the law,
> the truncheon. This time resistance meant insurrection, and
> the Englishman must be provoked for a long time before he
> breaks out in insurrection. Hence the counter-demonstration
> was confined, in the main, to hissing, jeering and whistling at
> the police-wagons, to isolated and feeble attempts at liberating
> the arrested, but above all to passive resistance in phlegmatically
> standing their ground.

Thus did 'the English revolution' fizzle out, only seven days after
Marx's bold fanfare; and all because of the natives' deferential
timidity when confronted by the majesty of institutionalised
power. It is all too like a scene from Gilbert and Sullivan in which
the bloodthirsty pirates of Penzance, having captured a posse of
police officers, are standing over their victims with drawn swords.
'We charge you yield,' a police sergeant commands from a
prostrate position, 'in Queen Victoria's name!' The pirate king
cannot but obey: 'We yield at once, with humbled mien,/Because,
with all our faults, we love our Queen.'

For the rest of his life, Marx's view of the English proletariat
oscillated between reverence and scorn. In January 1862 he cited
British workers' support for the North in the American Civil War
as 'a new, splendid proof of the indestructible thoroughness of
the English popular masses, that thoroughness which is the secret
of England's greatness'. But when anti-government demonstrators
tore down the Hyde Park railings in July 1866, he despaired of
their moderation. 'The Englishman first needs a revolutionary
education, of course,' he wrote to Engels. 'If the railings – and it
was touch and go – had been used offensively and defensively
against the police and about twenty of the latter had been knocked
out, the military would have had to "intervene" instead of only

parading. And then there would have been some fun. One thing
is certain, these thick-headed John Bulls, whose brainpans seem
to have been specially manufactured for the constables' bludgeons,
will never get anywhere without a really bloody encounter with
the ruling powers.' As he conceded, however, there was no great
likelihood of serious combat: the workers were 'slavish', 'sheepish'
and incurably enfeebled by a 'bourgeois infection'.

This disease had many small but telling symptoms. The
historian Keith Thomas has suggested that 'the preoccupation
with gardening, like that with pets, fishing and other hobbies . . .
helps to explain the relative lack of radical and political impulses
among the British proletariat'. Hence the popularity of allotments
in the nineteenth century, and the surprising dearth of large-scale
tenement blocks – which 'would have deprived working men of
the gardens which they regarded as a necessity'. For every worker
who ripped up railings in Hyde Park, there were dozens more
who wanted only to walk their dogs or inspect the flower-beds.

Even Ernest Jones, the Chartist leader whom Marx most
admired, soon revealed himself as a middle-class dilettante by
advocating a coalition between the Chartists and the thoroughly
bourgeois radicals. 'The business with Jones is very disgusting,'
Engels wrote after hearing him address a meeting in Manchester.
'One is really almost driven to believe that the English proletarian
movement in its old traditional Chartist form must perish
completely before it can develop in a new, viable form.' But what
form would this be? As Engels noted, with rueful prescience, 'the
English proletariat is actually becoming more and more bourgeois,
so that this most bourgeois of all nations is apparently aiming
ultimately at the possession of a bourgeois aristocracy and a
bourgeois proletariat *as well as* a bourgeoisie'. So it has come to
pass: in the England of today, toffs and workers alike buy their
food from Tesco superstores and watch the National Lottery draw
on Saturday nights. If the ghosts of Marx and Engels returned
they would also notice the most bizarre oxymoron of all, a
bourgeois monarchy, whose young princes wear baseball caps, eat

Big Macs and take their holidays at Eurodisney. In Hyde Park, where once the Chartists taunted aristocrats and Karl Marx thought the English revolution had begun, the largest mass assembly in living memory occurred on 6 September 1997 – for the funeral of Diana, Princess of Wales.

Marx's final verdict on his adopted country can be found in a letter written shortly before his death in 1883. After mocking the 'poor British bourgeois, who groan as they assume more and more "responsabilities" [*sic*] in the service of their historic mission, while vainly protesting against it', he concluded with a cry of exasperation: 'Drat the British!'

Ernest Jones's apostasy in joining forces with the middle-class liberals incurred the most severe punishment Marx and Engels could mete out: he was labelled an 'opportunist'. A few years later they passed the same sentence on Ferdinand Lassalle for his proposal that Prussian workers and noblemen should gang up against the industrial bourgeoisie. While railing against these cynical marriages of convenience, however, Marx himself was forming opportunistic partnerships with some pretty rum coves.

The rummiest of them all was David Urquhart, an eccentric Scottish aristocrat and sometime Tory MP who is now remembered, if at all, as the man who introduced Turkish baths to England. 'To most of his adherents, to the end of his life, Urquhart was the Bey, the Chief, the Prophet, almost "the sent of God",' one disciple recorded. 'To his little daughter dreaming of her father . . . it did not seem strange that that same father should change, after the strange fashion of dreams, into the Christ. "It is really the same thing, is it not, mother?" she said.' To less worshipful observers, he was a cantankerous old walrus with a lopsided moustache, a lopsided bow-tie and exceedingly lopsided opinions. 'There is no art I have practised so assiduously as the faculty of making men hate me,' Urquhart boasted. 'That removes apathy. You can get them into speech. Then you have their words to catch and hurl back at them to knock them down with.' Many mid-Victorian eminences could testify to the success of this technique: he had enemies galore.

Born in Scotland in 1805, educated in France, Switzerland and Spain, Urquhart discovered his long obsession with the East when at the age of twenty-one he sailed – at the suggestion of Jeremy Bentham, an admirer – to take part in the Greek war of independence, and was severely wounded at the siege of Scio. Having caught the attention of Sir Herbert Taylor, private secretary to William IV, he was then dispatched on secret diplomatic missions to Constantinople, where he abruptly changed his allegiance. 'This chap went to Greece as a Philhellene and, after three years of fighting the Turks, proceeded to Turkey and went into raptures about those selfsame Turks,' Marx wrote in March 1853 after chuckling over Urquhart's book *Turkey and Its Resources*.

> He enthuses over Islam on the principle, 'if I wasn't a Calvinist, I could only be a Mohammedan'. Turks, particularly those of the Ottoman Empire in its heyday, are the most perfect nation on earth in every possible way. The Turkish language is the most perfect and melodious in the world . . . If a European is maltreated in Turkey, he has only himself to blame; your Turk hates neither the religion of the Frank, nor his character, but only his narrow trousers. Imitation of Turkish architecture, etiquette, etc. is strongly recommended. The author himself was several times kicked in the bottom by Turks, but subsequently realised that he alone was to blame . . . In short, only the Turk is a gentleman and freedom exists only in Turkey.

Urquhart's hosts in Constantinople were dazzled by his extravagant Turkophilia. 'The Turkish officials placed such reliance on Urquhart,' according to the *Dictionary of National Biography*, 'that they kept him immediately informed of all communications made to them by the Russian ambassador. Lord Palmerston, however, took alarm . . . and wrote to the ambassador, Lord Ponsonby, to remove him from Constantinople as a danger to the peace of Europe.' As well he might. Urquhart's passionate partisanship – pro-Turkey, anti-Russia – left him at odds with British policy, and persuaded him that his own country's government had been hijacked by sinister forces. In short, he concluded that the Foreign Secretary, Lord Palmerston, must be a secret Russian agent. On his return to Britain he founded several newspapers and a national network of 'foreign affairs committees' to disseminate this bold conspiracy theory. After entering Parliament in 1847, he fired off a fusillade of speeches calling for an immediate inquiry into the conduct of the Foreign Office, 'with a view to the impeachment of the Right Honourable Henry John Temple, Viscount Palmerston'.

Essentially a romantic reactionary, Uruquhart nevertheless managed to convince some radicals that he was really on their side – speaking for the downtrodden workers against their devious and deceitful rulers. Though the more revolutionary Chartists dismissed him as a Tory spy whose populist crusade against Lord Palmerston was a 'red herring', others praised his exposure of 'the injury done to the labour and capital of this country by the expansion of the Russian Empire, and the almost universal exercise of Russian influence, all directed to the destruction of British commerce.'

This all chimed in most harmoniously with Karl Marx's own hatred and mistrust of Tsarist Russia. 'Excited but not convinced' by Urquhart's allegations, he set to work with characteristic diligence, poring over old copies of *Hansard* and the diplomatic *Blue Books* in search of evidence. His progress can be followed through the changing tone of his letters to Engels. In the spring of 1853 he mocked Urquhart as 'the mad MP who denounces Palmerston as being in the pay of Russia'. By that summer, he was already showing rather more respect: 'In the *Advertiser* four letters by D. Urquhart on the eastern question contained much that was interesting, despite quirks and quiddities.' Before autumn was out, the conversion to Urquhartism – if not to Urquhart himself – was complete. 'I have come to the same conclusion as that monomaniac Urquhart – namely that for several decades Palmerston has been in the pay of Russia,' he wrote on 2 November. 'I am glad that chance should have led me to take a closer look at the foreign policy – diplomatic – of the past twenty years. We had very much neglected this aspect, and one ought to know with whom one is dealing.'

The first fruit of these researches was a series of articles for the *New York Tribune* at the end of 1853, describing Palmerston's clandestine 'connections' with the Russian government. Urquhart, understandably delighted, arranged a meeting with the author early in 1854 at which he paid him the highest compliment in his lexicon by saying that 'the articles read as though written by a Turk'. Marx, rather crossly, pointed out that he was in fact a German revolutionist.

'He is an utter maniac,' Marx reported soon after this strange encounter:

> is firmly convinced that he will one day be Premier of England. When everyone else is downtrodden, England will come to him and say, Save us, Urquhart! And then he will save her. While speaking, particularly if contradicted, he goes into *fits* . . . The fellow's most comical idea is this: Russia rules the world through having a specific superfluity of *brain*. To cope with her, a man must have the *brain* of an Urquhart and, if one has the misfortune not to be Urquhart himself, one should at least be an Urquhartite, i.e. believe what Urquhart believes, his 'metaphysics', his 'political economy' etc etc. One should have been in the 'East', or at least have absorbed the Turkish 'spirit', etc.

When some of Marx's Palmerston articles from the *Tribune* were reprinted as a pamphlet, he was horrified to discover that polemics by Urquhart were appearing in the same series – and promptly forbade any further publication. 'I do not wish to be numbered among the followers of that gentleman,' he explained to Ferdinand Lassalle, 'with whom I have only one thing in common, viz. my views on Palmerston, but to whom in all other matters I am diametrically opposed.'

One might infer from this that any further offers or inducements from the maniac would be rejected with a brisk 'Get thee behind me, Satan!' But Marx could not afford to maintain his principled posture for long. Harried by impatient creditors, he found it hard to resist a commission to write a series for one of Urquhart's journals, the Sheffield *Free Press*, in the summer of 1856. 'The Urquhartites are being damned importunate,' he grumbled. 'A good thing financially. But I don't know whether, *politically*, I ought to get too involved with the fellows.' The articles were suitably sensational: he claimed to have discovered, among the diplomatic manuscripts at the British Museum, 'a series of documents going back from the end of the eighteenth century to the time of Peter the Great, which revealed the secret and permanent collaboration of the Cabinets at London and St Petersburg'. More alarmingly still, the aim of Russia throughout this period had been nothing less than the conquest of the earth. 'It is yet the policy of Peter the Great, and of modern Russia, whatever changes of name, seat and character the hostile power used may have undergone. Peter the Great is indeed the inventor of modern Russian policy, but he became so only by divesting the old Muscovite method of its merely local character and its accidental admixtures, by distilling it into an abstract formula, by generalising its purpose, and exalting its object from the overthrow of certain given limits of power to the aspiration of unlimited power.'

There was a rather obvious flaw in the theory that Britain and Russia had been in cahoots for the previous 150 years: the Crimean War. Urquhart and Marx had a ready explanation. The war had been a cunning ploy to throw sleuths off the scent of Palmerston's corrupt alliance with Russia; and Britain had deliberately pro-secuted the war as incompetently as possible. To the dedicated conspiracy theorist, all is explicable, and any inconvenient facts are merely further confirmation of the diabolical deviousness of his prey.

Marx may have convinced himself, but few others were persuaded. His philippics against Palmerston and Russia were reissued in 1899 by his daughter Eleanor as two pamphlets, *The Secret Diplomatic History of the Eighteenth Century* and *The Story of the Life of Lord Palmerston* – though with some of the more provocative passages quietly excised. For most of the twentieth century they remained out of print and largely forgotten. The Institute of Marxism–Leninism in Moscow omitted them from its otherwise exhaustive collected works, presumably because the Soviet editors could not bring themselves to admit that the presiding spirit of the Russian revolution had in fact been a fervent Russophobe. Marxist hagiographers in the West have also been reluctant to draw attention to this embarrassing partnership between the revolutionist and the reactionary. An all-too-typical example is *The Life and Teaching of Karl Marx* by John Lewis, published in 1965; the curious reader may search the text for any mention of David Urquhart, or of Marx's contribution to his obsessive crusade – but will find nothing.

Urquhart himself later turned his attention to other, equally quixotic causes. A devout if unorthodox Roman Catholic, he spent many years appealing to Pope Pius IX for the restoration of Canon Law while also proselytising tirelessly on behalf of the Turkish bath. ('Did you overlook, in one of the *Guardian*s you sent me, the item in which David Urquhart figures as an infanticide?' Marx wrote to Engels in 1858. 'The fool treated his thirteen-month-old baby to a Turkish bath which, as chance would have it, contributed to congestion of the brain and hence its subsequent death. The coroner's inquest on this case lasted for three days and it was only by the skin of his teeth that Urquhart escaped a verdict of manslaughter.') Urquhart's house in Rickmansworth, Hertfordshire, was described by one visitor as 'an Eastern palace, with a Turkish bath . . . which in luxuriousness was inferior to none in Constantinople'. A session in this ornate sweat-chamber might have done Marx's carbuncles a power of good, but as far as one can discover he never had the pleasure.

8

The Hero on Horseback

Shortly before dawn on 16 January 1855 Jenny Marx gave birth to another daughter, Eleanor. The father was none too ecstatic. 'Unfortunately of the "sex" *par excellence*,' he told Engels. 'If it had been a male child, well and good.' His announcement of Franziska's arrival, four years earlier, had been equally joyless. It would be easy to infer that Marx felt only lukewarm affection for his daughters; easy, but wrong. Their own letters and auto-biographical scraps all testify that 'Moor' was an adoring father who inspired utter devotion in return. Unlike many men of his generation, he treated girls as intelligent adults-to-be. To Eleanor, as to her sisters before her, he read the whole of Homer, Shakespeare, the *Niebelungen Lied*, *Gudrun*, *Don Quixote*, the *Arabian Nights* and much else. For her sixth birthday she was given her first novel, *Peter Simple*, which was soon followed by the complete works of Marryat, Cooper and Walter Scott. Subjects that would have been taboo *devant les enfants* in other middle-class Victorian households – atheism, socialism – were not merely permitted but encouraged. After a family outing to hear the sung mass in a Roman Catholic church, when Eleanor was about five, she confessed to feeling 'certain religious qualms'. Her father then 'made everything straight', patiently elucidating the story of the carpenter whom the rich men killed. 'We can forgive Christianity much,' he told her, 'because it taught us the worship of the child.'

Marx's hand-wringing at the 'unfortunate' gender of his new baby should not, therefore, be taken as evidence of misogyny or paternal coldness. He was simply facing the social and economic facts: since middle-class girls couldn't be expected to earn a living or fend for themselves, Eleanor would be one more financial burden on an already overdrawn exchequer.

Even so, there can be no doubt that Edgar – the impish, round-faced Colonel Musch – was the favourite. A sickly lad, whose huge head seemed far too heavy for his feeble body, he was nevertheless an inexhaustible source of drollery and high spirits. When his parents lapsed into despondency, he could always cheer them up by singing nonsensical ditties – or the Marseillaise, for that matter – with tremendous feeling and at the top of his voice. After giving the boy a fine travelling bag as a fifth-birthday present, Marx's secretary Wilhelm Pieper regretted the impulsive gift and threatened to take it back. 'Moor, I've hiddened it well,' Musch confided to his papa, 'and if Pieper asks for it, I'll tell him I've given it to a poor man.'

Marx adored this cunning little slyboots, 'a friend who was more dear to me personally than any other'. The order of precedence is confirmed by a letter to Engels on 3 March 1855, in which he listed the various ailments that were turning their apartment into a cottage hospital: Edgar had been laid low by some kind of gastric fever; Karl himself was confined to bed with a frightful cough; Jenny had a painful and irritating whitlow on one of her fingers; baby Eleanor was perilously frail and growing weaker every day. 'This,' he said of Edgar's illness, 'is the worst of all.' A surprising judgement, since Eleanor's very life appeared to be threatened whereas Edgar was making 'rapid strides towards convalescence' within a few days.

But the remission was horribly brief. When Edgar took a serious turn for the worse at the end of March, the doctor diagnosed consumption and warned that there was no hope of recovery. 'Though my heart is bleeding and my head afire, I must, of course, retain my composure,' Marx wrote. 'Never for one moment throughout his illness has the child been untrue to his own good-natured, and at the same time independent, self.' Edgar died in his father's arms shortly before six o'clock on the morning of 6 April. It was Good Friday, the grimmest day in the Christian calendar, and so the boy's passing was marked by solemn peals of church bells. Wilhelm Liebknecht arrived at Dean Street soon afterwards to find Jenny sobbing quietly over the corpse while Laura and Jennychen clung feverishly to her skirt as if to defend themselves against the malign force that had robbed them of their brothers and sister. Marx, almost out of his wits, was angrily and violently resisting any condolence.

The funeral took place two days later at the Whitefield Tabernacle in Tottenham Court Road, already the final resting place of Fawkesy and Franziska. During the short coach journey to the graveyard Liebknecht stroked Marx's forehead and tried, rather fatuously, to remind him of how many people still loved him – his wife, his daughters, his friends. 'You can't give my boy back to me!' Marx howled, burying his head in his hands. As the coffin was being lowered into the earth he stepped forward, and for a moment the other mourners thought he might hurl himself in after it. Liebknecht stuck out a restraining arm, just in case.

Marx could hardly bring himself to return to Dean Street, which seemed unbearably desolate without its court jester. 'I've already had my share of bad luck,' he told Engels, 'but only now do I know what real unhappiness is. I feel broken down.' For several days afterwards, he was 'fortunate enough' to have such splitting headaches that he could neither think nor hear nor see. One of the few things that sustained him was the friendship of Engels, who invited Karl and Jenny to spend a few days in Manchester for a change of scene from the accursed apartment in Soho. (Years later, long after he had moved out of the district, Marx said that 'the region round Soho Square still sends a shiver down my spine if I happen to be anywhere near there'.) But as soon as they were back in London the old marks of Edgar's presence – his books, his toys – plunged them into deeper grief. 'Bacon says that really important people have so many relations to nature and the world, so many objects of interest, that they easily get over any loss,' he wrote to Ferdinand Lassalle three months later. 'I am not one of those important people. The death of my child has shattered me to the very core and I feel the loss as keenly as on the first day. My poor wife is also completely broken down.'

From July until September the family decamped to the south London suburb of Camberwell, where the German émigré Peter Imandt had offered the use of his apartment while he was away in Scotland. Though they were glad enough to keep away from Dean Street, the main reason for the change of address was to hide from the many creditors who were closing in again – especially that avenging fury Dr Freund, now threatening legal action over the unpaid medical bills. In mid-September, when Freund discovered his whereabouts, Marx had to execute another quick getaway – inspired, or so he claimed, by the hasty tactical retreat of the Russian troops from the south end of Sebastopol the previous week, following their defeat by the French at the Battle of the Chernaya. 'I have been compelled by *force supérieure* to evacuate the southern side without, however, blowing everything up behind me,' he informed Engels in a battlefront dispatch from Camberwell. 'Indeed, my garrison will remain quietly here, whither I also propose to return in a week or so. In other words, I am obliged to withdraw to Manchester for a few days and shall arrive there tomorrow evening. I shall have to stay there incognito, so don't let anyone know about my presence.'

Two days after reading this letter Engels sent the *New York Daily Tribune* a long article on 'Crimean Prospects' – under Marx's name, as usual – in which he justified the Russians' apparently unnecessary flight from southern Sebastopol. 'Resistance in a besieged place is of itself demoralising in the long run,' he argued. 'It implies hardships, want of rest, sickness, and the presence, not of that acute danger which braces, but of that chronic danger which must ultimately relax the mind ... It is not astonishing that this demoralisation should at last seize the garrison; it is astonishing that it had not done so long before.' It's hard to believe that Engels composed this tactical assessment without at least half an eye on his own weary and beleaguered ally.

During the spring of 1855, between Eleanor's birth and Musch's death, there was one item of family news that gave Marx unalloyed pleasure. 'Yesterday we were informed of a VERY HAPPY EVENT,' he wrote on 8 March. 'The death of my wife's uncle, aged ninety.' He had no particular grudge against Heinrich Georg von Westphalen, a harmless lawyer and historian, except that the old boy's longevity had delayed the redistribution of his considerable wealth. For the previous few years this indestructible uncle had been referred to in the Marx household as 'the inheritance-thwarter'. Jenny's legacy of about £100 arrived at the end of the year, and in the summer of 1856 she received another £120 following the death of her mother. On this occasion even Marx was tactful enough not to rejoice openly, especially as Jenny had been at the Baroness's bedside in Trier during the final days. 'She seems greatly affected by the old lady's death,' he observed, in tones of slight surprise.

These two windfalls at last gave him the wherewithal to escape from the 'old hole' in Soho. After tramping the streets for two weeks in search of more salubrious lodgings he settled on an unfurnished four-storey house at 9 Grafton Terrace, Kentish Town, not far from Hampstead Heath. The annual rent of £36 was cheap for north London – probably because, as Marx explained to Engels, this end of Hampstead remained 'somewhat unfinished'. More than somewhat: the street was neither paved nor lit, and the immediate neighbourhood was a huge and muddy building site. The land had been green fields until the 1840s, but the coming of the railway transformed London's rural outskirts into a suburban girdle of speculative developments for middle-class commuters. As with today's 'executive estates' in even further-flung suburbs, the architectural style was a riotous hybrid of whimsical flourishes – quoins and coping-stones, arched windows and rococo balconies.

The house at Grafton Terrace was officially classified as 'third-class' by the Metropolitan Building Office. Still, Marx thought it 'very nice'. Jenny revelled in the forgotten delights of domestic comfort and hired Helene Demuth's stepsister, Marianne Creuz, to help with the extra chores. 'It is indeed a princely dwelling compared with the holes we lived in before,' she told a friend, 'and although it was furnished from top to bottom for little more than £40 (in which second-hand rubbish played a leading role), I felt quite grand at first in our snug parlour.' After redeeming her Argyll linen and silver from 'Uncle's' – the pawnshop – she took great pleasure in laying out damask napkins at the dinner table. There were more intimate celebrations, too: only a few weeks after her arrival at Grafton Terrace, Jenny found herself pregnant for the seventh time.

The three children loved their new middle-class life. Jennychen and Laura, now aged twelve and eleven, transferred to the South Hampstead College for Ladies and were soon winning prizes in every subject. The two-year-old Eleanor – nicknamed Tussy, to rhyme with pussy – established herself as a mini-*châtelaine*, keeping open house for any children who wished to drop by. In fine weather she would eat her tea sitting on the front doorstep, gadding off between mouthfuls to join in the street games. Such was her fame that most neighbours referred to the whole Marx family simply as 'the Tussies'.

Even the back garden, though little more than a few square yards of grass and gravel, was a delicious novelty. One of Eleanor's earliest childhood memories was of Marx carrying her on his shoulder round the garden in Grafton Terrace, and putting convolvulus flowers in her brown curls.

Moor was admittedly a splendid horse. In earlier days – I cannot remember them, but have heard tell of them – my sisters and little brother – whose death just after my own birth was a lifelong grief to my parents – would 'harness' Moor to chairs which they 'mounted', and that he had to pull . . .

Personally – perhaps because I had no sisters of my own age – I preferred Moor as a riding-horse. Seated on his shoulder, holding tight to his great mane of hair, then black with but a hint of grey, I have had magnificent rides round our little garden, and over the fields – now built over – that surrounded our house.

On Sundays the Marxes and any visiting friends would stroll over to nearby Hampstead Heath for a picnic, often their only substantial meal of the week. In spite of her tiny budget Lenchen usually managed to conjure up a large joint of veal, supplemented by bread, cheese, shrimps and periwinkles bought from vendors on the heath and flagons of beer from the local pub, Jack Straw's Castle. After lunch the children played hide-and-seek among the gorse bushes while the adults snoozed or read the Sunday papers – but as so often happens on family outings, the reluctant papa would soon be dragged from his postprandial torpor by squealing youngsters. 'Let's see who can bring the most down!' the daughters yelled one day, pointing at a chestnut tree laden with ripe nuts, and for the next hour or two Marx maintained a ceaseless bombardment until the tree was entirely bare. He was unable to move his right arm for a week afterwards.

Sometimes they ventured further afield to the green meadows and hills beyond Highgate, seeking out wild forget-me-nots and hyacinths while blithely ignoring the 'No Trespassing' signs. Wilhelm Liebknecht, who went on several of these expeditions, was amazed to see how many spring flowers grew in the dank English climate. 'We looked down from our fragrant Asphodel meadows proudly upon the world,' he wrote, 'the mighty boundless city of the world which lay before us in its vastness, shrouded in the ugly mystery of the fog.' On the walk home, Marx led his daughters in renditions of German folk-songs and Negro spirituals, or recited long passages from Shakespeare and Dante. 'We really thought that we were living in a magic castle,' Jenny Marx sighed. But the magic depended on financial legerdemain. It was

at this time, fittingly enough, that Marx began amusing little
Eleanor with his tales of Hans Röckle, the hard-up magician
'who could never meet his obligations either to the devil or the
butcher, and was therefore – much against the grain – constantly
obliged to sell his toys to the devil'. Jenny's inheritance had all
gone on paying off debts and setting up house. One by one, the
new pieces of furniture and the precious old linen found their
way back to the pop-shop.

'The clouds gathering over the money market are sombre
indeed,' Engels wrote in the very week of the move to Grafton
Terrace. 'This time there'll be a day of wrath such as has never
been seen before: the whole of Europe's industry in ruins, all
markets over-stocked (already nothing more is being shipped to
India), all the propertied classes in the soup, complete bankruptcy
of the bourgeoisie, war and profligacy to the nth degree. I, too,
believe that it will all come to pass in 1857, and when I heard you
were again buying furniture I promptly declared the thing to be a
dead certainty and offered to take bets on it. Adieu for today;
cordial regards to your wife and children . . .' A rather tactless
joke in the circumstances. No sooner was Marx installed in the
magic castle than he realised, to his horror, that there was no
money for the rent. 'So here I am,' he wrote to Engels in January
1857, 'without any prospects and with growing domestic liabilities,
completely stranded in a house into which I have put what little
cash I possessed and where it is impossible to scrape along from
day to day as we did in Dean Street. I am utterly at a loss what to
do, being, indeed, in a more desperate situation than five years
ago. I thought I had tasted the bitterest dregs of life. *Mais non!*
And the worst of it is that this is no mere passing crisis. I cannot
see how I am to extricate myself.'

Engels was flabbergasted: 'I had believed that everything was
going splendidly at last – you in a decent house and the whole
business settled, and now it turns out that everything's in
doubt . . .' He promised to send £5 every month, plus extra one-
off payments whenever needed. 'Even if it means my facing the

new financial year with a load of debts, no matter. I only wish you had told me about the business a fortnight earlier.' For, as he confessed guiltily, he had just bought a splendid new hunter with some Christmas money from his father. 'I'm exceedingly vexed that I should be keeping a horse here while you and your family are down on your luck in London.'

It was Jenny Marx who felt the misfortune most painfully. Her husband could withdraw into his study, where books and newspapers formed an impregnable barricade; the girls had the consoling distraction of new friends and a busy school timetable. But Jenny was marooned. She missed her long walks through the bustling streets of the West End, the meetings, the clubs and pubs, the conversations with fellow Germans who shared the misery of exile:

Our attractive little house, though it was like a palace for us in comparison with the places we had lived in before, was not easy to get to. There was no smooth road leading to it, building was going on all around, one had to pick one's way over heaps of rubbish and in rainy weather the sticky red soil caked to one's boots so that it was a tiring struggle and with heavy feet that one reached our house. And then it was dark in those wild districts, so that rather than have to tackle the dark, the rubbish, the clay and the heaps of stones one preferred to spend the evenings by a warm fire. I was very unwell that winter and was always surrounded with stacks of medicine bottles . . .

On 7 July her new baby was stillborn, but she could hardly muster the energy to mourn. 'One day,' she found, 'was just like any other . . .' Her only involvement in the world beyond 9 Grafton Terrace came from copying out Karl's twice-weekly article for the *Daily Tribune*. Then even this lifeline was cut. Noticing that the newspaper was using fewer and fewer of his contributions – and, of course, he was paid only for what was printed – Marx went on strike. 'It's truly nauseating that one should be condemned to count it a blessing when taken aboard by a blotting-paper vendor such as this,' he raged. He saw himself as a pauper in the workhouse, crushing up bones and boiling them into soup.

His threat to transfer allegiance to some other paper worked – but only up to a point. The *Tribune*'s editor, Charles Dana, said that in future he would pay for one column a week, whether or not it was published. 'They are in effect cutting me down by one half,' Marx complained. 'However, I shall agree to it and must agree to it.' As a sop, Dana added that he was compiling a *New American Cyclopaedia* and wondered if Marx would like to write the entries on great generals and the history of warfare. Though it was Grub Street hack work of the dullest kind, Marx was in no position to refuse a fee of $2 per page.

The self-styled General Engels was happy to take on most of the labour – it would, he said, give him something to do in the evenings – and started on the first batch at once: Abensberg, Actium, Adjutant, Alma, Ammunition, Army, Artillery ... But then an attack of glandular fever laid him low. For the rest of the summer he was effectively *hors de combat* while recuperating in the felicitously named Lancashire resort of Waterloo. This left Marx with the ticklish problem of explaining to Dana why the supply had suddenly dried up. 'What am I to tell him?' he wailed. 'I can't plead sickness, since I am continuing to send articles to the *Tribune*. It's a very awkward case.' He stalled for time by pretending that a parcel of manuscripts had been lost in the post.

The revolt by Sepoy soldiers against British rule in India added to his troubles, since the *Tribune* naturally expected a lengthy analysis from its expert. Fortunately Marx had learned enough artful dodging from the late lamented Musch to bluff his way out. 'As to the Delhi affair,' he confided to Engels, 'it seems to me that the English ought to begin their retreat as soon as the rainy season has set in in real earnest. Being obliged for the present to hold the fort for you as the *Tribune*'s military correspondent, I have taken it upon myself to put this forward ... It's possible that I shall make an ass of myself. But in that case one can always get out of it with a little dialectic. I have, of course, so worded my proposition as to be right either way.' By September, Engels felt well enough to have another crack at the *Cyclopaedia*, and from his new place of convalescence on the Isle of Wight there emerged a torrent of articles – on Battle, Battery, Blücher and many more. While visiting Jersey in October he moved on to the next letter of the alphabet, starting with Cannon. Could Campaign and Cavalry be far behind?

This burst of productivity was, however, interrupted by the most glorious news imaginable: the international financial cataclysm had at last arrived. Beginning with a bank collapse in New York, the crisis spread through Austria, Germany, France and England like a galloping apocalypse. Engels scuttled back to Manchester in mid-November to witness the fun – plummeting prices, daily bankruptcies and panic galore. 'The general appearance of the [Cotton] Exchange here was truly delightful,' he told Marx. 'The fellows are utterly infuriated by my sudden and inexplicable onset of high spirits.' One factory owner had already sold all his hunters and foxhounds, dismissed his servants and put his mansion up for let. 'Another fortnight, and the dance will really be in full swing here.'

Would revolution ensue immediately? He doubted it: the workers were bound to be pretty lethargic after such a long period of prosperity. But this was just as well, since the would-be leaders of the masses must first prepare themselves for the fray. As Engels saw it, he would command the insurrectionary army – crushing any bourgeois resistance with breakneck cavalry charges through the streets of Manchester and Berlin – while Marx directed the civilian side of the campaign, enlightening the proletariat in the mysteries of political economy. 'It's a case of do or die,' Engels announced, strapping on his spurs. 'This will at once give a more practical side to my military studies. I shall apply myself without delay to the existing organisation and elementary tactics of the Prussian, Austrian, Bavarian and French armies, and apart from that confine my actitvities to riding, i.e. fox-hunting, which is the best school of all.' The members of the Cheshire Hunt little guessed, as they sipped their stirrup-cups, that the charming Mr Engels on his powerful new steed was secretly preparing to become the Napoleon of north-west England. But he was in deadly earnest: 'After all, we want to show the Prussian cavalry a thing or two when we get back to Germany. The gentlemen will find it difficult to keep up with me for I've already had a great deal of practice and am improving every day . . . Only now am I getting to grips with the real problems of riding over difficult country; it's a highly complicated business.' Equitation, he believed, was the 'material basis' of all military success. Why did the French petty bourgeois regard the wretched Louis Bonaparte as a hero? 'Because he sits elegantly on a horse.' This must have been rather galling for Marx, whose ungainliness in the saddle – demonstrated during Sunday donkey rides on Hampstead Heath – was a family joke.

By the end of December, Engels's training scheme had transformed the sickly cotton merchant into a dashing cavalier. 'On Saturday I went out fox-hunting – seven hours in the saddle,' he noted breathlessly on New Year's Eve. 'That sort of thing always keeps me in a state of devilish exhilaration for several days; it's the greatest physical pleasure I know. I saw only two out of the whole field who were better horsemen than myself, but then they were also better mounted. This will really put my health to rights. At least twenty of the chaps fell off or came down, two horses were done for, one fox killed (I was in AT THE DEATH) . . . And now, a happy New Year to all your family and to the year of strife 1858.'

Marx, not wholly convinced that all this gallivanting served a greater purpose, wondered how he would earn any more dollars from the *Cyclopaedia* while his co-author was leaping hedges and ditches. He was deep in debt, and the hungry wolves were again threatening to blow his house down. 'I try to avoid mentioning the matter to you because the last thing I want is to subject you to any strain that might damage your health,' he suggested gently.

'Yet sometimes it seems to me that, if you could manage to do a little every two days or so, it might act as a check on your junketings.' Engels refused: how could he be expected to read or write while his head was throbbing and buzzing with visions of 'a general crash'? Marx took the point. For all his protestations about the need to earn a living, he too was infected by the melodramatic spirit of the moment. If fate had appointed him chief theoretician of the revolution, so be it. Fortified by 'mere lemonade on the one hand but an immense amount of tobacco on the other', he sat in his study until about 4 a.m. every night through the long winter of 1857–8, collating his economic studies 'so that I at least get the outlines clear before the *déluge*'.

The deluge never came: those dark storm clouds portended nothing worse than a scattered shower. But Marx continued to build his ark, certain that a drenching flood would come sooner or later. When schoolboy arithmetic proved inadequate for complex economic formulae he took a hasty revision course in algebra. As he explained, 'for the benefit of the public it is absolutely essential to go into the matter thoroughly'. Very thoroughly indeed: these nocturnal scribblings filled more than 800 manuscript pages. They remained unseen until the Marx–Engels Institute of Moscow released them from the archives in 1939, and became widely available only with the publication of a German edition in 1953, titled *Grundrisse der Kritik der Politischen Oekonomie* ('Outlines of a Critique of Political Economy'). The first English translation appeared as recently as 1971.

The *Grundrisse* – as it is now generally called – is a fragmentary and sometimes incoherent tome, described by Marx himself as a real hotchpotch. But as the missing link connecting the *Economical and Philosophical Manuscripts* (1844) with the first volume of *Capital* (1867), it does at least dispel the common misconception that there is some sort of 'radical break' between the thought of Young Marx and Old Marx. Wine may mature and improve in the bottle, but it remains wine for all that. There are long sections on alienation, dialectics and the meaning of money which take up where he left off with the Paris manuscripts, the most striking difference being that now he merges philosophy and economics whereas before they were treated seriatim. (In Lassalle's words, he was 'a Hegel turned economist, a Ricardo turned socialist'.) Elsewhere, the analysis of labour power and surplus value anticipates his fuller exposition of these theories in *Capital*.

On the first page he proposes that material production – 'individuals producing in society' – should be the foundation of any serious enquiry into economic history. 'The individual and isolated hunter or fisher who forms the starting point with Smith or Ricardo belongs to the insipid illusions of the eighteenth century.' Humans are social animals, and the belief that 'production' began with lone pioneers acting independently 'is as great an absurdity as the idea of the development of language without individuals living together and talking to one another'. The subheadings in this introduction – 'The General Relation of Production to Distribution, Exchange and Consumption', 'The Method of Political Economy', etc. – give the impression that it is to be a rigidly schematic work. But Marx can never stick to a schedule for long, and in no time he is wandering off on picturesque detours and digressions. In his notes on the relation between production and the general development of society at any given time, he suddenly pauses to wonder about the enduring appeal of cultural artefacts. Why do we still value the Parthenon or the *Odyssey*, even though the mythology from which they arose is now wholly alien?

Is the view of nature and social relations which shaped Greek imagination and Greek art possible in the age of automatic machinery and railways and locomotives and electric telegraphs? Where does Vulcan come in, as against Roberts & Co.? Jupiter, as against the lightning conductor . . . Is the *Iliad* at all compatible with the printing press and even printing machines? Do not singing and reciting and the muses necessarily go out of existence with the appearance of the printer's bar, and do not, therefore, the prerequisites of epic poetry disappear?

Manifestly not: Marx was writing only a few years after the appointment as poet laureate of Alfred Tennyson, whose 'Ulysses' had become one of the most popular verses of the age. Why, then, did the aesthetics of ancient Greece remain not only a source of pleasure but also the standard or model to which many Victorian artists and writers aspired?

An excellent question – but Marx's brief answer scarcely did justice to it. Though no man can become a child, he wrote, 'does he not enjoy the artless ways of the child, and must he not strive to reproduce its truth on a higher plane?' Similarly, 'why should the childhood of human society, where it had attained its most beautiful development, not exert an eternal charm as an age that will never return?' Perhaps he was thinking of his own games of leap-frog and giddy-up with the girls on Hampstead Heath: inside that thirty-nine-year-old body, prematurely decaying and crumbling, there was a teenager wildly signalling to be let out. Sometimes, as he watched the children disporting themselves, he yearned to be able to turn somersaults or cartwheels, to clear his mind of the accumulated muck and misery.

The biggest headache of all was what he called 'the economic shit'. As long ago as 1845 he had claimed that his treatise on political economy was almost finished, and over the next thirteen years he repeated and embellished the lie so often that his friends' expectations were raised to an impossible pitch. To judge by the time taken, they reasoned, it must indeed be an explosive *magnum opus* that would dissolve the baseless edifices of capitalism – the cloud-capp'd towers, the gorgeous palaces, the solemn temples, the great globe itself – leaving not a rack behind. The regular bulletins from London to Manchester kept up the pretence of splendid progress. 'I have completely demolished the theory of profit as hitherto propounded,' he wrote triumphantly to Engels in January 1858. In truth, all he had to show for those long days in the British Museum and even longer nights at his desk was a tottering pile of unpublishable notebooks, filled with random scribble.

The arrival later that month of Ferdinand Lassalle's new book on the philosophy of Heraclitus – a huge two-volume doorstopper – made him even more conscious of his own inability to deliver the goods. How could Lassalle, the self-appointed leader of German socialism, have found the time to finish such a substantial theoretical tome? Marx dealt with his own guilty conscience by belittling Lassalle's achievement, assuring Engels that the Heraclitus book was 'a very silly concoction'. True, it had a tremendous show of learning – but 'provided one has the time and money and, like Mr Lassalle, can have Bonn University Library delivered *ad libitum* to one's home, it is easy enough to assemble such an array of quotations. One can see what an amazing swell the fellow himself thinks he is ... Every other word a howler, but set forth with remarkable pretentiousness.'

Lassalle was seven years Marx's junior, and although they had much in common – both bourgeois German Jews weaned on Heine and Hegel, with a weakness for aristocratic women – the contrast in their fortunes was painfully acute. While he was still a philosophy student Lassalle had taken up the cudgels on behalf of the Countess von Hatzfeldt, who was fighting a celebrated divorce action. She seemed an unlikely heroine of the socialist cause, but for this ambitious young barrack-room lawyer her plight demonstrated the larcenous villainy of the upper classes: the Count had effectively stolen his wife's dowry, and under German law at the time she had little chance of retrieving it. Lassalle hurled himself into the case with a fine disregard for legal niceties – suborning witnesses, stealing documents – until, after ten years and dozens of lawsuits, the exhausted husband handed over the loot. Lassalle's share of the spoils set him up for life: he installed himself in a palatial Berlin residence, furnished in the most exotic and expensive style; his box at the opera was next to that of the King, and no less grand. Even Bismarck came to pay homage, recognising a fellow Man of Destiny when he saw one.

Unsurprisingly, some of the workers whom Lassalle claimed to represent were deeply mistrustful of his intentions – and troubled by Marx's apparent support for him. In the spring of 1856 the Düsseldorf communists sent an emissary to London, one Gustav Lewy, in the hope of persuading Marx to break off relations: for a whole week Lewy regaled his host with stories of Lassalle's skulduggery, opportunism and dictatorial ambitions. 'He [Lassalle] seems to see himself quite differently from the way we see him,' Marx wrote to Engels immediately afterwards. 'The whole thing made a distinct impression on myself and Freiligrath, however prejudiced in Lassalle's favour and mistrustful of workers' tittle-tattle I may have been. I told Lewy that it was, of course, impossible to reach any conclusion on the strength of a report from one side only.'

It was most unusual for Marx to give anyone the benefit of the doubt; but Lassalle was not just anyone. His fearlessness and enthusiasm had greatly impressed Marx at their first encounter, in Germany during the '48 revolution, and though their friendship since then had been purely epistolary he had heard nothing to make him revise his opinion. Perhaps it was true, as Lewy warned, that Lassalle was a tyrant-in-waiting, a dangerous megalomaniac who would happily trample on the workers and form alliances with Prussian absolutism in his feverish quest for power; if so, however, he had never mentioned it in his letters. Even at the height of his fame, Lassalle remained loyal to his indigent chum in London – praising his ideas, encouraging him to get on with his book, sending occasional donations. Should one disown such a generous benefactor merely because of workers' tittle-tattle? Marx's only advice to Lewy and the communists of Düsseldorf was that 'they should continue to keep an eye on the man but for the time being avoid any public row'.

By the spring of 1858 he had another reason for avoiding 'any public row', since Lassalle was now offering to arrange a contract for him with a Berlin publisher, Franz Duncker (whose wife happened to be Lassalle's mistress). While sneering at the Heraclitus book in his private correspondence with Engels, Marx delivered a strikingly different verdict to the author: 'I carefully perused your Heraclitus. Your reconstruction of the system from the scattered fragments I regard as brilliant, nor was I any less impressed by the perspicacity of your polemic . . . It is incomprehensible to me, by the by, how you found the time in the midst of all your other work to acquire so much Greek philology.' Having paid these disingenuous respects, he went on to describe the structure of his own masterpiece.

> The work I am presently concerned with is a Critique of Economic Categories or, if you like, a critical exposé of the system of bourgeois economy . . . The whole is divided into six books: 1. On Capital (contains a few introductory chapters). 2. On Landed Property. 3. On Wage Labour. 4. On the State. 5. International Trade. 6. World Market.

Marx wanted it issued in instalments. The first volume – on capital, competition and credit – would be ready for the printers in May, followed by the second within a few months, and so on.

This was a tight series of deadlines; and, as often happened when he found himself under pressure to deliver the goods, his body rebelled. 'I've been so ill with my bilious complaint this week that I am incapable of thinking, reading, writing or, indeed, of anything,' he wrote to Engels on 2 April. 'My indisposition is disastrous, for I can't begin working on the thing for Duncker until I'm better and my fingers regain their vigour and grasp.' For the rest of the month he was unable to work at all. 'Never before have I had such a violent attaque of liver trouble and for some time there was a fear that it might be sclerosis of the liver . . . Whenever I sit down and write for a couple of hours I have to lie quite fallow for a couple of days.'

It was a familiar lament. 'Alas, we are so used to these excuses for the non-completion of the work!' Engels commented many years later, after rereading some of Marx's old letters. 'Whenever the state of his health made it impossible for him to go on with it, this impossibility preyed heavily on his mind, and he was only too glad if he could only find out some theoretical excuse why the work should not then be completed.' This assumes that it was his health which sabotaged his work, but one could argue that cause and effect were the other way round. Though Marx's many ailments over the years were real enough, there was undoubtedly a psychosomatic influence. As he admitted, 'my sickness always originates in the mind'.

In the summer of 1851, when starting his regular column for the *New York Daily Tribune*, he fell ill immediately and begged Engels to take over. A few months later, when asked for a contribution to Weydemeyer's newspaper *Die Revolution*, he took to his bed for a week. In the summer of 1857, when poverty forced him to take on hack work for the American *Cyclopaedia*, he was out of action for three weeks with liver trouble. Now that Lassalle and Duncker were demanding his economic manuscript, anyone who knew Marx would have guessed the consequence. Jenny, for one, was not at all surprised by the sudden bilious bother. In April 1858, at a time when Marx himself was too ill even to write a letter, she told Engels that 'the worsening of his condition is largely attributable to mental unrest and agitation which now, of course, after the conclusion of the contract with the publisher are greater than ever and increasing daily, since he finds it impossible to bring the thing to a close'. Soon afterwards he spent a week in Manchester, where Engels prescribed his favourite remedy of energetic equestrianism. 'Moor has been out riding for two hours today,' Engels revealed in a medical bulletin to Jenny Marx, 'and feels so well after it that he's waxing quite enthusiastic about the thing.' But as soon as he returned to his desk in Grafton Terrace all the old anxieties descended again.

Marx was an incorrigible fidget, forever breaking off to search for one more fragment of evidence, or pacing up and down his study while brooding on how to improve his argument. (A strip of

carpet between the door and window became threadbare from
these exertions, as clearly defined as a track across a meadow.)
Back in August 1846, when his 'economic shit' was already overdue
for delivery to another German publisher, he had explained the
delay thus: 'Since the all but completed manuscript of the first
volume of my book has been lying idle for so long, I shall not have
it published without revising it yet again, both as regards matter
and style. It goes without saying that a writer who works
continuously cannot, at the end of six months, publish word for
word what he wrote six months earlier.' Many authors will know
this syndrome – the dread of letting one's ship finally slide down
the slipway, the irresistible need to splash on another coat of
paint or add a few more rivets. In that summer of 1846 he had
thought it would take about four months to apply the finishing
touches: 'The revised version of the first volume will be ready for
publication at the end of November. The second volume, of a
more historical nature, will be able to follow soon after it.'

More than a decade later, Marx's great ark was still in dry dock.
'Now let me tell you how my political economy is coming on,' he
wrote to Lassalle at the end of February 1858. 'I have in fact been
at work on the final stages for some months. But the thing is
proceeding very slowly because no sooner does one set about
finally disposing of subjects to which one has devoted years of
study than they start revealing new aspects and demand to be
thought out further.' So long as there was one source unconsulted,
one treatise unread – as there always would be – he could not let
go.

And, of course, there was the unending struggle against those
other notorious enemies of promise – illness, poverty and domestic
duty. Eleanor went down with whooping cough; Jenny was 'a
nervous wreck'; the butcher, the pawnbroker and the tallyman
were all clamouring for payment. As Marx joked grimly, 'I don't
suppose anyone has ever written about "money" when so short
of the stuff.' Trapped in a quagmire of vexations, he wrote almost
nothing throughout the summer. At the end of September he

claimed that the manuscript would be ready for dispatch 'in two weeks', but a month later he admitted that 'it will be weeks before I am able to send it'. Everything seemed to conspire against him: the world economic crisis, so cheerfully expected, had fizzled out all too soon and Marx's 'very bad humour' at this turn of events had its predictable physical consequence – 'the most appalling toothache and ulcers all over my mouth'.

By the middle of November, six months after the deadline, the publisher in Berlin began to wonder if the book was anything more than a chimera. With heroic chutzpah, Marx explained to Lassalle that the procrastination 'merely signified the endeavour to give him [Duncker] the best value for his money'. How so?

All that I was concerned with was the form. But to me the style of everything I wrote seemed tainted with liver trouble. And I have a twofold motive for not allowing this work to be spoiled on medical grounds:

1. It is the product of fifteen years of research, i.e. the best years of my life.

2. In it an important view of social relations is scientifically expounded for the first time. Hence I owe it to the Party that the thing shouldn't be disfigured by the kind of heavy, wooden style proper to a disordered liver . . .

I shall have finished about four weeks from now, having only just begun the actual writing.

Only just begun! This must have come as quite a shock to Lassalle and Duncker, who had been told back in February that the text was in its 'final stages'. Still, if the work was as weighty and profound as Marx maintained, no doubt it would be worth the wait.

As Christmas approached, the house in Grafton Terrace seemed more woebegone than ever. Jenny had no time to organise any festivities for the children, being fully occupied copying out Karl's manuscript when not running errands to the pawnshop and answering the dunning letters from creditors that arrived almost daily. 'My wife is quite right when she says that, after all the *misère* she has had to go through, the revolution will only make things worse and afford her the gratification of seeing all the humbugs from here once again celebrating their victories over there,' Marx remarked. 'Women are like that.'

By late January the book was ready to go – but he hadn't a farthing for postage or insurance. After stumping up the necessary £2, Engels was rewarded with a horrific and astounding confession: 'The manuscript amounts to about twelve sheets [192 pages] of print (three instalments) and – don't be bowled over by this – although entitled Capital in General, these instalments contain nothing as yet on the subject of capital.' Engels may have suspected that something was amiss: uncharacteristically, Marx had declined to show him any of the work in progress. Even so, it was a grievous disappointment after the years of boasting. The mountains had heaved in labour, and given birth to a ridiculous mouse. Half of this slim volume was little more than a critical summary of other economists' theories, and the only section of lasting interest was an autobiographical preface describing how he had reached the conclusion that 'the anatomy of civil society is to be found in political economy' through his reading of Hegel and his journalism at the *Rheinische Zeitung*.

The general result at which I arrived and which, once won, served as a guiding thread for my studies, can be briefly formulated as follows. In the social production of their life, men enter into definite relations that are indispensable and independent of their will, relations of production which correspond to a definite stage of development of their material productive forces. The sum total of these relations constitutes the economic structure of society, the real foundation, on which rises a legal and political superstructure and to which correspond definite forms of social consciousness. The mode of production of material life conditions the social, political and

intellectual process in general. It is not the consciousness of
men that determines their being, but, on the contrary, their
social being that determines their consciousness.

At a certain stage of development these 'material relations'
become intolerably restrictive, and then begins an epoch of social
revolution in which the whole immense 'superstructure' of
consciousness – legal, political, religious, aesthetic – melts as
quickly as snowfall on a sunny winter morning. This had happened
with every previous mode of production, from the Asiatic to the
feudal, and would most assuredly be the fate of the modern
bourgeois tyranny. But there was one difference: 'The bourgeois
relations of production are the last antagonistic form of the social
process of production – antagonistic not in the sense of individual
antagonism, but of one arising from the social conditions of life
of the individuals; at the same time the productive forces
developing in the womb of bourgeois society create the material
conditions for the solution of that antagonism. This social
formation brings, therefore, the prehistory of human society to a
close.'

A pretty extravagant 'therefore', some might say. These few
paragraphs alone have produced an entire industry of disputation,
in which Marxist philosophers quarrel among themselves about
the precise significance of 'base and superstructure' while sceptics
wonder why Victorian capitalism must necessarily be the last
form of antagonistic production before the creation of a communist nirvana. Mightn't bourgeois society merely mutate into a
sharper if subtler version of itself, with more sophisticated
instruments of torture and more persuasive justifications for its
hegemony?

A Contribution to the Critique of Political Economy, as Marx called it,
thus provided much to chew on – but little to satisfy the hunger of
his admirers. As publication day loomed he kept up a splendid
show of hyperbolic huckstering, declaring that the book would be
translated and admired throughout the civilised world. But his

body knew better: in the middle of July 1859, shortly after the finished copies reached London, he was 'overcome by a kind of cholera as a result of the heat and was vomiting from morning to night'. And no wonder. The reaction of his friends, when they at last got their hands on the long-promised *opus*, was one of consternation. Wilhelm Liebknecht said that 'never had a book disappointed him so much'.

There were no advertisements and few reviews: the explosive bombshell had turned out to be a very damp squib indeed. 'The secret hopes we had long nourished in regard to Karl's book were all set at naught by the Germans' conspiracy of silence,' Jenny complained at the end of the year, 'only broken by a couple of wretched, belletristic *feuilleton* articles which confined themselves to the preface and ignored the contents of the book. The second instalment may startle the slugabeds out of their lethargy. . .' Ah yes, the second instalment – due a few months after the first, or so its author had once promised. He now adjusted the timetable slightly, imposing an 'extreme limit' of December 1859 for completion of his thesis on capital, which had been so eccentrically omitted from the *Critique*. Connoisseurs of Marx's working habits would have predicted that he was most unlikely to stick to this plan – and, sure enough, for the next year his economic notebooks lay unopened on the desk as he distracted himself with a spectacular, pointless feud against one Karl Vogt, the professor of natural science at Berne University.

This absurd interlude began with a chance remark by the radical author Karl Blind, who shared the platform with Marx at an anti-Russian rally organised by the Urquhartites in May 1859. Whenever two or three German socialists were gathered together it was a safe bet that they would soon begin swapping slanderous gossip about fellow émigrés, and on this occasion Blind happened to mention that Karl Vogt – a former liberal member of the Frankfurt Assembly now exiled in Switzerland – was receiving clandestine payments from Napoleon III.

Since Vogt had recently written a pro-Bonapartist political tract, Marx thought this titbit interesting enough to pass on to the journalist Elard Biskamp, who duly published it in his new weekly paper for London refugees, *Das Volk*. Meanwhile, Blind produced an anonymous flysheet repeating the accusation, which was reprinted in the *Augsburg Allgemeine Zeitung*, a respectable German newspaper. Vogt, wrongly assuming Marx to be the author, issued libel writs against the paper – whereupon the man responsible for the *brouhaha*, Blind, went into a blue funk and refused to testify, pretending that the flysheet had nothing to do with him. Though the case was dismissed on a technicality, Vogt claimed a moral victory since the defence had been unable to prove its allegations. (A few years later, documents found in the French archives showed that Bonaparte had indeed been paying him a secret stipend.)

There it might have ended, had not Vogt decided to gloat over his success in a small book called *Mein Prozess gegen die Allgemeine Zeitung* ('My Lawsuit Against the *Allgemeine Zeitung*') which denounced Marx as a revolutionary charlatan who sponged off the workers while consorting with the aristocracy. He was also identified as the leader of a 'Brimstone Gang' which blackmailed German communists by threatening to expose them unless they paid hush money. The many pages of supporting evidence included a particularly damning letter from Gustav Techow, an ex-lieutenant in the Baden campaign, describing a meeting of the Communist League soon after his arrival in London in 1850:

First we drank port, then claret (which is red Bordeaux), then champagne. After the red wine he [Marx] was completely drunk. That was exactly what I wanted, because he would be more openhearted than he would probably otherwise have been. I became certain of many things which would otherwise have remained mere suppositions. In spite of his condition Marx dominated the conversation up to the last moment.

He gave the impression not only of rare intellectual superiority but also of outstanding personality. If he had had

as much heart as intellect and love as hate, I should have gone
through fire for him, even if he had not just occasionally hinted
at his complete contempt for me, which he finally expressed
quite openly. He is the first and only one among us all whom I
would trust to have the capacity for leadership and for never
losing himself in small matters when dealing with great events.

In view of our aims, I regret that this man, with his fine
intellect, is lacking in nobility of soul. I am convinced that the
most dangerous personal ambition has eaten away at all the
good in him. He laughs at the fools who parrot his proletarian
catechism, just as he laughs over the communists à la Willich
and over the bourgeoisie. The only people he respects are the
aristocrats, the genuine ones who are well aware of it. In order
to drive them from government, he needs a source of strength,
which he can find only in the proletariat. Accordingly, he has
tailored his system to them. In spite of all his assurances to the
contrary, and perhaps because of them, I took away with me
the impression that the acquisition of personal power was the
aim of all his endeavours.

Engels and all his old associates, in spite of their many fine
talents, are all far inferior to him, and if they should dare to
forget it for a moment, he would put them in their place with
an unashamedness worthy of a Napoleon.

Though some modern critics have found this picture 'only too
credible', as did Karl Vogt, it is a blotchy caricature. Marx may
have been uxoriously proud of Jenny's innate nobility, but there is
no evidence whatever that he admired the aristocracy as a class.
He had rather more respect for the bourgeoisie, as he proved in
the *Communist Manifesto* with that lyrical celebration of capitalism's
progressive achievements. And the portrayal of Engels as a
cowering subordinate is laughable. Nevertheless, the description
of Marx's domineering style had just enough verisimilitude to be
very damaging indeed.

Vogt's book was an instant bestseller in Germany, but copies were hard to find in London. For some weeks Marx had to rely on hearsay about the 'horrible scurrilities' and 'absurd calumnies' in its pages. 'Needless to say,' he warned Engels, 'I have kept the whole squalid business from my wife.' She found out soon enough. At the end of January 1860 the *National-Zeitung* in Berlin carried two long articles based on the Vogt indictment, confirming Marx's suspicion that 'he is obviously seeking to represent me as an insignificant and rascally bourgeois blackguard'; he began libel proceedings against the newspaper forthwith. When the book itself arrived, on 13 February 1860, he found it to be 'nothing but shit, sheer tripe'.

Defending his honour would be a costly business. Postage stamps alone came to several pounds, as he dashed off dozens of letters inviting old comrades – some of whom he hadn't seen since 1848 – to act as character witnesses. There was a retaining fee of 15 thalers (£2.10) for the Berlin lawyer he had hired, J. M. Weber, plus a payment to 'that bastard Zimmerman', an official at the Austrian embassy who supplied the wording for Weber's power of attorney. 'You will have gathered from the foregoing,' he told Engels, 'that I'm now stone-broke.' He even borrowed a pound from his baker – a splendidly ironic gesture by a man seeking to refute the slur that he cadged off the workers.

The Berlin lawsuit might have cost him nothing if, instead of instituting a private action for libel, he had used the services of the Royal Prussian Public Prosecutor, but he doubted that this worthy gent would 'display especial zeal in upholding the honour of my name'. Quite so: unbeknown to Marx, his lawyer did try this route and was informed that no public interest would be served by the case. He pressed ahead with a civil action but that too was dismissed (on 5 June 1860) when the court ruled that the *National-Zeitung* articles 'do not exceed the bounds of legitimate criticism' and had no 'intention to insult'. ('Like the Turk who cut off the head of a Greek, but without intending to injure him,' Marx muttered.)

Very well then: he would find some other way of avenging

himself. The only surprise is that he didn't challenge Vogt to a
duel: perhaps the fare to Switzerland deterred him, or perhaps he
was simply feeling his age. He shut himself away in his study and
composed a rip-roaring counterblast which in both length and
savagery far outdid the original pamphlet to which it was
supposedly a riposte. 'Tit for tat, reprisals make the world go
round!' he hummed merrily while venting his sarcasm over more
than 300 pages. One minute Vogt was a cut-price Cicero, the next
a humourless Falstaff. He was a buffoon, a windbag, a clammy-
handed pot-boy, a performing dog. Mostly, however, he was a
skunk – 'which has only one method of defending itself at
moments of extreme danger: its offensive smell'.

Anyone who had ever aided or abetted the gruesome Vogt was
given the same treatment. Several steaming buckets of scatological
insults were tipped over a London newspaper which had reprinted
the *National-Zeitung* articles:

> By means of an ingenious system of concealed plumbing, all
> the lavatories of London empty their physical refuse into the
> Thames. In the same way every day the capital of the world
> spews out all its social refuse through a system of goose quills,
> and it pours out into a great central paper *cloaca* – the *Daily
> Telegraph* ... At the entrance which leads to the sewer, the
> following words are written in sombre colours: '*Hic quisquam
> faxit oletum!*', or as Byron translated it so poetically, 'Wanderer,
> stop and – piss!'

When Marx was in this sort of mood there was no stopping him
– more's the pity. Joseph Moses Levy, the *Telegraph*'s editor, was
subjected to many pages of heavy-handed and anti-Semitic taunts
for changing the spelling of his surname from 'Levi'.

> Levy is determined to be an Anglo-Saxon. Therefore, at least
> once a month, he attacks the unEnglish policies of Mr Disraeli,
> for Disraeli, 'the Asiatic mystery', is, unlike the *Telegraph*, not an

Anglo-Saxon by descent. But what does it profit Levy to attack Mr D'Israeli and to change 'I' into 'y', when Mother Nature has inscribed his origins in the clearest possible way right in the middle of his face. The nose of the mysterious stranger of Slawkenbergius (see *Tristram Shandy*) who had got the finest nose from the promontory of noses was just a nine days' wonder in Strasbourg, whereas Levy's nose provides conversation throughout the year in the City of London ... Indeed the great skill of Levy's nose consists in its ability to titillate with a rotten smell, to sniff it out a hundred miles away and to attract it. Thus Levy's nose serves the *Daily Telegraph* as elephant's trunk, antenna, lighthouse and telegraph.

Pretty rich coming from a man whose own rabbinical forebears were also called Levi, a name dropped purely to assimilate themselves into Prussian society.

No publisher in Germany would touch the book, and so Marx had *Herr Vogt* printed in London after a whip-round to cover the production costs: Lassalle and the Countess von Hatzfeldt provided £12, another £12 came from the wine merchant Sigismund Borkheim, an old ally from the '48 uprising; and Engels sent a fiver. Anyone reading the book today will feel that these well-wishers might have performed a more useful service if they had dissuaded him from wasting so much time on this nonsense; but apparently the madness was contagious. Engels praised *Herr Vogt* as 'the best polemical work you have ever written', superior even to *The Eighteenth Brumaire of Louis Bonaparte*; Jenny, who transcribed the manuscript, found it a source of 'endless glee and delight'. As usual, Marx expected to cause a sensation and become the sole topic of conversation throughout Germany, if not the whole of Europe; as usual, he was disappointed. *Herr Vogt* made its entrance on 1 December 1860 with as little fanfare or applause as the *Critical Economy*.

He consoled himself in traditional fashion. 'A circumstance that has been of great help to me was having an appalling toothache,' he wrote to Engels in publication week. 'The day before yesterday, I had a tooth pulled out. While the fellow (Gabriel, he's called) did, in fact, pull out the root, after causing me great physical pains, he left in a splinter. So, the whole of my face is sore and swollen, and my throat half closed up. This physical pressure contributes much to the disablement of thought and hence to one's powers of abstraction for, as Hegel says, pure thought or pure being or *nothingness* is one and the same thing.'

This mental anaesthetic was more necessary than ever; quite apart from his disappointment at the failure of *Herr Vogt*, he was also numbing his grief at the condition of his wife, who had succumbed to smallpox a couple of weeks earlier. While Karl and Helene nursed the invalid, the girls went off to stay with the Liebknechts for a month – though sometimes they returned to stand forlornly outside the window, so that she could at least catch a glimpse of them from her sick-bed. 'The poor children are very scared,' Marx told Engels. The physician, Dr Allen, said that if Jenny hadn't been twice vaccinated she would not have pulled through, and her own account in a letter to Louise Weydemeyer confirms that it was touch and go:

I became hourly more ill, the smallpox assuming horrifying proportions. My sufferings were great, very great. Severe, burning pains in the face, complete inability to sleep, and mortal anxiety in regard to Karl, who was nursing me with the utmost tenderness, finally the loss of all my outer faculties while my inner faculty – consciousness – remained unclouded throughout. All the time, I lay by an open window so that the cold November air must blow in me. And all the while hell's fire in the hearth and ice on my burning lips, between which a few drops of claret were poured now and then. I was barely able to swallow, my hearing grew ever fainter and, finally, my eyes closed up and I did not know whether I might not remain shrouded in perpetual night.

When the three children were at last allowed to return home, on Christmas Eve, they wept at the sight of their beloved mother. Five weeks earlier she had been a well-preserved woman of forty-six, without a grey hair on her head, who 'didn't look too bad alongside my blooming daughters'. Now her face was disfigured by scars and a dark purple-red tinge. She saw herself as a rhinoceros or hippopotamus 'which belonged in a zoological garden rather than in the ranks of the Caucasian race'. Meanwhile her husband, anxious and exhausted, was once again suffering tortures from his liver; and then there was the problem of how to pay the hefty medical bills, especially as he had been unable to work for more than a month. The only pleasure in an otherwise miserable Christmas was Engels's gift of a few bottles of port, which Jenny found a most effective medicine. But even this pick-me-up was denied to Karl, whose doctor had imposed a strict diet of lemonade and castor oil. 'I am as tormented as Job,' he moaned, 'though not as God-fearing.'

By all the laws of aerodynamics the bumble-bee should be unable to fly. Marx had a similar gravity-defying talent: just when he seemed certain to crash under his weight of woes, news arrived from Germany which kept him airborne. On 12 January 1861 the new Prussian King, Wilhelm I, celebrated his coronation by declaring an amnesty for political émigrés, thus raising the hope that Marx could regain his long-lost citizenship; one week later Lassalle proposed that Marx and Engels return home to edit a new 'party organ' modelled on the *Neue Rheinische Zeitung*.

Though Marx had no faith in the project, guessing that 'the tide in Germany hasn't risen high enough yet to bear our ship', he was nevertheless tempted – especially when he learned that the newspaper would be backed by 300,000 thalers from the Countess von Hatzfeldt's fortune. Now that the *New York Daily Tribune* had more or less abandoned him because of the American Civil War, he needed an income of some kind more desperately than ever. At the very least, Lassalle's proposition justified some on-the-spot reconnaissance. Travelling with a false passport and money borrowed from Lassalle, he set off for Germany at the end of February – stopping en route at Zaltbommel in the Netherlands, where he squeezed £160 out of his rich uncle Lion Philips as an advance against the inheritance that would be due to him under Henriette Marx's will when that redoubtable old buzzard finally fell off her perch.

Lassalle and the Countess entertained Marx regally during his month-long visit to Berlin – thus showing how little they understood his character, since the last thing an anti-monarchist wants is to be treated like royalty. One evening they took him to see a new comedy, full of Prussian self-glorification, which disgusted him. The next night he was at the opera-house, forced to endure three hours of ballet ('deadly dull'), sitting in a private box only a few feet away from King Wilhelm himself. At a dinner in his honour, attended by a swarm of Berlin celebrities, Marx was stuck next to the literary editor Ludmilla Assing ('the most ugly creature I ever saw in my life'), who flirted with him throughout the meal – 'eternally smiling and grinning, always speaking poetical prose, constantly trying to say something extraordinary, playing at false enthusiasm, and spitting at her auditor during the trances of her ecstasies'.

After a month of Lassalle's excruciating hospitality, Marx was screaming with boredom. 'I am treated as a kind of lion and am forced to see a great many professional "wits", both male and female,' he wrote to the German poet Carl Siebel, a friend of Engels. 'It's awful.' The only reason for prolonging the ordeal was that he still awaited a decision on his application for citizenship, which Lassalle had delivered in person to the chief of the Prussian police. The reply came on 10 April. Since Marx had given up his rights as a Prussian subject voluntarily in 1845, the Police Presidium 'can only regard you as a foreigner'. He was thus ineligible for the royal amnesty.

The Countess pleaded with him to stay for yet more dinners and *divertissements*. 'This, then, is the thanks for the friendship we have shown you,' she chided, 'that you leave Berlin as soon as your business will permit?' But he couldn't abide the place any longer: the prevalence of men in uniform and ardent bluestockings made him exceedingly uncomfortable. Germany, he decided, was a beautiful country only if you didn't have to live there. 'If I were quite free, and if, besides, I were not bothered by something you may call "political conscience", I should never leave England for Germany, and still less for Prussia, and least of all for that ghastly Berlin.' Jenny, too, was vehemently opposed to any more uprooting. During his absence she confided to Engels that 'I myself feel small longing for the fatherland, for "dear", beloved, trusty Germany, that *mater dolorosa* of poets – and as for the girls! The idea of leaving the country of their precious Shakespeare appals them; they've become English to the marrow and cling like limpets to the soil of England.' Besides, she had no wish to see her little darlings fall under the influence of the giddy, gilded 'Hatzfeldt circle'.

Marx himself was rather fond of the Countess – 'a very distinguished lady, no bluestocking, of great natural intellect, much vivacity, deeply interested in the revolutionary movement, and of an aristocratic *laissez aller* very superior to the pedantic grimaces of professional "clever women" ' – even if she did wear far too much make-up to conceal the ravages of age and decay. For him, the clinching argument against taking a job in Berlin was his unwillingness to be a colleague or neighbour of Ferdinand Lassalle. In more than a decade of regular correspondence he had somehow failed to detect the man's vanity, pomposity and incipient megalomania, but after a month under the same roof he understood why the Düsseldorf communists had tried to warn him off. In letters to Engels, Lassalle was now dubbed 'Lazarus', 'Baron Izzy' or 'the Jewish nigger'. This last epithet began as a piece of whimsy: though Lassalle was certainly dark – as was Marx – he had no Negro ancestry. But Marx repeated the joke so often that he came to believe its essential veracity: 'It is now quite plain to me – as the shape of his head and the way his hair grows also testify – that he is descended from the negroes who accompanied Moses's flight from Egypt (unless his mother or paternal grandfather interbred with a nigger),' he wrote. 'Now, this blend of Jewishness and Germanness, on the one hand, and basic negroid stock, on the other, must inevitably give rise to a peculiar product. The fellow's importunity is also niggerlike.' As with his comments about the amazing nose of Mr Levy, editor of the *Daily Telegraph*, one can only assume that it seemed funny at the time.

The German trip was not wholly unprofitable: before leaving the country Marx spent two days in Trier with his mother, who rewarded this rare effort at filial solicitude by cancelling several of his ancient debts. He thus returned to London on 29 April with £160 in cash from Uncle Lion and a pocketful of torn-up IOUs. By the middle of June, however, he was sponging off Engels once again. 'The fact that I have already spent what I brought back with me will not surprise you,' he wrote, 'since, besides the debts which occasioned the trip, nothing has been coming in for nearly four months, while school and doctor alone ate up nearly £40.' He was soon back in the old routine of subterfuges and emergency measures. Whenever the landlord came to collect the rent Jenny would send him off empty-handed, explaining that Karl was away on business – while in fact he was cowering in his upstairs study. More and more household effects were sent to the pop-shop, including the children's clothes 'right down to their boots and shoes'. Through the winter of 1861–2 Jennychen was continuously ill: Marx deduced that at the age of seventeen she 'is now already old enough to feel the full strain and also the stigma of our circumstances, and I think this is one of the main causes of her physical indisposition'. Engels immediately sent his patent restorative for 'weak blood' – eight bottles of claret, four of hock and two of sherry – which lifted her spirits but did nothing for her weak and emaciated body.

The mood in the Marx household became even more forlorn during the summer of 1862 while the rest of London was *en fête* for the second Great Exhibition, a fanfaronade of mid-Victorian pride and achievement. 'Every day my wife says she wishes she and the children were safely in their graves, and I really cannot blame her, for the humiliations, torments and alarums that one has to go through in such a situation are indeed indescribable,' he wrote. 'I feel all the more sorry for the unfortunate children in that all of this is happening during the Exhibition season, when their friends are having fun, whereas they themselves live in dread lest someone should come and see them and realise what a mess they are in . . . No one comes to see me, and I'm glad of it.'

He spoke too soon. Three weeks later who should turn up on his doorstep but 'Baron Izzy' Lassalle, in town to inspect the industrial marvels on display in Hyde Park. It was a hideously inopportune moment, but Marx felt duty-bound to make some show of returning the hospitality he had accepted – if not enjoyed – in Berlin the previous year. Everything not actually nailed or bolted down was taken to the pawnbroker, and for the next three weeks Lassalle played the part of the guest from hell – eating and drinking like a starved glutton while holding forth about his limitless talents and ambitions. Though he knew that Marx's income from the *New York Daily Tribune* had dried up, Lassalle seemed astonishingly insensitive to the family's plight: he boasted of losing £100 on a rash stock-market speculation as if it were nothing, and spent more than a pound a day on cabs and cigars without offering a penny to his hosts. Instead he had the insolence to ask Karl and Jenny if they would mind handing over one of their teenage daughters to *la* Hatzfeldt as a 'companion' – i.e. a glorified maidservant.

'The fellow has wasted my time,' Marx noted during the third week of this ordeal, 'and, what is more, the dolt opined that, since I was not engaged upon any "business" just now, but merely upon a "theoretical work", I might just as well kill time with him!' The whole family had to escort Lassalle on sightseeing tours of London – and further afield, to Windsor and Virginia Water – while listening to his interminable self-aggrandising monologues.

Looking at the Rosetta Stone in the British Museum, he turned to Marx and asked. 'What do you think? Should I spend six months making my mark as an Egyptologist?' Had Marx not been so infuriated by the way 'this parvenu flaunted his moneybags', he might have found it all quite amusing. 'Since I last saw him a year ago he's gone quite mad,' he told Engels. 'He is now indisputably not only the greatest scholar, the profoundest thinker, the most brilliant man of science, and so forth, but also and in addition, Don Juan *cum* revolutionary Cardinal Richelieu. Add to this the incessant chatter in a high falsetto voice, the unaesthetic, histrionic gestures, the dogmatic tone!' One day Lassalle disclosed the 'profound secret' that the Italian liberators Mazzini and Garibaldi, like the government of Prussia, were pawns directed by his guiding hand. Unable to contain themselves, Karl and Jenny began teasing him about these Napoleonic fantasies – whereupon the German messiah lost his temper, screaming that Marx was too 'abstract' to comprehend the realities of politics. After Lassalle had gone to bed, Marx disappeared into his study to write another letter to Engels mocking his guest's 'niggerlike' characteristics.

Jenny's account of the Lassalle invasion has rather less rancour and more humour:

He was almost crushed under the weight of the fame he had achieved as scholar, thinker, poet and politician. The laurel wreath was fresh on his Olympian brow and ambrosian head or rather on his stiff bristling Negro hair. He had just victoriously ended the Italian campaign – a new political *coup* was being contrived by the great men of action – and fierce battles were going on in his soul. There were still fields of science that he had not explored! Egyptology lay fallow: 'Should I astonish the world as an Egyptologist or show my versatility as a man of action, as a politician, as a fighter, or as a soldier?' It was a splendid dilemma. He wavered between the thoughts and sentiments of his heart and often expressed that struggle in really stentorian accents. As on the wings of wind he swept through our rooms, perorating so loudly, gesticulating and raising his voice to such a pitch that our neighbours were scared by the terrible shouting and asked what was the matter. It was the inner struggle of the 'great' man bursting forth in shrill discords.

It was only when he was leaving, on 4 August, that Lassalle acknowledged the Marxes' predicament – as he could hardly fail to, since the landlord and a posse of other creditors had chosen this moment to batter on the front door, loudly threatening to send in bailiffs. Even then his generosity was pretty strained. He offered Marx £15, but only as a short-term loan and then only subject to a promise from Engels that he would guarantee it.

Over the next couple of months Lassalle made such a fuss about this minor transaction – insisting on 'signed bonds' from Engels, haggling over the repayment date – that Marx regretted ever taking the money. After a thoroughly ill-tempered exchange of letters, however, he offered a semi-apology. 'Is there to be an outright split between us because of this? . . . I trust that, despite everything, our old relationship will continue untroubled.' He was a man sitting on a powder-barrel, a despairing wretch who would like nothing better than to blow his brains out: was this not enough to excuse his thoughtless ingratitude?

Lassalle never replied. Though he blamed 'financial reasons' for the end of the friendship, the two men's political differences would have caused a rupture soon enough. Lassalle had an Old Hegelian respect for the might of the Prussian state, and was now advocating co-operation between the old *Junker* ruling class (represented by Bismarck) and the new industrial proletariat (represented, naturally, by himself) to thwart the political aspirations of the rising liberal bourgeoisie. In June 1863, two weeks after founding the General German Workers' Association, Lassalle wrote to the Iron Chancellor, bragging about the absolute power he had over his members, 'which perhaps you'd have to envy me! But this miniature picture will plainly convince you how

true it is that the working class feels instinctively inclined to
dictatorship if it can first be rightfully convinced that such will be
exercised in its interests, and how very much it would therefore be
inclined, as I recently told you, in spite of all republican sentiments
– or perhaps on those very grounds – to see in the Crown the
natural bearer of the social dictatorship, in contrast to the egoism
of bourgeois society.' (This letter gives the lie to a claim by one
of Marx's biographers, Fritz J. Raddatz, that 'the notorious
"conspiracy" with Bismarck never took place'.) What the workers
required was not a monarchy created by the bourgeoisie, like that
of Louis Philippe in France, but 'a monarchy that still stands as
kneaded out of its original dough, leaning upon the hilt of the
sword . . .'

One wonders if the Prussian King would have been flattered
by this bizarre image of a sabre-rattling *baguette*. Probably not: in
spite of this gushing allegiance, Lassalle actually envisaged a ruling
triumvirate of King Wilhelm, Bismarck and himself, and once
the middle classes had been forcibly cut down to size he would
have no further use for his two partners. His dictatorial scheme,
which has been well described as 'social Caesarism', was anathema
to Marx – and all the more annoying because its rhetoric included
much 'brazen plagiarism' from the *Communist Manifesto* to which
Lassalle had added his own reactionary, self-serving embellishments. He was the Master, the Redeemer, the Hero on Horseback.
Even at the age of twenty, in a 'Manifesto of War Against the
World', his melodramatic egoism had been uncontainable: 'Alike
to me are all means; nothing is so sacred that I shunned it; and I
have won the right of the tiger, the right to tear to pieces . . .
Insofar as I have power over the mind of a person, I will abuse it
without mercy . . . From head to toe I am nothing but Will.' If he
hadn't existed, Nietzsche would have invented him.

That was the spirit in which he lived – and died. In 1864
Lassalle became infatuated with a Titian-haired young beauty
called Helene von Dönniges who was already engaged to one
Janko von Rakowitz, a Wallachian prince. The aggrieved fiancé

challenged the Superhero to a duel and shot him fatally in the
stomach. It was observed that Lassalle did not even lift his pistol,
but smiled enigmatically as his rival took aim. Had he come to
believe in his own invincibility? Or had he decided that a romantic
and premature death would guarantee immortal fame? It was all
a great mystery. As Engels commented, 'Such a thing could only
happen to Lassalle, with his strange and altogether unique mixture
of frivolity and sentimentality, Jewishness and chivalry.' The news
distressed Marx more than he might have expected. Whatever
else he might have been, Lassalle was 'the foe of our foes', one of
the old guard of *quarante-huitards*. 'Heaven knows, our ranks are
being steadily depleted, and there are no reinforcements in sight.'
To the Countess von Hatzfeldt he offered the consolation that at
least 'he died young, at a time of triumph, as an Achilles'.

This was a generous tribute in the circumstances. Two years
earlier Marx had nearly bankrupted himself while entertaining
Lassalle at Grafton Terrace; he had been repaid with tetchiness,
mistrust and ultimately silence. Since that visit – and partly
because of it, Marx suspected – the family finances had gone
from bad to worse. In August 1862, a few days after Lassalle left
London, Marx travelled to Zaltbommel in the hope of arranging
another loan from Lion Philips only to find that his uncle was
away. He then proceeded to Trier, but his mother refused to give
him anything. At Christmas that year Jenny Marx tried working
her charm on Monsieur Abarbanel, a French banker of their
acquaintance, with even more disastrous results. Her ferry to
Boulogne nearly sank in a storm; the train taking her to
Abarbanel's house was two hours late; when she finally arrived it
turned out that the banker had just been paralysed by a stroke
which left him helpless and confined to bed. While returning to
London empty-handed, she endured yet more mishaps: a bus in
which she was travelling turned over, and then her London cab
crashed into another vehicle, losing a wheel. After making her
way back to Grafton Terrace on foot, accompanied by two boys
carrying her luggage, she learned that Marianne Creuz, Helene

Demuth's stepsister, had died of a heart attack two hours earlier. Imagine the scene: one maid dead in the front room, another howling in grief, a mud-spattered and exhausted wife – and the master of the house wondering where on earth he could find £7.10 in cash to pay the undertakers. Marx allowed himself a bleak laugh at this tragicomic tableau: 'A fine Christmas show for the poor children.'

For once, however, grotesque misfortune did not have the usual debilitating effect on his health and productivity. Those Lassallean sneers at 'theory' had been the goad he needed to finish the book which had been so catastrophically interrupted by the feud with Vogt. 'If only I knew how to start some sort of business!' he wrote to Engels in a low moment soon after Lassalle's trip to London. 'All theory, dear friend, is grey, and only business green. Unfortunately, I have come to realise this too late.' It was at about this time that Marx applied for a clerical job on the railways but was rejected because of his poor handwriting. No matter: he could still put his pen to good use, as long as Jenny was there to transcribe the scrawl into something a typesetter could recognise. With few journalistic commissions to distract him, he started writing the next instalment of his critical economy.

'It is a curious and not unmeaning circumstance that the country where Karl Marx is least known is that in which he has for the last thirty years lived and worked,' the economist John Rae commented in the *Contemporary Review* of October 1881, two years before Marx's death. 'His word has gone into all the earth and evoked in some quarters echoes which governments will neither let live nor let die; but here, where it was pronounced, its sound has scarcely been heard.' When Engels sent a detailed analysis of *Capital* to the liberal *Fortnightly Review* in 1869, the editorial board returned it with a brief note explaining that it was 'too scientific for the English *Review*-reader'. A few years later, at a lecture delivered by an English economist on the 'harmony of interests', a socialist in the audience questioned the blithe assumption that all classes of society had the same interests, backing his scepticism with references to *Capital*. 'I know of no such work,' the speaker retorted.

Almost none of Marx's major works was translated into English during his lifetime and the most important exception, the *Communist Manifesto*, was available only to the handful of Chartists who subscribed to George Julian Harney's *Red Republican* in November 1850. Ten months later, however, a copy turned up belatedly at *The Times*, which hastened to warn its readers of 'cheap publications containing the wildest and most anarchical doctrines . . . in which religion and morality are perverted and scoffed at, and every rule of conduct which experience has sanctioned, and on which the very existence of society depends, openly assailed'. There followed two extracts from the *Manifesto* – though the source went unacknowledged, since *The Times* was 'not anxious to give it circulation by naming its writers, or the works of which it is composed'. The Tory politician John Wilson Croker tried to prolong the red-scare by penning a lurid de-nunciation of 'Revolutionary Literature' (complete with the same quotations from the *Manifesto*) in the *Quarterly Review* of September 1851. But nobody else seemed inclined to join in. The *Communist Manifesto* disappeared from view in England until Samuel Moore issued his new translation in 1888, five years after its author's death.

John Rae may have thought it 'curious' that the English paid so little attention to the presence of this old mole burrowing away in the very heart of London, but in fact it was entirely reasonable. How could they have heard of him? After falling out with the radical Harney and the crackpot Urquhart, Marx lost his lines of communication to English workers and intellectuals. The journalism with which he supported his family during the 1850s appeared in the *New York Tribune*. To the British public he was all but invisible, spending his days at the museum and his evenings in the company of fellow Germans. In May 1869 he joined the Royal Society for the Encouragement of Arts, Manufactures &

Commerce, which had become famous for its involvement in the
Great Exhibitions of 1851 and 1862, but there is no evidence that
he attended any lectures or used the library. He may have been
put off by his experience at the Society's summer party, a
'*Conversazione*' held at the South Kensington Museum on 1 July
1869. Jennychen, his escort for the evening, sent a full report to
Engels:

> Of all dreary concerns a *conversazione* is certainly the dreariest.
> What genius the English have for the inventing of melancholy
> pleasures! Fancy a crowd of some 7,000 in full evening dress,
> wedged in so closely as to be unable either to move about or to
> sit down in the chairs, and they were few and far between, a
> few imperturbable dowagers had taken by storm . . . Nothing
> was to be seen but silks, satins, brocades and laces, and these
> too on the ugliest of pegs – on women, vulgar, coarse-featured,
> dull-eyed, and either short and stumpy or tall and lank. Of the
> much talked-of beauty of the English aristocracy there wasn't
> a trace. We saw only two passably pretty girls. Among the men
> there was a sprinkling of interesting faces, the owners of which
> were probably artists, but the great majority consisted of insipid-
> looking 'Dundrearys' and parsons all run to fat.

Her father relieved the tedium by getting squiffy and giggling
ostentatiously at a notice that had been handed to all guests,
headed 'Mobbing of Distinguished Persons', which asked that
royal patrons and other eminences should be allowed to walk
about unmolested 'like any private person'. As Jennychen vowed,
'they won't catch us there a second time'.

Marx's encounters with the natives were almost always
disastrous, especially if he had a few drinks inside him. One night
he set off with Edgar Bauer and Wilhelm Liebknecht for a
drunken jaunt up the Tottenham Court Road, intending to have
at least one glass of beer in every pub between Oxford Street and
the Hampstead Road. Since the route included no fewer than

eighteen pubs, by the time they reached the last port of call he was ready for a rumpus. A group of Oddfellows, enjoying a quiet dinner, found themselves accosted by this drunken trio and taunted about the feebleness of English culture. No country but Germany, Marx declared, could have produced such masters as Beethoven, Mozart, Handel and Haydn; snobbish, cant-ridden England was fit only for philistines. This was too much even for the mild-mannered Oddfellows. 'Damned foreigners!' one growled, while several others clenched their fists. Choosing the better part of valour, the German roisterers fled outside. Liebknecht takes up the story:

Now we had enough of our 'beer trip' for the time being, and in order to cool our heated blood, we started on a double-quick march, until Edgar Bauer stumbled over a heap of paving stones. 'Hurrah, an idea!' And in memory of mad students' pranks he picked up a stone, and Clash! Clatter! a gas lantern went flying into splinters. Nonsense is contagious – Marx and I did not stay behind, and we broke four or five street lamps – it was, perhaps, two o'clock in the morning and the streets were deserted . . . But the noise nevertheless attracted the attention of a policeman who with quick resolution gave the signal to his colleagues on the same beat. And immediately counter-signals were given. The position became critical. Happily, we took in the situation at a glance; and happily we knew the locality. We raced ahead, three or four policemen some distance behind us. Marx showed an agility that I should not have attributed to him. And after the wild chase had lasted some minutes, we succeeded in turning into a side street and there through an alley – a back yard between two streets – whence we came behind the policemen who lost the trail. Now we were safe. They did not have our description and we arrived at our homes without further adventures.

While strolling through the London streets Marx would often

pause to stroke the hair of some young urchin or ragamuffin sitting in a doorway, and to slip a halfpenny into its little hand. But experience taught him that British adults do not take kindly to strangers with alien accents. Riding up Tottenham Court Road on an omnibus one day, he and Liebknecht noticed a large crowd outside a gin palace and heard a piercing female voice call out 'Murder! Murder!' Though Liebknecht tried to restrain him, Marx leaped off the bus and shoved his way into the throng. Alas, the woman was merely a drunken wife enjoying a noisy argument with her husband; and Marx's arrival at the scene instantly reunited the couple, who turned their anger on the interfering busybody. 'The crowd closed more and more around us,' Liebknecht reported, 'and assumed a threatening attitude against the "damned foreigners". Especially the woman went full of rage for Marx and concentrated her efforts on his magnificent shining black beard. I endeavoured to soothe the storm – in vain. Had not two strong constables made their appearance in time, we should have had to pay dearly for our philanthropic attempt at intervention.' Thereafter, Liebknecht noticed, Marx was 'a little more cautious' in his encounters with the London proletariat.

Not that he minded. As the historian Kirk Willis has pointed out, 'by 1860 Marx was not interested in acquiring English disciples or propagandists, for he had another project under way which was much more important – the intellectual destruction of classical political economy'. For the next four years he again took refuge in the anonymity of the British Museum's reading room, preparing for his final assault on capitalism. 'I myself, by the by, am working away hard and, strange to say, my grey matter is functioning better in the midst of the surrounding *misère* than it has done for years,' he told Engels in June 1862, adding that he had hit upon 'one or two pleasing and surprising novelties' in his analysis. Between 1861 and 1863 he filled more than 1,500 pages. 'I am expanding this volume,' he explained, 'since those German scoundrels estimate the value of a book in terms of its cubic capacity.'

Theoretical problems which had formerly defeated him were suddenly as clear and invigorating as a glass of gin. Take the question of agricultural rents – or this 'shitty rent business' as he preferred to call it. 'I had long harboured misgivings as to the absolute correctness of Ricardo's theory, and have at length got to the bottom of the swindle.' Ricardo had simply confused value and cost price. In mid-Victorian England, the prices of agricultural products were higher than their actual value (i.e. the labour time embodied in them), and the landlord pocketed the difference in the form of higher rent. Under socialism, however, this surplus would be redistributed for the benefit of the workers. Thus, even if the market price remained the same, the value of the goods – their 'social character' – would change utterly.

He was so pleased with this progress that sometimes optimism got the better of him – as when a doctor from Hanover, Ludwig Kugelmann, wrote at the end of 1862, enquiring when the sequel to *A Contribution to the Critique of Political Economy* could be expected. 'I was delighted to see from your letter how warm an interest is taken by you and your friends in my critique of political economy,' Marx replied at once. 'The second part has now at last been finished, i.e. save for the fair copy and the final polishing before it goes to press.' He concluded with a suggestion that 'you could write to me occasionally about the situation at home'. Thus began a friendly correspondence that continued for more than ten years, until Marx suddenly decided that he wanted nothing more to do with this 'hair-splitting philistine'.

The manuscript was nowhere near completion, of course: plenty more carpentry was needed before it would be ready for 'final polishing'. Even so, this was at least the raw timber from which he built the great baroque masterpiece that finally emerged in 1867. The cumbersome working title – *A Contribution to the Critique of Critical Economy, Volume II* – was now abandoned. By some inverse logic, big books deserved short names. And so, as he revealed for the first time in that letter to Kugelmann, 'it will appear on its own under the title *Capital*'.

9

The Bulldogs and the Hyena

Jenny Marx could never quite share her husband's fondness for Friedrich Engels. She was grateful for his largesse, of course, just as she appreciated the intellectual companionship and encouragement he gave Karl. She was touched, too, by his interest in the children, who adored their avuncular 'General'. To Jenny, however, he always remained Mr Engels. An unshockable woman in many ways, happy to contemplate violent revolution and the overthrow of the bourgeoisie, she still had enough middle-class propriety – or prudery – to be scandalised by the idea of a man and woman living together out of wedlock, especially when the woman concerned was an illiterate 'factory girl'.

Engels had met Mary Burns on his first visit to Manchester in 1842, while he was collecting material for *The Condition of the Working Classes in England*, and they soon became lovers. Though largely uneducated, this lively redhead of proletarian Irish stock taught Engels at least as much as she learned from him. As with her sister Lydia, who eventually joined them in a *ménage à trois*, he admired her 'passionate feeling for her class, which was inborn, [and] was worth infinitely more to me and had stood by me in all critical moments more strongly than all the aesthetic nicey-niceness and wiseacreism of the "eddicated" and "senty-mental" daughters of the bourgeoisie could have done'.

The affair was renewed when Engels and Marx came over in 1845; he then paid for Mary to come and visit him in Brussels for a while. After resigning himself to a life of vile commerce in

Manchester, Engels set her up in a little house near his own, and by the end of the 1850s they were living together. On the rare occasions when Jenny Marx was forced to acknowledge Mary's existence she referred to her as 'your wife', though in fact the relationship was never legally solemnised. The addition of Lydia ('Lizzy') to the household was an even greater affront to Frau Marx's puritanical sensibilities. But Engels didn't give a damn.

His devotion to Mary Burns also caused the only *froideur* in his otherwise warm and uninterrupted partnership with Karl Marx. Although Marx had no objection to his friend's unorthodox domestic set-up (in fact it gave him a certain amount of vicarious titillation), out of deference to Jenny he tended to underestimate the importance of the Burns sisters – and never more disastrously than when he received this short, ghastly note from Engels, dated 7 January 1863:

Dear Moor,

Mary is dead. Last night she went to bed early and, when Lizzy wanted to go to bed shortly before midnight, she found she had already died. Quite suddenly. Heart failure or an apoplectic stroke. I wasn't told till this morning; on Monday evening she was still quite well. I simply can't convey what I feel. The poor girl loved me with all her heart.

Your
FE

Marx replied the following day. 'The news of Mary's death surprised no less than it dismayed me. She was so good-natured, witty and closely attached to you.' So far so good; but this was merely the cue for a lengthy recitation of his own woes. 'The devil alone knows why nothing but ill luck should dog everyone in our circle just now. I no longer know which way to turn either . . .' Attempts to raise money in France and Germany had come to naught, no one would let him buy anything on credit, he was being dunned for the school fees and the rent, it was impossible to get on with work. After plenty more in this vein, Marx briefly remembered himself. 'It is dreadfully selfish of me to tell you about these *horreurs* at this time,' he conceded. 'But it's a homeo-pathic remedy. One calamity is a distraction from the other. And, in the final count, what else can I do?' Well, he could have tried offering his condolences rather more tactfully, for a start. In mitigation one must allow that Marx was in a truly calamitous predicament: the children hadn't been back to school since Christmas, partly because the bill for the previous term was still unpaid but also because their only presentable clothes and shoes were in hock. Even his parting thought had more to do with his own troubles than Engels's loss: 'Instead of Mary, ought it not to have been my mother, who is in any case a prey to physical ailments and has had her fair share of life? You can see what strange notions come into the heads of "civilised men" under the pressure of certain circumstances. *Salut.*'

Engels read all this with anger and amazement. How dare Marx go on about money at such a time – especially when he knew that Engels himself had been feeling the pinch lately because of a slump in the price of cotton? He held his silence for five days before sending an icy acknowledgement. His letters usually began 'Dear Moor', but such informality would no longer do:

Dear Marx,
    You will find it quite in order that, this time, my own misfortune and the frosty view you took of it should have made it positively impossible for me to reply to you any sooner. All my friends, including philistine acquaintances, have on this occasion, which in all conscience must needs affect me deeply, given me proof of greater sympathy and friendship than I could have looked for. You thought it a fit moment to assert the superiority of your 'dispassionate turn of mind'. So be it, then!

There was nothing dispassionate about Marx's turn of mind now.

For the next three weeks sour recriminations flew back and forth across the kitchen table at Grafton Terrace, as Jenny blamed Karl for not alerting Engels to their wretched state of affairs earlier and he blamed her for assuming that they could always rely on subventions from Manchester. ('The poor woman had to suffer for something of which she was in fact innocent, for women are wont to ask for the impossible,' Marx said afterwards, rather ungallantly. 'Women are funny creatures, even those endowed with much intelligence.') After many a long argument they agreed that Karl should have himself declared insolvent in the bankruptcy court. Jennychen and Laura would find employment as governesses, Lenchen would enter service elsewhere, while little Tussy and her parents would move into the City Model Lodging House, a refuge for the destitute.

Did he really have any such intention, or was this self-inflicted martyrdom just a ruse to win Engels's sympathy? Hard to say. But there is no doubting the sincerity of his contrition:

> It was very wrong of me to write you that letter, and I regretted it as soon as it had gone off. However, what happened was in no sense due to heartlessness. As my wife and children will testify, I was as shattered when your letter arrived (first thing in the morning) as if my nearest and dearest had died. But, when I wrote to you in the evening, I did so under the pressure of circumstances that were desperate in the extreme. The landlord had put a broker in my house, the butcher had protested a bill, coal and provisions were in short supply, and little Jenny was confined to bed. Generally, under such circumstances, my only recourse is to cynicism.

Though the self-laceration was still mixed in with a ladleful of self-pity, this constitutes the only sincere apology Marx ever gave anyone in his life.

Engels, with his usual generosity, recognised Marx's penitence at once. 'Dear Moor,' he wrote, resuming the old affectionate greeting:

Thank you for being so candid. You yourself have now realised what sort of impression your last letter but one made on me. One can't live with a woman for years on end without being fearfully affected by her death. I felt as though with her I was burying the last vestige of my youth. When your letter arrived she had not been buried. That letter, I tell you, obsessed me for a whole week; I couldn't get it out of my head. Never mind. Your last letter made up for it and I'm glad that, in losing Mary, I didn't also lose my oldest and best friend.

The estrangement was not mentioned again: without further ado Engels applied himself to the task of rescuing the Marx family from bankruptcy. Unable to borrow money, he simply filched a £100 cheque from the in-tray at Ermen & Engels which he then endorsed in Marx's favour. 'It is an exceedingly daring move on my part,' he acknowledged, 'but the risk must be taken.' Another £250 followed a few months later to keep Marx afloat through the summer – which was just as well, since a plague of carbuncles made work almost impossible.

That November a telegram arrived from Trier announcing the death of Henriette Marx at the age of seventy-five. She had predicted her end with suspicious accuracy – 4 p.m. on 30 November, the very hour and day of her fiftieth wedding anniversary – but no one seems to have paused to wonder if the old girl assisted her own passage into oblivion. Karl's only comment on hearing the news was predictably cool: 'Fate laid claim to one of our family. I myself have already had one foot in the grave. Circumstances being what they were, I, presumably, was needed more than my mater.' Engels sent off a tenner to pay for the journey to Trier but offered no word of condolence: he knew Marx well enough to realise that bogus regrets would cause more offence than none at all.

The execution of the will dragged on for several months, and once all the advances and loans from Uncle Lion had been discounted Marx was left with little more than £100. Still, it was enough to justify a spree. In his contempt for bourgeois financial prudence Marx practised what he preached: if there was no cash in the house he survived by ducking and diving, bluffing and juggling; but whenever he did get his hands on a fistful of sterling he spent recklessly, with no thought for the morrow. The Marxes had moved to Grafton Terrace in 1856 on the strength of Jenny's small inheritance from Caroline von Westphalen, although they must have known that the house was beyond their means. Now the folly was repeated. In March 1864, as soon as the first payment from Henriette's legacy arrived, they took a three-year lease on a spacious detached mansion at 1 Modena Villas, Maitland Park. The new address was only about 200 yards from Grafton Terrace but a world away in style and status – the sort of residence favoured by well-to-do doctors and lawyers, with a large garden, a 'charming conservatory' and enough space for each girl to have her own bedroom. A room on the first floor overlooking the park was commandeered by Marx as his study.

The annual rent for Modena Villas was £65, almost twice that of Grafton Terrace. Quite how Marx expected to pay for all this luxury is a mystery: as so often, however, his Micawberish faith was vindicated. On 9 May 1864 Wilhelm 'Lupus' Wolff died of meningitis, bequeathing 'all my books furniture and effects debts and moneys owning to me and all the residue of my personal estate and also all real and leasehold estates of which I may die seized possessed or entitled or of which I may have power to dispose by this my Will unto and to the use of the said Karl Marx'. Wolff was one of the few old campaigners from the 1840s who never wavered in his allegiance to Marx and Engels. He worked with them in Brussels on the Communist Correspondence Committee, in Paris at the 1848 revolution and in Cologne when Marx was editing the *Neue Rheinische Zeitung*. From 1853 he lived quietly in Manchester, earning his living as a language teacher and relying largely on Engels to keep him up to date with political news. 'I don't believe anyone in Manchester can have been so universally beloved as our poor little friend,' Karl wrote to Jenny after delivering the funeral oration, during which he broke down several times.

As executors of the will, Marx and Engels were amazed to discover that modest old Lupus had accumulated a small fortune through hard work and thrift. Even after deducting funeral expenses, estate duty, a £100 bequest for Engels and another £100 for Wolff's doctor, Louis Borchardt – much to Marx's annoyance, since he held this 'bombastic bungler' responsible for the death – there was a residue of £820 for the main legatee. This was far more than Marx had ever earned from his writing, and explains why the first volume of *Capital* (published three years later) carries a dedication to 'my unforgettable friend Wilhelm Wolff, intrepid, faithful, noble protagonist of the proletariat', rather than the more obvious and worthy candidate, Friedrich Engels.

The Marxes wasted no time in spending their windfall. Jenny had the new house furnished and redecorated, explaining that 'I thought it better to put the money to this use rather than to fritter it away piecemeal on trifles'. Pets were bought for the children (three dogs, two cats, two birds) and named after Karl's favourite tipples, including Whisky and Toddy. In July he took the family on vacation to Ramsgate for three weeks, though the eruption of a malignant carbuncle just above the penis rather spoiled the fun, leaving him confined to bed at their guest-house in a misanthropic sulk. 'Your philistine on the spree lords it here as do, to an even greater extent, his better half and his female offspring,' he noted, gazing enviously through his window at the beach. 'It is almost sad to see venerable Oceanus, that age-old Titan, having to suffer these pygmies to disport themselves on his phiz, and serve them for entertainment.' The boils had replaced the bailiffs as his main source of irritation. Mostly, however, he dispatched them with the same careless contempt. That autumn he held a grand ball at Modena Villas for Jennychen and Laura, who had spent many years declining invitations to parties for fear that they would be unable to reciprocate. Fifty of their young friends were entertained until four in the morning, and so much food was left over that little Tussy was allowed to have an impromptu tea-party for local children the following day.

Writing to Lion Philips in the summer of 1864, Marx revealed an even more remarkable detail of his prosperous new way of life:

> I have, which will surprise you not a little, been speculating – partly in American funds, but more especially in English stocks, which are springing up like mushrooms this year (in furtherance of every imaginable and unimaginable joint stock enterprise), are forced up to a quite unreasonable level and then, for the most part, collapse. In this way, I have made over £400 and, now that the complexity of the political situation affords greater scope, I shall begin all over again. It's a type of operation that makes small demands on one's time, and it's worth while running some risk in order to relieve the enemy of his money.

Since there is no hard evidence of these transactions, some scholars have assumed that Marx simply invented the story to impress his businesslike uncle. But it may be true. He certainly kept a close eye on share prices, and while badgering Engels for the next payment from Lupus's estate he mentioned that 'had I had the money during the past ten days, I'd have made a killing on the Stock Exchange here. The time has come again when, with wit and very little money, it's possible to make money in London.'

Playing the markets, hosting dinner-dances, walking his dogs in the park: Marx was in severe danger of becoming respectable. One day a curious document arrived, announcing that he had been elected, without his knowledge, to the municipal sinecure of 'Constable of the Vestry of St Pancras'. Engels thought this hilarious: '*Salut, ô connétable de Saint Pancrace!* Now you should get yourself a worthy outfit: a red nightshirt, white nightcap, down-at-heel slippers, white pants, a long clay pipe and a pot of porter.'

But Marx boycotted the swearing-in, quoting the advice of an Irish neighbour that 'I should tell them that I was a foreigner and that they should kiss me on the arse'.

Ever since the split in the Communist League he had been a resolute non-joiner, spurning any committee or party that tried to recruit him. 'I am greatly pleased by the public, authentic isolation in which we two, you and I, now find ourselves,' he had told Engels as long ago as February 1851, and it would certainly take more than St Pancras philistines to entice him out of this long hibernation. Nevertheless, after thirteen years of 'authentic isolation' (if not exactly peace and quiet) Marx did now feel ready to emerge. The first hint of a new mood can be seen in his enthusiastic reaction to the 1863 uprising in Poland against Tsarist oppression. 'What do you think of the Polish business?' he asked Engels on 13 February. 'This much is certain, the era of revolution has now fairly opened in Europe once more.' Four days later he decided that Prussia's intervention on behalf of the Tsar against the Polish insurgents 'impels us to speak'. At that stage he was thinking merely of a pamphlet or manifesto – and indeed he published a short 'Proclamation on Poland' in November. Little did he imagine that within another twelve months he would be the *de facto* leader of the first mass movement of the international working classes.

Marx's adult life has a tidal rhythm of advance and retreat, in which foaming surges forward are followed by a long withdrawing roar. This alternation of involvement and isolation was largely beyond his control, dictated as it was by accident and circumstance – illness, exile, domestic disaster, political reverses, fractured friendships. But it can also be seen as a wilful experiment in reconciling the demands of theory and practice, private contemplation and social engagement. Like many writers he was a kind of gregarious loner, yearning for a bit of solitude in which he could get down to work without interruption yet also craving the stimulus of action and argument. And he felt the dilemma more keenly than most, since the estrangement of individuals from society was one of his preoccupying obsessions.

In a schoolboy essay from 1835, brimming with the facile certitude of a seventeen-year-old who has just bought his first razor, the problem was eliminated as briskly as youthful stubble. 'The chief guide which must direct us in the choice of a profession is the welfare of mankind and our own perfection,' he wrote. 'It should not be thought that these two interests could be in conflict.' And why not? Because human nature was so constituted that individuals reached the zenith of perfection when devoting themselves to others. Someone who works only for himself 'may perhaps become a famous man of learning, a great sage, an excellent poet, but he can never be a perfect, truly great man'. History acclaims only those people who have ennobled themselves by enriching their tribe, and 'religion itself teaches us that the ideal being whom all strive to copy sacrificed himself for the sake of mankind ... Who would dare to set at naught such judgements?'

Marx himself would, as it happened. After realising that religion was no cure for alienation but merely an opiate to dull the pain, he was forced to look elsewhere for wholeness – first in the grand unifying self-consciousness of Hegelian philosophy, and then in historical materialism. But there was no escape from the old theological argument about faith versus works: it simply assumed a secular form, as theory versus practice or words versus deeds. 'Philosophers have only *interpreted* the world in various ways; the point is to *change* it,' he declared in 1845, as if abolishing the division of labour by a stroke of his pen: in future everyone would be both philosopher and soldier, just as we should all tend our sheep in the morning, paint a picture in the afternoon and go fishing in the evening. Aglow with existentialist fervour, Marx had no patience in those days with the ivory-tower mentality. In a little-known article from 1847 he derided the Belgian journalist Adolphe Bartels, who had taken fright at the activities of revolutionary German émigrés in Brussels:

M. Adolphe Bartels claims that public life is finished for him. Indeed, he has withdrawn into private life and does not mean to leave it; he limits himself, each time some public event occurs, to hurling protests and proclaiming loudly that he believes he is his own master, that the movement has been made without him, M. Bartels, and in spite of him, M. Bartels, and that he has the right to refuse it his supreme sanction. It will be agreed that this is just as much a way of participating in public life as any other, and that by all those declarations, proclamations and protestations the public man hides behind the humble appearance of the private individual. This is the way in which the unappreciated and misunderstood genius reveals himself.

Within a few years, however, Marx came to believe that a misunderstood genius such as himself might well participate in public life by dashing off protests and proclamations from the solitude of his desk. To everything there was a season: a time to rend, and a time to sew; a time of war, and a time of peace. Or, to mix references, why imitate the action of the tiger when the blast of war has fallen silent?

Hence the striking contrast between his sardonic swipe at Bartels and the autobiographical preface to *A Contribution to the Critique of Political Economy* (1859), where he confessed that the closure of the *Rheinische Zeitung* in 1843 had given him a longed-for opportunity 'to withdraw from the public stage into the study', which he 'eagerly seized'. That preface was written during a far longer withdrawal from public business – an abstinence which he showed no great desire to break, even though German newspapers sometimes chided him for inactivity. In 1857 a group of New York revolutionaries wrote begging him to resurrect the old Communist League in London; he took more than a year to answer, and then only to point out that 'since 1852 I had not been associated with *any* association and was firmly convinced that my theoretical studies were of greater use to the working class than my meddling

with associations which had now had their day on the Continent'.
As he told Ferdinand Freiligrath in February 1860, 'whereas you
are a *poet*, I am a *critic* and for me the experiences of 1849–52 were
quite enough. The "League", like the *société des saisons* in Paris and
a hundred other societies, was simply an episode in the history of
a party that is everywhere springing up naturally out of the soil of
modern society.' This organic metaphor is a most apt description
of how the International Working Men's Association emerged
into the daylight, four years later.

It seems almost oxymoronic that an organisation rejoicing in
the name 'International' could be started in England, where
insularity has long been not so much a geographical fluke as a
way of life and generations of schoolchildren have learned to
chant the Shakespearean cadences about this scepter'd isle, this
other Eden:

> This precious stone set in the silver sea,
> Which serves it in the office of a wall,
> Or as a moat defensive to a house,
> Against the envy of less happier lands,
> This blessed plot, this earth, this realm, this England . . .

When the English talk about 'Europe' or 'the Continent' they do
not include their own country: they are referring to Abroad, a
strange and savage place where the natives piss on your shoes and
eat garlic in bed. One can visit Abroad, of course – and indeed
conquer it to create the largest empire ever known – but the
purpose of such expeditions, whether by Victorian gunboat-
diplomats or modern football hooligans, is to remind Johnny
Foreigner that he will always remain a lesser breed. After all,
which other nation can boast that it arose from the azure main at
heaven's command? The nineteenth-century humorist Douglas
Jerrold, friend of Dickens and contributor to *Punch* magazine, was
kidding on the level when he wrote, 'The best thing I know
between France and England is – the sea.' These quasi-jokes are

still a staple of English tabloid headlines today. The very thought of England can transform even intelligent people into babbling tosh-merchants. 'When you come back to England from any foreign country, you have immediately the sensation of breathing a different air,' George Orwell wrote in a famous and vastly overpraised essay. 'In the first few minutes dozens of small things conspire to give you this feeling. The beer is bitterer, the coins are heavier, the grass is greener . . .' Poor old Abroad: it can't even produce a decent lawn.

Alongside the history of bragging and xenophobia, however, there is another tradition – quieter but no less enduring – of English internationalism, particularly among trade unionists. One thinks of their campaigns against South African apartheid, or their refusal to produce goods for the Chilean dictatorship in the 1970s: time and again, at least some British workers have been willing to demonstrate an instinctive kinship with the oppressed. As the Chartist George Julian Harney said at the time of the 1847 Portuguese uprising, 'People are beginning to understand that foreign as well as domestic questions do affect them; that a blow struck at Liberty on the Tagus is an injury to the friends of Freedom on the Thames; that the success of Republicanism in France would be the doom of Tyranny in every other land; and the triumph of England's democratic Charter would be the salvation of the millions throughout Europe.' It would be easy to assume, as the ruling élite of the time did, that these friends of Freedom on the Thames existed only in Harney's imagination. Why else did England remain immune from the revolutionary epidemic that afflicted the rest of Europe in 1848? Harney's society of Fraternal Democrats – whose committee included refugees from France, Germany, Switzerland and Scandinavia – might hold meetings to discuss the stirring events on the Continent, but did ordinary British workers care two hoots about the struggle in far-away countries of which they knew nothing?

The answer was provided by the astonishing 'Haynau incident' of 1850 – which, by happy coincidence, did indeed take place right beside the Thames. Field Marshal Baron von Haynau was a brutal Austrian commander known as 'the Hyena' who had fully earned the sobriquet by torturing prisoners and flogging women while suppressing revolts in Italy and Hungary. In August 1850, as a respite from these exhausting duties, he took a short holiday in London, where his sightseeing itinerary included a tour of Barclay and Perkins's Brewery on the south bank of the river. Though George Julian Harney encouraged all friends of Freedom to protest at the visit he had little hope of success – and was as surprised as anyone by what happened next. As soon as the Hyena entered the brewery, a posse of draymen threw a bale of hay on his head and pelted him with manure. He then ran out into the street, where lightermen and coal-heavers joined the chase – ripping his clothes, yanking out great tufts of his moustaches and shouting 'Down with the Austrian butcher!' Haynau tried to hide in a dustbin at the George Inn on Bankside, but was soon routed out and pelted with more dung. By the time the police reached the pub, rowing him across the Thames to safety, the bedraggled and humiliated butcher was in no fit state to continue his holiday. Within hours, a new song could be heard in the streets of Southwark:

> Turn him out, turn him out, from our side of the Thames,
> Let him go to great Tories and high-titled dames.
> He may walk the West End and parade in his pride,
> But he'll not come back again near the 'George' in Bankside.

Harney's *Red Republican* newspaper saw the debagging of Haynau as proof of 'the progress of the working classes in political knowledge, their uncorrupted love of justice, and their intense hatred of tyranny and cruelty'. A celebratory rally in the Farringdon Hall, at which Engels spoke, was so oversubscribed that hundreds had to be turned away. Letters of congratulation arrived from workers' associations as far afield as Paris and New York. Even Palmerston was secretly amused, reckoning that the Field

Marshal could only be improved by a sip of his own medicine. But conservative newspapers such as the *Quarterly Review* found nothing to laugh at: the riotous scenes in Bankside were a most alarming 'indication of foreign influence even amongst our own people' – foreign influence being the standard mid-century euphemism for the dread virus of socialism.

The *Quarterly Review* needn't have worried; not yet, anyway. For the next ten years the spirit of Bankside was invisible, as the few socialist groups in Britain – the Communist League, the Chartists, the Fraternal Democrats – either died or fell asleep. It was not until about 1860 that the proletariat began to wake from its long doze. As the historian Eric Hobsbawm has remarked, this revival manifested itself in 'a curious amalgam of political and industrial action, of various kinds of radicalism from the democratic to the anarchist, of class struggles, class alliances and government or capitalist concessions. But above all it was *international*, not merely because, like the revival of liberalism, it occurred simultaneously in various countries, but because it was inseparable from the international solidarity of the working classes.'

The London Trades Council, founded in 1860, was behind much of this activity. It organised a demonstration to welcome the Italian liberator Giuseppe Garibaldi (who drew a crowd of about 50,000), and in March 1863 it held a public meeting at St James's Hall to pledge support for Abraham Lincoln's fight against slavery in the American Civil War. Marx, who made a rare journey into town for the occasion, was pleased to note that 'the working men themselves spoke *very well indeed*, without a trace of bourgeois rhetoric'. But one shouldn't overlook the unwitting contribution of Napoleon III, who paid for a delegation of French workers to visit London during the Exhibition of 1862, thus giving them the chance to establish contact with men such as George Odger, secretary of the Trades Council. When several of these representatives returned to London for a rally in July 1863 to mark the Polish insurrection, Odger wrote an 'Address to the Workmen of France from the Working Men of England', proposing that they

should formalise their cross-Channel solidarity. Yet another
meeting was called – this time at the cavernous St Martin's Hall
in Covent Garden, on 28 September 1864 – to consecrate their
new union in the International Working Men's Association.

Note the title: if this was to be more than merely an Anglo-
French entente they would need at least a few token figures from
elsewhere. Which is why, one September morning in 1864, a
young Frenchman named Victor Le Lubez knocked on the door
of 1 Modena Villas and asked if Karl Marx would suggest the
name of someone to speak on behalf of the 'German workers'.
Marx himself was far too bourgeois to be eligible so he
recommended the émigré tailor Johann Georg Eccarius, an old
ally from the Communist League. One wonders why Le Lubez
and Odger hadn't thought of Eccarius already, since he was well
known to them through his involvement in the London Trades
Council. Perhaps familiarity had bred contempt, as it usually did
with Eccarius: his gauche and humourless manner antagonised
almost all who had to work with him, and they may have hoped
that Marx could recruit a rather more inspiring proletarian orator
for this important assembly.

It is worth pausing for a moment to consider what Marx's
patronage of Eccarius tells us about his own character. According
to the legend tirelessly peddled by his critics, Marx was an
incorrigible snob who despised working-class socialists, regarding
them as dolts and asses who had acquired ideas above their station.
The biographer Robert Payne, for example, refers to 'Marx's
contempt for humanity and especially for that section of it which
he called the proletariat'. Even a sophisticated Marxologist such
as Professor Shlomo Avineri can write that 'Marx's sceptical view
of the proletariat's ability to conceive its own goals and realise
them without outside intellectual help has often been documented.
It suits his remark that revolutions never start with the "masses"
but originate in élite groups.' Where have these views and remarks
been documented? You will search the works of Marx – and
indeed the footnotes of Avineri – in vain. Avineri mentions the

'snubbing' of Wilhelm Weitling: as we have seen, however, Marx was in fact remarkably generous to Weitling, arguing that one shouldn't be too beastly to a poor tailor who had genuinely suffered for his beliefs, and what caused their eventual rift was not lordly disdain for the underclass but terminal exasperation at the political and religious delusions of an insufferable egomaniac. Had Weitling been a middle-class intellectual, Marx would have treated him far more savagely.

Which brings us to Avineri's second exhibit. 'Even one of his most loyal followers, George Eccarius, also a tailor by trade, came in for a generous measure of unearned contempt from his master and teacher.' Once again no sources are cited: clearly Marx's lofty scorn for tailors, cobblers and other pond-life is so universally accepted as to need no verification.

This is the exact opposite of the truth. It was Marx who gave Eccarius his first break by publishing his study of 'Tailoring in London' in the short-lived London journal *NRZ Revue*. 'The author of this article,' Marx informed readers, 'is himself a *worker* in one of London's tailoring shops. We ask the German bourgeoisie how many authors it numbers capable of grasping the real movement in a similar manner? . . . The reader will note how here, instead of the sentimental, moral and psychological criticism employed against existing conditions by Weitling and other workers who engage in authorship, a purely materialist understanding and a freer one, unspoilt by sentimental whims, confronts bourgeois society and its movement.'

No sign there of contempt, unearned or otherwise. Throughout the darkest days of the 1850s Marx remained attentive and sympathetic, helping Eccarius place articles in German-language newspapers abroad in the hope of rescuing him from the treadmill of tailoring from five in the morning until eight in the evening. 'If any money is forthcoming, I would suggest that Eccarius get some first so that he doesn't have to spend all day tailoring,' he advised a journalistic comrade in Washington. 'Do try and see that he gets *something*, if at all possible.' However dire his own financial straits might be, he insisted that Eccarius's needs should take priority.

When Eccarius went down with consumption, in February 1859, Marx described it as 'the most tragic thing I have yet experienced here in London'. A few months later he noted sadly that Eccarius 'is again going to pieces in his sweatshop', and asked if Engels could send the poor chap a few bottles of port to sustain him. In 1860, forced by ill health to give up tailoring for a while, Eccarius was installed in lodgings rented at Marx's own expense and fixed up with regular work for the American press at $3 an article. When three of Eccarius's children died during the scarlet-fever epidemic of 1862, it was the poverty-stricken Marx who organised an appeal fund to cover the funeral expenses. Finally, when invited to nominate a speaker for the historic public meeting in September 1864, he again pressed the claims of his old friend. Eccarius put on a 'splendid performance', Marx reported to Engels afterwards, adding that he himself had been happy to remain mute on the platform. And yet, even now, many authors continue to repeat the old nonsense about Marx's mean-spirited and snooty disdain for mere tailors.

In fact, it was the presence of so many genuine workers – and the refreshing lack of preening middle-class dilettantes – that attracted him to the International's inaugural rally, persuading him 'to waive my usual standing rule to decline any such invitations'. Although he came to St Martin's Hall only as a silent observer, by the end of the evening he had been co-opted on to the General Council.

Now there seems to be a slight paradox here. Marx himself was indisputably a bourgeois intellectual. By joining the Council was he not in danger of diluting the proletarian purity which he so admired? To answer the question we need to look more closely at the composition of the International. The General Council consisted of two Germans (Marx and Eccarius), two Italians, three Frenchmen and twenty-seven Englishmen – almost all of them working class. It was a muddled *mélange*: English trade unionists who cared passionately about the right to free collective bargaining but had no interest in socialist revolution; French Proudhonists who dreamed of utopia but disliked trade unions; plus a few republicans, disciples of Mazzini and campaigners for Polish freedom. They disagreed about almost everything – and particularly about what role, if any, the enlightened middle classes should be allowed to play in the International. In a letter to Engels two years after its foundation, Marx reported an all-too-typical contretemps:

> By way of demonstration against the French monsieurs – who wanted to exclude everyone except '*travailleurs manuels*', in the first instance from membership of the International Association, or at least from eligibility for election as delegate to the congress – the English yesterday proposed *me* as President of the General Council. I declared that under *no* circumstances could I accept such a thing, and proposed Odger [the English trade union leader] in my turn, who was then in fact re-elected, although some people voted for me despite my declaration.

The minute-book for this meeting records that Marx 'thought himself incapacitated because he was a head worker and not a hand worker', but it is not quite as simple as that. (His desire to get on with writing *Capital* may have exerted a stronger tug at the sleeve.) A few years later, when a doctor called Sexton was proposed for membership, there were the usual mutterings about 'whether it was desirable to add professional men to the Council'; according to the minutes, however, 'Citizen Marx did not think there was anything to fear from the admission of professional men while the great majority of the Council was composed of workers.' In 1872, when there were problems with various crackpot American sects infiltrating the International, it was Marx himself who proposed – successfully – that no new section should be allowed to affiliate unless at least two-thirds of its members were wage labourers.

In short, while accepting that most office-holders and members must be working class, Marx was unembarrassed by his own lack of proletarian credentials: men such as himself still had much to offer the association as long as they didn't pull rank or hog the limelight. Engels followed this example, though as an affluent capitalist he was understandably more reluctant to impose himself. After selling his stake in the family firm and moving down to London in 1870, he accepted a seat on the General Council almost at once but declined the office of treasurer. 'Citizen Engels objected that none but working men ought to be appointed to have anything to do [with] the finances,' the minutes record. 'Citizen Marx did not consider the objection tenable: an ex-commercial man was the best for the office.' Engels persisted with his refusal – and was probably right to do so. As the Marxian scholar Hal Draper has pointed out, handling money was the touchiest job in a workers' association, for charges of financial irregularity were routine ploys whenever political conflict started; and a Johnny-come-lately businessman from Manchester would have been an obvious target for any 'French monsieurs' who wanted to stir up trouble.

Marx may have preferred to work behind the scenes, but he worked exceptionally hard all the same: without his efforts the International would probably have disintegrated within a year. The Council met every Tuesday at its shabby HQ in Greek Street, Soho – on the site which, almost exactly a century later, was to become the Establishment night-club, where satirists such as Lenny Bruce and Peter Cook used rather different techniques to undermine prevailing orthodoxy. The minute-books show that he was happy to take on his share of the donkey-work. ('Citizens Fox, Marx and Cremer were deputed to attend the Compositors' Society . . . Citizen Marx proposed, Citizen Cremer seconded, that the Central Council thank Citizen Cottam for his generous gift . . . Citizen Marx stated that societies in Basle and Zurich had joined the Association . . . Citizen Marx reported that he had received £3 from Germany for members' cards, which he paid to the Financial Secretary. . .') His influence was apparent from the outset. The initial item of business at the Council's very first meeting, on 5 October 1864, was a proposal by Marx that William Randal Cremer of the London Trades Council should be appointed secretary. ('Mr Cremer was unanimously elected.') Later that evening Marx was elected to a subcommittee whose task was to draw up rules and principles of the new Association.

So far so good. But then Marx fell ill, thus missing the next two meetings. He was roused from his sick-bed on 18 October by an urgent letter from Eccarius, who warned that if he didn't come to the General Council that evening a hopelessly insipid and confused statement of aims would be adopted in his absence. Marx staggered down to Greek Street and listened aghast as the worthy Le Lubez read out 'a fearfully cliché-ridden, badly written and totally unpolished preamble pretending to be a declaration of principles, with Mazzini showing through the whole thing from beneath a crust of the most insubstantial scraps of French socialism'. After long debate, Eccarius proposed that this un-appetising menu be sent back to the subcommittee for further editing, cunningly forestalling any suspicion of a *coup* by promising that its 'sentiments' would remain unchanged.

This was the opportunity Marx needed. Putting on his most innocent expression, he suggested that the subcommittee meet two days later at his house, which offered rather more comfort (and a better stocked cellar) than the poky little room in Greek Street. When the team assembled *chez* Marx, he then spun out a discussion about the rules at such interminable length that by one in the morning they had still not even begun their 'editing' of the preamble. How were they to have it ready in time for the next gathering of the General Council five days later? His weary colleagues, yawning fit to bust, gratefully accepted Marx's suggestion that he should try to cobble something together himself. All the draft papers were left in his hands, and they departed to their beds.

'I could see that it was impossible to make anything out of the stuff,' he told Engels. 'In order to justify the extremely peculiar way in which I intended to edit the sentiments that had already been "carried", I wrote *An Address to the Working Classes* (which was not in the original plan: a sort of review of the adventures of the working class since 1845); on the pretext that all the necessary facts were contained in this "Address" and that we ought not to repeat the same things three times over, I altered the whole preamble, threw out the *déclaration des principes* and finally replaced the forty rules by ten.' As a sop to the more pious and less revolutionary members, he threw in a few references to truth, morality, duty and justice, and avoided the belligerent rhetorical flourishes that had so enlivened the *Communist Manifesto*. As he explained to Engels, 'It will take time before the revival of the movement allows the old boldness of language to be used. We must be *fortiter in re, suaviter in modo*.' Which, being translated from the Latin, essentially means: speak softly and carry a big stick.

Despite the years of seclusion, Marx had lost none of his old procedural guile. At its meeting of 1 November, partly at his suggestion, the General Council co-opted several new members. They included Karl Pfänder, the Communist League veteran who had once examined Wilhelm Liebknecht's skull; Hermann Jung, a Swiss watchmaker; Eugène Dupont, a French musical-instrument maker; and Friedrich Lessner, the tailor who had rushed the manuscript of the *Communist Manifesto* to the printers in 1848. All were stalwart supporters of Marx – and he needed all the support he could get, since some of the English members were none too happy with his new text. One of the milder suggestions, as the minutes record, was that 'some explanation should be given (in the form of a footnote) of the terms "nitrogen" and "carbon" '. (Marx thought this quite unnecessary. 'We need hardly remind the reader,' he commented wearily in the footnote, 'that, apart from the elements of water and certain inorganic substances, carbon and nitrogen form the raw materials of human food.') A more hostile complaint came from a printer, William Worley, who had made his opinions clear at the previous meeting by objecting to the statement that 'the capitalist was opposed to the labourer'. This time, his reformist conscience was outraged by Marx's description of capitalists as 'profitmongers'. By eleven votes to ten, the council agreed that the inflammatory word be erased. The address was then passed *nem. con.*

The unanimous acceptance of this 'review of the adventures of the working class' is a tribute to Marx's skill in judging how far he could go. There were no revolutionary predictions, no spectres or hobgoblins stalking Europe – though he did his best to make the reader's flesh creep with a description of British industry as a vampire which could survive only by sucking the blood of children. Mostly, he allowed the facts to speak for themselves, larding the document with official statistics plagiarised from his own work in progress, *Capital*, to justify his claim that 'the misery of the working masses has not diminished from 1848 to 1864'. But, as ever, his attempt to imagine an alternative was as formless if sweet as a bowl of blancmange: 'Like slave labour, like serf labour, hired labour is but a transitory and inferior form, destined to disappear before associated labour plying its toil with a willing hand, a ready mind and a joyous heart.'

The address ended with the words 'Proletarians of all countries, Unite!'; the equally familiar phrase encouraging them to throw off their chains was tactfully omitted. Even so, one can't help wondering how closely his colleagues scrutinised the text before approving it. 'The lords of land and the lords of capital will always use their political privileges for the defence and per-petuation of their economical monopolies,' he announced in the final pages. 'To conquer political power has therefore become the great duty of the working classes.' Such a notion was anathema to many of the English representatives on the General Council, who thought that the great duty of the working classes was to form trade unions which could bargain for better pay and conditions, while leaving politics to Members of Parliament. This was certainly the view of the impeccably moderate general secretary, William Randal Cremer, who later became a Liberal

MP and ended his career as a knight of the realm. The fact that even he voted for the address tells us much about Marx's powers of persuasion. As old Communist Leaguers such as Pfänder and Lessner knew, Marx's intimidating presence – his dark eyes, his slashing wit, his formidable analytical brain – would always dominate any committee. Scarcely a month after sitting silently on the stage at St Martin's Hall, he was already taking charge.

But mere force of personality was not enough to quell the feuds and animosities that inevitably characterised such as incongruous hybrid as the International. Even the small French contingent on the General Council was itself split into two irreconcilable factions of republicans and Proudhonists. The republicans, represented by Le Lubez, were essentially middle-class radicals – red hot for *liberté, égalité* and *fraternité* but rather less excited by arguments about industry or property. Proudhon's earnest disciples, led by the engraver Henri Louis Tolain, regarded republics and governments as centralised tyrannies that were inimical to the interests of the small shopkeepers and artisans whose cause they championed; all they wanted was a network of mutual-credit societies and small-scale co-operatives. Another Proudhonist, who joined the General Council in 1866, was the young medical student Paul Lafargue, later to become the husband of Laura Marx. His first encounters with his future father-in-law were unpromising. 'That damned boy Lafargue pesters me with his Proudhonism,' Karl complained to Laura, 'and will not rest, it seems, until I have administered to him a sound cudgelling.' After one of Lafargue's many speeches declaring nations and nationalities to be the purest moonshine, Marx raised a laugh among his English colleagues by pointing out that 'our friend Lafargue, and others who had abolished nationalities, had addressed us in "French", i.e. in a language which nine-tenths of the audience did not understand'. He added mischievously that by denying the existence of nationalities the young zealot 'seemed quite unconsciously to imply their absorption by the model French nation'.

If the doughty English trade unionists were incredulously amused by these Gallic squabbles, they were downright astonished to learn that the great Mazzini – a heroic figure in London – was regarded by the Germans and French as a posturing ninny whose passion for national liberation had quite eclipsed any awareness of the central importance of class. 'The position is difficult now,' Marx admitted after another bruising session at Greek Street, 'because one must oppose the silly Italianism of the English, on the one hand, and the mistaken polemic of the French, on the other.'

It was a time-consuming business. In a letter to Engels of March 1865 he described a fairly typical week's work. Tuesday evening was given over to the General Council, at which Tolain and Le Lubez bickered until midnight, after which he had to adjourn to a nearby pub and sign 200 membership cards. The next day he attended a meeting at St Martin's Hall to mark the anniversary of the Polish insurrection. On Saturday and Monday there were subcommittee meetings devoted to 'the French question', both of which raged on until one in the morning. And so to Tuesday, when another stormy session of the General Council 'left the English in particular with the impression that the Frenchmen stand really in need of a Bonaparte!' In between all these meetings, there were 'people dashing this way and that to see me' in connection with a conference on household suffrage which was to be held the following weekend. 'What a waste of time!' he groaned.

Engels thought so too. After Marx's death he said that 'Moor's life without the International would be a diamond ring with the diamond broken out', but at first he simply couldn't understand why his friend wished to spend hours suffering in dingy Soho back rooms when he could be at his desk in Hampstead writing *Capital*. 'I have always half-expected that the naïve *fraternité* in the International Association would not last long,' he commented smugly in 1865, after another bout of internecine squabbling among the French. 'It will pass through a lot more such phases and will take up a great deal of your time.' Until he retired to London in 1870 Engels played no part in the association.

By 1865 Marx was the *de facto* leader of the International, though his official title was 'corresponding secretary for Germany'. Even this was a misnomer: the death of Lassalle left him with only a couple of friends in the whole of Germany – Wilhelm Liebknecht and the gynaecologist Ludwig Kugelmann – and most of his 'corresponding' took the form of sniggers about the alleged homosexuality of Lassalle's successor, Johann Baptist von Schweitzer, plus a few dismissive remarks about the appalling political backwardness of the Teutonic race. 'There is *nothing* I can do in Prussia at the moment,' he wrote to Dr Kugelmann. 'I prefer my agitation here through the "International Association" a hundred times. The effect on the English proletariat is direct and of the greatest importance. We are now stirring the General Suffrage Question here, which is, naturally, of quite different significance here than in Prussia.'

Extending the franchise was the dominant parliamentary issue of the moment – though it should be added that the various proposals for reform put forward by Tories and Whigs in the mid-1860s owed less to high principle than to the jostle for party advantage. There were debates galore, which today seem as remote and incomprehensible as the Schleswig-Holstein question, about the voting rights of 'copyholders', '£6 ratepayers' and '£50 tenants-at-will'. But amid all the arcane arguments over fancy franchises and plural voting, one point was accepted by all peers and MPs: there must be some sort of property qualification to prevent the great unwashed from having any say in the nation's affairs. 'What I fear,' Walter Bagehot wrote in his *English Constitution*, 'is that both our political parties will bid for the support of the working man; that both of them will promise to do as he likes . . .' Even the National Reform Union, a supposedly radical pressure group, desired only the enfranchisement of householders and ratepaying lodgers.

In the spring of 1865, after a packed meeting at St Martin's

Hall, a Reform League was founded to campaign for universal manhood suffrage. (The possibility that women might be either willing or able to vote was, apparently, too far-fetched to merit consideration.) Marx and his colleagues from the International took charge: 'The whole leadership is in our hands,' he revealed triumphantly to Engels. For the next year or so he threw himself into the crusade with gusto while also attending to the International, the manuscript of *Capital*, the demands of his family and creditors – and, of course, those blossoming boils on his bum, which were more prolific than ever. He hacked away at them with a cut-throat razor, watching with vicious satisfaction as the bad blood spurted over the carpet. Sometimes, having staggered to bed at 4 a.m. several nights running, he felt 'infernally harassed' and wished he had never emerged from hibernation.

Was the game worth so many late-night candles? He convinced himself that it was. 'If we succeed in re-electrifying the political movement of the English working class,' he wrote after launching the Reform League, 'our Association will already have done more for the European working class, without making any fuss, than was possible in any other way. And there is every prospect of success.' Not so. Reformist trade union leaders such as Cremer and Odger soon made concessions, deciding that they would be quite content with household suffrage rather than one man one vote. And that, more or less, is what they got. In the summer of 1867, Parliament approved Disraeli's Reform Bill, which lowered the property qualification for county voters and extended the franchise to all urban householders – thus doubling the size of the electorate. But the vast majority of the working population remained as voteless as ever.

The International, too, never quite lived up to Marx's hyperbole. There were some early successes, notably in sabotaging attempts by English employers to recruit foreign workers as strikebreakers, and the ensuing notoriety persuaded several small craft societies to affiliate – among them such exotic bodies as the Amalgamated Cordwainers of Darlington, the Hand-in-Hand

Society of Coopers, the West-End Cabinet Makers, the Day-Working Bookbinders, the English Journeymen Hairdressers, the Elastic Web Weavers' Society and the Cigar Makers. But the big industrial unions stayed aloof. William Allen, general secretary of the Amalgamated Society of Engineers, refused even to meet a deputation from the International. More galling still was the failure to enrol the London Trades Council, even though its secretary, George Odger, was also president of the International. By the time of the Association's first pan-European Congress, held in Geneva during the summer of 1866, the total number of members in affiliated societies was 25,173 – by no means negligible, but hardly proof that the English proletariat had been 're-electrified'. If the International was to expand any further it would have to live up to its name and broaden its horizons far beyond the Cordwainers of Darlington.

Marx himself missed the Geneva Congress, yet still managed to dominate the proceedings. When the French Proudhonists issued their well-rehearsed protest against middle-class socialists ('all men who have the duty of representing working-class groups should be workers'), William Randal Cremer defended the record of the few non-manual workers on the General Council. 'Among those members I will mention one only, Citizen Marx, who has devoted his life to the triumph of the working classes.' The baton was then taken up by James Carter of the Journeymen Hairdressers:

> Citizen Marx has just been mentioned; he has perfectly understood the importance of this first congress, where there should be only working-class delegates; therefore he refused the delegateship he was offered in the General Council. But this is not the reason to prevent him or anyone else from coming into our midst; on the contrary, men who devote themselves completely to the proletarian cause are too rare for us to push them aside. The middle class only triumphed when, rich and powerful as it was in numbers, it allied itself with men of science . . .

After this barber-shop testimonial even the leader of the Proudhon faction, Henri Tolain, felt obliged to congratulate the absent hero. 'As a worker, I thank Citizen Marx for not accepting the delegateship offered him. In doing that, Citizen Marx showed that workers' congresses should be made up only of manual workers.' Citizen Marx had not intended to show anything of the kind, and there is no evidence that he stayed away from Geneva to avoid offending proletarian sensibilities. A more likely explanation is that he didn't wish to endure tedious harangues from the French exclusionists when he could have a few days' uninterrupted work on *Capital*.

A year earlier he had told Engels that the draft required only a few 'finishing touches', which would be done by September 1865. 'I am working like a horse at the moment.' His friends had heard many such hopeful forecasts over the years, but this time he really did seem to be in the final furlongs – even if the spavined old nag was proceeding at a limping trot rather than full gallop. Through the summer of 1865 he was vomiting every day ('in consequence of the hot weather and related biliousness'), and a sudden influx of house guests provided further unwelcome distraction. Jenny's buffoonish brother, Edgar von Westphalen, came to stay for six months, drinking the wine cellar dry and 'pondering the needs of his stomach from morn till night'; other visitors included Marx's brother-in-law from South Africa, a niece from Maastricht and the Freiligrath family. This was the price he paid for moving to a house with spare rooms, but it was a price he could ill afford. 'For two months I have been living solely on the pawnshop,' he fretted. 'A queue of creditors has been hammering on my door, becoming more and more unendurable every day.' And yet, at the still point in the centre of this whirlwind, his masterpiece was nearing completion. By the end of 1865 *Capital* was a manuscript of 1,200 pages, a baroque mess of ink-blots and crossings-out and squiggles. On New Year's Day 1866 he sat down to make a fair copy and polish the style – 'licking the infant clean after long birth pangs'. But then the carbuncles returned. On doctor's orders he was banished to Margate for a month, where he did little except bathe in the sea, swallow arsenic three times a day and feel thoroughly sorry for himself. 'I can sing with the Miller of the Dee: "I care for nobody and nobody cares for me".' At the end of his sea cure the carbuncles had gone – only to be replaced by rheumatism and toothache. Then the old liver trouble returned for an encore. Even on days when he was fit to work some new misfortune usually descended, as when his stationer refused to supply any more paper until the last batch had been paid for.

With exquisitely bad timing, Paul Lafargue chose this un-propitious moment to ask for the hand of the twenty-year-old Laura Marx in marriage. The Creole medical student, having met Marx through the International, had transferred his attention to the old man's green-eyed daughter and begun wooing her with an enthusiasm which Karl thought most indecorous. Lafargue was suspect anyway, not only for Proudhonist tendencies but also because of his exotic Franco-Spanish-Indian-African ancestry, which to his prospective father-in-law suggested a certain genetic flightiness. As soon as writing paper could be found Marx sent the overzealous suitor a letter of which any Victorian paterfamilias would have been proud.

My dear Lafargue,

Allow me to make the following observations:

1. If you wish to continue your relations with my daughter, you will have to give up your present manner of 'courting'. You know full well that no engagement has been entered into, that as yet everything is undecided. And even if she were formally betrothed to you, you should not forget that this is a matter of long duration. The practice of excessive intimacy is especially inappropriate since the two lovers will be living at the same place for a necessarily prolonged period of severe testing and purgatory ... To my mind, true love expresses itself in reticence, modesty and even the shyness of the lover towards his object of veneration, and certainly not in giving free rein to

one's passion and in premature demonstrations of familiarity. If you should urge your Creole temperament in your defence, it is my duty to interpose my sound reason between your temperament and my daughter. If in her presence you are incapable of loving her in a manner in keeping with the London latitude, you will have to resign yourself to loving her from a distance.

In fact it was Marx and not Lafargue who attributed this ardour – and almost everything else – to the 'Creole temperament'. As late as November 1882 he was still going on about it, telling Engels that 'Lafargue has the blemish customarily found in the negro tribe – *no sense of shame*, by which I mean shame about making a fool of oneself.'

Before consenting to the marriage, Marx required a full account of the young man's prospects. 'You know that I have sacrificed my whole fortune to the revolutionary struggle,' he wrote to Lafargue. 'I do not regret it. Quite the contrary. If I had to live my life over again, I would do the same. I would not marry, however. As far as it lies within my power, I wish to save my daughter from the reefs on which her mother's life was wrecked ... You must have achieved something in life before thinking of marriage, and a long period of testing is required of you and Laura.' Not that long, as it turned out: Laura Marx's engagement to Paul Lafargue was announced in September 1866, only a month after Marx dispatched his letter, and they were married in St Pancras register office on 2 April 1868. Her father, rather unromantically, described the union as 'a great relief for the entire household, since Lafargue is as good as living with us, which perceptibly increases expenses'. At the wedding lunch Engels cracked so many jokes about the bride that she burst into tears.

Lacking the vivacity of Jennychen and Eleanor, Laura never enjoyed being the centre of attention. ('As I am in the habit of keeping in the background, I am very apt to be overlooked and forgotten.') Of all the Marx girls she was probably the most like Jenny Marx: while her sisters dreamed of careers on the stage, Laura's only ambition was to be a good wife. Her first child, Charles Etienne (nicknamed 'Schnapps'), was born on 1 January 1869, almost exactly nine months after the wedding, followed over the next two years by a daughter and another son. All died in infancy. There was, it seemed, no escaping those reefs on which her mother's life had been wrecked. 'In all these struggles we women have the harder part to bear,' Jenny Marx wrote, mourning the loss of her grandchildren, 'because it is the lesser one. A man draws strength from his struggle with the world outside, and is invigorated by the sight of the enemy, be their number legion. We remain sitting at home, darning socks.'

10

The Shaggy Dog

The house at 1 Modena Villas has long since crumbled into dust, but Paul Lafargue left an evocative description of the chaotic upstairs den in which Marx worked. It should gladden the hearts of untidy authors everywhere:

> Opposite the window and on either side of the fireplace the walls were lined with bookcases filled with books and stacked up to the ceiling with newspapers and manuscripts. Opposite the fireplace on one side of the window were two tables piled up with papers, books and newspapers; in the middle of the room, well in the light, stood a small, plain desk (three foot by two) and a wooden armchair; between the armchair and the bookcase, opposite the window, was a leather sofa on which Marx used to lie down for a rest from time to time. On the mantelpiece were more books, cigars, matches, tobacco boxes, paperweights and photographs of Marx's daughters and wife, Wilhelm Wolff and Friedrich Engels . . .
>
> He never allowed anybody to put his books or papers in order – or rather in disorder. The disorder in which they lay was only apparent, everything was really in its intended place so that it was easy for him to lay his hand on the book or notebook he needed. Even during conversations he often paused to show in the book a quotation or figure he had just mentioned. He and his study were one: the books and papers in it were as much under his control as his own limbs.

This is almost identical to the report written by a Prussian police spy twelve years earlier, describing the disorderly front room in Dean Street, Soho – 'manuscripts, books and newspapers, as well as the children's toys, and rags and tatters of his wife's sewing basket, several cups with broken rims, knives, forks, lamps, an inkpot, tumblers, Dutch clay pipes, tobacco ash – in a word, everything topsy-turvy.' His working habits hadn't changed at all: he still got through hundreds of matches relighting the pipes and cigars that he had forgotten to finish. '*Capital*,' he told Lafargue, 'will not even pay for the cigars I smoked writing it.'

His inability to afford decent Havanas inspired a bizarre flight of economic fancy when he noticed a tobacconist in Holborn selling cigars with the slogan 'the more you smoke the more you save', which were even cheaper and nastier than his usual cut-price cheroots. By switching to the new brand, he told friends, he would save one shilling and sixpence a box, and consequently if he forced himself to smoke enough of them he might one day be able to live on his 'savings'. The theory was tested with such lung-rasping commitment that eventually the family doctor had to intervene, ordering the wheezing patient to find some other way of enriching himself.

Marx was plagued by his usual physical ailments through the winter of 1866–7 but even they could no longer thwart his determination to finish Volume One of *Capital*. He wrote the last few pages of Volume One standing at his desk when an eruption of boils around the rump made sitting too painful. (Arsenic, the usual anaesthetic, 'dulls my mind too much and I needed to keep my wits about me'.) Engels's experienced eye immediately spotted certain passages in the text 'where the carbuncles have left their mark', and Marx agreed that the fever in his groin might have given the prose a rather livid hue. 'At all events, I hope the bourgeoisie will remember my carbuncles until their dying day,' he cursed. 'What swine they are!'

Nevertheless, after twenty years of gestation the egg was finally hatched. 'I had resolved not to write to you until I could announce completion of the book,' he told Engels on 2 April 1867, 'which is now the case.' A week later he set off for Hamburg to deliver the manuscript to Meissner, the publisher, after first sending the inevitable begging letter to Engels so that he could reclaim his clothes and watch from the pawnbroker. 'I can also hardly leave my family in their present situation, they being *sans sou* and the creditors becoming more brazen each day. Finally, before I forget, all the money that I could afford to spend on Laura's champagne treatment has gone the way of all flesh. She now needs red wine, of better quality than I can command. *Voilà la situation.*' As ever, Engels was equal to *la situation*: seven five-pound notes were posted to London forthwith.

Having seen off both his carbuncles and his *Capital*, Marx left England feeling 'as voraciously fit as 500 hogs': even a ghastly fifty-two-hour voyage buffeted by gales and rain couldn't dampen his high spirits. 'With all that riff-raff being seasick and falling about to left and right of us, it would all have become *ennuyant* in time, if a certain nucleus had not held firm,' he reported. The nucleus included a London cattle-dealer ('a true John Bull, bovine in every respect'), a German explorer who had been roaming eastern Peru for fifteen years, and a deeply pious old lady with a Hanoverian accent. 'What was keeping this beautiful creature so spellbound in these inimical circumstances? Why did she not withdraw to the ladies' chamber? Our savage German was regaling us with an enthusiastic account of the sexual depravities of savages.'

Marx delivered his precious cargo to Meissner, who sent it off for typesetting with a view to publication by the end of May. For the next month the elated author lodged with Dr Ludwig Kugelmann in Hanover so that he could be on hand to check the proof-sheets. 'Kugelmann is a doctor of great eminence in his special field, which is gynaecology,' he wrote to Engels. 'Kugelmann is secondly a fanatical supporter (and for my taste excessively Westphalian in his admiration) of our ideas and the two of us personally. He sometimes bores me with his enthusiasm . . .' Though the two men hadn't met before, Kugelmann had been sending him fan mail for several years. He had a more comprehensive collection of the works of Marx and Engels than they did themselves: while staying in the house Marx came upon *The Holy Family*, which he hadn't seen since his own copy went astray soon after publication.

In spite of Kugelmann's suffocating adulation, Marx wrote, 'he *understands*, and he is a really *excellent man*, unaffected by qualms, capable of making sacrifices, and, most important of all, *convinced*. He has a charming little wife [Gertruda] and an eight-year-old daughter [Franziska] who is positively sweet.' Marx immediately awarded them nicknames, a sure sign of approval: Mrs K. became 'Madame la Comtesse' because of her social grace and insistence on good manners, while her husband was dubbed 'Wenzel' after two old Bohemian rulers of contrasting reputations. 'My father was very outspoken in his sympathies and antipathies,' Franziska Kugelmann recalled, 'and Marx would call him the good or the bad Wenzel according to his attitude.' If the doctor started discussing politics in the presence of Franziska and Madame la Comtesse, Marx would silence him at once: 'That is not for young ladies, we'll speak of that later.' Instead, the frolicsome sage entertained his hostess with jokes, literary anecdotes and folksongs. The only time he lost his temper was when a visitor asked who would clean the shoes under communism. 'You should,' Marx retorted crossly. Frau Kugelmann quickly saved the day with a tease, commenting that she couldn't imagine Herr Marx in a truly egalitarian society since his tastes and habits were so thoroughly aristocratic. 'Neither can I,' he agreed. 'These times will come, but we must be away by then.' He was immensely flattered when the Kugelmanns pointed out his resemblance to a bust of Zeus in their hall – the powerful head, the abundant hair, the Olympian brow, the authoritative yet kind expression.

It was not only the Kugelmanns who lionised Marx while he was in Hanover. 'The standing the two of us enjoy in Germany,' he wrote to Engels, 'particularly among the "educated" officials, is of an altogether different order from what we imagined. Thus e.g. the director of the statistical bureau here, Merkel, visited me and told me he had been studying questions of money for years to no avail, and I had immediately clarified the matter once and for all.' He was invited to dinner by the head of the local railway company, who thanked Dr Marx profusely for 'doing me such an honour'. More flattering still was the arrival of an emissary from Bismarck, who announced that the Chancellor wished 'to make use of you and your great talents in the interests of the German people'. Rudolf von Bennigsen, chairman of the right-wing National Liberal Party, turned up in person to pay his respects.

No wonder Marx was so chirpy. He was in excellent health, with no carbuncle daring to show its ugly face and not even a trace of liver trouble in spite of boozy dinner parties every night. The sleepless years of sickness, squalor and obscurity were consigned to the dustbin of history. 'I always had the feeling,' Engels wrote on 27 April, 'that that damn book, which you have been carrying for so long, was at the bottom of all your misfortune, and you would and could never extricate yourself until you had got it off your back.' A delay at the printers meant that he didn't receive the proofs until 5 May, his forty-ninth birthday; but even this inconvenience, which would usually have provoked foul temper for a day or two, couldn't cloud his sunny mood. 'I hope and confidently believe that in the space of a year I shall be made,' he predicted, 'in the sense that I shall be able to funda-mentally rectify my financial affairs and at last stand on my own feet again.' *Again?* There had never been a moment in his adult life when Marx didn't need hand-outs. As he admitted in a letter to Engels, 'Without you I would never have been able to bring the work to a conclusion, and I can assure you it always weighed like a nightmare on my conscience that you were allowing your fine energies to be squandered and to rust in commerce, chiefly for my sake, and, into the bargain, you had to share all my *petites misères* as well.' Only a few sentences later, however, angst and despondency began their nagging chorus once more. The publisher expected delivery of Volumes Two and Three before the end of the year; his creditors in London were waiting to pounce as soon as he returned; 'and then the torments of family life, the domestic conflicts, the constant harassment, instead of settling down to work refreshed and free of care'.

The torments of a middle-class Londoner are not quite the same as those of the truly destitute. His first request to Engels after returning to London was for several cases of claret and Rhenish wine, since 'my children are obliged to invite some other girls for dancing on 2 July, as they have been unable to invite anyone for the whole of this year, to respond to invitations, and are therefore about to lose caste'. Where once he had struggled to find a few pence for bread and newspapers, now his domestic necessities were those of a suburbanite anxious to keep up appearances. He was 'exceedingly vexed' to learn that the poet Freiligrath, having lost his managerial job with the London branch of a Swiss bank, now lived off the proceeds of a subscription fund raised by admirers in Britain, America and Germany which allowed him to entertain in grand style. The best cure for vexation was to send his children away for a summer holiday in Bordeaux (financed by Engels, of course) so that he could scribble without interruption at the proof-sheets of *Capital*. Early word of mouth among those who had glimpsed parts of the work led him to hope that on the morning after publication his name and fame would resound throughout Europe. Johann Georg Eccarius told friends that 'the Prophet Himself is just now having the quintessence of all wisdom published'.

After weeks of revising and correcting, Marx finished the last proof of Volume One in the early hours of 16 August and dashed off a heartfelt note of thanks to his sponsor. 'So, *this volume is finished*. I owe it to *you* alone that it was possible! Without your self-sacrifice for me I could not possibly have managed the immense labour demanded by the three volumes. I embrace you, full of thanks . . . *Salut*, my dear, valued friend.'

*

Exactly a century after its publication, the British Prime Minister Harold Wilson boasted that he had never read *Capital*. 'I only got as far as page two – that's where the footnote is nearly a page long. I felt that two sentences of main text and a page of footnotes were too much.' Wilson had a first-class degree in politics, philosophy and economics, but he guessed that his profession of ignorance would endear him to the educated middle classes – who, particularly in Britain and America, are often perversely proud of their refusal to engage with Marx. Hence the mad circular argument one hears from people who haven't ventured even as far as page two. '*Capital* is all hooey.' And how do you know it's hooey? 'Because it's not worth reading.'

A rather more sophisticated objection to the book, put by the philosopher Karl Popper, is that one cannot tell whether or not Marx was writing nonsense, since his 'iron laws' of capitalist development are no more than unconditional historical prophecies, as vague and slippery as the quatrains of Nostradamus. Unlike proper scientific hypotheses, they cannot be either proved or – the crucial Popperian test – falsified. 'Ordinary predictions in science are conditional,' Popper argues. 'They assert that certain changes (say, of the temperature of water in a kettle) will be accompanied by other changes (say, the boiling of the water).' Actually, it would be easy to subject Marx's economic assertions to a similar experiment by studying what has happened in practice during the past century or so. As capitalism matured, he predicted, we would see periodic recessions, an ever-growing dependence on technology and the growth of huge, quasi-monopolistic corporations, spreading their sticky tentacles all over the world in search of new markets to exploit. If none of this had happened, we might be forced to agree that the old boy was talking poppycock. The boom–bust cycles of Western economies in the twentieth century, like the globe-girdling dominance of Bill Gates's Microsoft, suggest otherwise.

Ah yes, critics say, but what about Marx's belief in the

'progressive immiseration' of the proletariat? Did he not forecast that capitalism's swelling prosperity would be achieved by an absolute reduction in the workers' wages and standard of living? Look at the working classes of today, with their cars and their satellite dishes: not very immiserated, are they? The economist Paul Samuelson has declared that Marx's entire *œuvre* can safely be ignored because the impoverishment of the workers 'simply never took place' – and, since Samuelson's textbooks have been the staple fare for generations of undergraduates in both Britain and America, this has become the received wisdom. But it is a myth, based on a misreading of Marx's 'General Law of Capitalist Accumulation' in chapter twenty-five of the first volume. 'Pauperism,' he writes, 'forms a condition of capitalist production, and of the capitalist development of wealth. It forms part of the incidental expenses of capitalist production: but capital usually knows how to transfer these from its own shoulders to those of the working class and the petty bourgeoisie.' In the context, however, he is referring not to the pauperisation of the entire proletariat but to the 'lowest sediment' of society – the unemployed, the ragged, the sick, the old, the widows and orphans. These are the 'incidental expenses' which must be paid by the working population and the petty bourgeoisie. Can anyone deny that such an underclass still exists? Another Jewish outcast once said that 'the poor ye have always with you', but no economist has yet suggested that the teachings of Jesus are entirely discredited by his forecast of perpetual immiseration.

What Marx did predict was that under capitalism there would be a *relative* – not an absolute – decline in wages. This is self-evidently true: few if any firms which enjoy a twenty per cent increase in surplus value will instantly hand over the loot to their workforce in the form of a twenty per cent pay rise. So labour lags further and further behind capital, however many microwave ovens the workers can afford. 'It follows therefore that in proportion as capital accumulates, the situation of the worker, *be his payment high or low*, must grow worse.' (My italics.)

Marx's definition of poverty, like Christ's, was as much spiritual as economic. What is a man profited if he shall gain the whole world and lose his own soul? Or, as Marx wrote in *Capital*, the means by which capitalism raises productivity

> distort the worker into a fragment of a man, they degrade him to the level of an appendage of a machine, they destroy the actual content of his labour by turning it into a torment; they alienate from him the intellectual potentialities of the labour process in the same proportion as science is incorporated in it as an independent power; they deform the conditions under which he works, subject him during the labour process to a despotism the more hateful for its meanness; they transform his lifetime into working time, and drag his wife and child beneath the wheels of the juggernaut of capital ... Accumulation of wealth at one pole is, therefore, at the same time accumulation of misery, the torment of labour, slavery, ignorance, brutalisation and moral degradation at the opposite pole.

That last sentence, taken alone, could be adduced as another prediction of absolute financial impoverishment for the workers, but only a halfwit – or an economics lecturer – could maintain this interpretation after reading the thunderous indictment that precedes it.

'It must be borne in mind,' admits Leszek Kolakowski, one of the most influential modern obituarists of Marxism, 'that material pauperisation was not a necessary premiss either of Marx's analysis of the dehumanisation caused by wage labour, or of his prediction of the inescapable ruin of capitalism.' Quite so. Yet Kolakowski then ignores his own advice by placing another lump of hard cheese in Karl Popper's old mousetrap. 'As an interpretation of economic phenomena,' he warns, 'Marx's theory of value does not meet the normal requirements of a scientific hypothesis, especially that of falsifiability.' Well, of course it doesn't: no litmus paper or electron microscope or computer program can discern the presence of such intangibles as 'aliena-tion' and 'moral degradation'.

Capital is not really a scientific hypothesis, nor even an economic treatise, though zealots on both sides of the argument have persisted in regarding it thus. The author himself was quite clear about his intentions. 'Now, regarding my work, I will tell you the plain truth about it,' Marx wrote to Engels on 31 July 1865. 'There are three more chapters to be written to complete the theoretical part . . . But I cannot bring myself to send anything off until I have the whole thing in front of me. Whatever shortcomings they may have, the advantage of my writings is that they are an artistic whole . . .' Another letter, a week later, refers to the book as a 'work of art' and cites 'artistic considerations' as a reason for his delay in submitting the manuscript.

Had Marx wished to produce a straightforward text of classical economics, rather than a work of art, he could have done so. In fact he did: two lectures delivered in June 1865, later published as *Value, Price and Profit*, give a concise and lucid précis of his conclusions:

As the exchangeable values of commodities are only social functions of those things, and have nothing at all to do with their natural qualities, we must first ask: what is the common social substance of all commodities? It is *labour*. To produce a commodity a certain amount of labour must be bestowed upon it, or worked up in it. And I say not only *labour*, but *social labour*. A man who produces an article for his own immediate use, to consume it himself, creates a *product* but not a *commodity* . . . A commodity has a *value*, because it is a *crystallisation of social labour* . . . *Price*, taken by itself, is nothing but the *monetary expression of value* . . . What the working man sells is not directly his *labour*, but his *labouring power*, the temporary disposal of which he makes over to the capitalist . . . Now suppose that the average amount of the daily necessaries of a labouring man require six hours of average labour for their production. Suppose, moreover, six hours of average labour to be also realised in a quantity of gold equal to three shillings. Then three shillings would be the *price*, or the monetary expression of the daily value of that man's labouring power . . . But by paying the daily or weekly value of the spinner's labouring power, the capitalist has acquired the right of using that labouring power during the *whole day or week*. He will, therefore, make him work daily, say, *twelve* hours . . . By advancing three shillings, the capitalist will, therefore, realise a value of six shillings, because, advancing a value in which six hours of labour are crystallised, he will receive in return a value in which twelve hours of labour are crystallised. By repeating this same process daily, the capitalist will daily advance three shillings and daily pocket six shillings, one half of which will go to pay wages anew, and the other half of which will form *surplus value*, for which the capitalist pays no equivalent. It is this sort of exchange between capital and labour upon which capitalistic production, or the wages system, is founded, and which must constantly result in reproducing the working man as a working man, and the capitalist as a capitalist.

Whatever its merits as an economic analysis, this can be understood by any intelligent child: no elaborate metaphors or metaphysics, no confusing digressions or philosophical orotundities, no literary flourishes. Why then is *Capital*, which covers exactly the same ground, so utterly different in style? Did Marx suddenly lose the gift of plain speaking? Manifestly not: at the time he gave these lectures he was also completing the first volume of *Capital*. A clue can be found in one of the very few analogies he permitted himself in *Value, Price and Profit*, when explaining his belief that profits arise from selling commodities at their 'real' value, and not – as one might assume – from adding a surcharge. 'This seems paradox and contrary to everyday observation,' he wrote. 'It is also paradox that the earth moves round the sun, and that water consists of two highly inflammable gases. Scientific truth is always paradox, if judged by everyday experience, which catches only the delusive nature of things.'

This sounds like an invitation to judge his master-work by
scientific standards. But listen more closely: he is taking on 'the
delusive nature of things', a subject which cannot be confined
within an existing genre such as political economy, anthropological
science or history. As Marx points out, 'A commodity appears, at
first sight, a very trivial thing, and easily understood. Its analysis
shows that it is, in reality, a very queer thing, abounding in
metaphysical subtleties and theological niceties.' He admired the
objective, unsentimental methodology of Ricardo and Adam
Smith: indeed, the aspects of *Capital* that are most often ridiculed
today – such as the labour theory of value – derived from these
classical economists and were the prevailing orthodoxy of the
time. Nevertheless, he felt that for all its achievements 'the
bourgeois science of economics had reached the limits beyond
which it could not pass'. Empirical measurements could never
quantify the human cost of exploitation and estrangement.

In the British Museum, Marx had discovered a reservoir of
data about capitalist practice – government Blue Books, statistical
tables, reports from factory inspectors and public health officers –
which he used to the same drenching effect as Engels had in *The
Condition of the Working Class in England*. But his other main source,
less often noticed, is literary fiction. Discussing the effects of
machinery on labour power, he uses the 1861 census figures to
show that the number of workers employed in mechanised
industries such as textile factories and metalworks is lower than
the number of domestic servants. ('What a splendid result of the
capitalist exploitation of machinery!') How can capitalists shrug
off their responsibility for the human casualties of technological
progress? Putting aside his census figures, Marx turns to a speech
from the dock by Bill Sykes in Dickens's *Oliver Twist*. 'Gentlemen
of the jury, no doubt the throat of this commercial traveller has
been cut,' Sykes explained. 'But that is not my fault, it is the fault
of the knife. Must we, for such a temporary inconvenience, abolish
the use of the knife? . . . If you abolish the knife – you hurl us
back into the depths of barbarism.'

More use-value and indeed profit can thus be derived from *Capital* if it is read as a work of the imagination: a Victorian melodrama, or a vast Gothic novel whose heroes are enslaved and consumed by the monster they created ('Capital which comes into the world soiled with mire from top to toe and oozing blood from every pore'); or perhaps a satirical utopia like Swift's land of the Houyhnhnms, where every prospect pleases and only man is vile. In Marx's vision of capitalist society, as in Swift's equine pseudo-paradise, the false Eden is created by reducing ordinary humans to the status of impotent, exiled Yahoos. All that is solid melts into air, he wrote in the *Communist Manifesto*; now, in *Capital*, all that is truly human becomes congealed or crystallised into an impersonal material force, while dead objects acquire menacing life and vigour. Money, once no more than an *expression* of value – a kind of lingua franca in which commodity could speak unto commodity – becomes value itself.

In the simplest of all worlds, exchange-value hardly exists: people produce to satisfy their needs – a leg of lamb, a loaf of bread, a candle – and barter these goods only if there is a surplus to their own requirements. But then along come the butcher, the baker and the candlestick-maker, rogues all three. To buy their alluring products we must become paid labourers; instead of living for our work, we work for our living. Gradually but unstoppably, we are dragged into the social nexus of commodities and wages, prices and profits, a fantasy land where nothing is what it seems. Look at the very first sentence of the very first chapter of *Capital*: 'The wealth of societies in which the capitalist mode of production prevails appears as an "immense collection of commodities"; the individual commodity appears as its elementary form.' What ought to strike the alert reader at once is the choice of verb, repeated for emphasis – '*appears as* . . .' Though less dramatic than the opening sentence of the *Communist Manifesto*, it has a similar purpose: we are entering a world of spectres and apparitions, as he reminds us regularly throughout the next 1,000 pages.

> Exchange-value *appears* to be something accidental and purely relative ... Let us now look at the residue of the products of labour. There is nothing left of them in each case but the same *phantom-like* objectivity ... This led to the rise of a restored mercantile system which sees in value nothing but a social form, or rather the *unsubstantial ghost* of that form ... The distinction between higher and simple labour, 'skilled labour' and 'unskilled labour', rests in part on *pure illusion* ... Instead of revealing the capital-relation, they [political economists] show us the *false semblance* of a relation ... [My italics.]

To expose the difference between heroic appearance and inglorious reality – stripping off the gallant knight's disguise to reveal a tubby little man in his underpants – is, of course, one of the classic methods of comedy.

The absurdities to be found in *Capital*, which have been seized on so readily by those who wish to expose Marx as a crackpot, reflect the madness of the subject, not of the author. This is obvious almost from the outset, when he plunges into a wild and increasingly surreal meditation on the relative values of a coat and twenty yards of linen.

> Now it is true that the tailoring which makes the coat is concrete labour of a different sort from the weaving which makes the linen. But the act of equating tailoring with weaving reduces the former in fact to what is really equal in the two kinds of labour, to the characteristic they have in common of being human labour ... Yet the coat itself, the physical aspect of the coat-commodity, is purely a use-value. A coat as such no more expresses value than does the first piece of linen we come across. This proves only that, within its value relation to the linen, the coat signifies more than it does outside it, just as some men count for more when inside a gold-braided uniform than they do otherwise.

The ludicrous simile ought to forewarn us that we are in fact reading a shaggy-dog story. This becomes more and more evident as Marx goes on:

Despite its buttoned-up appearance, the linen recognises in it [the coat] a splendid kindred soul, the soul of value. Nevertheless, the coat cannot represent value towards the linen unless value, for the latter, simultaneously assumes the form of a coat. An individual, A, for instance, cannot be 'your majesty' to another individual, B, unless majesty in B's eyes assumes the physical shape of A, and, moreover, changes facial features, hair and many other things, with every new 'father of his people' ... As a use-value, the linen is something palpably different from the coat; as value, it is identical with the coat, and therefore looks like the coat.

Then, just as the reader's head is beginning to spin uncontrollably, Marx delivers the punch-line:

Thus the linen acquires a value-form different from its natural form. Its existence as value is manifested in its equality with the coat, just as the sheep-like nature of the Christian is shown in his resemblance to the Lamb of God.

Short of printing the page upside-down in green ink, Marx could hardly give a clearer signal that we have embarked on a picaresque odyssey through the realms of higher nonsense. One is reminded of the last lines from his beloved *Tristram Shandy*:

—L—d! said my mother, what is all this story about?
— A *Cock* and a *Bull*, said Yorick; — and one of the best of its kind I ever heard.

In his first youthful infatuation with Laurence Sterne, Marx tried writing a comic shaggy-dog novel of his own. Nearly thirty years on, he at last found a subject and a style. Sterne, according to his biographer Thomas Yoseloff, 'broke with the tradition of contemporary writing: his novel was no more a novel than it was an essay, or a book of philosophy, or a memoir, or a local satire after the manner of the pamphleteers. He wrote as he talked as he thought; his book was loose and disjointed in structure, full of curious and difficult oddities . . .' Much the same could be said of Marx and his epic. Like *Tristram Shandy*, *Capital* is full of systems and syllogisms, paradoxes and metaphysics, theories and hypotheses, abstruse explanations and whimsical tomfoolery. One of the running gags concerns a slightly dim embryonic capitalist, Mr Moneybags. 'In order to be able to extract value from the consumption of a commodity, our friend Moneybags must be so lucky as to find, within the sphere of circulation, in the market, a commodity whose use-value possesses the peculiar property of being a source of value . . . and consequently a creation of value.' Lucky old Moneybags finds just such a commodity in labour power, which has the unique ability to multiply its own value.

To do justice to the deranged logic of capitalism, Marx's text is saturated, sometimes even waterlogged, with irony – an irony which has yet escaped almost every reader for more than a century. One of the very few exceptions is the American literary critic Edmund Wilson, who hailed Marx as 'certainly the greatest ironist since Swift'. This is such an extravagant tribute that supporting evidence may be required; so let us quote a passage from *Theories of Surplus Value*, the so-called fourth volume of *Capital*:

DIGRESSION: ON PRODUCTIVE LABOUR

A philosopher produces ideas, a poet poems, a clergyman sermons, a professor compendia and so on. A criminal produces crimes. If we take a closer look at the connection between this latter branch of production and society as a whole, we shall rid ourselves of many prejudices. The criminal produces not only crime but also criminal law, and with this also the professor who gives lectures on criminal law and in addition to this the inevitable compendium in which this same professor throws his lectures on to the general market as 'commodities' . . . The criminal moreover produces the whole of the police and of criminal justice, constables, judges, hangmen, juries, etc; and all these different lines of business, which form just as many categories of the social division of labour, develop different capacities of the human mind, create new needs and new ways of satisfying them. Torture alone has given rise to the most ingenious mechnical inventions, and employed many honourable craftsmen in the production of its instruments. The criminal produces an impression, partly moral and partly tragic, as the case may be, and in this way renders a 'service' by arousing the moral and aesthetic feelings of the public. He produces not only compendia on Criminal Law, not only penal codes and along with them legislators in this field, but also art, belles-lettres, novels, and even tragedies, as not only Müllner's *Schuld* and Schiller's *Räuber* show, but *Oedipus* and *Richard the Third* . . . The effects of the criminal on the development of productive power can be shown in detail. Would locks ever have reached their present degree of excellence had there been no thieves? Would the making of banknotes have reached its present perfection had there been no forgers? . . . And if one leaves the sphere of private crime, would the world market ever have come into being but for national crime? Indeed, would even the nations have arisen? And has not the Tree of Sin been at the same time the Tree of Knowledge ever since the time of Adam?

This stands comparison with Swift's modest proposal for curing the misery of Ireland by persuading the starving poor to eat their surplus babies. (It may be worth recording, parenthetically, that in 1870 Marx bought a fourteen-volume edition of Swift's collected works for the bargain price of four shillings and sixpence.) As

Wilson rightly observes, the purpose of Marx's theoretical abstractions – the dance of commodities, the zany cross-stitch of logic – is primarily an ironic one, juxtaposed as they are with grim, well-documented portraits of the misery and filth which capitalist laws create in practice. 'The meaning of the impersonal-looking formulas which Marx produces with so scientific an air is, he reminds us from time to time as if casually, pennies withheld from the worker's pocket, sweat squeezed out of his body, and natural enjoyments denied his soul,' Wilson continues. 'In competing with the pundits of economics, Marx has written something of a parody...'

Ultimately, however, even Edmund Wilson loses the plot: only a few pages after elevating Marx to the pantheon of satirical genius alongside Swift, he protests at 'the crudity of the psychological motivation which underlies the world view of Marx' and complains that the theory propounded in *Capital* is 'simply, like the dialectic, a creation of the metaphysician who never abdicated before the economist in Marx'. This gripe doesn't even have the merit of originality. Some German reviewers of the first edition accused Marx of 'Hegelian sophistry', a charge to which he happily pleaded guilty. As he reminded them in an afterword to the second German edition, published in 1873, he had criticised the 'mystificatory side of the Hegelian dialectic' nearly thirty years earlier, when it was still the fashion. 'But just when I was working at the first volume of *Capital*, the ill-humoured, arrogant and mediocre epigones who now talk large in educated German circles began to take pleasure in treating Hegel ... as a "dead dog". I therefore openly avowed myself the pupil of that mighty thinker, and even, here and there in the chapter on the theory of value, coquetted with the mode of expression peculiar to him.'

These dialectical flirtations which so offended Edmund Wilson are all of a piece with the irony he praised so highly: both techniques up-end apparent reality to expose the hidden truth. 'The mealy-mouthed babblers of German vulgar economics grumbled about the style of my book,' Marx wrote in 1873. 'No one can feel the literary shortcomings of *Capital* more strongly than I myself.' But critics elsewhere, even when hostile to the theories, acknowledged its stylistic merits. The *Saturday Review*, a London magazine, commented that 'the author's views may be as pernicious as we conceive them to be, but there can be no question as to the plausibility of his logic, the vigour of his rhetoric, and the charm with which he invests the driest problems of political economy'. The *Contemporary Review*, while patriotically scornful of German economics ('we do not suspect that Karl Marx has much to teach us'), complimented the author on not forgetting 'the human interest – the "hunger and thirst interest" which underlies the science'. Marx was particularly gratified by a notice in the *St Petersburg Journal* which praised the 'unusual liveliness' of his prose. 'In this respect,' it added, 'the author in no way resembles . . . the majority of German scholars, who . . . write their books in a language so dry and obscure that the heads of ordinary mortals are cracked by it.'

In spite of its lively charms the first volume of *Capital* was still too forbidding for the heads of many ordinary mortals, whose task was made all the harder by Marx's decision to place the most impenetrable chapters at the front of the book. 'Beginnings are always difficult in all sciences,' he explained in the preface. 'The understanding of the first chapter, especially the section that contains the analysis of commodities, will therefore present the greatest difficulty. I have popularised the passages concerning the substance of value and the magnitude of value as much as possible.' The value-form, he reassured readers, was really simplicity itself: 'Nevertheless, the human mind has laboured for more than 2,000 years to get to the bottom of it . . . With the exception of the section on the form of value, therefore, this volume cannot stand accused on the score of difficulty. I assume, of course, a reader who is willing to learn something new and therefore to think for himself.'

A rather ambitious assumption, as it turned out. While the book was being typeset Engels had advised him that it was 'a serious mistake' not to clarify the abstract arguments by splitting them up into shorter sections with their own headings. 'The thing would have looked somewhat like a school textbook, but a very large class of readers would have found it considerably easier to understand. The *populus*, even the scholars, just are no longer at all accustomed to this way of thinking, and one has to make it as easy for them as one possibly can.' Marx made a few changes on his proof-sheets, but they were mere tinkerings at the margin. 'How could you leave the *outward* structure of the book in its present form!' Engels asked in some exasperation after inspecting the final set of proofs. 'The fourth chapter is almost 200 pages long and only has four sub-sections . . . Furthermore, the train of thought is constantly interrupted by illustrations, and the point to be illustrated is *never* summarised after the illustration, so that one is forever plunging straight from the illustration of *one* point into the exposition of another point. It is dreadfully tiring, and confusing, too.' However, he added lamely, 'all that is of no import'.

Even some of Marx's most adoring disciples found their eyes glazing over as they tried to make sense of the obscure early chapters. 'Please be so good as to tell your good wife,' he wrote to Ludwig Kugelmann, 'that the chapters on "The Working Day", "Co-operation, Division of Labour and Machinery" and finally on "Primitive Accumulation" are the most immediately readable. You will have to explain any incomprehensible terminology to her. If there are any other doubtful points, I shall be glad to help.' When the great English socialist William Morris read *Capital*, years later, he 'suffered agonies of confusion of the brain . . . Anyhow, I read what I could, and will hope that some information stuck to me from my reading.' Sheer incomprehension, rather than political prejudice, may explain the muted reaction to *Capital* when it was published. 'The silence about my book makes me fidgety,' Marx wrote to Engels in October, revealing that insomnia had begun to persecute him again. 'My sickness always originates in the mind.' Engels did his best to stir up a commotion by submitting hostile pseudonymous reviews to the bourgeois press in Germany, and urged Marx's other friends to do likewise. 'The main thing is that the book should be discussed over and over again, in any way whatsoever,' he told Kugelmann. 'And as Marx is not a free agent in the matter, and is furthermore as bashful as a young girl, it is up to the rest of us to see to it . . . In the words of our old friend Jesus Christ, we must be as innocent as doves and wise as serpents.' Dr Kugelmann did his eager best, placing articles in one or two of the Hanover newspapers, but they were of little assistance since he barely understood the book himself. 'Kugelmann becomes more simple-minded every day,' Engels complained. Jenny Marx was rather more gracious: the Hanoverian acolyte might be a clodhopping dunce but at least he meant well. Depressed by the universal indifference to her husband's *magnum opus*, and alarmed by his worsening health, she was grateful for any gesture of support. 'There can be few books that have been written in more difficult circumstances,' she said, 'and I am sure I could write a secret history of it which would tell of many, extremely many unspoken troubles and anxieties and torments. If the workers had an inkling of the sacrifices that were necessary for this work, which was written only for them and for their sakes, to be completed they would perhaps show a little more interest.'

Two days before Christmas 1867, while Karl lay on the couch in carbuncular agony, Jenny was in the kitchen joylessly preparing the seasonal pudding – seeding raisins, chopping up almonds and orange peel, shredding suet, kneading eggs and flour – when a voice called down the stairs, 'A great statue has arrived.' It was the Kugelmanns' bust of Zeus, sent from Germany as a Christmas gift and only slightly chipped from its long journey. 'You can have no idea of the delight and surprise you occasioned us,' she wrote to the Doctor. 'My warmest thanks to you also for your great interest and indefatigable efforts on behalf of Karl's book.' The form of applause preferred by most Germans, she added bitterly, 'is utter and complete silence'.

For the first three months of 1868 Marx was unable to work at all. If he walked to the British Museum, the carbuncle on his inner thigh rubbed against his trousers; if he sat at his desk, the carbuncle on his bottom soon forced him to retreat to a couch and lie on his side; if he tried to write, the carbuncle below his shoulder-blade took a painful revenge. Even his letters to Engels became noticeably shorter. 'During the whole of last week I had many bleeding shingles; particularly obstinate and hard to obliterate the mess under my left armpit,' he reported on 23 March. 'But generally I feel much better...' Not for long: the very next day, while he was reading a book, 'there was something like a black veil before my eyes. In addition, a frightful headache and chest constriction.' If only he didn't have to produce the next 'two damned volumes' of *Capital* and seek out an English publisher, he would move to Switzerland forthwith. In London the Marxes' living costs were between £400 and £500 a year, but in Geneva he reckoned they could muddle along quite comfortably on about £200.

The only reasons for staying in London were those two institutions that occupied so much of his time – the British Museum and the General Council of the International Working Men's Association. However, one other consideration may have crossed his mind: Geneva was now the home of Michael Bakunin, whom Marx had already identified as the man most likely to destroy the International.

11

The Rogue Elephant

Michael Bakunin was a hairy Russian giant, the very model of a thunderbolt-hurling revolutionist, all impulse and passion and pure will. The composer Richard Wagner, a comrade-in-arms during the Dresden uprising of 1849, is said to have modelled the character of Siegfried on him; his presence can also be detected in Dostoyevsky's novel *The Possessed*. Legends naturally attached themselves to such a figure, many of his own invention. There was the story of how, during a revolt in Italy, the fearless colossus marched out of a besieged house straight through a crowd of soldiers: none dared touch him. He roamed the world claiming to be the leader of vast insurrectionary Brotherhoods or Leagues, which usually turned out to be no more than a dozen cronies in a pub. He had a boyish enthusiasm for the paraphernalia of plotting – cyphers, passwords, invisible ink. Marx referred to him as the Russian hierophant (high priest), but Engels suggested that elephant would be more accurate: the gigantic frame, the lumbering gait, the habit of trampling anything that stood in his path.

Bakunin is often described as the Father of Modern Anarchism (Proudhon being his main rival for the title); but he bequeathed no great theoretical scripture. His legacy was the single idea that the state was evil and must be destroyed. Communist states were no better than capitalist: authority would still be centralised in the hands of the few, and even if the state were run by 'workers' they would soon become as corrupt and despotic as the tyrants they had overthrown. He proposed instead a form of federal anarchy in which power was so widely dispersed that nobody could abuse it.

Or so his disciples would have you believe. It is remarkable how many of them there are: during his lifetime he may have been a general without an army or a Mohammed without a Koran, but in the twentieth century he acquired a legion of admirers – many not in the least revolutionary or anarchistic – who hailed him as the one person to foresee that Marx's ideas could lead only to the Gulag. The two men are consistently juxtaposed, and always to Marx's discredit. 'The struggle between the two lies at the very heart and core of all debates about the history of the workers' movement even to the present day,' writes the German Marx-ologist Professor Fritz Raddatz. 'There is no way of evading the answer . . . Marx and Bakunin = Stalin and Trotsky.' The British historian E. H. Carr contrasts Bakunin and Marx as 'the man of generous, uncontrollable impulses, and the man whose feelings were so perfectly subdued to his intellect that superficial observers disbelieved in their existence . . . the man of magnetic personal attraction, and the man who repelled and intimidated by his coldness'. True, Carr concedes that Bakunin was sometimes reckless and incoherent. But even these failings become virtues when set against the icy, inhuman discipline of a desiccated Marxist calculating machine.

According to Isaiah Berlin, 'Bakunin differed from Marx as poetry differs from prose.' The apparent implication – that Bakunin was a lyrical free spirit and Marx a literal-minded plodder – is little more than a donnish rephrasing of that crude Trotsky/ Stalin formula: the humane libertarian versus the ruthless authoritarian. It is a myth that has just enough truth to keep it alive. Bakunin was indeed a creature of pure emotion who despised Marx's meticulous rationalism and attention to detail. His lack of interest in the complex mechanics of capital was matched or balanced by Marx's contempt for cloak-and-dagger skulduggery. Beyond that, however, almost everything said and written about this battle of the giants is nonsense.

They had met in Paris in 1844 and then in Brussels shortly before the revolutions of 1848, at a time when Bakunin was still more of a communist than an anarchist. Though four years older than Marx, he acknowledged the young man's superior learning ('I knew nothing at that time of political economy') while guessing that their irreconcilable temperaments would never permit 'any frank intimacy'. That summer, Marx's *Neue Rheinische Zeitung* published a gossip item from Paris, attributed to George Sand, alleging that Bakunin was a secret agent of the Tsar: Marx's willingness to spread this rumour can probably be attributed to his instinctive mistrust of Russia and the Russians. Nevertheless, he happily printed a letter from George Sand denying that she had ever said anything of the sort, and appended a brief editorial note apologising for the mistake. A few weeks later the two men met by chance in Berlin. 'You know,' Marx revealed melo-dramatically, 'I am now at the head of a communist secret society, so well disciplined that if I told one of its members, "Go kill Bakunin," he would kill you.' However, since the source of this alleged remark is Bakunin himself, an incorrigible fantasist, we should not necessarily believe it. If Marx really had issued such a threat, would the short-fused Russian ever have spoken to him again?

As it happened they didn't see each other for another sixteen years, but this was a purely geographical estrangement. After his adventures with Richard Wagner in 1849, Bakunin spent the next eight years as a peripatetic prisoner in Dresden, Prague and St Petersburg. In 1857, following the death of Tsar Nicholas, his sentence was commuted to 'exile for life' in Siberia. Four years later he escaped by stowing away aboard a ship bound for San Francisco, whence he returned via New York to Europe.

As with Lassalle, Marx could recognise a big man when he saw one, however much he disliked the fellow's airs and affectations. Engels made the point very well in 1849, when publicly de-nouncing Bakunin's scheme to create a pan-Slavic nation: 'Bakunin is our friend. That will not deter us from criticising his pamphlet.' Or mocking his habits, come to that. Like Lassalle, Bakunin was a regular comic butt in the Marx–Engels correspondence. 'Bakunin has become a monster, a huge mass of flesh and fat, and is barely capable of walking any more,' Marx noted merrily in 1863. 'To crown it all, he is sexually perverse and jealous of the seventeen-year-old Polish girl who married him in Siberia because of his martyrdom. He is presently in Sweden, where he is hatching "revolution" with the Finns.' At the time he wrote this Marx hadn't actually set eyes on the monster since 1848, but they renewed their acquaintance in the autumn of 1864 when Bakunin stopped off in London, en route from Sweden to Italy, to order some bespoke suits from the socialist tailor Friedrich Lessner.

Some historians have claimed that Marx always hated Bakunin, but the facts of this encounter prove otherwise. For one thing, it was Marx who requested the meeting, having heard from Lessner (a fellow member of the International's General Council) that Bakunin was in town. Why bother to seek out a man he despised? Marx's letter to Engels the following day confirms that this was a comradely reunion. 'I must say I liked him very much, more so than previously . . . On the whole, he is one of the few people whom after sixteen years I find to have moved forwards and not backwards.' In a gushingly affectionate message from Florence a few weeks later, Bakunin addressed Marx as 'my dearest friend', praised his Inaugural Address for the International and begged for a signed photograph.

During their conversation in London, Bakunin said that he had now abandoned his juvenile obsession with furtive plots and secret societies: from now on, he vowed, he would involve himself only in the wider 'socialist movement', i.e. the International. But after arriving in Italy he soon reverted to his old conspiratorial capers – aided and abetted by a rich new Russian patron, the Princess Obolensky, who apparently found this fat, toothless giant irresistible. For the next three years or so he had no dealings with the International at all.

In 1867 the Princess and her pet anarchist moved to Switzerland, where Bakunin soon noticed that the International was establishing itself as a significant force. Making up for lost time, he determined to hijack the organisation for himself and devised what his biographer E. H. Carr calls a 'bold plan'. Bold, but also utterly absurd. As the self-styled leader of the 'International Alliance of Socialist Democracy' – the latest of his many grand-sounding but tiny groupuscules – he wrote to the workers' International proposing a merger, and a merger on equal terms. He would thus effectively become co-president of the new organisation. Naturally enough, Marx and his colleagues on the General Council scorned the idea: through their affiliated unions and associations they represented tens of thousands of workers, whereas the entire membership of Bakunin's 'International Alliance' was probably no more than twenty. Having had his frontal assault rebuffed, Bakunin decided to tiptoe in through the back door instead. He informed the General Council that the International Alliance had been disbanded. But his new outfit, a mere 'Alliance' for Socialist Democracy, wished to become an ordinary, humble affiliate of the workers' International, just like any other local section. Marx could see no harm in it, and recommended acceptance.

Those who portray Bakunin as a heroic opponent of centralised power structures and rigid hierarchies find it difficult to explain his subsequent conduct – which may be why they often prefer to ignore it altogether. At the first and only International congress he attended (at Basle in 1869), he argued for 'the construction of the international state of millions of workers, a state which it will be the role of the International to constitute' – temporarily forgetting that 'states' of any and every kind were anathema to a true anarchist such as himself. During another debate, he actually proposed *strengthening* the power of the General Council to veto new applicants and expel existing members. And no wonder: as Carr admits, 'Bakunin's ambition at this stage was to capture the General Council, not destroy it.' The closer one looks, the clearer it becomes that his later rage against the General Council owed less to a high-minded dislike of authority than to sour grapes at his own failure to seize control of it.

Behind the scenes, he was scheming away as usual. A perfect example of Bakunin's *modus operandi* can be found in a conversation with one of his acolytes, Charles Perron:

> Bakunin assured him that the International was an excellent institution in itself, but that there was something better which Perron should also join – the Alliance. Perron agreed. Then Bakunin said that, even in the Alliance, there might be some who were not genuine revolutionaries, and who were a drag on its activities, and it would therefore be a good thing to have at the back of the Alliance a group of 'International Brothers'. Perron again agreed. When next they met a few days later, Bakunin told him that the 'International Brothers' were too wide an organisation, and that behind them there must be a Directorate or Bureau of three – of whom he, Perron, should be one. Perron laughed, and once more agreed.

Thus spake the great advocate of power to the people.

At the Basle congress of 1869 it was agreed that delegates should reconvene a year later in Paris. But the plan was overtaken by the outbreak of the Franco-Prussian war in July 1870 – a last desperate attempt by Napoleon III to shore up his tottering Second Empire by challenging the mighty Bismarck. The International had long been preparing itself for this moment. Its 1868 congress in Brussels had passed a motion calling for a general strike the moment war began – though Marx dismissed the idea as 'Belgian nonsense', arguing that the working class 'is not yet sufficiently organised to throw any decisive weight on to the scales'. All it should do, he believed, was issue some suitably 'pompous declamations and high-faluting phrases' to the effect that a war between France and Germany would be ruinous for both countries and for Europe as a whole.

This he duly did. On 23 July 1870, four days after the declaration of hostilities, the General Council approved an Address written by Marx. The defeat of his old *bête noire*, Louis Bonaparte, was cheerfully (and correctly) predicted. But he warned that if German workers allowed the war to lose 'its strictly defensive character' and to degenerate into an attack on the French people, victory and defeat alike would be equally disastrous. Fortunately, the German working classes were far too enlightened to permit any such outcome:

> Whatever turn the impending horrid war may take, the alliance of the working classes of all countries will ultimately kill war. The very fact that while official France and Germany are rushing into a fratricidal feud, the workmen of France and Germany send each other messages of peace and goodwill; this great fact, unparalleled in the history of the past, opens the vista of a brighter future. It proves that in contrast to old society, with its economical miseries and its political delirium, a new society is springing up, whose International rule will be *Peace*, because its natural ruler will be everywhere the same – *Labour*! The Pioneer of that new society is the International Working Men's Association.

All most inspiring. John Stuart Mill sent a message of congratulation, declaring himself 'highly pleased with the Address. There was not one word in it that ought not to be there; it could not have been done with fewer words.' While maintaining an official neutrality, however, Marx couldn't resist privately calculating the odds and brooding on what result would best suit his purposes.

As long ago as February 1859 he had written to Lassalle that war between France and Germany 'would naturally have serious consequences, and in the long run revolutionary ones for sure. But at the start it will bolster up Bonapartism in France, drive back the internal movement in England and Russia, arouse anew the pettiest passions in regard to the nationality issue in Germany, and will therefore, in my opinion, have first and foremost a counter-revolutionary effect in every respect.' Eleven years on, this game of consequences had become an obsession. 'I have been totally unable to sleep for four nights now, on account of the rheumatism,' he told Engels in August 1870, 'and I spend this time in fantasies about Paris, etc.' One beguiling fantasy was that the two sides would thrash each other alternately, thus weakening both Bonaparte and Bismarck. Then, ultimately, the Germans would win. 'I wish this because the definite defeat of Bonaparte is likely to provoke Revolution in France, while the definite defeat of Germany would only protract the present state of things for twenty years.'

Neither Marx's wife nor his best friend needed any such convoluted justifications for taking sides. Jenny thought that France deserved a damn good walloping for having the impudence to try and export its 'civilis-a-a-ation' into the sacred soil of Germany. 'All the French, even the tiny number of better ones, have an element of chauvinism in some remote corner of their hearts,' she wrote to Engels. 'This will have to be knocked out of them.' Engels, who spent the war profitably knocking out military analyses for the *Pall Mall Gazette*, also felt the tug of atavistic allegiance. 'My confidence in the military achievements of the Germans grows daily,' he enthused. 'We really do seem to have won the first serious encounter.' Once Bonaparte had been smashed, his long-suffering citizens would at last have the chance to take power for themselves.

But did the Parisians have either the means or the leaders to effect a revolution while resisting the Prussian army? This question, more than any other, tormented Marx during those sleepless nights. 'One cannot conceal from oneself that the twenty-year-long Bonapartist farce has caused enormous demoralisation,' he wrote to Engels. 'One is hardly justified in counting on revolutionary heroism. What do you think about it?' Engels barely had time to reply before Bonaparte surrendered at Sedan and a new regime – the Third Republic – was proclaimed in Paris.

If you wait by the river for long enough, you will see the corpses of your enemies float by. The installation of the pipsqueak Napoleon had provoked Marx's *Eighteenth Brumaire of Louis Bonaparte* almost twenty years earlier; now he had the pleasure of writing the obituary. On 9 September the International issued a Second Address on the war, which began with the rather smug confirmation that 'we were not mistaken as to the vitality of the Second Empire'. Alas, Marx continued, 'we were not wrong in our apprehension lest the German war should "lose its strictly defensive character and degenerate into a war against the French people".' Anyone referring back to the First Address might notice that he had in fact denied this possibility, insisting that the heroic German working class would forestall it. But the purely 'defensive' campaign had ended with the capitulation at Sedan, and now that the Germans were demanding the annexation of Alsace and Lorraine he quickly rewrote history to spare his own blushes.

Not that we should be too hard on old Marx. His earlier tribute to Teutonic restraint had been a triumph of hope over experience, but with that notable exception his entrail-reading was amazingly accurate. If the fortune of arms and the arrogance of success led Prussia to dismember France, what then? In the Second Address he warned that Germany would either 'become the avowed tool of Russian aggrandisement, or, after some short respite, make again ready for another "defensive" war, not one of those new-fangled "localised" wars, but a *war of races* – a war of the combined Slavonian and Roman races'. A letter to the International's American organiser, Friedrich Adolph Sorge, was even more prescient. 'What the Prussian jackasses do not see is that the present war is leading . . . inevitably to a war between Germany and Russia. And such a war No. 2 will act as the midwife of the inevitable social revolution in Russia.' Marx did not live to see the drama of 1917, but it would not have surprised him in the least. Sometimes he seemed to be looking even further ahead:

If limits are to be fixed by military interests, there will be no
end to claims, because every military line is necessarily faulty,
and may be improved by annexing some more outlying territory; and, moreover, they can never be fixed finally and fairly,
because they must always be imposed by the conqueror upon
the conquered, and consequently carry within them the seed
of fresh wars.

Those who cite Marx's occasional misjudgements as proof of his
historical myopia might care to tell us if any other mid-Victorian
had such an acute premonition of the rise of Adolf Hitler.

Marx's Second Address welcomed the new French Republic
('*Vive la République!*'), but with profound misgivings. 'That Republic
has not subverted the throne, but only taken its place become
vacant,' he noted. 'It has been proclaimed, not as a social
conquest, but as a national measure of defence.' The provisional
government was an unstable coalition of Orleanists and
Republicans, Bonapartists and Jacobins, which might turn out to
be a mere bridge or stopgap for a royal restoration. Nevertheless,
the French workers must do their duty as citizens and banish all
thoughts of revolution. 'Any attempt at upsetting the new
government in the present crisis, when the enemy is almost
knocking at the doors of Paris, would be a desperate folly.'

Desperate folly was, of course, the favourite pastime of Michael
Bakunin, who had been following the news from France at his
Swiss villa. Hearing of an insurrection in Lyons after the Sedan
defeat, he hastened there at once, strutted into the Hotel de Ville
and appointed himself leader of the 'Committee of French
Salvation'. In a proclamation from the balcony of the town hall
he then decreed the Abolition of the State – adding that anyone
who disagreed with him would be executed. (*Very* libertarian.)
The state, in the form of a platoon of National Guards, promptly
entered the town hall through a door which had been inad-
vertently left unguarded and forced the Messiah of Lyons to
scuttle back to the safe shores of Lake Geneva.

Marx's admonishment against upsetting the apple-cart had no more influence than Bakunin's vainglorious buffoonery. Adolphe Thiers, a veteran liberal lawyer, was installed as president of the Third Republic, and soon set about suing for peace with Prussia on behalf of his ill-named 'Government of National Defence'. The rage of Parisians at this capitulation was redoubled when he announced that reparations would be financed by the immediate repayment of all outstanding bills and rents, which had been suspended during the siege. On 18 March 1871 an indignant crowd took to the streets – backed by the city's National Guard, which had refused to obey an order to hand over its weapons to the government. Thiers and his followers decamped to Versailles, leaving the nation's capital in the hands of its citizens.

Once again, the Gallic cock had crowed. The rulers of Europe affected deafness at first, perhaps hoping that the squawks would fade if they took no notice. When this failed, their panic was delightful to behold. *The Times* of London thundered against 'this dangerous sentiment of the Democracy, this conspiracy against civilisation in its so-called capital'. Even Karl Marx, it reported, was so horrified by the uprising that he had sent a stern message of rebuke to French members of the International. The paper then had to publish a denial from Marx, who revealed that the alleged letter was 'an impudent forgery'. ('You must not believe a word of all the stuff you get to see in the bourgeois papers about the internal events in Paris,' he advised Liebknecht in Germany. 'It is all lies and deception. Never has the vileness of the reptile bourgeois newspaper hacks displayed itself more splendidly.')

Marx's excitement at 'the internal events in Paris' was tempered only by a fear that the revolutionaries might be too decent for their own good. Instead of marching on Versailles at once to finish off Thiers and his wretched crew, they 'lost precious moments' organising a city-wide election for the Commune. He also disapproved of their willingness to allow the National Bank to continue with business as usual: if Marx had been in charge he'd have ransacked the vaults at once. Even so, bliss was it in that dawn to be alive. 'What resilience, what historical initiative, what a capacity for sacrifice in these Parisians!' he exclaimed. 'After six months of hunger and ruin, caused rather by internal treachery than by the external enemy, they rise, beneath Prussian bayonets, as if there had never been a war between France and Germany and the enemy were still not at the gates of Paris! History has no like example of such greatness.'

Of the ninety-two Communards elected by popular suffrage on 28 March, seventeen were members of the International. At a meeting in London that same day, the General Council unanimously agreed that Marx should draft a new 'Address to the People of Paris'. But then nothing happened. Throughout the two months of the Commune's existence, the International made no public statement whatever. By the time Marx delivered his fifty-page Address, on 30 May, it was an epitaph: Thiers's troops had retaken the city three days earlier, and the cobblestones of Paris were red with the blood of at least 20,000 murdered Communards.

Why the delay? His biographers usually attribute it to 'Marx's personal ambivalence to the Commune'. He was certainly haunted by fears that the Commune would fall, but apprehension is not the same as ambivalence. The main reason, more banal and familiar, is that for much of April and May he had bronchitis and liver trouble which prevented him from attending the General Council – let alone gathering the necessary evidence for a magisterial fifty-page tribute that would do justice to the Parisians' historic *levée en masse*. 'The present state of things causes our dear Moor intense suffering,' his daughter Jenny wrote in mid-April, 'and no doubt is one of the chief causes of his illness. A great number of our friends are in the Commune.' One was Charles Longuet, editor of the daily *Journal Officiel*, who moved to London after the fall of the Commune and married Jennychen in 1872. Another Communard, Prosper Olivier Lissagaray, later became the secret fiancé of Eleanor Marx – though the engagement was eventually broken off. Paul and Laura Lafargue had escaped from

Paris shortly before the Prussians laid siege to the city, but were busily agitating on behalf of the Commune from their bolt-hole in Bordeaux.

Weighed down by illness and foreboding, Marx also had to struggle against his own obsessive perfectionism: whether in *Capital* or a brief pamphlet, he was reluctant to issue a definitive pronouncement on any subject until he had gleaned and winnowed all the available evidence. During the weeks of the Commune he dashed off dozens of letters to comrades on the Continent, badgering them for yet more documents and press cuttings. To judge by the more scurrilous passages in his long-awaited Address – which was published as *The Civil War in France* – the research also included close study of the gossip columns. Within the first couple of pages we are treated to this charming portrait of Thiers's foreign minister: 'Jules Favre, living in concubinage with the wife of a drunkard resident at Algiers, had, by a most daring concoction of forgeries, spread over many years, contrived to grasp, in the name of the children of his adultery, a large succession, which made him a rich man.' The finance minister Ernest Picard is dubbed 'the Joe Miller of the government of National Defence', a reference to one of London's music-hall comedians. Since Marx's knowledge of English popular culture was almost zero, one guesses that his stage-struck daughters suggested the line. But the rest of the indictment against Picard is pure Marx, as each new item on the charge-sheet is produced with a legalistic flourish. Picard, we learn, 'is the brother of one Arthur Picard, an individual expelled from the Paris *Bourse* as a blackleg (see report of the Prefecture of Police, dated the 31st July, 1867), and convicted, on his own confession, of a theft of 300,000 francs, while manager of one of the branches of the *Société Générale*, rue Palestro, No. 5 (see report of the Prefecture of Police, 11th December 1868). This Arthur Picard was made by Ernest Picard the editor of his paper, *l'Électeur Libre* . . .' The Communards may have left the bank vaults unmolested, but they had certainly enjoyed rummaging in the police archives.

Having introduced the bit players, Marx ushers in Thiers himself – the 'monstrous gnome':

> A master in small state roguery, a virtuoso in perjury and treason, a craftsman in all the petty stratagems, cunning devices, and base perfidies of parliamentary party-warfare; never scrupling, when out of office, to fan a revolution, and to stifle it in blood when at the helm of the state; with class prejudices standing him in the place of ideas, and vanity in the place; his private life is as infamous as his public life is odious – even now, when playing the part of a French Sulla, he cannot help setting off the abomination of his deeds by the ridicule of his ostentation.

Marx then sketches the background to the Commune. Far from being some sort of mutiny against a legitimate government, it was a valiant attempt to save the Third Republic from Thiers's unconstitutional demand that the National Guard surrender its arms and leave Paris undefended. He adds proudly that the popular uprising of 18 March was more or less untainted by 'the acts of violence in which the revolutions, and still more the counter-revolutions, of the "better classes" abound'.

For an example of these better classes he turns again to the president himself, sparing his readers nothing:

> Thiers opened his second campaign against Paris in the beginning of April. The first batch of Parisian prisoners brought into Versailles was subjected to the most revolting atrocities while Ernest Picard, with his hands in his trousers' pockets, strolled about jeering them, and while Mesdames Thiers and Favre, in the midst of their ladies of honour (?), applauded, from the balcony, the outrages of the Versailles mob. The captured soldiers of the line were massacred in cold blood; our brave friend, General Duval, the iron-founder, was shot without any form of trial. Gallifet, the kept man of his wife, so notorious for her shameless exhibitions at the orgies of

the Second Empire, boasted in a proclamation of having commanded the murder of a small troop of National Guards ... With the elated vanity of a parliamentary Tom Thumb, permitted to play the part of a Tamerlane, he [Thiers] denied the rebels against his littleness every right of civilised warfare, up to the right of neutrality for ambulances. Nothing more horrid than that monkey, allowed for a time to give full fling to his tigerish instincts, as foreseen by Voltaire.

Before we are surfeited with all this gore and fury Marx executes a skilful change of tone, pausing to consider the lessons of the Commune. He quotes a manifesto of 18 March which boasted that the proletarians of Paris had made themselves 'masters of their own destiny by seizing upon the government power'. A naïve delusion, he argues. The working class cannot simply 'lay hold of the ready-made state machinery and wield it for its own purposes': one might as well try playing a piano sonata on a tin whistle. Fortunately the Commune had quickly taken the point by getting rid of the political police, replacing the standing army with an armed populace, disestablishing the Church, liberating schools from the interference of bishops and politicians, and introducing elections for all public servants – including judges – so that they would be 'responsible and revocable'. The Communal constitution restored to society all the forces hitherto absorbed by the state, and the transformation was visible at once: 'Wonderful indeed was the change the Commune had wrought in Paris! ... No longer was Paris the rendezvous of British landlords, Irish absentees, American ex-slaveholders and shoddy men, Russian ex-serfowners, and Wallachian boyards. No more corpses at the morgue, no nocturnal burglaries, scarcely any robberies; in fact, for the first time since the days of February 1848 the streets of Paris were safe, and that without any police of any kind.'

Not for long, however. As Marx points out, Thiers cannot have it both ways: if the Commune was the work of a few 'usurpers' who had held the citizens of Paris hostage for two months, why did the bloodhounds of Versailles have to murder tens of thousands of people in order to kill the revolution? He concludes with another roar of *saeva indignatio* at the government's brutality and a promise that the spirit of the Commune will not be suppressed, in France or anywhere else.

> The soil out of which it grows is modern society itself. It cannot be stamped out by any amount of carnage. To stamp it out, the governments would have to stamp out the despotism of capital over labour – the condition of their own parasitical existence.
>
> Working men's Paris, with its Commune, will be for ever celebrated as the glorious harbinger of a new society. Its martyrs are enshrined in the great heart of the working class. Its exterminators history has already nailed to that eternal pillory from which all the prayers of their priests will not avail to redeem them.

The Civil War in France was one of Marx's most intoxicating tracts – far too heady for the temperate English trade unionists Benjamin Lucraft and George Odger, who resigned from the General Council as soon as the text was approved, protesting that the International had no business meddling in politics. (Henceforth they would pursue their modest ambitions through the dear old non-political Liberal Party.) The first two printings of 3,000 copies were sold out within a fortnight; German and French editions followed soon afterwards. Perhaps Marx's most impressive achievement was to make the rival factions of the Left quite forget their squabbles. 'The French translation of the *Civil War* has had an excellent effect on the refugees,' his daughter Jenny wrote, 'for it has equally satisfied all parties – Blanquists, Proudhonists and Communists.'

It also had an excellent effect on the notoriety of Karl Marx and his Association. Those who uphold the status quo can never believe that ordinary people might be able or willing to challenge it, and so any act of civil disobedience or defiance is invariably followed by a hunt for the hidden hand – whether a single Mr Big or a 'tightly knit group of politically motivated men' – that has been pulling the strings. (One of the most delicious examples of this paranoid tendency can be found in Agatha Christie's novel *The Secret Adversary*, published in 1922, in which the dauntless private detectives Tommy and Tuppence investigate a sudden spate of industrial strikes. 'The Bolshevists are behind the labour unrest,' they learn, 'but this man is *behind the Bolshevists*.' The villain, who masterminded and manipulated the entire Russian revolution without drawing attention to himself, turns out to be an Englishman named Mr Brown.) The Victorian versions of Tommy and Tuppence did not have far to look for the criminal force behind the Paris Commune. The evidence was all there on the last page of *The Civil War in France*. 'The police-tinged bourgeois mind naturally figures to itself the International Working Men's Association as acting in the manner of a secret conspiracy, its central body ordering, from time to time, explosions in different countries,' Marx noted sarcastically. 'Our Association is, in fact, nothing but the international bond between the most advanced working men in the various countries of the civilised world. Wherever, in whatever shape, and under whatever conditions the class struggle obtains any consistency, it is but natural that members of our Association should stand in the foreground.'

Although a few of its individual members had been elected to the Commune, the International itself had said and done nothing throughout those two months apart from commissioning Marx to compose an Address, which appeared too late to have any influence on the outcome. But his exaggerated claim that the Association was 'in the foreground' set off a hue and cry across the continent. Jules Favre, now reinstated as foreign minister, asked all European governments to outlaw the International at once. A French newspaper identified Marx as the 'supreme chief' of the conspirators, alleging that he had 'organised' the uprising of 18 February from his lair in London. The International was said to have seven million members, all awaiting Marx's orders to

revolt. The great Mazzini, romantic hero of republican
nationalism, seized the chance to settle an old score, informing
the Italian and British press that Marx was 'a man of domineering
disposition; jealous of the influence of others; governed by no
earnest, philosophical, or religious belief; having, I fear, more
elements of anger than of love in his nature'.

Other European governments fanned the panic. Spain agreed
to extradite Communard refugees, and the German ambassador
in London urged Lord Granville, the British Foreign Secretary, to
treat Marx as a common criminal because of his outrageous
'menaces to life and property'. After consulting the Prime Minister
and the Queen, Granville replied that 'extreme socialist opinions
are not believed to have gained any hold upon the working men
of this country' and 'no practical steps with regard to foreign
countries are known to have been taken by the English branch of
the Association'. Besides, one couldn't arrest a man who had
broken no law.

Lord Aberdare, the Home Secretary, was continually badgered
to do something about Marx and the International, particularly
by a noisy backbench MP called Alexander Baillie-Cochrane.
Before offering an opinion, Aberdare asked his private secretary
to obtain copies of the International's supposedly incendiary
literature. Marx was happy to co-operate: on 12 July he sent the
Home Office a parcel of papers that included the Inaugural
Address, the Provisional Rules and a copy of *The Civil War in
France*. When news of this reached Bakunin, he denounced Marx
as a 'sneaky and calumniatory police spy' – a libel that has been
repeated periodically ever since. One of Marx's most recent
biographers, Robert Payne, concludes that 'there is some truth in
the charge'.

But why shouldn't Marx strive to dispel nonsense that might
otherwise have been believed by the British government? Unlike
Bakunin, he had no time for clandestine conspiracies. The
International was an association of legally constituted trade
unions, so why behave as if there were some guilty secret lurking

in the wainscoting? His belief in openness was fully vindicated when Aberdare told Parliament, after studying the documents, that Marx and his supporters were harmless malcontents who needed only 'education with some religious training' to put themselves to rights. *The Times* was unconvinced, fearing that solid English trade unionists who wanted nothing more than 'a fair day's wage for a fair day's work' might be corrupted by 'strange theories' imported from abroad.

Thanks to Marx's pamphlet, British newspapers were now fully alert to the enemy within. 'Little as we saw or heard openly of the influence of the "International", it was in fact the real motive force whose hidden hand guided, with a mysterious and dreaded power, the whole machine of the Revolution,' *Fraser's Magazine* reported in June 1871. A Catholic magazine, the *Tablet*, warned its readers about the sinister significance of an unprepossessing bookseller's shop in central London. 'We would venture to set that undistinguished shop above more than one palace and monument. For there are the headquarters of a society whose behests are obeyed by countless thousands from Moscow to Madrid, and in the New World as in the Old, whose disciples have already waged desperate war against one government, and whose proclamations pledge it to wage war against every government – the ominous, the ubiquitous International Association of Workmen.' A *Spectator* editorial, while praising Marx's prose style ('as vigorous as Cobbett's'), thought the Address was 'perhaps the most significant and ominous of the political signs of the times'. Even the *Pall Mall Gazette*, for which Engels had been a valued contributor during the Franco-Prussian war, joined the witchhunt, describing Marx as 'an Israelite by birth' who had placed himself at the head of 'a vast conspiracy having for its object to create political communism'.

After years of obscurity, Karl Marx suddenly woke up to find himself infamous. 'It is true, no doubt, that the secretary of that body, who assumes to direct it and to speak and write in its name, is a mischievous, hot-headed, and intemperate German, named

Karl Marx,' the *Quarterly Review* reported. 'It is true, too, that many of his English colleagues are disgusted at his violence and resist his imperious behaviour, and altogether refuse to be dragged through the mire and blood which have no repugnant qualities for him.' At first he was rather flattered by all the hullaballoo. 'I have the honour to be at this moment the most calumniated and the most menaced man in London,' he bragged to his German friend Ludwig Kugelmann. 'That really does one good after a tedious twenty years' idyll in the backwoods. The government paper – the *Observer* – threatens me with legal prosecution. Let them dare! I don't care a damn about these scoundrels!' But this insouciant defiance soon gave way to injured pride at the falsehoods and fantasies that were repeated in the press almost daily. When Jenny offered to help out by demanding an apology on his behalf from the weekly magazine *Public Opinion*, he instructed her to enclose her old calling card ('Mme Jenny Marx, *née* Baronesse de Westphalen') – which, he hoped, 'will be bound to put fear into those Tories'. Mostly, however, he preferred less subtle forms of counter-attack. 'If your paper continues to spread such lies, legal action will be taken against it,' he warned the editor of a French newspaper in London, *L'International*, which had claimed that 'infatuated' European workers were bankrupting themselves to provide Marx with 'every desirable comfort for leading a pleasant life in London'. Fresh libels in the *Pall Mall Gazette* provoked yet another riposte:

Sir,

From the Paris correspondence in your yesterday's publication I see that while fancying to live in London, I was, in reality, arrested in Holland on the request of Bismarck-Favre. But, maybe, this is but one of the innumerable sensational stories about the International which for the last two months the Franco-Prussian police has never tired of fabricating, the Versailles press of publishing, and the rest of the European press of reproducing.

I have the honour, Sir, to be
Yours obediently,
Karl Marx

1, Modena Villas, Maitland Park.

The *Pall Mall Gazette* retaliated by accusing Marx of libelling the
French politician Jules Favre – and the obedient correspondent
from Modena Villas once again took up his pen. 'I declare you to
be a libeller,' he told the editor, Frederick Greenwood. 'It is no
fault of mine that you are as ignorant as arrogant. If we lived on
the Continent, I should call you to account in another way.
Obediently, Karl Marx.' To English readers, of course, the
publication of such a letter merely confirmed their worst fears
about this dangerous German ruffian.

In mid-July a correspondent from the New York *World* travelled
to Modena Villas to inspect the ogre in his den. The first surprise
was that Marx's surroundings and appearance were those of a
well-to-do man of the middle class – a thriving stockbroker,
perhaps.

It was comfort personified, the apartment of a man of taste
and of easy means, but with nothing in it peculiarly characteristic of its owner. A fine album of Rhine views on the table,
however, gave a clue to his nationality. I peered cautiously into
the vase on the side-table for a bomb. I sniffed for petroleum,
but the smell was the smell of roses. I crept back stealthily to
my seat, and moodily awaited the worst.

He has entered and greeted me cordially, and we are sitting
face to face. Yes, I am *tête à tête* with the revolution incarnate,
with the real founder and guiding spirit of the International
Association, with the author of the address in which capital
was told that if it warred on labour it must expect to have its
house burned down about its ears – in a word, with the apologist
for the Commune of Paris. Do you remember the bust of

Socrates, the man who died rather than profess his belief in the gods of the time – the man with the fine sweep of profile for the forehead running meanly at the end into a little snub, curled-up feature like a bisected pothook that formed the nose? Take this bust in your mind's eye, colour the beard black, dashing it here and there with puffs of grey; clap the head thus made on a portly body of the middle height, and the Doctor is before you. Throw a veil over the upper part of the face and you might be in the company of a born vestryman. Reveal the essential feature, the immense brow, and you know at once that you have to deal with that most formidable of all composite forces – a dreamer who thinks, a thinker who dreams.

The interview itself scarcely lived up to the elaborate *mise en scène*. Was Marx the shadowy puppetmaster behind the International? 'There is no mystery to clear up, dear sir,' he chuckled, 'except perhaps the mystery of human stupidity in those who perpetually ignore the fact that our Association is a public one and that the fullest reports of its proceedings are published for all who care to read them. You may buy our rules for a penny, and a shilling laid out in pamphlets will teach you almost as much about us as we know ourselves.' The American newsman was unconvinced. The International might be a society of genuine working men, but were they not mere instruments in the hands of an evil genius masquerading as a respectable middle-class citizen of north-west London? 'There is,' Marx answered curtly, 'nothing to prove it.'

He grew weary of refuting the sensational rumours that were surfacing all over western Europe and beyond. A French newspaper, *L'Avenir Libéral*, reported that he had died; he then read his own obituary in the New York *World*, which eulogised 'one of the most devoted, most fearless and most selfless defenders of all oppressed classes and peoples'. Quite gratifying, perhaps – but also an unwelcome reminder of mortality, since he was indeed in feeble health. By mid-August his doctor diagnosed 'overstrain' and recommended two weeks of rest and sea air. 'I have not brought my liver medicine with me,' Marx wrote to Engels from the Globe Hotel, Brighton, 'but the air does me a world of good.' He neglected to add that it was raining continuously and he had caught a beastly cold.

Notoriety followed him everywhere. Shortly after arriving in Brighton he recognised a man lurking on the street corner as a rather inept spy who had often tailed him and Engels in London. A few days later, fed up with having his every footstep dogged, Marx stopped in mid-stride, turned round and fixed his pursuer with a menacing glare. The snoop humbly doffed his hat and scarpered, never to be seen again.

Had they known the truth, these sleuth hounds could have saved themselves much wasted shoe leather. Marx's vast, disciplined army of revolutionists existed only in the imagination of excitable politicians and editors. Once the Commune had been crushed, the International itself soon began to disintegrate. The French section was outlawed, its members either killed or transported to the distant colony of New Caledonia; the English trade-union leaders fell into the embrace of Gladstone's Liberal Party; and many of the American branches were hijacked by middle-class disciples of the weird sisters Victoria Woodhull and Tennessee Claflin, who advocated spiritualism, necromancy, free love, teetotalism and a Universal Language. (Woodhull, who used her undoubted seductive charms to con large sums of money from the tycoon Cornelius Vanderbilt, had begun her career as a snake-oil saleswoman in the travelling medicine-shows. She was a beneficiary of Marx's open-door policy, which held that anyone who roughly subscribed to the Association's statement of aims should be allowed in; but even his patience ran out when she announced her intention to stand for the American presidency as the candidate of the International Working Men's Association and the National Society of Spiritualists.) During Marx's absence at the seaside, several Parisian refugees in London were co-opted on to the General Council, but since most of them were

Proudhonist windbags the old factional squabbles began all over again.

And, of course, there was still the menace of Michael Bakunin, who observed the wounded and limping International like a hungry hyena eyeing up its lunch. He was now intriguing more ruthlessly than ever with his new henchman Sergei Nechayev, a deranged Russian anarcho-terrorist who had come to Switzerland in 1869. Bakunin, no mean fantasist himself, was awestruck by Nechayev's boast of having organised a network of revolutionary cells across Russia, and the dramatic account of his jailbreak from the Peter and Paul Fortress in St Petersburg. Although most of these tales were pure fiction, Nechayev's appetite for violence was real enough: before fleeing from Russia he had murdered a fellow student in St Petersburg, apparently for no better reason than to prove that he could do it. Having teamed up with Bakunin he published a series of incendiary articles and proclamations, ostensibly from 'the International', warning of the wrath to come.

The antics of the Bakuninists split the Federation Romande, the International's Swiss section, down the middle and caused endless confusion – not least because both factions continued to issue statements in the name of the Federation. To settle the dispute the London HQ called a special conference in September 1871, held at the Blue Posts pub off Tottenham Court Road. 'It was hard work,' Marx wrote to his wife, who wisely took herself off to Ramsgate for the duration. 'Morning and evening sessions, commission sessions in between, hearing of witnesses, reports to be drawn up and so forth. But more was done than at all the previous Congresses put together, because there was no audience in front of which to stage rhetorical comedies.'

Marx, always a good performer in pubs, dominated the proceedings. He pointed out that although Bakunin had promised to disband his so-called Alliance of Socialist Democracy as a condition of admission to the International, 'the Alliance was never really dissolved; it has always maintained a sort of organisation'. There was no direct condemnation of Bakunin but the delegates passed a motion noting that Nechayev, who had never been a member or agent of the International, 'has fraudulently used the name of the International Working Men's Association in order to make dupes and victims in Russia'. The Bakuninists were also ordered to stop using the name of the Federation Romande; as a sop, they were allowed to form a separate Swiss section to be known as the Jurassian Federation.

Bakunin had been let off quite lightly. But he knew that Marx was preparing for a final showdown, since the International clearly wasn't big enough for both of them. Soon after the London conference the new Jurassian Federation held a congress of its own, at the Swiss town of Sonvillier, where there was much huffing and puffing about the 'unrepresentative' nature of the London conference. True enough: at the Blue Posts there had been thirteen members of the General Council but just ten delegates from the rest of the world – two from Switzerland (both anti-Bakunin), one each from France and Spain, and no fewer than six from Belgium. The Sonvillier gathering was, however, even less representative: sixteen delegates and every one a Bakuninist. They produced a circular which was distributed to International branches throughout the Continent: 'If there is an undeniable fact, attested a thousand times by experience, it is the corrupting effect of authority on those in whose hands it is placed . . . The functions of members of the General Council have come to be regarded as the private property of a few individuals . . . They have become in their own eyes a sort of government; and it was natural that their own particular ideas should seem to them to be the official and only authorised doctrine of the Association, while divergent ideas expressed by other groups seemed no longer a legitimate expression of opinion equal in value to their own, but a veritable heresy.' The only cure for rampant authoritiarianism, they said, was to strip the General Council of its powers and reduce it to a mere 'letter-box'.

Over the next few months Bakunin issued a series of increasingly hysterical, phlegm-spattered circulars to International members in Spain and Italy, presenting himself as the victim of 'a dire conspiracy of German and Russian Jews' who were 'fanatically devoted to their dictator-messiah Marx'. Only the 'Latin race', he added flatteringly, could foil the Hebrews' secret plans for world domination.

> This whole Jewish world which constitutes a single exploiting sect, a sort of bloodsucker people, a collective parasite, voracious, organised in itself, not only across the frontiers of states but even across all the differences of political opinion – this world is presently, at least in great part, at the disposal of Marx on the one hand and of the Rothschilds on the other. I know that the Rothschilds, reactionaries as they are and should be, highly appreciate the merits of the communist Marx; and that in his turn the communist Marx feels irresistibly drawn, by instinctive attraction and respectful admiration, to the financial genius of Rothschild. Jewish solidarity, that powerful solidarity that has maintained itself through all history, united them.

These putrid ravings were at least sincere, if nothing else. Back in 1869 he had written a lengthy tirade against the Jews ('devoid of all moral sense and all personal dignity') in which he named only five exceptions to the rule: Jesus Christ, St Paul, Spinoza, Lassalle and Marx. When a friend asked why Marx had been granted absolution, Bakunin explained that he wanted to put the enemy off guard: 'It could happen, even in a short time, that I will begin a battle with him . . . But there is a time for everything, and the hour for the struggle has not yet sounded.' Now that battle had commenced, he no longer needed to hide his true feelings.

There is an important distinction to be made here. Until the Second World War, popular novelists such as Agatha Christie sometimes included throwaway anti-Semitic remarks in their books ('He's a Jew, of course, but an awfully nice one'); no one, however, has ever accused Christie of wanting to round up six million Jews and slaughter them. Similarly, the stereotype of the 'economic Jew' was almost universal in the nineteenth century: Marx himself used it in his early essay *On the Jewish Question*. But Bakunin directed his vicious diatribes at 'blood Jews', regardless of their actual religious observances, business methods, social class or political ideology. Where Marx had argued that the emancipation of mankind would free Jews from the tyranny of Judaism, Bakunin wished only to annihilate them. 'In all countries the people detest the Jews,' he wrote in a circular letter to the Bologna section of the International. 'They detest them so much that every popular revolution is accompanied by a massacre of Jews: a natural consequence . . .'

Understandably, the General Council felt obliged to distance itself from these genocidal rants, especially at a time when every editor in Europe was looking for mud to throw at the International Working Men's Association. In June 1872 it issued a pamphlet written by Marx, *The Fictitious Splits in the International*, whose very first page served only to disprove the title by confirming that there was indeed a split as big as the English Channel: 'The International is undergoing the most serious crisis since its foundation.' Bakunin was accused of inciting 'racial war' and organising secret societies as part of his anarchistic master plan to wreck the working-class movement.

He retaliated by demanding that a full congress should be summoned to settle the dispute once and for all. As there had been no congress since 1869 – first because of the Franco-Prussian war and then because of police persecution following the Paris Commune – the General Council could hardly refuse. It duly announced that a plenary assembly would open at the Hague on 2 September 1872. This was the cue for yet more howls of protest from Bakunin, who wanted it held in his own stronghold of Geneva, but the Council pointed out that Switzerland had already been the location for three of the International's four congresses and one could have too much of a good thing. Bakunin decided to boycott the event altogether, while instructing his followers 'to send their delegates to the Hague, but with *imperative mandates*, clearly set forth, ordering them to walk out of the congress in solidarity as soon as the majority has declared itself in the Marxian direction on any question whatever'.

After these preliminary skirmishes the Hague congress opened in a mood of conspiratorial frenzy at the inappropriately named Concordia Hall. There were sixty-five delegates but many more reporters, spies and curious sightseers who came to gaze at the dangerous revolutionaries as if they were lions in a circus. A Belgian newspaper broke the sad news to its readers that Dr Marx, godfather of terrorism and chaos, looked like a 'gentleman farmer'. The liberal Dutch journalist S. M. N. Calisch noted that Marx was said to have relations in Amsterdam: 'If that is correct, then his family will have no worries about introducing him to society or drinking tea with him in the Zoo Café. The impression he makes in his grey suit is exactly *comme il faut*. Anyone who did not know him and had no connection with the nightmare of the feared International would take him for a tourist making a sortie on foot.' Even so, jewellers locked and barred their shops for fear that the communists would otherwise smash the windows and steal all the trinkets. A local paper, the *Haager Dagblaad*, advised women and children to stay indoors.

To the dismay of police agents and pressmen, the congress immediately went into closed session while delegates' bona fides were checked. A spy from Berlin wrote dejectedly to his masters that 'the public is not even allowed a look into the ground floor where the meetings are held, or even so much as make an attempt to overhear through the open window a single word of what is taking place within'. *The Times*'s correspondent did manage to press his ear to a keyhole, but heard only 'the tinkling of the President's bell, rising now and again above a storm of angry voices'. The arguments were both angry and prolonged: for three days the rival factions jostled for advantage by challenging the credentials of almost all their opponents. When someone pointed out that Maltman Barry, present on behalf of the German workers in Chicago, was in fact a Tory from London and 'not a recognised leader of English working men', Marx replied that this was no disgrace since 'almost every recognised leader of English working men was sold to Gladstone' – a remark scarcely calculated to win the other English representatives to his side. Still, at least he could rely on the Germans and the French, who included Jennychen's fiancé, Charles Longuet. Marx's son-in-law Paul Lafargue had cunningly smuggled himself into the Spanish delegation, the rest of which was solidly pro-Bakunin.

At the end of the three-day marathon it was clear that the anarchists were heavily outnumbered. Some delegates, unable to stay away from work any longer, then returned home without waiting for the actual debates and votes; others wandered off in search of more stimulating congress in the local brothels.

'At last we have had a real session of the International congress,' the newspaper Le Français reported after the doors had opened to the public on the evening of 5 September, 'with a crowd ten times greater than the hall could accommodate, with applause and interruptions and pushing and jostling and tumultuous cries, and personal attacks and extremely radical but nevertheless extremely conflicting declarations of opinion, with recriminations, denunciations, protests, calls to order, and finally a closure of the session, if not of the discussion, which at past ten o'clock, in a tropical heat and amid inexpressible confusion, imposed itself by the force of things.' Although he was trying to make himself inconspicuous by sitting discreetly behind Engels, no one doubted that the gentleman farmer was running the show. In the very first debate, on extending the powers of the General Council, a delegate from New York argued that the International needed a strong head 'with plenty of brains'. There was laughter in the hall as all eyes turned simultaneously to Marx. The motion was carried by thirty-two votes to six, with sixteen abstentions.

When the result was announced, Engels suddenly rose from his chair and asked for permission to 'make a communication to the congress'. In view of the International's manifest disunity and the unlikelihood of ever reconciling the French with the Spaniards or the English with the Germans, he and Marx wished to propose that the home of the General Council should be moved to New York.

Unable to believe what they had heard, the delegates sat in numbed silence for a minute or two. As an English observer wrote, 'It was a *coup d'état*, and each one looked to his neighbour to break the spell.' Europe was the cradle of the new revolutionary movement, as the Paris Communards had shown little more than a year before: how could the International nurture and educate its infant from the other side of the Atlantic Ocean? Engels's tribute to the superior 'capacity and zeal' of organised labour in the United States was particularly unconvincing, since everyone knew that for the past couple of years the International's American section had been preoccupied with the struggle against Victoria Woodhull and her crackpot cult. True, an all-American General Council might suffer from fewer quarrels between Proudhonists, Blanquists and Communists, but it would also lack the mighty brain of Karl Marx. Some of his bitterest enemies thoroughly approved of the idea for this very reason, just as many allies felt obliged to vote against. 'His personal supervision and direction are absolutely essential,' one distraught Marxist pleaded. Another said that they might as well transfer the HQ to the moon as to New York. Thanks to the anarchists' block vote, however, Marx and Engels got their way: twenty-six votes for, twenty-three against, and six abstentions.

By exiling the International to America, Marx had deliberately condemned it to death. 'The star of the Commune has already passed its not very elevated meridian altitude,' the *Spectator* commented on 14 September, 'and, unless it be in Russia, we shall hardly ever see it so high again.' So why did he do it? Marxian scholars have treated the question as an insoluble riddle, but there is no great mystery: he was simply exhausted by the effort of holding the warring tribes together. One or two comrades had already been let in on the secret. 'I am so overworked,' he wrote to a Russian friend three months before the congress, 'and in fact so much interfered with in my theoretical studies, that, after September, I shall withdraw from the *commercial concern* [a code-phrase for the General Council] which, at this moment, weighs principally on my own shoulders, and which, as you know, has its ramifications all over the world. But moderation in all things, and I can no longer afford – for some time at least – to combine two sorts of business of so very different a character.' In a letter to the Belgian socialist César de Paepe, dated 28 May 1872, he sounded even more demob happy: 'I can hardly wait for the next congress. It will be the end of my slavery. After that I shall become a free man again; I shall accept no more administrative functions any more . . .' Marx knew that without his commanding presence the General Council would disintegrate anyway and might do serious damage to communism before expiring. Far better to put the wounded beast out of its misery.

After the New York decision, the subsequent debates at the Hague congress could only be something of an anti-climax. But Marx had prepared one more *coup de théâtre* with which to quit the public stage. Two weeks before travelling to Holland he had obtained a document from St Petersburg which seemed to prove that Michael Bakunin was a homicidal maniac. This he now produced, thus igniting a final bonfire of the vanities.

Back in the winter of 1869, short of money as usual, Bakunin had accepted 300 roubles from a publisher's agent called Lyubavin to translate *Capital* into Russian. It would be hard to think of anyone less suited to the task: quite apart from being an incorrigible procrastinator, he was unlikely to do anything that would enhance Marx's reputation. But Lyubavin apparently knew nothing of this, and after a few months he sent a gentle reminder that the manuscript was now due. By way of reply, in February 1870 he received a terrifying letter from Bakunin's rabid attack-dog, young Sergei Nechayev, who claimed to be acting on behalf of a secret 'bureau' of revolutionary assassins. After denouncing Lyubavin as a parasite and extortioner who sought to prevent Bakunin from 'working for the supremely important cause of the

Russian people' by forcing him on to the literary treadmill, Nechayev ordered the publisher to tear up the contract and let Bakunin keep the money – or else.

> Recognising with whom you are dealing, you will therefore do everything necessary to avoid the regrettable possibility that we may have to address ourselves to you *a second time in a less civilised way* ... We are always rigorously punctual, and we have calculated the exact day on which you will receive this letter. You, in turn, should be no less punctual in submitting to these demands, so that we shall not be placed under the necessity of having recourse to extreme measures which will prove a trifle more severe ... It depends entirely on you whether our relations become more amicable and a firmer understanding is created between us or whether our relationship takes a more unpleasant course.
>
> I have the honour to be, Sir, yours truly ...

As a clue as to the nature of his 'extreme measures', Nechayev embellished the writing paper with a crest featuring a pistol, an axe and a dagger.

This is not a technique one would recommend to an author who has missed his deadline. Bakunin later maintained that he was unaware of the letter, just as he had no idea that Nechayev was wanted for the murder of a student in St Petersburg: as soon as he discovered the ghastly truth, in the spring of 1870, he disowned his bloodthirsty associate at once. His plea of innocence has been accepted by historians and biographers ever since, but it is no more reliable than anything else emanating from this world-class fantasist.

The truth resides in the archives of the Bibliothèque Nationale in Paris, where in 1966 Professor Michael Confino discovered a long letter from Bakunin to Nechayev dated 2 June 1870 – that is, *after* the father of anarchism had supposedly disinherited his delinquent son. Far from repudiating him, Bakunin proposed that they continue to plot and scheme together, the only proviso being that 'Boy' (as he fondly called Nechayev) should be more discriminating in his choice of victims. 'This simple law,' he wrote, 'must be the basis of our activity: truth, honesty, mutual trust between all Brothers and towards any man who is capable of becoming and whom you would wish to become a Brother; lies, cunning, entanglement, and, if necessary, violence towards enemies.' So much for Bakunin's repudiation of 'gangsterism'.

That other incriminating letter, from Nechayev to the hapless Lyubavin, had the desired effect when Marx showed it to delegates at the Hague. On the last day of the congress, by a majority of twenty-seven votes to seven, they agreed that Bakunin should be expelled from the association.

The International went into rapid decline after the relocation to New York and formally dissolved itself in 1876. Michael Bakunin died in the same year. Nechayev, his beloved Boy, was deported from Switzerland to Russia in the autumn of 1872, convicted of murder and sent to the St Peter and Paul Fortress – where, after ten years of solitary confinement in a damp dungeon, he died at the age of thirty-five. Marx outlived them all.

The Shaven Porcupine

Paradox, irony and contradiction, the animating spirits of Marx's work, were also the impish trinity that shaped his own life. He would, one guesses, have applauded Ralph Waldo Emerson's defiant creed: 'A foolish consistency is the hobgoblin of little minds, adored by little statesmen and philosophers and divines. With consistency a great soul has simply nothing to do.'

It is no surprise, then, that a man who was perpetually skint throughout his working career should find financial security only when he abandoned the struggle to earn a living. In the summer of 1870 Engels sold his partnership in the family business to one of the Ermen brothers, and with the proceeds he was able to guarantee his improvident friend a pension of £350 a year. 'I am quite knocked down by your too great kindness,' Marx gasped. For two decades Engels had been the breadwinner for an extended tribe of dependants – the Burns sisters, the Marx family, Helene Demuth – while also writing and campaigning energetically for his political cause. He had never once complained. As Jenny Marx said, 'He is always healthy, vigorous, cheerful and in good spirits, and he thoroughly relishes his beer (especially when it's the Viennese variety)'. Accompanied by Lizzy Burns and her simple-minded niece Mary Ellen ('Pumps') – yet another waif for whom he had assumed responsibility – Engels moved down to London, taking a lease on a handsome town house at 122 Regent's Park Road.

Not all the ironies of destiny were so benign. The years of

strife in the International had left Marx with a violent allergy to French socialists, which he had hoped to cure by resigning from the General Council; now fate inflicted two of these chafing irritants on him as sons-in-law. On 2 October 1872, a couple of weeks after the Hague congress, Jennychen married Charles Longuet in a civil ceremony at St Pancras register office.

The bride's mother, who did not always share Karl's more extreme prejudices, certainly endorsed this one. Almost everything about the French set her teeth on edge – their *hauteur*, their *élan*, their *savoir faire*, their *idées fixes*, their *grandes passions* and quite probably a certain *je ne sais quoi* as well. 'Longuet is a very gifted man,' she wrote to Liebknecht when the engagement was announced, 'and he is good, honest and decent . . . On the other hand I cannot contemplate their union without great uneasiness and would really have preferred if Jenny's choice had fallen (for a change) on an Englishman or German, instead of a Frenchman, who of course possesses all the charming qualities of his nation, but is not free of their foibles and inadequacies.'

Sure enough, Longuet proved to be a sullen, selfish and hectoring brute who condemned his wife to a treadmill of ceaseless housework. 'Though I drudge like a nigger,' she told her sister Eleanor, 'he never does anything but scream at me and grumble every minute he is in the house.' For Karl Marx, the only consolations of this miserable marriage were the arrival of grandchildren – five boys, of whom one died young – and the fact that Longuet had a regular income as a lecturer at London University which kept Jennychen fed and housed. (Two years before the wedding, when the Marx family finances plummeted to a hellish new nadir, she had been reduced to seeking work as a governess.)

Laura's husband, by contrast, seemed a hopeless case. Paul Lafargue renounced his medical ambitions because the deaths of their three children had shattered his faith in doctors; he embarked instead on a career in business, buying the patent rights to a 'new process' for photo-engraving. This implausible enterprise was hobbled from the start by constant quarrels with his partner, the Communard refugee Benjamin Constant Le Moussu, and to save the family's honour Marx felt obliged to buy out Lafargue's stake (financed, one need hardly add, by good old Engels). Marx himself then fell out with Le Moussu over the ownership of the patent. Rather than suffer the embarrassment and expense of going to court, they submitted the dispute to private arbitration by a left-wing barrister, Frederic Harrison. In his memoirs he recalled:

Before they gave evidence I required them in due form to be sworn on the Bible, as the law then required for legal testimony. This filled both of them with horror. Karl Marx protested that he would never so degrade himself. Le Moussu said that no man should ever accuse him of such an act of meanness. For half an hour they argued and protested, each refusing to be sworn first in the presence of the other. At last I obtained a compromise, that the witnesses should simultaneously 'touch the book', without uttering a word. Both seemed to me to shrink from the pollution of handling the sacred volume, much as Mephistopheles in the Opera shrinks from the Cross. When they got to argue the case, the ingenious Le Moussu won, for Karl Marx floundered about in utter confusion.

The débâcle fortified Marx's conviction that, beneath their 'French fiddlededeee', Parisian socialists were all liars and rascals. Le Moussu immediately joined his private bestiary of scallywags, damned as an embezzler 'who cheated me and others out of significant sums of money and who then resorted to infamous slanders in order to whitewash his character and present himself as an innocent whose beautiful soul has gone unappreciated'. But Marx's wrath was soon redirected against Paul Lafargue, the incompetent oaf who had got him into this mess. Quite apart from their personal 'foibles and indequacies', both Lafargue and Longuet were political flibbertigibbets who refused to heed the countless sermons and tutorials from their exasperated father-in-law. 'Longuet as the last Proudhonist and Lafargue as the last Bakuninist!' he complained to Engels. 'May the devil take them!'

To lose two daughters to Frenchmen might be regarded as a misfortune; to lose a third would be unthinkably careless. So one can imagine the horrified reaction when Eleanor fell in love with the dashing Hippolyte Prosper Olivier Lissagaray, who at thirty-four was exactly twice her age. It was Lissagaray's misfortune to arrive at Modena Villas when the Gallic wars against Lafargue and Longuet had already begun; in other circumstances he might have seemed quite acceptable. 'With one exception, all the books on the Commune that have hitherto appeared are mere trash. That one exception to the general rule is Lissagaray's work,' Jennychen told the Kugelmanns in 1871, apparently echoing her father's opinion. When Lissagaray published a fuller *History of the Commune* a few years later, Marx even helped Eleanor to prepare an English translation. Nevertheless, the man was indubitably French: his pomaded quiff, supercilious smirk and careless flamboyance all seemed to betoken a fickle individualist, and the onus was on Lissagaray to show that he could become a responsible husband. 'I asked nothing of him,' Marx wrote to Engels, 'but that he should provide proof instead of words that he was better than his reputation and that there was some good reason to rely on him . . . The damned nuisance is that I must be very circumspect and indulgent because of the child.'

Not so: for long periods he forbade 'Tussy' to see 'Lissa' at all, while the more truly circumspect and indulgent Jenny Marx connived at their secret assignations. But these snatched meetings merely aggravated the pain of separation. In May 1873 Eleanor took a teaching post at a ladies' seminary in Brighton, hoping to escape from Marx's baleful glare (and perhaps her financial dependence); by September she was back home in a state of nervous collapse. If forced to choose between her father and her lover she could not defy the gravitational pull of filial devotion – but why should such a choice be imposed? A letter she left on his desk a few months later revealed both her agony and her undiminished obedience:

My dearest Moor,

I am going to ask you something, but first I want you to promise me that you will not be very angry. I want to know, dear Moor, when I may see L. again. It is so *very* hard *never* to see him. I have been doing my best to be patient, but it is so difficult and I don't feel as if I could be much longer. I do not expect you to say that he can come here. I should not even wish it, but could I not, now and then, go for a little walk with him? . . .

When I was so very ill at Brighton (during a time when I fainted two or three times a day), L. came to see me, and each time left me stronger and happier; and more able to bear the rather heavy load left on my shoulders. [Marx was entirely unaware of these visits.] It is *so* long since I saw him and I am beginning to feel so very miserable notwithstanding all my efforts to keep up, for I have tried hard to be merry and cheerful. I cannot much longer . . .

At any rate, dearest Moor, if I may not see him now, could you not say *when* I may. It would be something to look forward to, and if the time were not so indefinite it would be less wearisome to wait.

My dearest Moor, please don't be angry with me for writing this, but forgive me for being selfish enough to worry you again.

Your

Tussy

Marx refused to yield.

Eleanor tried to divert herself by keeping busy, just as her father always had. She enrolled for acting classes with a Mrs Vezin, in the hope of realising childhood fantasies of a stage career; she joined the New Shakespeare Society and the Browning Society, two of the many groups founded by the socialist teacher

Frederick James Furnivall; like Marx before her, she discovered the warm sanctuary of the British Museum, where she undertook freelance research and translations for Furnivall. (It was while working in the reading room that she met a young Irishman named George Bernard Shaw, newly arrived in England, who became a firm friend.) Years later, after giving a recitation at the annual meeting of the Browning Society in June 1882, she wrote excitedly to Jennychen,

> The place was crowded – and as all sorts of 'literary' and other 'swells' were there I felt ridiculously nervous but went on capitally. Mrs Sutherland Orr (the sister of Frederick Leighton, the president of the Royal Academy) wants to take me to see Browning and recite his own poems to him! I have been asked to go this afternoon to a 'crush' at Lady Wilde's. She is the mother of that very limp and nasty young man, Oscar Wilde, who has been making such a d—d ass of himself in America. As the son has not yet returned and the mother is nice I may go ... What a fine thing enthusiasm is!

The exclamation marks, like the name-dropping awe with which she mentions the 'swells', are worthy of Charles Pooter himself.

Though enthusiasm brought some joy and consolation it could not entirely distract her from the Lissagaray *impasse*. What most grieved Eleanor was that Jenny, who never understood her, should be so sweetly sympathetic while the beloved Moor seemed oblivious to her sacrifice – even though 'our natures were so exactly alike'. As many visitors remarked, there was a startling physical resemblance too: a broad, low forehead above dark bright eyes and a prominent nose. Draw a beard on Eleanor's photograph and you have the very image of the young Karl Marx. 'I unfortunately only inherited my father's nose,' she joked, 'and not his genius.' When comparing his daughters Marx would acknowledge that 'Jenny is most like me, but Tussy *is* me'. Following his example, she sought to calm her nerves with chain-smoking, a habit common enough among literary gents but rare and shocking for a well-educated Victorian girl still in her teens.

Even their ailments achieved a gruesome synchronicity. Tussy's depression manifested itself in headaches, insomnia, biliousness and almost all the other symptoms (except carbuncles) which Marx knew so well. 'What neither Papa nor the doctors nor anyone will understand,' she complained, 'is that it is chiefly *mental worry* that affects me' – a strange lapse for the man who had himself once admitted that 'my sickness always originates in the mind'. For much of the 1870s this pair of wheezing semi-invalids traipsed around the spas of Europe in search of a cure, but it is hard to avoid the conclusion that they were making each other ill. In August 1873, when Tussy was having her fainting fits in Brighton, Marx wrote to a comrade in St Petersburg, 'I have since months suffered severely, and found myself, for some time, even in a dangerous state of illness, consequent upon overwork. My head was so seriously affected that a paralytic strike was to be apprehended . . .' Two weeks later, while drinking a spoonful of raspberry vinegar in the belief that it might do him good, he had a terrible choking fit: 'My face went quite black, etc. Another second or so and I would have departed this life.' After Tussy's return to London he began to brood on 'the serious possibility of my succumbing to apoplexy'. At first his doctor thought he might have had a stroke, but the diagnosis was then revised to nervous exhaustion. On 24 November, much to Jenny Marx's relief, father and daughter left London to take the waters at Harrogate.

Both of them enjoyed their three weeks of rest and mineral baths, though Marx did his tortured brain no favours by reading Saint-Beuve, an author he had always disliked. 'If the man has become so famous in France,' he wrote to Engels, 'it must be because he is in every respect the most classical incarnation of French *vanité* . . . strutting about in a romantic disguise and newly minted idioms.' Hardly the ideal book to take his mind off that other strutting Frenchman for whom his daughter was pining. But he seemed cheerful enough, even when his return to Modena

Villas for Christmas was accompanied by an outbreak of carbuncles and a spate of newspaper gossip about his health. 'I myself allow the English papers to announce my death from time to time, without showing any sign of life,' he said. 'I don't give a farthing for the public, and, if my occasional illness is exaggerated, it at least has the advantage that it spares me all sorts of requests (theoretical and otherwise) from unknown people in every corner of the earth.'

On the way back from Harrogate he had spent a day in Manchester being examined by Engels's friend Dr Eduard Gumpert, who found 'a certain elongation of the liver' for which the only known cure was a trip to the fashionable Bohemian spa-town of Carlsbad. Since this entailed travelling through Germany, where he would probably be arrested as a subversive, Marx thought it impossible. But then an idea struck him: an émigré who had lived in England for more than a year was entitled to British citizenship and, therefore, the full protection of Her Britannic Majesty against foreign border-guards. After submitting an application to the Home Office, together with affidavits from four Hampstead neighbours testifying to his 'good character', he and Eleanor set off for Germany on 15 August 1874 in the belief that the certificate of naturalisation would be forwarded within a few days. On 26 August, however, the Home Secretary wrote to inform Marx's solicitor that his application had been turned down. No reason was given; but a confidential letter sent from Scotland Yard to the Home Office on 17 August, now to be found in the Public Record Office, reveals all:

Carl Marx – Naturalisation

With reference to the above I beg to report that he is the notorious German agitator, the head of the International Society, and the advocate of Communistic principles. He has not been loyal to his own King and Country.

The referees Messrs 'Seton', 'Matheson', 'Manning' and

'Adcock' are all British born subjects, and respectable householders. The statements made by them with reference to the time they have known the applicant are correct.

W. Reimers, Sergeant
F. Williamson, Supt.

As it happened, Marx reached Carlsbad without requiring the assistance of Queen Victoria and her plenipotentiaries – possibly because he was accompanied by Eleanor, a British subject from birth. But he remained wary, registering at the Hotel Germania as 'Mr Charles Marx, private gentleman' in the hope that no one would guess his identity. Although the local police saw through this disguise at once, after a month of continuous surveillance they were forced to admit that he gave 'cause for no suspicion' – hardly surprising, since his health regime left no time for fomenting revolution among the palsied inmates and their physicians. 'We are both living in strict accordance with the rules,' he wrote to Engels. 'We go to our respective springs at six every morning, where I have to drink seven glasses. Between each two glasses there has to be a break of fifteen minutes during which one marches up and down. After the last glass, an hour's walk and, finally, coffee. Another cold glass in the evenings before bed.' In the afternoons they explored the wooded granite foothills of the Schlossberg, where other patients were scandalised by the sight of Eleanor puffing away incessantly at her cigarettes.

All those mineral-water sluicings may have done wonders for Marx's liver but they gave him a foul temper – not helped by the arrival of Ludwig and Gertrud Kugelmann, who installed themselves in an adjoining room. Of late he had been increasingly irritated by the doltishness and indiscretion of this self-appointed disciple; now, through the thin hotel walls, he was kept awake by the din of Herr Kugelmann berating his wife. 'My patience came to an end finally when he inflicted his family scenes on me,' Marx reported. 'The fact is that this arch-pedant, this pettifogging bourgeois philistine has got the idea that his wife is unable to understand him, to comprehend his Faustian nature with its aspirations to a higher world outlook, and he torments the woman, who is his superior in every respect, in the most repulsive manner.' He moved to a bedroom on a higher floor and never spoke to Dr Kugelmann again.

One might expect Marx to have been bored out of his wits with the shallow, narrow society of health resorts, but he soon became an *aficionado*. There were further vacations at Carlsbad in 1875 and 1876; after that, when Germany's new anti-socialist laws made the journey too perilous, he transferred his affections to the insuperably bourgeois Isle of Wight, favoured watering-hole of Queen Victoria and Lord Tennyson. Wherever he went, fellow guests were amazed to find that the terrifying communistic bogeyman was in fact the life and soul of the house party. During his 1875 visit to Carlsbad a Viennese newspaper described him as the most popular raconteur in town:

> He always has to hand the *mot juste*, the striking simile, the suddenly illuminating joke. If you share his society accompanied by a woman of evident wit – women and children are the best *agents provocateurs* in conversation and, because they appreciate the general only in relationship to the personal, constantly summon one into the cosy arbour of personal encounters – then Marx will bestow on you with full hands the rich and well-ordered treasure of his memories. He then prefers to direct his steps back into past days when romanticism was singing its last free woodland song, when . . . Heine brought poems into his study with the ink still wet.

Tellingly, the same newspaper recorded that 'Marx is now sixty-three years old'; in fact he was fifty-seven. Three years later, an interviewer from the *Chicago Tribune* noted that 'he must be over seventy years of age'. Though still working on the next two volumes of *Capital* when his doctors permitted, it was as if he had tacitly accepted defeat and settled down to benign anecdotage, content to observe and reminisce. The years of passionate engagement – pamphlets and petitions, meetings and manoeuvres – were over.

With the two older daughters married and settled elsewhere in Hampstead, the villa on Maitland Park Road had become too spacious for the requirements of his shrunken *ménage*. In March 1875 the remaining members of the household – Karl, Jenny, Eleanor, Helene – moved a hundred yards down the street to number 44, a four-storey terraced property which was slightly smaller and far cheaper. He stayed there for the rest of his life.

As he grew older, Marx's domestic habits became more regular and temperate. He no longer had the stamina for pub-crawls up the Tottenham Court Road, epic chess games or all-night sessions at his desk. Rising at a conventional hour he would read *The Times* over breakfast, just like any other middle-class gent, and then retire to his study for the day. At dusk he put on his black cloak and soft felt hat (looking, as Eleanor said, 'for all the world like a conspirators' chorus') and strolled through the streets of London for an hour or so. He was very short-sighted by now: on his return from these excursions he sometimes returned to a neighbouring front door by mistake, discovering his error only when the key didn't fit.

Sundays were devoted to the family: a roast-beef lunch (cooked to perfection by Helene) followed by long walks over the Heath with Laura, Jennychen and her sons. August Bebel, one of the founders of German Social Democracy, was 'pleasantly surprised to see with what warmth and affection Marx, who was described everywhere in those days as the worst misanthrope, could play with his grandchildren and what love the latter showed for their grandfather'. When little Edgar Longuet was eighteen months old he was caught biting at a raw kidney which he thought was a piece of chocolate – and which he continued to chew despite the mistake. Marx promptly nicknamed the lad 'Wolf', though this was later amended to 'Mr Tea' because of his insatiable thirst.

Except on Sunday, callers were discouraged during the hours of daylight, but since Marx's doctor (and indeed his wife) had banned him from working in the evenings he was happy to play the genial host at dinner, dispensing wine and anecdotes to foreign pilgrims who came to make the great man's acquaintance. 'He was most affable,' the Russian revolutionary Nikolai Morozov reported. 'I did not notice in him any of the moroseness or unapproachableness that somebody had spoken to me about.'

Everyone who visited Maitland Park Road made the same startling discovery: under that leonine mane was a playful, purring pussy-cat. 'He spoke in the quietly detached tones of a patriarch, quite the opposite of the picture I had formed of him,' the German journalist Eduard Bernstein reported. 'From descriptions that originated, I must admit, from his enemies, I had expected to meet a fairly morose and very irritable old gentleman; yet now I saw opposite me a white-haired man whose laughing dark eyes spoke of friendship and whose words contained much that was mild. When a few days later I expressed to Engels my surprise at having found Marx so very different from expectations, he asserted, "Well, Marx can nevertheless get most awfully stormy".'

Another German socialist, Karl Kautsky, arrived at Maitland Park Road almost catatonic with anxiety, having heard plenty of stories about these tempests. He was terrified of making a fool of himself like the young Heinrich Heine – who, on meeting Goethe, was so intimidated that he could think of nothing better to talk about than the delicious sweet plums that could be found on the road from Jena to Weimar. But Marx wasn't nearly so distant or forbidding as old Goethe: he received Kautsky with a friendly smile and asked if he took after his mother, the popular novelist Minna Kautsky. Not at all, Kautsky replied cheerfully – little guessing that Marx, who had taken an instant dislike to this bumptious youth, was silently congratulating Frau Kautsky on her good fortune. 'Whatever Marx might have thought of me,' Kautsky wrote many years later, 'he nowhere betrayed the slightest sign of ill-will. I left him highly satisfied.' Since Marx privately considered Karl Kautsky to be a 'small-minded mediocrity', his forbearance proves how much the Jupiter Tonans had mellowed.

He no longer bothered to correct libels or inaccuracies from his enemies. 'If I denied everything that has been said and written of me,' he told an American interviewer in 1879, 'I would require a score of secretaries.' A tendentious 'biography' issued by a publisher in Haarlem was loftily ignored. 'I do not reply to pinpricks,' he explained, when invited by a Dutch journal to review this slipshod portrait. 'In my younger days I sometimes did some hard hitting, but wisdom comes with age, at least in so far as one avoids useless dissipation of force.' Age conferred eminence, too: even the English, who had ignored the giant in their midst for thirty years (when not blackguarding him as an assassin), now began to show a certain curiosity and respect. In 1879 no less a figure than Crown Princess Victoria, daughter of the English Queen and wife of the future German Emperor Friedrich Wilhelm, asked a senior Liberal politician what he knew of this Marx fellow. The MP, Sir Mountstuart Elphinstone Grant Duff, had to plead ignorance but promised to invite the 'Red Terrorist Doctor' to lunch and report back.

To judge by Sir Mountstuart's subsequent letter to the Princess, Marx was on his best behaviour throughout their three-hour meeting in the ornate dining-room of the Devonshire Club, St James's:

> He is a short, rather small man with grey hair and beard which contrast strangely with a still dark moustache. The face is somewhat round, the forehead well shaped and filled up – the eye rather hard but the whole expression rather pleasant than not, by no means that of a gentleman who is in the habit of eating babies in their cradles – which is I daresay the view which the Police takes of him.
>
> His talk was that of a well-informed, nay learned man – much interested in comparative grammar which had led him

into the Old Slavonic and other out-of-the-way studies and was
varied by many quaint turns and little bits of dry humour...

Having exhausted the conversational possibilities of Slavonic
grammar, Marx turned to politics. He expected a 'great and not
distant crash' in Russia, starting with reforms from above and
culminating in the collapse of Tsarism; there would then be a
revolt against 'the existing military system' in Germany. When
Grant Duff suggested that the rulers of Europe might forestall
revolution by agreeing to reduce their spending on armaments,
thus lightening the economic burden on their people, Marx
assured him that 'all sorts of fears and jealousies' would make this
impossible. 'The burden will grow worse and worse as science
advances,' he predicted, 'for the improvements in the art of
destruction will keep pace with its advance and every year more
and more will have to be devoted to costly engines of war.' Very
well, Grant Duff conceded, but even if a revolution did occur it
would not necessarily realise all the dreams and plans of the
communists. 'Doubtless,' Marx replied, 'but all great movements
are slow. It would merely be a step to better things as your
Revolution of 1688 was.' *Touché!*

Although unaware that his comments would be written down,
Marx had enough caution and common sense to sidestep the
little traps laid by his wily interrogator. As Sir Mountstuart told
the Princess:

In the course of conversation Karl Marx spoke several times
both of your Imperial Highness and of the Crown Prince and
invariably with due respect and propriety. Even in the case of
eminent individuals of whom he by no means spoke with
respect there was no trace of bitterness or savagery – plenty of
acrid and dissolvent criticism but nothing of the Marat tone.

Of the horrible things that have been connected with the
International he spoke as any respectable man would have
done . . .

Altogether my impression of Marx, allowing for his being at the opposite pole of opinion from oneself, was not at all unfavourable and I would gladly meet him again. It will not be he who, whether he wishes it or not, will turn the world upside down.

In gloomier moments, Marx himself sometimes feared as much. He found an exact description of his anxieties in Balzac's novel *The Unknown Masterpiece*, the story of a brilliant artist so obsessive in his perfectionism that he spends many years refining and retouching the portrait of a courtesan to achieve 'the most complete representation of reality'. When he shows the masterpiece to his friends, all they can see is a formless mass of colour and random lines: 'Nothing! Nothing! After ten years of work . . .' He hurls the worthless canvas on to the flames – 'the fire of Prometheus' – and dies that very night.

However, Karl Marx's unknown masterpiece did have at least one famous and appreciative reader – or so he thought. In October 1873, a few months after publication of the second German edition of *Capital*, he had received the following letter:

Downe, Beckenham, Kent

Dear Sir:

I thank you for the honour which you have done me by sending me your great work on Capital; & I heartily wish that I was more worthy to receive it, by understanding more of the deep & important subject of political Economy. Though our studies have been so different, I believe that we both earnestly desire the extension of Knowledge, & that this is in the long run sure to add to the happiness of Mankind.

I remain, Dear Sir
Yours faithfully,
Charles Darwin

Marx and Darwin were the two most revolutionary and influential thinkers of the nineteenth century; and since they lived only twenty miles apart for much of their adult lives, with several acquaintances in common, the temptation to search for a missing link is hard to resist. Even as Marx's coffin was being lowered into the earth of Highgate cemetery, Engels was already making the connection. 'Just as Darwin discovered the law of evolution in human nature,' he declared, 'so Marx discovered the law of evolution in human history.' The small group of mourners at the graveside included Professor Edwin Ray Lankester, an intimate friend of both Marx and Darwin, who apparently had no objection to this attempted marriage of the evolutionist and the revolutionist. The one man who might have protested, Marx himself, was in no position to do so.

His first reaction to Darwin's *On the Origin of Species*, published in 1860, might seem to justify Engels's posthumous judgement. 'Although it is developed in the crude English style,' he wrote in December 1860, 'this is the book which contains the basis in natural history for our view.' A month later, he told Lassalle that 'Darwin's book is very important and serves me as a basis in natural science for the class struggle in history'. But this initial enthusiasm was modified and diluted over the next few years: though the Darwinian 'struggle for life' might be applicable to flora and fauna, as an explanation of human society it led to the Malthusian fantasy that over-population was the motive force of political economy.

Marx's loathing of Malthus led him to take refuge in an even wackier theory, proposed by the French naturalist Pierre Trémaux in 1865. In his book *Origine et Transformations de l'Homme et des Autres Êtres*, Trémaux postulated that evolution was governed by geological and chemical changes in the soil. The idea attracted little attention at the time and is now entirely forgotten, but for a few weeks Marx could think of little else. 'It represents a *very significant* advance over Darwin,' he wrote. 'For certain questions, such as nationality etc., only here has a basis in nature been found.' The 'surface-formations' of the Russian landscape had tartarised and mongolised the Slavs, just as the secret of how 'the common negro type is only a degeneration of a far higher one' could be found in the dusty plains of Africa. Engels, who usually phrased his rare criticisms of Marx as mildly and respectfully as possible, didn't trouble to hide his belief that the old boy had gone barmy. Trémaux was quietly removed from the Marxist pantheon soon afterwards, and Darwin rehabilitated. The edition of *Capital* which he sent out in 1873, inscribed to 'Mr Charles Darwin on the part of his sincere admirer Karl Marx', included a footnote referring to the 'epoch-making' effect of *On the Origin of Species*.

The history of the Marx–Darwin partnership might have ended there but for another letter, which was discovered seventy years ago and has misled countless Marxian scholars ever since. It is dated 13 October 1880:

Downe, Beckenham, Kent

Dear Sir:

I am much obliged for your kind letter & the Enclosure.— The publication in any form of your remarks on my writings really requires no consent on my part, & it would be ridiculous in me to give consent to what requires none. I shd prefer the Part or Volume not to be dedicated to me (though I thank you for the intended honour) as this implies to a certain extent my approval of the general publication, about which I know nothing.— Moreover though I am a strong advocate for free thought on all subjects, yet it appears to me (whether rightly or wrongly) that direct arguments against christianity and theism produce hardly any effect on the public; & freedom of thought is best promoted by the gradual illumination of men's minds, which follow from the advance of science. It has, therefore, always been my object to avoid writing on religion, & I have confined myself to science. I may, however, have been unduly biased by the pain which it would give some members of my family, if I aided in any way direct attacks on religion.— I am sorry to refuse you any request, but I am old & have very little strength, & looking over proof-sheets (as I know by present experience) fatigues me much.—

I remain Dear Sir
Your faithfully,
Ch. Darwin

This was first published in 1931 by a Soviet newspaper, *Under the Banner of Marxism*, which hypothesised that the 'Enclosure' must have been two chapters from the English edition of *Capital* dealing with the theory of evolution. Palpable nonsense, of course, since the book was not translated into English until 1886, three years after Marx's death.

Isaiah Berlin then added to the confusion. In his hugely influential study of Karl Marx, published in 1939, he claimed that it was the *original German edition* which Marx had wished to dedicate to Darwin, 'for whom he had a greater intellectual admiration than for any other of his contemporaries'. According to Berlin, 'Darwin declined the honour in a polite, cautiously phrased letter, saying that he was unhappily ignorant of economic science, but offered the author his good wishes in what he assumed to be their common end – the advancement of human knowledge.' Berlin thus managed to fuse the two letters into one while entirely overlooking the fact that *Capital* – with its dedication to Wilhelm Wolff – appeared in 1867, a full thirteen years before Marx supposedly offered 'the honour' to Darwin.

Since the Second World War, all authors on Marx (and many on Darwin) have accepted the legend of the rebuffed dedication, differing only on the question of which particular version of the book it concerned. 'Marx certainly wished to dedicate the second volume of *Capital* to Darwin,' David McLellan wrote in his 1973 biography, an assertion that is still there in the most recent paperback (1995). This is no more plausible than Isaiah Berlin's theory: Volume Two was assembled by Engels from various notes and manuscripts only after Marx's death. Darwin could not have been asked to 'look over proof-sheets' in 1880 since no such sheets existed. Besides, Engels's introduction to the second volume confirmed that 'the second and third books of *Capital* were to be dedicated, *as Marx had stated repeatedly*, to his wife'.

Everything about that second 'letter to Marx' rings false. Why should Darwin fret about 'attacks on religion' if he had been sent a work on political economy? Yet no quizzical eyebrow was raised until 1967, when Professor Shlomo Avineri argued in *Encounter* magazine that Marx's misgivings about the political application of Darwinism made it 'quite unthinkable' for the great communist to have sought the great evolutionist's imprimatur. How then to explain the 1880 letter? 'Marx's dedication of *Capital* to Darwin,' he proposed, rather lamely, 'was evidently made tongue in cheek.'

Avineri's scepticism – if not his conclusion – struck a chord with Margaret Fay, a young graduate student at the University of California, when she came across the *Encounter* article seven years later. 'My gut-feeling persisted in taking me on repeated and rather aimless trips to the Biology library,' she wrote, 'where I wandered around dipping into biographies of Darwin and Marxist interpretations of his theory of evolution to see if, after all, there was perhaps some political significance in Darwin's work which had escaped me.' Instead, and quite by chance, she found a slim volume called *The Students' Darwin*. The contents were unremarkable enough, simply a rather schoolmasterish exposition of evolutionary theory. But what caught her eye was the publication date, 1881, and the name of the author – Edward B. Aveling, later to be the lover of Eleanor Marx. What if Darwin's second letter had not been addressed to Marx at all, but rather to Aveling?

In this moment of inspiration Margaret Fay solved the mystery that had eluded Isaiah Berlin and innumerable other professors for half a century. *The Students' Darwin* was the second volume in a series, 'The International Library of Science and Freethought',

edited by the crusading atheists Annie Besant and Charles
Bradlaugh. Hence Darwin's reference to 'the Part or Volume' of
a more general publication 'about which I know nothing', and his
reluctance to be associated with 'arguments against christianity
and theism'. Fay's hunch was confirmed by the discovery among
Darwin's papers at Cambridge University Library of a letter from
Edward Aveling, dated 12 October 1880, attached to a few sample
chapters from *The Students' Darwin*. After requesting 'the illustrious
support of your consent' Aveling added that 'I purpose, again
subject to your approval, to honour my work and myself by
dedicating the former to you'.

The only remaining question – of how a letter to Aveling had
ended up in the Marx archive – was easily answered. In 1895
Eleanor Marx and Edward Aveling began sorting through her
father's letters and manuscripts, which had come into their
possession following the death of Engels. Two years later Aveling
wrote an article comparing his two heroes, in which he quoted
the 1873 letter and mentioned that he too had corresponded with
Darwin. Having finished the piece he filed all his research
materials in one folder, little guessing that he was thus laying a
false scent which would be pursued over hill and dale for most of
the next century. As recently as October 1998, the British historian
Paul Johnson wrote that 'unlike Marx, Darwin was a genuine
scientist who, on a famous occasion, politely but firmly refused
Marx's invitation to strike a Faustian bargain'.

In fact, the only known contact between these two Victorian
sages was the indisputably genuine letter of acknowledgement
from 1873, which Marx showed proudly to his friends and family
as proof that Darwin had saluted *Capital* as a 'great work'. But the
book in question, which still sits on a shelf at Downe House in
Kent, tells a sadly different story. It has none of the pencilled
notes with which Darwin habitually embellished anything that he
read, and only the first 105 pages of the 822-page volume have
been cut open. One is forced to conclude that he did no more
than glance at the first chapter or two before sending his note of

thanks – and never looked at the unwanted gift again.

'Typical Englishman,' Marx would probably have muttered had he known the truth. On first reading *On the Origin of Species* he had warned Engels that 'one does, of course, have to put up with the clumsy English style of argument', and the muted, incomprehending reaction to *Capital* convinced him that 'the peculiar gift of stolid blockheadedness' was every true Briton's birthright. Thanks to yet another of fate's practical jokes, the master of nimble dialectics had been exiled to the most philistine country on earth – a land governed by instinct and crude empiricism, where the word 'intellectual' was a mortal insult. 'Though Marx has lived much in England,' the barrister Sir John Macdonnell wrote in the March 1875 *Fortnightly Review*, 'he is here almost the shadow of a name. People may do him the honour of abusing him; read him they do not.' The fact that no English edition was available in his lifetime seemed to Marx a symptom, not a cause, of the national myopia. ('We are much obliged by your letter,' Messrs Macmillan & Co. wrote to Engels's friend Carl Schorlemmer, the professor of organic chemistry at Manchester University, 'but we are not disposed to entertain the publication of a translation of *Das Kapital*.') The language barrier was an insurmountable obstacle to those few Britons who actually wished to study the text. An old colleague from the International, Peter Fox, said after being presented with a copy that he felt like a man who had acquired an elephant and didn't know what to do with it. Among Marx's papers there are several desperate letters from a working-class Scotsman, Robert Banner, pleading for help:

> Is there no hope of it being translated? There is no work to be had in English advocating the cause of the toiling masses, every book we young Socialists put our hands on is work in the interest of Capital, hence the backwardness of our cause in this country. With a work dealing with economics from the standpoint of Socialism, you would soon see a movement in this country that would put the nightcap on this bastard thing.

Those most likely to appreciate the book were the least able to understand it, while the educated élite who could read it had no desire to do so. As the English socialist Henry Hyndman complained, 'Accustomed as we are nowadays, especially in England, to fence always with big soft buttons on the point of our rapiers, Marx's terrible onslaughts with naked steel upon his adversaries appeared so improper that it was impossible for our gentlemanly sham-fighters and mental gymnasium men to believe that this unsparing controversialist and furious assailant of capital and capitalists was really the deepest thinker of modern times.'

Hyndman himself was an exception to this rule – as to every other rule. A product of Eton and Trinity College, Cambridge, a sometime batsman for Sussex County Cricket Club, he was said to have adopted socialism 'out of spite against the world because he was not included in the Cambridge eleven'. (There is more than a trace of him in P. G. Wodehouse's character Psmith, who converted to Marxism when he was expelled from Eton and thus deprived of the honour of playing cricket against Harrow at Lord's; thereafter he addressed everyone as 'Comrade'.) Hyndman never shed the trappings of his class, often appearing before left-wing audiences in a frock-coat and silk top hat. His politics, too, were *de haut en bas*: the proletariat could not be freed by the workers themselves but only by 'those who are born into a different position and are trained to use their faculties in early life'. And yet he convinced himself (if no one else) that he was the reddest and hottest radical in town. 'I could not carry on,' he said, 'unless I expected the revolution at ten o'clock next Monday morning.' Early in 1880, after reading a French translation of *Capital*, he bombarded the author with so many extravagant tributes that Marx eventually agreed to see him.

'Our method of talking was peculiar,' Hyndman wrote of their first meeting at 41 Maitland Park Road. 'Marx had a habit when at all interested in the discussion of walking actively up and down the room, as if he were pacing the deck of a schooner for exercise.

I had acquired, on my long voyages, the same tendency to pacing to and fro when my mind was much occupied. Consequently, master and student could have been seen walking up and down on opposite sides of the table for two or three hours in succession, engaged in discussing the affairs of the past and present.' Although Hyndman claimed that he was 'eager to learn', according to Marx it was the Old Etonian who did most of the talking.

Having gained his entrée, and knowing that Marx's doctor forbade him to work in the evenings, Hyndman acquired the habit of turning up at Maitland Park Road uninvited after dinner. Everyone in the household found this intensely tiresome – especially on the nights when a group of Eleanor's friends, the Dogberry Club, would gather in the drawing-room to recite a Shakespeare play. Marx adored these performances and always insisted on playing games of charades and dumb crambo after-wards ('laughing when anything struck him as particularly comic,' one Dogberry-ite recalled, 'until the tears ran down his cheeks'); but Hyndman had no compunction about barging in and treating the assembled company to his views on Mr Gladstone. As Marx wrote to Jennychen after one such occasion:

We were invaded by Hyndman and his wife, both of whom have too much staying-power. I quite like the wife on account of her brusque, unconventional and determined manner of thinking and speaking, but it's amusing to see how admiringly she hangs on the lips of her complacent chatterbox of a husband! Mama grew so weary (it was close on half past ten at night) that she withdrew.

The inevitable rupture occurred in June 1881 when Hyndman published his socialist manifesto *England For All*, in which Marx was astonished to find two chapters that had been largely plagiarised from *Capital* without permission. A note in the preface admitted that 'for the ideas and much of the matter contained in Chapters II and III, I am indebted to the work of a great thinker and original writer, which will, I trust, shortly be made accessible to the majority of my countrymen'. Marx thought this wholly inadequate. Why could Hyndman not acknowledge *Capital* and its author by name? His lame explanation was that the English had 'a horror of socialism' and 'a dread of being taught by a foreigner'. As Marx pointed out, however, the book was unlikely to assuage that horror by evoking 'the demon of Socialism' on page eighty-six, and even the densest English reader could guess from the preface that the anonymous thinker must be foreign. It was larceny, pure and simple – compounded by the insertion of idiotic mistakes in the few paragraphs that were not directly lifted from *Capital*. Hyndman was banished from Maitland Park Road. In his memoirs, written thirty years later, he babbled about Marx's enthusiasm for new ideas, adding, 'nor was he much concerned about the wholesale plagiarisms from himself of which he might have reasonably complained'. Like so many men of his class, Hyndman had all the sensitivity of an anaesthetised rhinoceros.

Happily, no sooner had Marx fallen out with one English disciple than he acquired another – though this time he took the precaution of never actually meeting the man, for fear of being stuck with another complacent chatterbox. Ernest Belfort Bax, born in 1854, came from a middle-class family of mackintosh manufacturers and devout Christians, but had been radicalised by the Paris Commune while still a schoolboy. In 1879 the highbrow monthly *Modern Thought* began publishing his long series of articles on the intellectual leaders of the age, including assessments of Schopenhauer, Wagner and (in 1881) Marx. Having studied Hegelian philosophy in Germany, Bax was the only English socialist of his generation to accept that dialectic was the inner dynamic of life. He described *Capital* as a book 'that embodies the working out of a doctrine in economy comparable in its revolutionary character and wide-reaching importance to the Copernican system in astronomy, or the law of gravitation in Mechanics generally'.

Marx was thrilled: at last he had found a John Bull who

understood him. 'Now this is the first publication of that kind which is pervaded by a real enthusiasm for the new ideas themselves and boldly stands up against British philistinism,' he wrote to Friedrich Adolph Sorge, an old '48 veteran now living in the United States. Better still, *Modern Thought* posted placards announcing the article on the walls of London's West End. When he read Bax's comments to his ailing wife, she cheered up at once.

Plagiarism and boorishness were undoubtedly the main reasons for Hyndman's expulsion from the inner circle, but he may have been right to suspect that Jenny's lingering illness had ruffled Marx's temper and 'disposed him to see the worst side of things'. In the summer of 1880 Karl was so worried by Jenny's deterioration that he took her up to Manchester for a consultation with his friend Dr Eduard Gumpert, who decided that she was suffering from a serious liver complaint. A long spell of *dolce far niente* was prescribed, preferably at the seaside, and so the entire tribe departed for a holiday in Ramsgate – Engels, Karl and Jenny, Laura and Paul Lafargue, Jenny and Charles Longuet, plus their children Jean, Henri and Edgar. 'The visit is proving especially beneficial to Marx, who, I hope, will be completely refreshed,' Engels wrote to a communist in Geneva. 'His wife has unfortunately been ailing for some time, but is as cheerful as could be expected.'

Not cheerful at all, in other words. Dissatisfied with Dr Gumpert's diagnosis, Marx encouraged her to seek a second opinion from a specialist in Carlsbad, Dr Ferdinand Fleckles – who, since he had never met Jenny, asked for a detailed account of her state. 'What has made my condition worse recently perhaps,' she told him, after listing the physical symptoms, 'is a great anxiety which weighs heavily upon us "old ones".' Now that the French government had declared an amnesty for political refugees, she pointed out, there was nothing to stop her son-in-law Longuet from returning to Paris, thus effectively robbing an old lady of her daughter and grandchildren. 'Dear, good Doctor,

I should so like to live a little longer. How strange it is that the nearer the whole thing draws to an end, the more one clings to this "vale of tears".' Though Marx never saw this letter he understood her mortal terrors well enough: after a month of idleness in Ramsgate, he reported that Jenny's illness 'has suddenly been aggravated to a degree which menaces to tend to a *fatal* termination'.

Marx himself felt slightly more chipper after the rest-cure, but any improvement was soon undone by a wet and freezing winter which 'blessed me with a perpetual cold and coughing, interfering with sleep, etc.,' as he informed a correspondent in St Petersburg, explaining why he could scarcely answer his mail let alone make any progress on the remaining volumes of *Capital*. 'The worst is that Mrs Marx's state becomes daily more dangerous notwith-standing my resort to the most celebrated medical men of London, and I have besides a host of domestic troubles.' One of these was the sudden removal of Jennychen and her sons to Paris, where Charles Longuet had been appointed editor of Georges Clemenceau's radical daily newspaper, *La Justice*. 'You understand how painful – in the present state of Mrs Marx – this separation must be. For her and myself our grandchildren, three little boys, were inexhaustible sources of enjoyment, of life.' Sometimes, hearing children's voices in the street, he would rush to the front window, momentarily forgetting that the beloved youngsters were now on the other side of the Channel. He felt another pang walking through Maitland Park one day when the park-keeper stopped him to ask what had become of little 'Johnny', a.k.a. Jean Longuet. Worse still was missing the arrival of his grandson Marcel, born at the Longuets' new home in Argenteuil in April 1881. Hence, perhaps, the rather grumpy tone of his con-gratulatory message: 'I am of course charged by Mama and Tussy . . . to wish you all possible good things, but I do not see that "wishes" are good for anything except the glossing over of one's own powerlessness.' Still, at least it was a boy. Though Jenny Marx had expected and hoped for a granddaughter, 'for my own part I prefer the "manly" sex for children born at this turning point of history. They have before them the most revolutionary period men have ever had to pass through. The bad thing now is to be "old" so as to be only able to foresee instead of seeing.'

Both he and his wife were feeling as ancient as Methuselah. Karl took Turkish baths to loosen his rheumatically stiff leg; Jenny retired to bed for days on end, becoming ever more emaciated. Now and again, her pain miraculously disappeared and she felt strong enough to go for walks or even visit the theatre, but Marx knew that there could be no recovery. Jenny had cancer. 'Between ourselves, my wife's illness is, alas, incurable,' he wrote in June 1881 to his old friend Sorge. 'In a few days' time I shall be taking her to the seaside at Eastbourne.' While there she was obliged to use a Bath chair – 'a thing that I, the pedestrian *par excellence*, should have regarded as beneath my dignity a few months ago'.

After two weeks on the south coast Jenny was strong enough to set off on a cross-Channel expedition with Karl to visit their new grandson, but by the time they reached Argenteuil she had severe diarrhoea. Their hostess was none too sprightly either. 'Jenny-chen's asthma is bad,' Marx wrote to Engels, 'the house being a very draughty one. The child is heroic, as always.' News then arrived from England that Tussy had been struck down by some dire if unspecified illness, and Marx hastened back to London alone to see what the matter was. He found her in a state of 'utter nervous dejection' that would nowadays be classified as anorexia. 'She has been eating next to nothing for weeks,' he wrote to Engels. 'Donkin [the doctor] says there's no organic trouble, heart sound, lungs sound, etc.; fundamentally the whole condition is attributable to a perfect derangement of action of stomach which has become unaccustomed to food (and she has made matters worse by drinking a great deal of tea; he at once forbade her all tea) and a dangerously overwrought nervous system.'

Jenny Marx returned a couple of weeks later, escorted by the indefatigable Helene Demuth, and immediately took to her bed. At the beginning of October, Marx felt certain that her illness was 'drawing closer to its consummation'. Marx himself was bedridden with bronchitis but perked up no end on learning that the German Social Democrats had won twelve seats in the Reichstag. 'If any one outside event has contributed to putting Marx more or less to rights again,' Engels wrote to Eduard Bernstein at the end of November, 'then it is the elections. Never has a proletariat conducted itself so magnificently . . . In Germany, after three years of unprecedented persecution and unrelenting pressure, during which any form of public organisation and even communication was a sheer impossibility, our lads have returned, not only in all their former strength, but actually stronger than before.'

Jenny Marx died on 2 December 1881. For the last three weeks she and her husband couldn't even see each other: his bronchitis had been complicated by pleurisy and he was confined to a neighbouring bedroom, unable to move. In her last words, spoken in English, she called out across the landing, 'Karl, my strength is ebbing . . .' Marx was forbidden by his doctor to attend the funeral, held three days later in an unconsecrated corner of Highgate cemetery. He consoled himself with the memory of Jenny's rebuke to a nurse on the day before her death, apropos some neglected formality: 'We are no such *external* people!' The other distraction from grief was his own wretched condition, which required him to anoint the chest and neck with iodine several times a day. 'There is only one effective antidote for mental suffering and that is physical pain,' he wrote. 'Set the end of the world on the one hand against a man with acute toothache on the other.'

Engels said that Marx himself was now effectively dead – a harsh observation which nevertheless had a horrible truth. During Jenny's last days, exhausted by sleeplessness and lack of exercise, he contracted the illness that eventually snatched him away. Though his German editor chose this inopportune moment to request a new edition of *Capital*, work was out of the question. On doctor's advice he tried the 'warm climate and dry air' of the

Isle of Wight for two weeks, accompanied by Eleanor – only to suffer gales, rain and sub-zero temperatures. The bronchial catarrh actually worsened, thanks to 'the caprices of the weather', and a local doctor had to give him a respirator to wear while out walking on the front at Ventnor.

Eleanor, still not eating or sleeping properly, veered between morose silence and outbursts of 'an alarmingly hysterical nature'. Her yearning for a career on the stage had now become an almost physical need: until this hunger could be satisfied she would not feed her other appetites either. The day of their return from Ventnor, 16 January 1882, coincided with Eleanor's twenty-seventh birthday, a painful reminder that her best years were being sacrificed on the altar of family duty. Marx knew that he had to set her free. 'As for future plans,' he wrote to Engels on 12 January, 'the first consideration must be to relieve Tussy of her role as my companion . . . The girl is under such mental pressure that it is undermining her health. Neither travelling, nor change of climate, nor physicians can do anything in this case.'

For Marx himself, however, a change of climate was urgently necessary: there could be no remission from his catarrh – 'this accursed English disease' – without fleeing the accursed English winter that had exacerbated it. Since Italy was barred to him (a man had recently been arrested in Milan merely for having the name Marx) he decided to leave Europe for the first time in his life, sailing to Algeria on 18 February.

Thus began a year of ceaseless wandering: three months in Algiers, a month in Monte Carlo, three months with the Longuets at Argenteuil, a month in the Swiss resort of Vevey. With comical consistency, his arrival in each of these places precipitated torrential rain and thunderstorms, even if the sun had been blazing for weeks beforehand. He returned to London in October but the damp and cold immediately forced him away to Ventnor again, where he remained until January 1883. In the 1840s he had been buffeted around the capitals of Europe by the gusts of revolution and reaction; now he became a nomad once more, driven only by a prickle in his bronchial tubes. History was repeating itself, this time as a rather tedious farce. In Algiers he seldom bothered to read the newspapers, preferring to visit the botanical gardens, chat to fellow hotel guests or simply to gaze out to sea. What use were his materialism and dialectics now? In a letter to Laura he recounted a local Arab fable which seemed all too applicable to his own situation:

A ferryman is ready and waiting, with his small boat, on the tempestuous waters of a river. A philosopher, wishing to get to the other side, climbs aboard. There ensues the following dialogue:

PHILOSOPHER: Do you know anything of *history*, ferryman?

FERRYMAN: No!

PHILOSOPHER: Then you've wasted half your life! Have you studied mathematics?

FERRYMAN: No!

PHILOSOPHER: Then you've wasted more than half your life.

Hardly were these words out of the philosopher's mouth when the wind capsized the boat, precipitating both ferryman and philosopher into the water. Whereupon,

FERRYMAN shouts: Can you swim?

PHILOSOPHER: No!

FERRYMAN: Then you've wasted your *whole* life.

In outward appearance he was still a formidable figure: an Englishwoman who met Marx at about this time remembered him as 'a big man in every way, with a very large head and hair rather like "shock-headed Peter's" way of wearing his'. Or, perhaps, like Samson in John Milton's poem, with 'bristles rang'd like those that ridge the back/Of chaf't wild Boars, or ruffl'd Porcupines'. But during the last years of his life, enfeebled by pleurisy and bronchitis, he could no longer summon the strength to smite the Philistines with the jawbone of an ass. Finally accepting that his power had vanished, he offered up his precious fleece to an Algerian barber. 'I have done away with my prophet's beard and my crowning glory,' he wrote to Engels on 28 April 1882.

Eyeless in Gaza; hairless in Algiers. A bald, clean-shaven Karl Marx is almost impossible to imagine – and he made sure that posterity would never see him thus. Before the symbolic shearing he had himself photographed, hirsute and twinkle-eyed, to remind his daughters of the man they knew. It is the last picture we have: a genial Jupiter, an intellectual Father Christmas. As he joked, 'I am still putting a good face on things.' And so he was, at least to his family. The pleurisy was stubbornly resistant to treatment, and while he was in Monte Carlo a local specialist confirmed that the bronchitis was now chronic; but all this was kept from his daughters. 'What I write and tell the children is the truth, but *not the whole truth*,' he explained. 'What's the point of alarming them?'

Jennychen, meanwhile, was keeping a secret of her own from him: she had cancer of the bladder. Heavily pregnant and exhausted by looking after her four lively boys, she somehow managed to hide her agony while Marx was at Argenteuil in the summer of 1882 – helped, no doubt, by the arrival of Eleanor and Helene. Little Johnny Longuet had been running wild since moving to France ('grown naughty out of boredom', Marx deduced) and when Eleanor returned to London in mid-August she took the six-year-old tearaway with her, promising to supervise his education and discipline for the next few months. So much for her hopes of escaping the slavery of duty: from father's nursemaid to nephew's governess in less than a year. Yet in fact this new responsibility brought Eleanor great joy, and before long she thought of Johnny as 'my boy'. His brothers Edgar and Harry went on holiday with their father to Calvados at the end of August, leaving Jennychen with only the infant Marcel. But she was still exhausted, and in constant pain. After giving birth to a baby girl (christened Jenny, known as Mémé) she finally confessed the truth about her bladder disease in a letter to Eleanor: 'To no one in the world would I wish the tortures I have undergone now since eight months, they are indescribable and the nursing added thereto makes life a hell to me.' She added a strict injunction that Moor must not be told. But a summer spent under the same roof had given plenty of clues that something was badly wrong. From his winter quarters on the Isle of Wight he sent out regular appeals for news of 'poor Jennychen' and her baby. 'It distresses me,' he told Eleanor in November. 'I fear that this burden is more than she can bear.'

Marx himself could do nothing to ease the burden. For much of December he was confined to his lodgings at 1 St Boniface Gardens, Ventnor, with a traccheal catarrh – though at least the pleurisy and bronchitis were now in abeyance. ('This, then, is most encouraging, considering that most of my contemporaries, I mean fellows of the same age, just now kick the bucket in gratifying numbers.') On 5 January 1883 he learned from the Lafargues that Jennychen's illness was now critical; the next morning he awoke with such a violent coughing fit that he thought he was suffocating. Were the two events by any chance related? He asked the local doctor, a friendly young Yorkshireman called James Williamson, if mental anguish could somehow 'touch the movements of the mucus'.

Jenny Longuet died at five o'clock in the afternoon of 11 January, aged thirty-eight. Eleanor left for Ventnor as soon as she heard the news:

I have lived many a sad hour, but none so sad as that. I felt that I was bringing my father his death sentence. I racked my brain all the long anxious way to find how I could break the news to him. But I did not need to, my face gave me away. Moor said at once, 'Our Jennychen is dead.' Then he urged me to go to Paris at once and help with the children. I wanted to stay with him but he brooked no resistance. I had hardly been half an hour at Ventnor when I set out again on the sad journey back to London. From there I left for Paris. I was doing what Moor wanted me to do for the sake of the children.

I shall not say anything more about my return home. I can only think with a shudder of that time, the anguish, the torment. But enough of that. I came back and Moor returned home, to die.

Before leaving Ventnor, Marx scribbled a note to Dr Williamson, explaining his hasty departure. 'Please, dear Doctor, send your bill to 41 Maitland Park, London, NW. I regret that I had not the time of taking leave from you. Indeed I find some relief in a grim headache. Physical pain is the only "stunner" of mental pain.' As far as we know, it was the last letter he ever wrote. Marx attached a photograph of himself as a memento, inscribed in a shaky hand 'with the [sic] wishes for a happy new year'.

As Eleanor knew, her father had gone home to die. Racked by laryngitis, bronchitis, insomnia and night sweats, he was too weak even to read the Victorian novels which had often brought solace in such moments. He stared into space or occasionally browsed through publishers' catalogues while warming his feet in a mustard-bath. Helene Demuth tried to revive his spirits by inventing exotic new dishes for supper, but Marx preferred a diet of his own devising – a daily pint of milk (which he had always detested previously) fortified with generous slugs of rum and brandy. By February he had an abscess in the lung and retreated to bed. Engels noted on 7 March that Marx's health 'is still not really making the progress it should. If it were two months from now, the warmth and air would do their work but as it is there's a north-east wind, a storm almost, with flurries of snow, so how can a man expect to cure himself of a long-standing case of bronchitis!' When Engels went to the house on Wednesday 14 March at about 2.30 p.m., his usual time for visiting, Lenchen came downstairs to tell him that Marx was 'half-asleep' in his favourite armchair next to the fire. By the time they entered the bedroom, only a minute or two later, he was dead. 'Mankind is shorter by a head,' Engels wrote to a comrade in America, 'and by the most remarkable head of our time.'

Karl Marx was buried on 17 March 1883 in a remote corner of Highgate cemetery, in the plot where his wife had been laid fifteen months earlier. Only eleven mourners attended the funeral. In a graveside oration, Engels described him as a revolutionary genius who had become the most hated and calumniated man of his time, predicting that 'his name and work will endure through the ages'. Socialist newspapers in France, Russia and America printed eulogies under similarly fulsome headlines – 'The Workingmen's Best Friend and Greatest Teacher', 'A Misfortune for Humanity', 'His Memory Will Live Long After Kings Are Forgotten', 'One of the Noblest Men to Walk the Earth'. But in the country where he had lived for more than half of his sixty-five years, his passing went almost unnoticed. 'The death is announced of Dr Karl Marx, the German Socialist,' the London *Daily News* reported. 'He had lived to see the portions of his theories which once terrified Emperors and Chancellors die out . . . English working men would not care to be identified with these principles.' *The Times* carried a single-paragraph obituary with an error in every sentence, claiming that he had been born in Cologne and emigrated to France at the age of twenty. Only the *Pall Mall Gazette* guessed that he might be remembered: '*Capital*, unfinished as it is, will beget a host of smaller books, and exercise a growing influence on men of all classes who think earnestly on social questions.'

What epitaph would he have chosen for himself? While holidaying at Ramsgate in the summer of 1880 Marx had met the American journalist John Swinton, who was writing a series on 'travels in France and England' for the *New York Sun*. Swinton watched the old patriarch playing on the beach with his grand-children ('not less finely than Victor Hugo does Karl Marx understand the art of being a grandfather') and then, at dusk, was granted an interview. As he reported:

The talk was of the world, and of man, and of time, and of ideas, as our glasses tinkled over the sea. The railway train waits for no man, and night is at hand. Over the thought of the babblement and rack of the age and ages, over the talk of the day and the scenes of the evening, arose in my mind one question touching upon the final law of being, for which I would seek answer from this sage. Going down to the depths of language and rising to the height of emphasis, during an interspace of silence, I interrupted the revolutionist and philosopher in these fateful words: 'What is?'

And it seemed as though his mind were inverted for a moment while he looked upon the roaring sea in front and the restless multitude upon the beach. 'What is?' I had inquired, to which in deep and solemn tone, he replied: 'Struggle!' At first it seemed as though I had heard the echo of despair; but peradventure it was the law of life.

Consequences

Karl Marx died stateless and intestate. His estate was assessed at £250, largely based on the value of furniture and books in 41 Maitland Park Road. These, together with his vast collection of letters and notebooks, passed into Engels's keeping – as did Helene Demuth, who was employed as the housekeeper at 122 Regent's Park Road until her death from bowel cancer on 4 November 1890.

Engels devoted himself to collating the notes and manuscripts for *Capital*. Volume II was published (in Germany) in July 1885, Volume III in November 1894. The first official English translation (1887) sold badly, but a pirated English-language edition which appeared in New York three years later exhausted its print run of 5,000 copies almost at once – possibly because the publisher sent a circular to Wall Street bankers claiming that the book revealed 'how to accumulate capital'. Engels died of cancer of the oesophagus on 5 August, 1895. About eighty people attended the funeral at Woking crematorium; Eleanor Marx and three friends then travelled to Eastbourne, took a rowing boat six miles out from Beachy Head and consigned his ashes to the sea.

After Engels's death, the task of sorting and storing Marx's papers fell to Eleanor Marx and her lover, Edward Aveling. Although astonishingly ugly and notoriously unreliable, Aveling was also a silver-tongued charmer who 'needed but half an hour's start of the handsomest man in London' to seduce a woman. He and Eleanor lived together openly, but since most of their friends were actors, freethinkers and other bohemian types no one was unduly scandalised. What did shock many guests was how appallingly he treated her: the novelist Olive Schreiner described Aveling as a 'ruffian'; William Morris thought him a 'disreputable dog'. Eleanor discovered how right they were in March 1898, when she learned that he had secretly married a twenty-two-year-old actress the previous summer. Aveling's solution to the crisis was to propose a suicide pact. Eleanor duly wrote a tender note of farewell and swallowed the prussic acid which he provided. Aveling, needless to say, never intended to keep his side of the bargain: as soon as she had taken the lethal dose he left the house. Though not charged with murder, he undoubtedly killed her.

Laura and Paul Lafargue lived outside Paris, mostly on the money they had sponged from Engels. In November 1911, when he was sixty-nine and she sixty-six, they decided that there was nothing left to live for and committed suicide together. The main speaker at their joint funeral was a representative of the Russian communists, one Vladimir Ilyich Lenin, who said that the ideas of Laura's father would be triumphantly realised sooner than anyone guessed.

Four of Marx's children predeceased him, and the two survivors both killed themselves. The only member of the family to escape the curse was Freddy Demuth, who lived and worked quietly in east London. He died of cardiac failure on 28 January 1929, aged seventy-seven. To the end, neither he nor anyone else suspected that Freddy might be a son of the man whose face and name were, by then, known throughout the world.

Confessions

All three Marx daughters loved the Victorian parlour game 'Confessions' – nowadays often known as the Proust Question-naire – and in the mid-1860s invited their father to submit himself to interrogation. Here are his answers:

Your favourite virtue:	Simplicity
Your favourite virtue in man:	Strength
Your favourite virtue in woman:	Weakness
Your chief characteristic:	Singleness of purpose
Your idea of happiness:	To fight
Your idea of misery:	Submission
The vice you excuse most:	Gullibility
The vice you detest most:	Servility
Your aversion:	Martin Tupper [popular Victorian author]
Favourite occupation:	Book-worming
Favourite poet:	Shakespeare, Aeschylus, Goethe
Favourite prose-writer:	Diderot
Favourite hero:	Spartacus, Kepler
Favourite heroine:	Gretchen
Favourite flower:	Daphne

Favourite colour:	Red
Favourite name:	Laura, Jenny
Favourite dish:	Fish
Favourite maxim:	*Nihil humani a me alienum puto*
	[Nothing human is alien to me]
Favourite motto:	*De omnibus dubitandum*
	[Everything should be doubted]

Regicide

During his visit to Germany in 1867, while waiting for the proof-sheets of *Capital*, Karl Marx attended a party given by the chess master Gustav R. L. Neumann. A record survives of one game he played that night, against a man called Meyer.

	Marx	**Meyer**		**Marx**	**Meyer**
1.	e2–e4	e7–e5	16.	Nd5 × f4	Nc6–e5
2.	f2–f4	e5 × f4	17.	Qf3–e4	d7–d6
3.	Ng1–f3	g7–g5	18.	h2–h4	Qg5–g4
4.	Bf1–c4	g5–g4	19.	Bc4 × f7	Rg8–f8
5.	0–0	g4 × Nf3	20.	Bf7–h5	Qg4–g7
6.	Qd1 × f3	Qd8–f6	21.	d3–d4	Ne5–c6
7.	e4–e5	Qf6 × e5	22.	c2–c3	a7–a5
8.	d2–d3	Bf8–h6	23.	Nf4–e6+	Bc8 × Ne6
9.	Nb1–c3	Ng8–e7	24.	Rf1 × Rf8+	Qg7 × Rf8
10.	Bc1–d2	Nb8–c6	25.	Qe4 × Be6	Ra8–a6
11.	Ra1–e1	Qe5–f5	26.	Re1–f1	Qf8–g7
12.	Nc3–d5	Ke8–d8	27.	Bh5–g4	Nc6–b8
13.	Bd2–c3	Rh8–g8	28.	Rf1–f7	Black resigns
14.	Bc3–f6	Bh6–g5			
15.	Bf6 × Bg5	Qf5 × Bg5			

Acknowledgements

I am grateful to the following institutions for their assistance: the International Institute of Social History, Amsterdam, final resting place of Marx's letters and manuscripts as well as many other socialist archives of the period; the Karl Marx Museum (Friedrich Ebert Foundation) in Trier and its associated Karl Marx Study-Centre, not least for helping me find a record of Marx's one surviving chess game; the Marx Memorial Library, London; the British Library; the London Library; the Public Records Office, Kew; the Census Office. My thanks, too, to the people who provided books and documents that might otherwise have eluded me: Anna Cuss of the Royal Society of Arts, Paul Foot, Mark Garnett, Ed Glinert, Ronald Gray, Bruce Page, Christopher Hawtree, Professor Colin Matthew, Bob O'Hara, Nick Spurrier. Both my agent, Pat Kavanagh, and Victoria Barnsley of Fourth Estate said yes to my suggestion of a Marx biography with heartening alacrity. But my greatest debt of love and gratitude is to Julia Thorogood, who never lost her enthusiasm for the book even at odd moments when my own faith and eyelids were sagging. Jack, Frank and GeorgeAnna Thorogood also gave great encouragement. Any errors of fact or interpretation are, of course, the sole responsibility of my beloved sons Bertie and Archie.

Endnotes

In the endnotes that follow, I have used the following abbreviations:

MECW: *Karl Marx, Frederick Engels, Collected Works* (forty-seven volumes issued since 1975 by Progress Publishers, Moscow, prepared in collaboration with International Publishers Co. Inc., New York, and Lawrence & Wishart, London).

RME: *Reminiscences of Marx and Engels* (Foreign Languages Publishing House, Moscow, no date).

KMIR: *Karl Marx: Interviews and Recollections*, ed. David McLellan (Macmillan, London, 1981).

Details of other textual sources are given in the notes themselves.

Page numbers are given below to locate references in the text, rather than note numbers.

1 The Outsider

page

7. 'Blessed is he . . .' Letter from KM to FE, 21 June 1854.

8. 'He was a unique, an unrivalled storyteller . . .' From 'Karl Marx' by Eleanor Marx, *RME*, p. 251.

8. 'She could not countenance her brother . . .' From 'Meetings with Marx' by Maxim Kovalevsky in *RME*, p. 299.

9. 'We cannot always attain . . .' *MECW*, Vol. 1, p. 4.

9. 'The sons had been rabbis for centuries . . .' Eleanor Marx to Wilhelm Liebknecht in *Mohr und General: Erinnerungen an Marx und Engels* (Dietz Verlag, Berlin, 1965).

9. 'Within its walls it is burdened . . .' Goethe's *French Campaign*, quoted in *Karl*

Marx: Man and Fighter by Boris Nicolaievsky and Otto Maenchen-Helfen (Methuen, London, 1936; revised edition published by Penguin, Harmondsworth, 1973).

11. 'To the Prussian state, the members of its established religion . . .' From 'The Baptism of Karl Marx' by Eugene Kamenka, *The Hibbert Journal*, Vol. LVI (1958), pp. 340–51.

12. 'Allow me to note . . .' Letter from Henriette Marx to KM, 29 November 1835.

12. 'I am being dunned . . .' Letter from KM to FE, 8 January 1863.

14. 'I found the position of good Herr Wyttenbach . . .' Letter from Heinrich Marx to KM, 18 November 1835.

14. 'Herr Loers has taken it ill . . .' Letter from Heinrich Marx to KM, 18 November 1835.

14. 'Social reforms are never carried out . . .' From 'Speech of Dr Marx on Protection, Free Trade, and the Working Classes', *Northern Star*, 9 October 1847.

14. 'Nine lecture courses seem to me rather a lot . . .' Letter from Heinrich Marx to KM, 18–25 November 1835.

15. 'Youthful sins in any enjoyment . . .' Letter from Heinrich Marx to KM, early 1836.

15. 'You must avoid everything that could make things worse . . .' Letter from Henriette Marx to KM, early 1836.

15. 'He has incurred a punishment . . .' Certificate of Release from Bonn University, 22 August 1836, *MECW*, Vol. 1, pp. 657–8.

16. 'Is duelling then so closely interwoven with philosophy?' Letter from Heinrich Marx to KM, about May/June 1836.

17. 'Every day and on every side I am asked . . .' Letter from KM to Jenny Marx, 15 December 1863.

19. 'His respect for Shakespeare was boundless . . .' From 'Reminiscences of Marx' by Paul Lafargue, *RME*, p. 74.

19. 'The children are constantly reading Shakespeare . . .' Letter from KM to FE, 10 April 1856.

20. 'in a perpetual flurry of allusions . . .' From *Karl Marx and World Literature* by S. S. Prawer (Oxford University Press, 1976), p. 209.

20. 'There you are before me, large as life . . .' Letter from KM to Jenny Marx, 21 June 1856.

21. 'The mystificatory side of Hegelian dialectic I criticised nearly thirty years ago . . .' Afterword to second German edition of *Capital*, *MECW*, Vol. 35, p. 9.

22. 'Words I teach all mixed up . . .' From 'On Hegel' by Karl Marx, *MECW*, Vol. 1, p. 576.

23. 'the new immoralists who twist their words . . .' Letter from Heinrich Marx to KM, 9 December 1837.

24. 'diffuse and inchoate expressions of feeling . . .' Letter from KM to Heinrich Marx, 10–11 November 1837.

26. 'Hegel remarks somewhere . . .' From the original 1852 text of *The Eighteenth Brumaire*, *MECW*, Vol. 11, p. 103.

28. 'God's grief!!!' Letter from Heinrich Marx to KM, 9 December 1837.

29. 'It should redound to the honour of Prussia . . .' Letter from Heinrich Marx to KM, 2 March 1837.

2 The Little Wild Boar

31. 'If Marx, Bruno Bauer and Feuerbach come together . . .' Letter from Georg Jung to Arnold Ruge, *Marx-Engels Gesamtausgabe*, I i (2), p. 261

32. 'As long as a single drop of blood pulses . . .' From *The Early Texts* by Karl Marx (Oxford University Press, 1971), p. 13.

33. 'My little heart is so full . . .' Letter from Jenny von Westphalen to KM, 10 August 1841.

34. 'In a few days I have to go to Cologne . . .' Letter from KM to Arnold Ruge, 20 March 1842.

34. 'I have abandoned my plan to settle in Cologne . . .' Letter from KM to Arnold Ruge, 27 April 1842.

34. 'How glad I am that you are happy . . .' Letter from Jenny von Westphalen to KM, 10 August 1841.

35. 'Since every true philosophy is the intellectual quintessence of its time . . .' Article in *Rheinische Zeitung*, 14 July 1842, translated in *MECW*, Vol. 1, p. 195.

36. 'who think freedom is honoured by being placed in the starry firmament . . .' Article in *Rheinische Zeitung*, 19 May 1842, translated in *MECW*, Vol. 1, p. 172.

36. 'He is a phenomenon . . .' From *Briefwechsel* by Moses Hess, ed. E. Silberner (The Hague, 1959), translated in *KMIR*, pp. 2–3.

37. 'Who runs up next with wild impetuosity?' From 'The Insolently Threatened Yet Miraculously Rescued Bible', published as an anonymous pamphlet in December 1842, translated in *MECW*, Vol. 2, p. 336.

37. 'It is easy to overlook the obvious . . .' A lone exception is the great American scholar Hal Draper, who included an amusing endnote on 'Marx and Pilosity' in *Karl Marx's Theory of Revolution, Volume II: The Politics of Social Classes* (Monthly Review Press, New York and London, 1978).

38. 'London provided the much venerated man with a new, complex arena . . .' From *Great Men of the Exile* by Karl Marx and Friedrich Engels, translated in *The Cologne Communist Trial* (Lawrence & Wishart, London, 1971), p. 166.

39. 'Last Sunday we had a moustache evening . . .' Letter from FE to Marie Engels, 29 October 1840.

40. 'I subjected this idea to police-examination . . .' *Marx-Engels Gesamtausgabe*, I i (2), p. 257, translated in *Karl Marx* by Werner Blumenberg (New Left Books, London, 1972).

40. 'and then suddenly going to another table . . .' From *Erlebtes* by Karl Heinzen (Boston, Mass, 1874), translated in *KMIR*, pp. 5–6.

41. 'the most stupid person of the century . . .' See *Against the Current: The Life of Karl Heinzen 1809–80* by Carl Wittke (University of Chicago Press, 1945).

42. 'The style is the dagger used for a well-aimed thrust . . .' From *Karl Marx: Biographical Memoirs* by Wilhelm Liebknecht, translated by E. Untermann (London, 1901).

44. 'The *Rheinische Zeitung*, which does not even admit . . .' *Rheinische Zeitung*, 16 October 1842, translated in *MECW*, Vol. 1, p. 220.

44. 'I regard it as inappropriate . . .' Letter from KM to Arnold Ruge, 30 November 1842.

44. 'As editor of the *Rheinische Zeitung*, I experienced . . .' From *A Contribution to the Critique of Political Economy* (1859), translated in *The Portable Karl Marx* (Penguin Books, New York, 1983), p. 158.

45. 'By analogy with this, the legislator would have to draw the conclusion . . .' *Rheinische Zeitung*, 25 October 1842, translated in *MECW*, Vol. 1, p. 225.

45. 'Do not imagine that we on the Rhine live in a political Eldorado . . .' Letter from KM to Arnold Ruge, 9 July 1842.

46. 'One evening the censor had been invited . . .' From 'Karl Marx als Mensch' by Wilhelm Blos, *Die Glocke* v (1919), translated in *KMIR*, pp. 3–4.

47. 'Our newspaper has to be presented to the police to be sniffed at . . .' Letter from KM to Arnold Ruge, 25 January 1843.

48. 'I had begun to be stifled in that atmosphere . . .' Letter from KM to Arnold Ruge, 25 January 1843.

48. 'For my sake, my fiancée has fought the most violent battles . . .' Letter from KM to Arnold Ruge, 13 March 1843.

49. 'Ah, dear, dear sweetheart, now you get yourself involved in politics . . .' Letter from Jenny von Westphalen to KM, 10 August 1841.

50. 'I entered Jenny's room one evening . . .' From *Red Jenny: A Life with Karl Marx* by H. F. Peters (Allen & Unwin, London, 1986).

51. 'So, sweetheart, since your last letter I have tortured myself . . .' Letter from Jenny von Westphalen to KM, *c.* 1839–40.

54. 'The entire German police is at his disposal . . .' Letter from KM to Ludwig Feuerbach, 3 October 1843.

55. 'I am glad to have an opportunity of assuring you . . .' Letter from KM to Ludwig Feuerbach, 11 August 1844.

55. 'It is now quite plain to me . . .' Letter from KM to FE, 30 July 1862.

56. 'What is the secular basis of Judaism?' *Karl Marx: Early Writings*, translated

by Rodney Livingstone and Gregor Benton (Pelican Books, London, 1975), pp. 212–41.

58. 'Religious suffering is at one and the same time . . .' *Karl Marx: Early Writings*, translated by Rodney Livingstone and Gregor Benton (Pelican Books, London, 1975), pp. 243–57.

3 The Grass-eating King

62. 'The bourgeois King's loss of prestige among the people . . .' From *Zwei Jahre in Paris* by Arnold Ruge (Leipzig, 1846).

62. 'Frau Herwegh summed up the situation at first glance . . .' From *1848: Briefe von und an Herwegh*, edited by Marcel Herwegh (Munich, 1898), translated in *KMIR*, pp. 6–7.

62. 'finishes nothing, breaks off everything . . .' From *Arnold Ruges Briefwechsel und Tagebuchblätter aus den Jahren 1825–80*, edited by P. Nerrlich (Berlin, 1886), translated in *KMIR*, pp. 8–9.

63. 'His wife gave him for his birthday a riding switch . . .' Letter from Arnold Ruge to Julius Fröbel, 4 June 1844.

63. 'The poor little doll was quite miserable . . .' Letter from Jenny Marx to KM, 21 June 1844.

64. 'Marx was then much more advanced than I was . . .' From *Mikhail Bakunin and Karl Marx* by K. Kenafick (Melbourne, 1948), p. 25.

65. 'He loved the poet as much as his works . . .' From *KMIR*, p. 10.

66. 'had not other personal differences . . .' From *Karl Marx: Man and Fighter* by Boris Nicolaievsky and Otto Maenchen-Helfen (Methuen, London, 1936).

66. 'I was incensed by Herwegh's way of living . . .' From *Arnold Ruges Briefwechsel und Tagebuchblätter aus den Jahren 1825–80*, edited by P. Nerrlich (Berlin, 1886), translated in *Karl Marx: Man and Fighter*.

66. 'Although the spirit is willing, the flesh is weak . . .' Letter from Jenny Marx to KM, 11–18 August 1844.

67. 'Some would sit on the bed or on the trunks . . .' From *Fünfunsiebzig Jahre in der alten und neuen Welt* by Heinrich Börnstein (Leipzig, 1881).

68. 'it represents man's protest . . .' From 'Critical Marginal Notes on the Article "The King of Prussia and Social Reform. By a Prussian."' *Vorwärts!*, 7 and 10 August 1844. Translated in *MECW*, Vol. 3, pp. 189–206.

72. 'a second Frankenstein on my back . . .' Letter from KM to FE, 4 December 1863.

72. 'From the front, the man who regales *his inner man* . . .' Letter from KM to FE, 27 December 1863.

72. 'Of the many wonderful tales . . .' From 'Karl Marx: A Few Stray Notes' by Eleanor Marx, *RME*, pp. 251–2.

74. 'Although in political and economic discussion he was not wont to mince his words . . .' From *Karl Marx: Biographical Memoirs* by Wilhelm Liebknecht, translated by E. Untermann (London, 1901).

76. 'When I visited Marx in Paris in the summer of 1844 . . .' From 'On the History of the Communist League', by FE, 1885, translated in *The Cologne Communist Trial* (Lawrence & Wishart, London, 1971).

76. 'so pronounced that even in old age . . .' From *Friedrich Engels: A Biography* by Gustav Mayer, translated by Gilbert and Helen Highet, edited by R. H. S. Crossman (Chapman & Hall, London, 1936).

77. 'He's a terribly nice fellow . . .' Letter from FE to Friedrich and Wilhelm Graeber, 1 September 1838.

78. 'Go home again, exotic guests!' *MECW*, Vol. 2, p. 4.

78. 'It has become clear to me . . .' Letter from FE to Friedrich and Wilhelm Graeber, 17–18 September 1838.

78. 'It is extraordinarily good . . .' Letter from FE to Friedrich and Wilhelm Graeber, 1 September 1838.

79. 'What shall I, poor devil, do now?' Letter from FE to Friedrich Graeber, 8 April 1839.

80. 'Ha, ha, ha!' Letter from FE to Friedrich Graeber, 24 April 1839.

81. 'Masses of refuse, offal and sickening filth . . .' *The Condition of the Working Class in England* by Friedrich Engels (London, 1892).

83. 'I simply cannot understand how anyone can be envious of genius . . .' Letter from FE to Eduard Bernstein, 25 October 1881.

85. 'See to it that the material you've collected is soon launched . . .' Letter from FE to KM, beginning of October 1844.

85. 'I find all this theoretical twaddle daily more tedious . . .' Letter from FE to KM, 19 November 1844.

85. 'The *Critical Criticism* has still not arrived!' Letter from FE to KM, 22 February–7 March 1845.

86. 'If I get a letter, it's sniffed all over . . .' Letter from FE to KM, 17 March 1845.

86. 'pleasantly surprised to find that we have no need to feel ashamed . . .' Letter from KM to FE, 24 April 1867.

4: The Mouse in the Attic

89. 'If amazement at this peculiar movement makes one think again . . .' *Vorwärts!*, 17 August 1844, translated in *MECW*, Vol. 3, pp. 207–210.

91. 'I fear that in the end you'll be molested . . .' Letter from FE to KM, 22

February–7 March 1845.

91. 'Her jam tarts are a sweet and abiding memory...' From 'My Recollections of Karl Marx' by Marian Comyn, in *Nineteenth Century and After*, Vol. XCI (1922), pp. 161ff.

92.'The little house should do...' Letter from Jenny Marx to KM, after 24 August 1845.

92. 'It seemed to me very important...' Letter from KM to Karl Leske, 1 August 1846.

93. 'The chief defect of all previous materialism...' From 'Theses on Feuerbach' by Karl Marx, *MECW*, Vol. 5, pp. 3–5.

94. 'Once upon a time a valiant fellow...' *The German Ideology* by Karl Marx and Friedrich Engels, *MECW*, Vol. 5, pp. 19–531.

101. 'Where among the bourgeoisie...' From 'Critical Marginal Notes on the Article by a Prussian' by Karl Marx, *Vorwärts!*, 10 August 1844.

101. 'If I tell you what kind of life we have been leading here...' Letter from Joseph Weydemeyer to Louise Lüning, 2 February 1846, published in the *Münchner Post*, 30 April 1926.

102. 'He was now the great man...' From 'On the History of the Communist League' by Friedrich Engels, *MECW*, Vol. 26, p. 320.

102. 'the fellow's utter lack of respect while he conversed with me...' Quoted in *To the Finland Station* by Edmund Wilson (Macmillan, London, 1972 edition), pp. 193–4.

103. 'Marx was the type of man...' From 'A Wonderful Ten Years' by Pavel Annenkov, in *RME*, pp. 269–72.

105. 'presents communism as the love-imbued opposite of selfishness...' From 'Circular Against Kriege' by Marx and Engels, 11 May 1846; translated in *MECW*, Vol. 6, pp. 35–51.

106. 'So far as France is concerned...' Letter from KM to Pierre-Joseph Proudhon, 5 May 1846.

107. 'Let us, if you wish, collaborate in trying to discover the laws of society...' *Confessions d'un révolutionnaire* by Pierre-Joseph Proudhon (Paris, 1849).

107. 'Monsieur Proudhon has the misfortune of being peculiarly misunderstood...' *Misère de La Philosophie* by Karl Marx (published by A. Frank, Paris, and C. G. Vogler, Brussels, 1847).

109. 'Our affair will prosper greatly here...' Letter from FE to Communist Correspondence Committee, 19 August 1846.

110. 'It is disgraceful that one should have to pit oneself...' Letter from FE to KM, 18 September 1846.

110. 'By dint of a little patience and some terrorism...' Letter from FE to KM, about 18 October 1846.

111. 'The stench is like five thousand unaired featherbeds...' Letter from FE to KM, 9 March 1847.

111. 'If at all possible, do come here some time in April . . .' Letter from FE to KM, 9 March 1847.

112. 'give his word of honour to work loyally. . .' From 'Rules of the Communist League', adopted at the First Congress, June 1847.

112. 'However minor it may be . . .' Letter from KM to Herwegh, 26 October 1847.

112. 'We have tried on the one hand to refrain from all system-making. . .' From 'A Circular of the First Congress of the Communist League to the League Members, 9 June 1847', translated in *MECW*, Vol. 6, p. 589.

5 The Frightful Hobgoblin

115. '*Question 1*: Are you a Communist?' From 'Draft of a Communist Confession of Faith' by Friedrich Engels, *MECW*, Vol. 6, pp. 96–103.

116. 'Completely unopposed, I got them to entrust me . . .' Letter from FE to KM, 25–26 October 1847.

117. 'What is communism?' From 'Principles of Communism', by Friedrich Engels, *MECW*, Vol. 6, pp. 341–57.

117. 'Marx was a born leader of the people . . .' From 'Before 1848 and After' by Friedrich Lessner, in *RME*, pp. 149–66.

118. 'aims at the emancipation of humanity. . .' From *Gründungsdokumente des Bundes der Kommunisten (Juni bis September 1847)*, edited by Bert Andreas (Hamburg, 1969).

118. 'The aim of the League is the overthrow of the bourgeoisie . . .' From *Die Communisten-Verschwörungen des neunzehnten Jahrhunderts* by Karl Wermuth and Wilhelm Stieber (Berlin, 1853).

119. 'The Central Committee charges its regional committee . . .' Quoted in *The Communist Manifesto of Karl Marx and Friedrich Engels*, edited by David Ryazanov (Russell & Russell, New York, 1963).

120. 'a lyrical celebration of bourgeois works . . .' From *All That is Solid Melts into Air: The Experience of Modernity* by Marshall Berman (Verso, London, 1982).

125. 'Our age, the age of democracy, is breaking . . .' *Deutsche-Brüsseler-Zeitung*, 27 February 1848.

126. 'What an ass Flocon is!' Letter from FE to KM, 15 November 1847.

126. 'Good and loyal Marx . . .' *MECW*, Vol. 6, p. 649.

127. 'The German workers [in Brussels] decided to arm themselves . . .' From 'Short Sketch of an Eventful Life' by Jenny Marx, *RME*, p. 223.

127. 'When Jenny appeared in court the next day. . .' See 'To the Editor of the *Northern Star*' by Friedrich Engels, *Northern Star*, 25 March 1848, and

letter from Karl Marx in *La Réforme*, 8 March 1848.

131. 'There's damned little prospect for the shares here . . .' Letter from FE to KM, 25 April 1848.

131. 'The most bitter complaints about Marx came from Engels . . .' From *Erinnerungen eines Achtundvierzigers* by Stephan Born (Leipzig, 1898), translated in *KMIR*, p. 16.

133. 'For a fortnight Germany has had a Constituent National Assembly. . .' *Neue Rheinische Zeitung*, 1 June 1848.

135. 'He could not have been much more than thirty years old . . .' *The Reminiscences of Carl Schurz* (London, 1909), Vol. 1, p. 138.

136. 'A characteristic feature of the Rhineland . . .' Reported in the *Neue Rheinische Zeitung*, 13 September 1848.

137. 'Indescribable rejoicing broke out . . .' *Neue Rheinische Zeitung*, 9 September 1848.

138. 'Name: *Friedrich Engels*; occupation: merchant . . .' *Kölnische Zeitung*, 4 October 1848.

138. 'It is clear from this that the Belgian government . . .' *Neue Rheinische Zeitung*, 12 October 1848.

139. 'this newspaper, with its inventive maliciousness . . .' *Neue Rheinische Zeitung*, 29 October 1848.

140. 'What country in Europe can compare with France . . .' From 'From Paris to Berne' by Friedrich Engels, *MECW*, Vol. 7, pp. 507–29.

140. 'I am truly amazed that you should still not have received any money. . .' Letter from KM to FE, first half of November 1848.

141. 'I have devised an infallible plan . . .' Letter from KM to FE, 29 November 1848.

142. 'The overthrow of the bourgeoisie in France . . .' From 'The Revolutionary Movement', *Neue Rheinische Zeitung*, 1 January 1849.

144. 'In political trials the government nowadays has no luck . . .' *Deutsche Londoner Zeitung*, 16 February 1849.

144. 'becoming increasingly more audacious now that he has been acquitted . . .' Letter from Colonel Engels to Oberpräsident Eichmann, 17 February 1849.

145. 'Relaxation of discipline must have gone very far . . .' Letter from KM to Colonel Engels, 3 March 1849; see also letter from FE to Karl Kautsky, 2 December 1885.

146. 'Wonder was expressed . . .' From 'Marx and the *Neue Rheinische Zeitung*', by Frederick Engels, published in *Der Sozialdemokrat*, 13 March 1884.

147. 'that the much-vaunted bravery under fire is quite the most ordinary quality. . .' Letter from FE to Jenny Marx, 25 July 1849.

147. 'For all that, never has a colossal eruption . . .' Letter from KM to FE, 7 June 1849.

147. 'If my wife were not in an *état par trop intéressant*...' Letter from KM to FE, late July 1849.

148. 'I need hardly say that I shall not consent to this veiled attempt on my life...' Letter from KM to FE, 23 August 1849.

148. 'all Aliens who are now on board my said ship...' HO 3/53, Public Record Office, London.

148. 'You must leave for London at once...' Letter from KM to FE, 23 August 1849.

6 The Megalosaurus

149. 'Implacable November weather...' *Bleak House* by Charles Dickens (Chapman & Hall, London, 1853), p. 1.

150. 'Sur, May we beg and beseech...' *The Times*, 5 July 1849.

151. 'I am now in a really difficult situation...' Letter from KM to Ferdinand Freiligrath, 5 September 1849.

153. 'in view of the inimical relations...' Letter from KM to Louis Bauer, 30 November 1849.

153. 'all in all, things are going quite well here...' Letter from FE to Jakob Lukas Schabelitz, 22 December 1849.

153. 'Herr Heinzen, so far from serving as a shining light...' *Northern Star*, 1 December 1849.

154. 'I did not know what a private parlour was...' From *Karl Marx: Biographical Memoirs* by Wilhelm Liebknecht, translated by E. Untermann (London, 1901).

156. 'The *Neue Rheinische Zeitung. Politisch-ökonomische Revue*...' *Westdeutsche Zeitung*, 8 January 1850.

156. 'I have little doubt that by the time...' Letter from KM to Joseph Weydemeyer, 19 December 1849.

156. 'What succumbed in these defeats was not the revolution...' From 'The Class Struggles in France, 1848 to 1850', translated in *MECW*, Vol. 10, pp. 47–145.

157. 'the whole was tactfully seasoned with pungent attacks...' From *Karl Marx: A Study in Fanaticism* by E. H. Carr (J. M. Dent & Sons, London, 1934).

157. 'I beg you to send us as soon as possible any money...' Letter from Jenny Marx to Joseph Weydemeyer, 20 May 1850.

157. 'Pray do not be offended by my wife's agitated letters...' Letter from KM to Joseph Weydemeyer, 27 June 1850.

158. 'Let me describe for you, as it really was, just one day in our lives...' Letter from Jenny Marx to Joseph Weydemeyer, 20 May 1850.

160. 'My husband and all the rest of us have missed you sorely. . .' Letter from Jenny Marx to FE, 2 December 1850.

161. 'I am writing today just to tell you . . .' Letter from FE to KM, 25 November 1850.

161. 'With such a salary, all should be well . . .' Letter from FE to KM, *c.* 6 July 1851.

161. 'last year, thank God, I gobbled up half of my old man's profits . . .' FE to KM, 10 March 1853.

161. 'Really, Sir, we should never have thought . . .' *Spectator*, 15 June 1850.

163. 'The murder of Princes is formally taught and discussed . . .' FO 64/317, Public Record Office, London.

163. 'this report is oddly convincing. . .' *Marx* by Robert Payne (W. H. Allen, London, 1968).

166. 'A complete office has now been set up in our house . . .' Letter from Jenny Marx to Adolf Cluss, 30 October 1852.

167. 'A few minutes before, he was laughing and joking. . .' Letter from KM to FE, 19 November 1850.

167. 'For two whole days . . .' Letter from KM to FE, 23 November 1850.

168. 'For the letter you wrote yesterday. . .' Letter from KM to Eduard von Müller-Tellering, 12 March 1850.

170. 'He leads the existence of a real bohemian intellectual . . .' Report of anonymous German police spy, in *KMIR*, pp. 34–6.

171. 'I know from General [Engels] himself that Freddy Demuth is Marx's son . . .' Original in International Institute of Social History, Amsterdam; first published in *Karl Marx* by Werner Blumenberg (Rowohlt, 1962; English edition published by Verso, London, 1972).

173. 'there can be no reasonable doubt that he [Freddy] was Marx's son . . .' From *Eleanor Marx: Volume One, Family Life 1855–1883* by Yvonne Kapp (Lawrence and Wishart, London, 1972).

173. 'possibly by Nazi agents . . .' *Friedrich Engels: His Life and Thought* by Terrell Carver (Macmillan, London and Basingstoke, 1989).

174. 'Research into the life of Frederick Demuth and of his relations . . .' Letter from Terrell Carver, *Sunday Times*, London, 27 June 1982.

176. 'I, of course, would make a joke of the whole dirty business . . .' Letter from KM to Joseph Weydemeyer, 2 August 1851.

177. 'If only there were some means . . .' Letter from FE to KM, 20 April 1852.

7 The Hungry Wolves

181. 'Byron and Leibniz rolled into one . . .' Letter from KM to FE, 22 April 1854.

181. 'I can't conceive what you still need him for . . .' Letter from FE to KM, 1 June 1853.

181. 'he kept his rendezvous with the old cow . . .' Letter from KM to FE, 13 February 1856.

181. 'her entire person green . . .' Letter from KM to FE, 10 April 1856.

182. 'I am, *hélas*, once again saddled with Pieper . . .' Letter from KM to FE, 27 July 1854.

182. 'It transpired that his "indispensability" was merely a figment . . .' Letter from KM to FE, 23 April 1857.

182. 'The combination of dilettantism and sententiousness . . .' Letter from KM to FE, 7 January 1858.

183. 'I find myself in a fix . . .' Letter from KM to FE, 21 June 1854.

184. 'The sea is doing my wife a lot of good . . .' Letter from KM to FE, 13 August 1858.

184. 'I for my part wouldn't care a damn about living in Whitechapel . . .' Letter from KM to FE, 15 July 1858.

184. 'It is true my house is beyond my means . . .' Letter from KM to FE, 31 July 1865.

185. 'Though I've racked my brains . . .' Letter from FE to KM, 16 July 1858.

185. 'I wish some of our lads in London . . .' Letter from FE to KM, 11 January 1853.

186. 'I would long ago have been obliged . . .' Letter from KM to Ludwig Kugelmann, 25 October 1866.

186. 'Engels really has too much work . . .' Letter from KM to Adolf Cluss, 18 October 1853.

187. 'The Parliamentary debates of the week offer but little of interest . . .' *New York Daily Tribune*, 15 March 1853.

187. 'Days of general election . . .' *New York Daily Tribune*, 4 September 1852.

187. 'There is something in human history like retribution . . .' *New York Daily Tribune*, 16 September 1857.

187. 'What he aims at is not the substance . . .' *New York Daily Tribune*, 19 October 1853.

188. 'so far advanced that I will have finished . . .' Letter from KM to FE, 2 April 1851.

188. 'Marx lives a very retired life . . .' Letter from Wilhelm Pieper to FE, 27 January 1851.

188. 'The material I am working on is so damnably involved . . .' Letter from KM to Joseph Weydemeyer, 27 June 1851.

189. 'Well, our friend Dakyns is a sort of Felix Holt . . .' Letter from KM to Jenny Marx (daughter), 10 June 1869.

189. 'The process of curing these stockfish . . .' Letter from KM to Jenny Marx, 11 June 1852.

190. 'I await your answer by return of post . . .' Letter from KM to J. G. Kinkel, 22 July 1852.

190. 'If you believe that you can . . . provide proof . . .' Letter from J. G. Kinkel to KM, 24 July 1852.

191. 'Your letter – and this is precisely why it was *provoked* . . .' Letter from KM to J. G. Kinkel, 24 July 1852.

191. 'The cream of the jest . . .' Letter from KM to Adolf Cluss, 30 July 1852.

192. 'used to enjoy flirting with this old he-goat . . .' Letter from KM to FE, 22 May 1852.

192. 'and should my explanation not suffice . . .' Letter from KM to Baron A. von Brüningk, 18 October 1852.

192. 'Should this letter cause you offence . . .' Letter from KM to Karl Eduard Vehse, end of November 1852.

193. 'I am engaged in a fight to the death with the sham liberals.' Letter from KM to Karl Eduard Vehse, end of November 1852.

193. 'The democratic simpletons . . .' Letter from KM to Joseph Weydemeyer, 27 June 1851.

194. 'No running around, no advertisement . . .' From *The Great Men of the Exile* by Karl Marx and Friedrich Engels, in *The Cologne Communist Trial* (Lawrence & Wishart, London, 1971), p. 167.

196. 'Your prediction that we will get the Charter . . .' Letter from George Julian Harney to FE, 30 March 1846.

196. 'in for a surprise when once the Chartists make a start . . .' Letter from FE to Emil Blank, 15 April 1848.

198. 'impressionable, that is, to famous names . . .' Letter from KM to FE, 23 February 1851.

198. 'I am *fatigué* of this public incense . . .' Letter from KM to FE, 11 February 1851.

198. 'I find this inanity and want of tact . . .' Letter from FE to KM, 13 February 1851.

199. 'who should arrive but our Dear . . .' Letter from KM to FE, 24 February 1851.

200. 'more of a Frenchman than an Englishman . . .' See letter from George Julian Harney to FE, 30 March 1846.

200. 'After the experiments which undermined universal suffrage . . .' From *Neue Oder-Zeitung*, 8 June 1855.

201. 'There is one great fact . . .' Speech delivered by KM on 14 April 1856, published in the *People's Paper*, 19 April 1856.

202. 'Provided nothing untoward happens . . .' Letter from FE to KM, 30 July 1851.

202. 'the very pleasing prospect of a trade crisis . . .' Letter from KM to FE, 31 July 1851.

202. 'In six months' time the circumnavigation of the world . . .' Letter from FE to KM, 23 September 1851.

202. 'The iron trade is totally paralysed . . .' Letter from FE to KM, 15 October 1851.

203. 'From what Engels tells me . . .' Letter from KM to Ferdinand Freiligrath, 27 December 1851.

203. 'In England our movement can progress only under the Tories . . .' Letter from KM to Lassalle, 23 February 1852.

203. 'One is almost tempted to forecast . . .' Letter from FE to KM, 20 April 1852.

204. 'The state of the winter crops . . . [etc.]' See Letters from KM to FE, 29 January 1853, 10 March 1853, 28 September 1853.

204. 'We were spectators from beginning to end . . .' *Neue Oder-Zeitung*, 28 June 1855.

204. 'At once the constabulary rushed from ambush . . .' *Neue Oder-Zeitung*, 5 July 1855.

205. 'a new, splendid proof of the indestructible thoroughness . . .' *Die Presse* (Vienna), 2 February 1862.

205. 'The Englishman first needs a revolutionary education . . .' Letter from KM to FE, 27 July 1866.

206. 'the preoccupation with gardening . . .' From *Man and the Natural World: Changing Attitudes in England 1500–1800* by Keith Thomas (Allen Lane, London, 1983), p. 240.

206. 'the English proletariat is actually becoming more and more bourgeois . . .' Letter from FE to KM, 7 October 1858.

207. 'Drat the British!' Letter from KM to Eleanor Marx, 9 January 1883.

207. 'To most of his adherents . . .' From *David Urquhart: Some Chapters in the Life of a Victorian Knight Errant of Justice and Liberty* by Gertrude Robinson (Basil Blackwell, Oxford, 1920).

208. 'This chap went to Greece . . .' Letter from KM to FE, 10 March 1853.

209. 'In the *Advertiser* four letters by D. Urquhart . . .' Letter from KM to FE, 18 August 1853.

210. 'He is an utter maniac . . .' Letter from KM to FE, 9 February 1854.

211. 'I do not wish to be numbered . . .' Letter from KM to Ferdinand Lassalle.

211. 'The Urquhartites are being damned importunate . . .' Letter from KM to Jenny Marx, 8 August 1856.

212. 'The institute of Marxism–Leninism in Moscow omitted them . . .' The offending texts were left out of both the German and Russian collected works, but did finally appear in and English edition – though only as recently as 1986, and after many years of tenacious argument between the British editors and the authorities in Moscow.

212. 'Did you overlook, in one of the *Guardian*s you sent me . . .' Letter from KM to FE, 5 March 1858.

212. 'an Eastern palace, with a Turkish bath . . .' *In the Days of the Dandies*, by Lord Lamington (London, 1890).

8 The Hero on Horseback

215. 'Unfortunately of the "sex" *par excellence* . . .' Letter from KM to FE, 17 January 1855.

216. 'a friend who was more dear to me . . .' Letter from KM to Amalie Daniels, 6 September 1855.

216. 'Though my heart is bleeding . . .' Letter from KM to FE, 30 March 1855.

217. 'I've already had my share of bad luck . . .' Letter from KM to FE, 12 April 1855.

217. 'the region round Soho Square . . .' Letter from KM to FE, 13 February 1863.

217. 'Bacon says that really important people . . .' Letter from KM to Ferdinand Lassalle, 28 July 1855.

218. 'I have been compelled by *force supérieure* to evacuate . . .' Letter from KM to FE, 11 September 1855.

220. 'It is indeed a princely dwelling . . .' Letter from Jenny Marx to Louise Weydemeyer, 11 March 1861.

220. 'Moor was admittedly a splendid horse . . .' From 'Karl Marx: A Few Stray Notes' by Eleanor Marx, in *RME*, pp. 250–1.

222. 'The clouds gathering over the money-market . . .' Letter from FE to KM, after 27 September 1856.

222. 'So here I am, without any prospects . . .' Letter from KM to FE, 20 January 1857.

222. 'I had believed that everything was going splendidly . . .' Letter from FE to KM, *c.* 22 January 1857.

223. 'Our attractive little house . . .' From 'Short Sketch of an Eventful Life' by Jenny Marx, translated in *RME*, pp. 229–30.

224. 'They are in effect cutting me down . . .' Letter from KM to FE, 24 March 1857.

224. 'What am I to tell him?' Letter from KM to FE, 29 June 1857.

224. 'As to the Delhi affair . . .' Letter from KM to FE, 15 August 1857.

225. 'The general appearance of the [Cotton] Exchange here was truly delightful . . .' Letter from FE to KM, 15 November 1857.

225. 'Another fortnight, and the dance will really be in full swing . . .' Letter from FE to KM, 7 December 1857.

225. 'It's a case of do or die . . .' Letter from FE to KM, 15 November 1857.

226. 'After all, we want to show the Prussian cavalry a thing or two . . .' Letter from FE to KM, 11 February 1858.

226. 'I try to avoid mentioning the matter to you . . .' Letter from KM to FE, 5 January 1858.

227. 'mere lemonade on the one hand . . .' Letter from KM to FE, 8 December 1857.

227. 'for the benefit of the public it is absolutely essential . . .' Letter from KM to FE, 18 December 1857.

230. 'provided one has the time and money . . .' Letter from KM to FE, 1 February 1858.

231. 'He [Lassalle] seems to see himself quite differently . . .' Letter from KM to FE, 5 March 1856.

232. 'I carefully perused your Heraclitus . . .' Letter from KM to Lassalle, 31 May 1858.

232. 'The work I am presently concerned with . . .' Letter from KM to Lassalle, 22 February 1858.

232. 'Alas, we are so used to these excuses . . .' Letter from FE to Nikolai Danielson, 13 November 1885.

233. 'my sickness always originates in the mind . . .' Letter from KM to FE, 19 October 1867.

233. 'the worsening of his condition is largely attributable . . .' Letter from Jenny Marx to FE, 9 April 1858.

233. 'Moor has been out riding . . .' Letter from FE to Jenny Marx, 11 May 1858.

234. 'Since the all but completed manuscript of the first volume . . .' Letter from KM to Carl Friedrich Julius Leske, 1 August 1846.

234. 'Now let me tell you how my political economy is coming on . . .' Letter from KM to Lassalle, 22 February 1858.

234. 'I don't suppose anyone has ever written about "money" when so short . . .' Letter from KM to FE, 21 January 1859.

235. 'it will be weeks before I am able to send it . . .' Letter from KM to FE, 22 October 1858.

235. 'the most appalling toothache . . .' Letter from KM to FE, 10 November 1858.

235. 'All that I was concerned with was the form . . .' Letter from KM to Lassalle, 12 November 1858.

236. 'My wife is quite right . . .' Letter from KM to FE, 11 December 1858.

236. 'The manuscript amounts to about twelve sheets . .' Letter from KM to FE, 13–15 January 1859.

236. 'The general result at which I arrived . . .' From 'Preface to *A Critique of Political Economy*' by Karl Marx, translated in *MESW*, Vol. 1, pp. 361ff.

238. 'overcome by a kind of cholera . . .' Letter from KM to FE, 22 July 1859.

238. 'The secret hopes we had long nourished . . .' Letter from Jenny Marx to FE, 23 or 24 December 1859.

239. 'First we drank port, then claret . . .' From *Mein Prozess gegen die Allgemeine Zeitung* by Karl Vogt (Geneva, 1859), translated in *KMIR*, pp. 17–19.

242. 'By means of an ingenious system of concealed plumbing . . .' From *Herr Vogt* by Karl Marx, in *MECW*, Vol. 17, p. 243.

243. 'A circumstance that has been of great help to me . . .' Letter from KM to FE, 28 November 1860.

244. 'I became hourly more ill . . .' Letter from Jenny Marx to Louise Weydemeyer, 11 March 1861.

245. 'I am as tormented as Job . . .' Letter from KM to FE, 18 January 1861.

246. 'eternally smiling and grinning . . .' Letter from KM to Antoinette Philips, 24 March 1861.

247. 'If I were quite free . . .' Letter from KM to Antoinette Philips, 13 April 1861.

247. 'I myself feel small longing for the fatherland . . .' Letter from Jenny Marx to FE, beginning of April 1861.

247. 'a very distinguished lady, no bluestocking . . .' Letter from KM to Antoinette Philips, 24 March 1861.

247. 'It is now quite plain to me . . .' Letter from KM to FE, 30 July 1862.

248. 'The fact that I have already spent what I brought back . . .' Letter from KM to FE, 19 June 1861.

249. 'Every day my wife says she wishes she and the children were safely in their graves . . .' Letter from KM to FE, 18 June 1862.

250. 'Since I last saw him a year ago he's gone quite mad . . .' Letter from KM to FE, 30 July 1862.

250. 'He was almost crushed under the weight of the fame . . .' From 'Short Sketch of an Eventful Life' by Jenny Marx, translated in *RME*, p. 234.

251. 'Is there to be an outright split between us . . .' Letter from KM to Lassalle, 7 November 1862.

251. 'which perhaps you'd have to envy me!' Letter from Lassalle to Bismarck, 8 June 1863, translated in *Karl Marx's Theory of Revolution, Volume IV: Critique of Other Socialisms* by Hal Draper (Monthly Review Press, New York, 1990), p. 55.

253. 'Such a thing could only happen to Lassalle . . .' Letter from FE to KM, 4 September 1864.

253. 'Heaven knows, our ranks are being steadily depleted . . .' Letter from KM to FE, 7 September 1864.

253. 'he died young, at a time of triumph . . .' Letter from KM to Sophie von Hatzfeldt, 12 September 1864.

254. 'A fine Christmas show. . .' Letter from KM to FE, 24 December 1862.

254. 'If only I knew how to start some sort of business!' Letter from KM to FE, 20 August 1862.

254. 'It is a curious and not unmeaning circumstance . . .' From 'The Socialism of Karl Marx and the Young Hegelians' by John Rae, *Contemporary Review* vol. XL, October 1881, p. 585.

254. 'too scientific for the English *Review*-reader. .' Letter from KM to Collet Dobson Collet, 6 September 1871.

255. 'cheap publications containing the wildest and most anarchical doctrines . . .' *The Times*, 2 September 1851.

255. 'In May 1869 he joined the Royal Society. . .' See 'The "Red Doctor" Amongst the Virtuosi: Karl Marx and the Society' by D. G. C. Allan, *Journal of the Royal Society of Arts*, Vol. 129 (1981), pp. 259–61 and 309–311.

256. 'Of all dreary concerns a *conversazione* certainly is the dreariest . . .' Letter from Jenny Marx (daughter) to FE, 2 July 1869.

257. 'Now we had enough of our "beer trip" . . .' From *Karl Marx: Biographical Memories* by Wilhelm Liebknecht, translated by E. Untermann (London, 1901).

258. 'by 1860 Marx was not interested in acquiring English disciples . . .' From 'The Introduction and Critical Reception of Marxist Thought in Britain, 1850–1900' by Kirk Willis, *The Historical Journal*, 20, 2 (1977), pp. 417–459.

258. 'I myself, by the by, am working away hard . . .' Letter from KM to FE, 18 June 1862.

259. 'I was delighted to see from your letter . . .' Letter from KM to Ludwig Kugelmann, 28 December 1862.

9 The Bulldogs and the Hyena

263. 'Dear Marx, You will find it quite in order . . .' Letter from FE to KM, 13 January 1863.

264. 'It was very wrong of me to write you that letter . . .' Letter from KM to FE, 24 January 1863.

265. 'Thank you for being so candid . . .' Letter from FE to KM, 26 January 1863.

265. 'Fate laid claim to one of our family. . .' Letter from KM to FE, 2 December 1863.

266. 'all my books furniture and effects . . .' From *'Last will and testament of*

Johann Friedrich Wilhelm Wolff, Manchester Probate Court, Register No. 1 (1864), Folio 606.

267. 'Your philistine on the spree . . .' Letter from KM to FE, 25 July 1864.

268. 'I have, which will surprise you not a little, been speculating . . .' Letter from KM to Lion Philips, 25 June 1864.

268. 'had I had the money during the past ten days . . .' Letter from KM to FE, 4 July 1864.

268. '*Salut, ô connétable de Saint Pancrace!*' Letter from FE to KM, 28 June 1868.

269. 'I should tell them that I was a foreigner . . .' Letter from KM to FE, 27 June 1868.

271. 'M. Adolphe Bartels claims that public life is finished for him . . .' From 'Remarks on the Article by M. Adolphe Bartels' by Karl Marx, *Deutsche-Brüsseler-Zeitung*, 19 December 1847.

272. 'whereas you are a *poet*, I am a *critic* . . .' Letter from KM to Ferdinand Freiligrath, 29 February 1860.

273. 'When you come back to England from any foreign country . . .' From *The Lion and the Unicorn: Socialism and the English Genius* by George Orwell (Secker & Warburg, London, 1941).

273. 'People are beginning to understand . . .' *Northern Star*, 19 June 1847.

274. 'As soon as the Hyena entered the brewery . . .' For accounts of the Haynau affair, see *The Chartist Challenge: A Portrait of George Julian Harney* by A. R. Schoyen (Heinemann, London, 1958); *A History of the Chartist Movement* by Julius West (Constable, London, 1920); *The Common People 1746–1938* by G. D. H. Cole and Raymond Postgate (Methuen, London, 1938); and Harney's editorial in *Red Republican*, 14 September 1850.

275. 'a curious amalgam of political and industrial action . . .' From *The Age of Capital 1848–1875* by E. J. Hobsbawm (Abacus, London, 1977), pp. 134–5.

275. 'the working men themselves spoke *very well indeed* . . .' Letter from KM to FE, 9 April 1863.

275. 'Marx's contempt for humanity . . .' From *Marx* by Robert Payne (W. H. Allen, London, 1968), p. 322.

276. 'Marx's sceptical view of the proletariat's ability . . .' From *The Social and Political Thought of Karl Marx* by Shlomo Avineri (Cambridge University Press, 1968), p. 63.

276. 'You will search the works of Marx . . .' For a thorough dissection of Avineri's errors, see the appendix to *Karl Marx's Theory of Revolution – Volume II: The Politics of Social Classes* by Hal Draper (Monthly Review Press, New York, 1978), pp. 635ff.

277. 'The author of this article is himself a *worker* . . .' From the *Neue Rheinische Zeitung, Politisch-ökonomische Revue*, Nos. 5–6, 1850.

278. 'the most tragic thing . . .' Letter from KM to FE, 9 February 1859.

278. 'is again going to pieces in his sweatshop . . .' Letter from KM to FE, 18 May 1859.

279. 'By way of demonstration against the French monsieurs . . .' Letter from KM to FE, 26 September 1866.

279. 'Citizen Marx did not think there was anything to fear . . .' All quotations from the minutes are taken from *The General Council of the First International*, a five-volume collection of the Council's record-books, published by Foreign Languages Publishing House, Moscow.

281. 'a fearfully cliché-ridden, badly written and totally unpolished preamble . . .' Letter from KM to FE, 4 November 1864.

284. 'That damned boy Lafargue . . .' Letter from KM to Laura Marx, 20 March 1866.

284. 'our friend Lafargue, and others who had abolished nationalities . . .' Letter from KM to FE, 20 June 1866.

285. 'What a waste of time!' Letter from KM to FE, 13 March 1865.

285. 'Moor's life without the International would be a diamond ring . . .' Letter from FE to Laura Lafargue (née Marx), 24 June 1883

285. 'I have always half-expected that the naïve *fraternité* . . .' Letter from FE to KM, 12 April 1865.

286. 'There is *nothing* I can do in Prussia at the moment . . .' Letter from KM to Ludwig Kugelmann, 23 February 1865.

287. 'If we succeed in re-electrifying the political movement . . .' Letter from KM to FE, 1 May 1865.

289. 'For two months I have been living solely on the pawnshop . . .' Letter from KM to FE, 31 July 1865.

290. 'My dear Lafargue . . .' Letter from KM to Paul Lafargue, 13 August 1866.

291. 'Lafargue has the blemish customarily found in the negro tribe . . .' Letter from KM to FE, 11 November 1882.

291. 'You know that I have sacrificed my whole fortune . . .' Letter from KM to Paul Lafargue, 13 August 1866.

291. 'a great relief for the entire household . . .' Letter from KM to FE, 6 March 1868.

291. 'At the wedding lunch Engels cracked so many jokes . . .' See letter from Laura Lafargue to FE, 6 March 1893, in the Engels–Lafargue *Correspondence*, Vol. III, pp. 246–7.

291. 'As I am in the habit of keeping in the background . . .' Letter from Laura Marx to FE, 16 October 1893, in the Engels–Lafargue *Correspondence*, Vol. III, p. 304.

292. 'In all these struggle we women have the harder part . . .' Letter from Jenny Marx to Wilhelm Liebknecht, 26 May 1872.

10 The Shaggy Dog

293. 'Opposite the window and on either side of the fireplace . . .' From 'Reminiscences of Marx' by Paul Lafargue, in *RME*, p. 73.

294. 'What swine they are!' Letter from KM to FE, 22 June 1867.

295. 'I can also hardly leave my family in their present situation . . .' Letter from KM to FE, 2 April 1867.

295. 'What was keeping this beautiful creature so spellbound . . .' Letter from KM to FE, 13 April 1867.

296. 'he *understands*, and he is a really *excellent man* . . .' Letter from KM to FE, 24 April 1867.

298. 'and then the torments of family life . . .' Letter from KM to FE, 7 May 1867.

298. 'my children are obliged to invite some other girls for dancing . . .' Letter from KM to FE, 22 June 1867.

298. 'So, *this volume is finished*. I owe it to *you* alone . . .' Letter from KM to FE, 16 August 1867.

299. 'I only got as far as page two . . .' *Conversations* by Kenneth Harris (Hodder & Stoughton, London, 1967), p. 268. Wilson repeated the claim in an interview with *The Times*, 2 August 1976.

300. 'Pauperism forms a condition of capitalist production . . .' From *Capital: A Critique of Political Economy*, Vol. I, by Karl Marx, translated by Ben Fowkes (Pelican Books, London, in association with *New Left Review*, 1976), p. 797.

300. 'It follows therefore that in proportion as capital accumulates . . .' Ibid. p. 799.

301. 'It must be borne in mind . . .' *Main Currents of Marxism: Its Rise, Growth and Dissolution*, Vol. I, by Leszek Kolakowski (Clarendon Press, Oxford, 1978), p. 291.

301. 'As an interpretation of economic phenomena . . .' Ibid., p. 329.

302. 'As the exchangeable values of commodities . . .' Lectures by Karl Marx to the General Council of the First International, 20 and 27 June 1865, published as the pamphlet *Value, Price and Profit*, edited by Eleanor Marx-Aveling (London, 1898).

304. 'the bourgeois science of economics had reached the limits . . .' Afterword to the second German edition of *Capital*, 1873.

306. 'Now it is true that the tailoring . . .' *Capital*, Vol. I, pp. 142–3.

307. 'L—d! said my mother, what is all this story about?' From *The Life and Opinions of Tristram Shandy, Gent.* by Laurence Sterne, in *The Works of Laurence Sterne*, Vol. 1 (Bickers & Son, London, 1885).

308. 'broke with the tradition of contemporary writing . . .' *Laurence Sterne: A Fellow of Infinite Jest* by Thomas Yoseloff (Francis Aldor, London, 1948), p. 87.

308. 'A philosopher produces ideas, a poet poems . . .' *MECW*, Vol. 30, pp. 306–310.

310. 'The meaning of the impersonal-looking formulas . . .' *To the Finland Station* by Edmund Wilson (Macmillan, London, 1972), pp. 340–2.

310. 'the author's views may be as pernicious as we conceive them to be . . .' *Saturday Review of Politics, Literature, Science and Art*, London, 18 January 1868.

311. 'we do not suspect that Karl Marx has much to teach us . . .' *Contemporary Review*, London, June 1868.

312. 'The thing would have looked somewhat like a school textbook . . .' Letter from FE to KM, 16 June 1867.

312. 'How could you leave the *outward* structure . . .' Letter from FE to KM, 23 August 1867.

312. 'Please be so good as to tell your good wife . . .' Letter from KM to Kugelmann, 30 November 1867.

312. 'My sickness always originates in the mind.' Letter from KM to FE, 19 October 1867.

313. 'The main thing is that the book should be discussed . . .' Letter from FE to Ludwig Kugelmann, 8 and 20 November 1867.

313. 'There can be few books that have been written in more difficult circumstances . . .' Letter from Jenny Marx to Ludwig Kugelmann, 24 December 1867.

313. 'You can have no idea of the delight . . .' Ibid.

11 The Rogue Elephant

316. 'The struggle between the two lies at the very heart and core of all debates . . .' *Karl Marx: A Political Biography* by Fritz J. Raddatz, translated by Richard Barry (Weidenfeld & Nicolson, London, 1978), p. 207.

316. 'the man of generous, uncontrollable impulses . . .' *Karl Marx* by E. H. Carr (J. M. Dent & Sons, London, 1934), p. 224.

316. 'Bakunin differed from Marx as poetry differs from prose . . .' *Karl Marx: His Life and Environment* by Isaiah Berlin (Butterworth, London, 1939), p. 79.

317. 'I am now at the head of a communist secret society . . .' From *Archives Bakounine*, edited by A. Lehning (International Institute for Social History, Amsterdam, 1967).

317. 'Bakunin is our friend . . .' From 'Democratic Pan-Slavism' by Friedrich Engels, *Neue Rheinische Zeitung*, 15 February 1849.

318. 'Bakunin has become a monster . . .' Letter from KM to FE, 12 September 1863.

318. 'I must say I liked him very much . . .' Letter from KM to FE, 4 November 1864.

320. 'Bakunin assured him that the International was an excellent institution . . .' From *Michael Bakunin* by E. H. Carr (Vintage Books, New York, 1961).

321. 'Whatever turn the impending horrid war may take . . .' From an address 'To the Members of the International Working Men's Association in Europe and the United States', published by the IWMA, July 1870.

321. 'John Stuart Mill sent a message of congratulation . . .' General Council minutes, 22 August 1870.

321. 'would naturally have serious consequences . . .' Letter from KM to Ferdinand Lassalle, 4 February 1859.

322. 'I have been totally unable to sleep . . .' Letter from KM to FE, 17 August 1870.

322. 'I wish this because the definite defeat of Bonaparte . . .' Letter from KM to Paul and Laura Lafargue, 28 July 1870.

322. 'All the French, even the tiny number of better ones . . .' Letter from Jenny Marx to FE, 10 August 1870.

322. 'My confidence in the military achievements of the Germans grows daily . . .' Letter from FE to KM, 31 July 1870.

322. 'One cannot conceal from oneself . . .' Letter from KM to FE, 8 August 1870.

323. 'we were not mistaken as to the vitality . . .' From an Address 'To the Members of the International Working Men's Association in Europe and the United States', published by the IWMA, September 1870.

323. 'What the Prussian jackasses do not see . . .' Letter from KM to Friedrich Adolph Sorge, 1 September 1870.

325. 'an impudent forgery . . .' *The Times*, 22 March 1871.

325. 'You must not believe a word of all the stuff you get to see . . .' Letter from KM to Wilhelm Liebknecht, 6 April 1871.

326. 'What resilience, what historical initiative . . .' Letter from KM to Ludwig Kugelmann, 12 April 1871.

326. 'Marx's personal ambivalence to the Commune . . .' See, for example, *Karl Marx: A Biography* by David McLellan, p. 359.

326. 'The present state of things causes our dear Moor intense suffering . . .' Letter from Jenny Marx (daughter) to the Kugelmanns, 18 April 1871.

328. 'A master in small state roguery . . .' From *The Civil War in France* (Edward Truelove, London, June 1871).

332. 'a man of domineering disposition . . .' From 'The International: addressed to the Working Class' by Joseph Mazzini, Contemporary Review, XX (July 1872), 155.

333. 'a fair day's wage for a fair day's work . . .' *The Times*, 16 April 1872.

333. 'Little as we saw or heard openly...' From 'The Commune of 1871' by E.B.M., *Fraser's Magazine*, June 1871.

333. 'We would venture to set that undistinguished shop...' *The Tablet*, 15 July 1871.

333. 'perhaps the most significant and ominous of the political signs...' *Spectator*, 17 June 1871.

333. 'It is true, no doubt, that the secretary of that body...' From 'The proletariat on a false scent' by W. R. Greg, *Quarterly Review*, CXXXII (January 1872), p. 133.

334. 'I have the honour to be at this moment...' Letter from KM to Ludwig Kugelmann, 18 June 1871.

334. 'Sir, From the Paris correspondence...' *Pall Mall Gazette*, 9 June 1871.

335. 'I declare you to be a libeller...' *Pall Mall Gazette*, 3 July 1871.

335. 'It was comfort personified...' The *World*, New York, 18 July 1871.

338. 'It was hard work...' Letter from KM to Jenny Marx, 23 September 1871.

340. 'This whole Jewish world which constitutes a single exploiting sect...' From *Archives Bakounine*, translated in *Karl Marx's Theory of Revolution, Volume IV: Critique of Other Socialisms*, p. 296.

341. 'The International is undergoing the most serious crisis...' From *Les Prétendues Scissions Dans L'Internationale* (Co-operative Press, Geneva, 1872).

342. 'If that is correct, then his family will have no worries...' From *Een Zesdaagsch International Debat* (Dordrecht, 1872), translated in *KMIR*, pp. 114–15.

342. 'the public is not even allowed a look...' Nicolaievsky and Maenchen-Helfen, p. 382.

342. 'the tinkling of the President's bell...' *The Times*, 7 September 1872.

343. 'At last we have had a real session of the International congress...' Nicolaievsky and Maenchen-Helfen, p. 384.

344. 'It was a *coup d'état*...' From *Report of the Fifth Annual General Congress of the International Working Men's Association held at the Hague, Holland, 2–9 September 1872* by Maltman Barry (London, 1873).

344. 'I am so overworked...' Letter from KM to Nikolai Danielson, 28 May 1872.

345. 'I can hardly wait for the next congress...' Letter from KM to César de Paepe, 28 May 1872.

345. 'This simple law must be the basis of our activity...' *Violence dans la violence: le débat Bakounine-Necaev* by Michael Confino (Maspero, Paris, 1973), p. 88; see also *Karl Marx's Theory of Revolution, Volume IV: Critique of Other Socialisms*, p. 302.

12 The Shaven Porcupine

349. 'He is always healthy, vigorous, cheerful . . .' Letter from Jenny Marx to Friedrich Adolph Sorge, 20 or 21 January 1877.

350. 'Longuet is a very gifted man . . .' Letter from Jenny Marx to Wilhelm Liebknecht, 26 May 1872.

350. 'Though I drudge like a nigger . . .' Letter from Jenny Marx (daughter) to Eleanor Marx, 10 April 1882, quoted in *Eleanor Marx, Volume I: Family Life 1855–1883* by Yvonne Kapp (Lawrence & Wishart, London, 1972), p. 240.

351. 'Before they gave evidence . . .' From *Autobiographic Memoirs* by Frederic Harrison (London, 1911), Vol. II, p. 33.

351. 'who cheated me and others . . .' Letter from KM to Friedrich Adolphe Sorge, 4 August 1874.

352. 'Longuet as the last Proudhonist and Lafargue as the last Bakuninist!' Letter from KM to FE, 11 November 1882.

352. 'With one exception, all the books on the Commune . . .' Letter from Jenny Marx (daughter) to Ludwig and Gertrud Kugelmann, 21–22 December 1871.

352. 'I asked nothing of him . . .' Letter from KM to FE, 31 May 1873.

353. 'My dearest Moor, I am going to ask you . . .' Letter from Eleanor Marx to KM, 23 March 1874; translated in *Eleanor Marx, Volume I: Family Life 1855–1883* by Yvonne Kapp (Lawrence & Wishart, London, 1972), pp. 153–4.

354. 'The place was crowded . . .' Letter from Eleanor Marx to Jenny Longuet, 1 July 1882.

354. 'I unfortunately only inherited my father's nose . . .' Letter from Eleanor Marx to Karl Kautsky, 28 December 1896.

355. 'What neither Papa nor the doctors nor anyone will understand . . .' Letter from Eleanor Marx to Jenny Longuet, 8 January 1882.

355. 'I have since months suffered severely . . .' Letter from KM to Nikolai Danielson, 12 August 1873.

355. 'My face went quite black . . .' Letter from KM to FE, 30 August 1873.

355. 'the serious possibility of my succumbing to apoplexy . . .' Letter from KM to Friedrich Adolph Sorge, 27 September 1873.

356. 'I myself allow the English papers to announce my death from time to time . . .' Letter from KM to Ludwig Kugelmann, 19 January 1874.

356. 'Carl Marx – Naturalisation . . .' File HO45/9366/36228 in the Public Record Office, London.

357. 'We are both living in strict accordance with the rules . . .' Letter from KM to FE, 1 September 1874.

357. 'My patience came to an end . . .' Letter from KM to FE, 18 September 1874.

358. 'He always has to hand the *mot juste*, the striking simile . . .' From *Sprudel* (Vienna), 19 September 1875, translated in *KMIR*, pp. 124–5.

359. 'pleasantly surprised to see with what warmth and affection . . .' From 'Going to Canossa' by August Bebel, *RME*, p. 216.

360. 'He was most affable . . .' From 'Visits to Karl Marx' by Nikolai Morozov, *RME*, p. 303.

360. 'He spoke in the quietly detached tones of a patriarch . . .' From *Aus den Jahren meines Exils: Erinnerungen eines Sozialisten* by Eduard Bernstein (Berlin, 1919), translated in *KMIR*, pp. 152–3.

360. 'Whatever Marx might have thought of me . . .' From *Aus den Frühzeit des Marxismus* by Karl Kautsky (Prague, 1935), translated in *KMIR*, pp. 153–6.

361. 'If I denied everything that has been said and written of me . . .' *Chicago Tribune*, 5 January 1879.

361. 'I do not reply to pinpricks . . .' Letter from KM to Ferdinand Domela Nieuwenhuis, 22 February 1881.

361. 'He is a short, rather small man . . .' Letter from Sir Mountstuart Elphinstone Grant Duff MP to the Crown Princess Victoria, 1 February 1879; first printed in 'A Meeting with Karl Marx', *Times Literary Supplement*, 15 July 1949.

363. 'He found an exact description of his anxieties . . .' See 'Karl Marx. Persönliche Erinnerungen' by Paul Lafargue, *Die Neue Zeit*, Vol. IX, pt 1 (1890–1), translated in *KMIR*, p. 73; also 'Karl Marx and the Promethean Complex' by Lewis S. Feuer, *Encounter*, Vol. XXXI, No. 6 (December 1968), p. 15.

363. 'Dear Sir, I thank you for the honour . . .' Letter from Charles Darwin to KM, 1 October 1873.

364. 'Although it is developed in the crude English style . . .' Letter from KM to FE, 19 December 1860.

364. 'Darwin's book is very important . . .' Letter from KM to Lassalle, 16 January 1861.

364. 'It represents a *very significant* advance over Darwin . . .' Letter from KM to FE, 7 August 1866.

365. 'Dear Sir, I am much obliged for your kind letter . . .' Letter from Charles Darwin to Edward Aveling, 13 October 1880. This and Darwin's letter of October 1873 can be found in the IISH, Amsterdam. Both have identical blotches where someone – probably Aveling himself – has spilled ink over them; since the marks are slightly fainter on the Marx letter one deduces that the documents were together on his desk, with the 1880 letter on top, when the accident happened. For more on the Marx–Darwin myth, see the following: 'The Contacts Between Karl Marx and Charles Darwin' by Ralph Colp Jr., *Journal of the History of Ideas*, Vol. XXXV, No. 2 (April–June 1974), pp. 329–338); 'Did Marx Offer to Dedicate *Capital* to Darwin?' by Margaret A. Fay, *Journal of the History of Ideas*, Vol. XXXIX, No. 1 (January–March 1978), pp. 133–146; 'The Case of the "Darwin–Marx" Letter' by Lewis S.

Feuer, *Encounter*, Vol. LI, No. 4 (October 1978), pp. 62–77; 'Marx and Darwin: A Literary Detective Story' by Margaret A. Fay, *Monthly Review* (NY), Vol. 31, No. 10 (March 1980), pp. 40–57; 'The Myth of the Darwin–Marx Letter' by Ralph Colp Jr., *History of Political Economy* (Duke University, North Carolina), Vol. 14, No. 4 (Winter 1982), pp. 461–481.

366. 'Darwin declined the honour in a polite, cautiously phrased letter...' From *Karl Marx* by Isaiah Berlin (Thornton Butterworth, London, 1939), p. 218.

367. 'Marx's dedication of *Capital* to Darwin was evidently made tongue in cheek...' From 'From Hoax to Dogma: A Footnote on Marx and Darwin' by Shlomo Avineri, *Encounter*, Vol. XXVIII (March 1967), pp. 30–32.

368. 'unlike Marx, Darwin was a genuine scientist...' *Spectator*, 17 October 1998.

369. 'Though Marx has lived much in England...' From 'Karl Marx and German Socialism' by John Macdonnell, *Fortnightly Review*, 1 March 1875.

369. 'We are much obliged by your letter...' Letter from Macmillan & Co. (London) to Professor Carl Schorlemmer, 25 May 1883.

369. 'Is there no hope of it being translated?' Letter from Robert Banner to KM, 6 December 1880.

370. 'Accustomed as we are nowadays, especially in England, to fence always with big soft buttons...' From *The Record of an Adventurous Life* by H. M. Hyndman (Macmillan, London, 1911), pp. 271–2.

370. 'out of spite against the world because he was not included in the Cambridge eleven...' See *The Proud Tower: A Portrait of the World Before the War, 1890–1914* by Barbara Tuchman (Macmillan, London, 1980), p. 360.

370. 'Our method of talking was peculiar...' Hyndman, p. 273.

371. 'laughing when anything struck him as particularly comic...' From 'My Recollections of Karl Marx' by Marian Comyn in *Nineteenth Century and After* (London, 1922), pp. 161 ff.

371. 'We were invaded by Hyndman and his wife...' Letter from KM to Jenny Longuet, 11 April 1881.

372. 'Ernest Belfort Bax, born in 1854...' See *The Victorian Encounter with Marx: A Study of Ernest Belfort Bax* by John Cowley (British Academic Press, London & New York, 1992).

373. 'Now this is the first publication of that kind...' Letter from KM to Friedrich Adolphe Sorge, 15 December 1881.

373. 'The visit is proving especially beneficial to Marx...' Letter from FE to Johann Philipp Becker, 17 August 1880.

373. 'Dear, good Doctor, I should so like to live a little longer...' Quoted in *Eleanor Marx*, Vol. 1, by Yvonne Kapp (Lawrence & Wishart, London, 1972), pp. 215–16.

374. 'The worst is that Mrs Marx's state becomes daily more dangerous...' Letter from KM to Nikolai Danielson, 19 February 1881.

374. 'for my own part I prefer the "manly" sex for children . . .' Letter from KM to Jenny Longuet, 29 April 1881.

375. 'Between ourselves, my wife's illness is, alas, incurable . . .' Letter from KM to Friedrich Adolph Sorge, 20 June 1881.

375. 'Jennychen's asthma is bad . . .' Letter from KM to FE, 9 August 1881.

375. 'She has been eating next to nothing for weeks . . .' Letter from KM to FE, 18 August 1881.

376. 'drawing closer to its consummation . . .' Letter from KM to Karl Kautsky, 1 October 1881.

376. 'If any one outside event has contributed . . .' Letter from FE to Eduard Bernstein, 30 November 1881.

376. 'We are no such *external* people!' See letter from KM to Jenny Longuet, 7 December 1881.

378. 'A ferryman is ready and waiting, with his small boat . . .' Letter from KM to Laura Lafargue, 13 and 14 April 1882.

378. 'a big man in every way, with a very large head . . .' The woman was Virginia Bateman, mother of the novelist Compton Mackenzie. Her reminiscences can be found in *My Life and Times* by Compton Mackenzie (London, 1968), Vol. VII, p. 181.

379. 'What I write and tell the children is the truth . . .' Letter from KM to FE, 20 May 1882.

379. 'To no one in the world would I wish the tortures . . .' Letter from Jenny Longuet to Eleanor Marx, 8 November 1882.

380. 'This, then, is most encouraging . . .' Letter from KM to Laura Lafargue, 14 December 1882.

380. 'touch the movements of the mucus . . .' Letter from KM to Dr James M. Williamson, 6 January 1883. See also *Prometheus Bound: Karl Marx on the Isle of Wight* by Dr A. E. Lawrence and Dr A. N. Insole (Isle of Wight County Council Cultural Services Department, Newport, 1981).

380. 'I have lived many a sad hour, but none so sad as that . . .' From *RME*, p. 128.

381. 'is still not really making the progress it should . . .' Letter from FE to August Bebel, 7 March 1883.

381. 'Mankind is shorter by a head . . .' Letter from FE to Friedrich Adolph Sorge, 15 March 1883.

382. 'The death is announced of Dr Karl Marx . . .' *Daily News* (London), 17 March 1883.

382. '*Capital*, unfinished as it is, will beget a host of smaller books . . .' *Pall Mall Gazette*, 16 March 1883.

382. 'The talk was of the world, and of man, and of time . . .' *New York Sun*, 6 September 1880.

Index

GEORGE ELIOT: The Last Victorian

Kathryn Hughes

An immensely readable biography of the nineteenth-century writer whose territory comprised nothing less than the entire span of Victorian society. Kathryn Hughes provides a truly nuanced view of Eliot, and is the first to grapple equally with the personal dramas that shaped her personality.

'A triumph, intelligent, persuasive and beautifully written.' *Sunday Times*

1 85702 891 0   £8.99

JANE AUSTEN

David Nokes

A revolutionary biography of one of Britain's best-loved writers that ventures beneath the outwardly calm existence of Jane Austen to reveal the psychological drama that shaped her fiction.

'This book cries out to be read, not alone by fans of Jane Austen but by anyone who enjoys a great, witty, gossipy read.' *Irish Times*

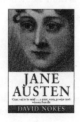

1 85702 667 5   £9.99

SHAKESPEARE: The Invention of the Human

Harold Bloom

A landmark work, this brilliant companion to
Shakespeare's plays explains why he has remained our
most popular and universal dramatist for more than
four centuries.

'This is unquestionably a fine work of Shakespearean
criticism. Filled with animation and fired by a
determination to extol the virtues of great literature.'
Peter Ackroyd, *The Times*

'Brilliant . . . a Shakespearean reading of Shakespeare
which is rich in asides and incidentals.' *Sunday Telegraph*

1 84115 048 7   £12.99

PUSHKIN'S BUTTON

Serena Vitale

A wonderful piece of literary detective work that charts
the colliding lives of Russia's greatest poet and the man
who killed him in their duel – cultural history that
reads like a thriller.

'Impossible to put down.' George Steiner

'*Pushkin's Button* should be bought, read and emulated.'
Literary Review

1 85702 937 2   £6.99

CAPTAIN BLIGH'S PORTABLE NIGHTMARE

John Toohey

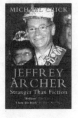

The account of an extraordinary journey, a great achievement in the history of European seafaring and a personal triumph for a man who has been misjudged by history.

'All the adrenalin of mutiny, marooning and maritime misdemeanours.' *Independent*

1 84115 078 9 £6.99

JEFFREY ARCHER: Stranger than Fiction

Revised Edition

Michael Crick

The book William Hague refused to read but now wishes he had. Michael Crick's widely praised biography of the extraordinarily invented life of Jeffrey Archer, fabulist, politician, fundraiser, and fibber on a grand scale.

'Utterly mesmerising.' *Sunday Times*

'I hate this book.' Jeffrey Archer

All Fourth Estate books are available from your local bookshop, or can be ordered direct (FREE UK p&p) from:

Fourth Estate, Book Service By Post, PO Box 29, Douglas, I-O-M, IM99 1BQ

Credit cards accepted.

Tel: 01624 836000   Fax: 01624 670923

Or visit the Fourth Estate website at: www.4thestate.co.uk

*Prices are correct at time of going to press, but may be subject to change. Please state when ordering if you do **not** wish to receive further information about Fourth Estate titles.*